SPY x FAMILY

6

I hope you enjoy this!

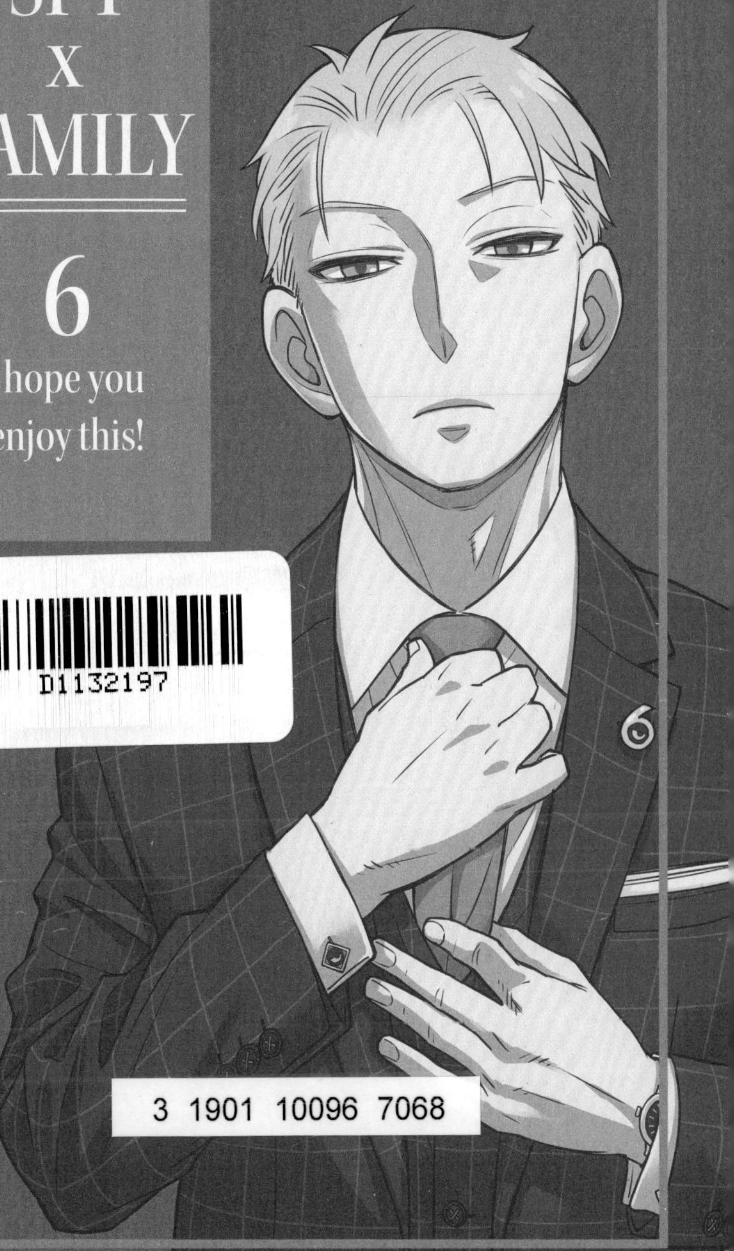

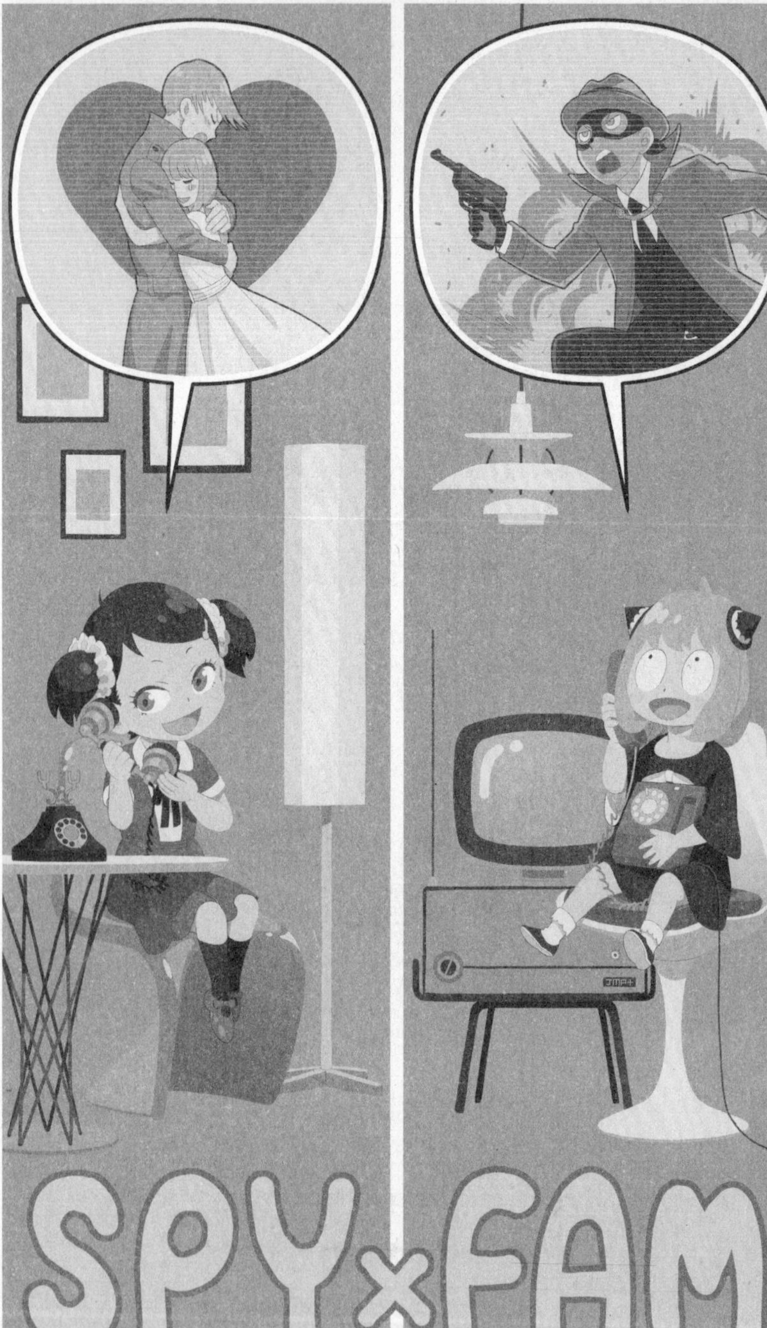
SPY×FAM

6

STORY AND ART BY
TATSUYA ENDO

SPY×FAMILY

SPY×FAMILY CHARACTERS

LOID FORGER

ROLE: **Husband**

Known as a skilled psychiatrist, Loid is actually "Twilight," a spy and master of disguise serving the nation of Westalis.

YOR FORGER

ROLE: **Wife**

A city hall clerk who also lives a secret life as a talented contract killer. Her code name is "Thorn Princess."

ANYA FORGER

ROLE: **Daughter**

Anya is a first grader at the prestigious Eden Academy. A telepath whose abilities were created in an experiment conducted by a certain organization. She can read minds.

BOND FORGER

ROLE: **Dog**

Anya's playmate and the family guard dog. As a former military test subject, he can see the future.

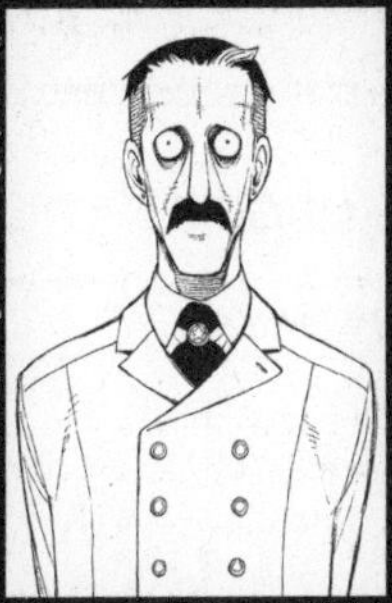

MISSION

OPERATION STRIX

Spy on Donovan Desmond, a dangerous figure who threatens to disrupt peace between the East and West. Must gain entry into the prestigious Eden Academy to breach the target's inner circle.

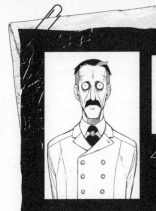

TARGET

DONOVAN DESMOND

The focus of Operation Strix. Chairman of Ostania's National Unity Party.

KEY PEOPLE

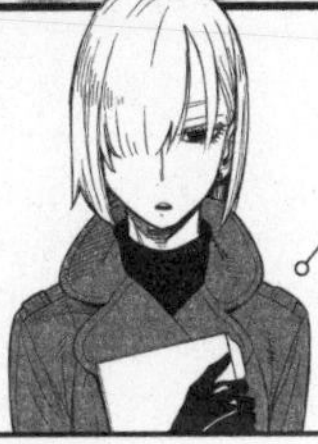

FIONA FROST

Loid's agent coworker, known as "Nightfall."

HENRY HENDERSON

Housemaster at Eden Academy.

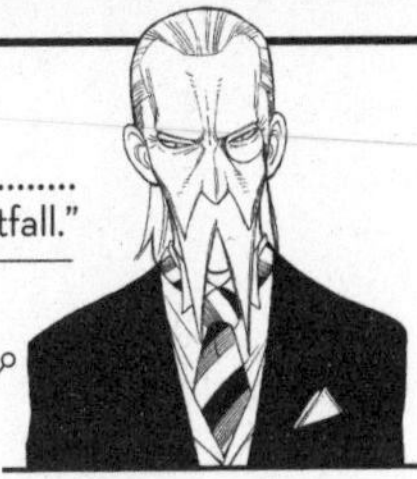

BECKY BLACKWELL

Anya's friend.

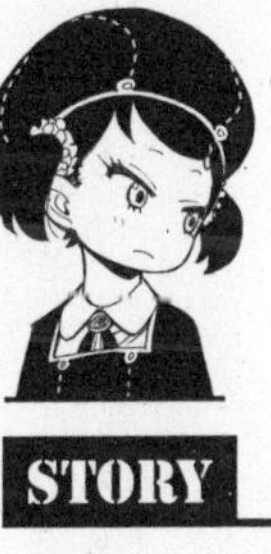

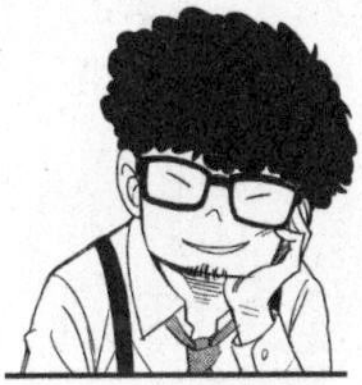

FRANKY

Intelligence asset who works with Twilight.

DAMIAN DESMOND

Second son of Donovan Desmond.

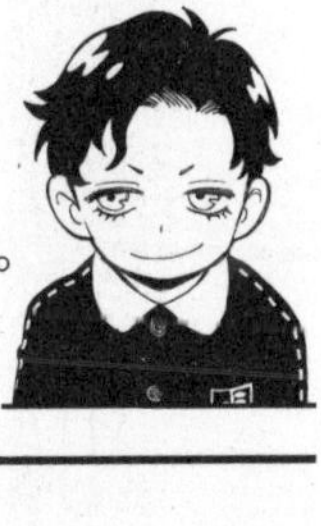

STORY

Westalis secret agent Twilight receives orders to uncover the plans of Donovan Desmond, the warmongering chairman of Ostania's National Unity Party. To do so, Twilight must pose as Loid Forger, create a fake family and enroll his child at the prestigious Eden Academy. However, by sheer coincidence, the daughter he selects from an orphanage is secretly a telepath! Also, the woman who agrees to be in a sham marriage with him is secretly an assassin! While concealing their true identities from one another, the three now find themselves living together as a family.

Anya realizes she'll be unable to use her telepathic ability on the midterm exams and might even flunk out. When her uncle Yuri comes to tutor her, however, she gets inspiration from his pep talk and manages to avoid failing any of her tests. Meanwhile, Westalis agent Fiona visits the Folgers' home. Is she making a play for Yor's role as Mrs. Forger?!

CONTENTS

SPY×FAMILY 6

MISSION 31

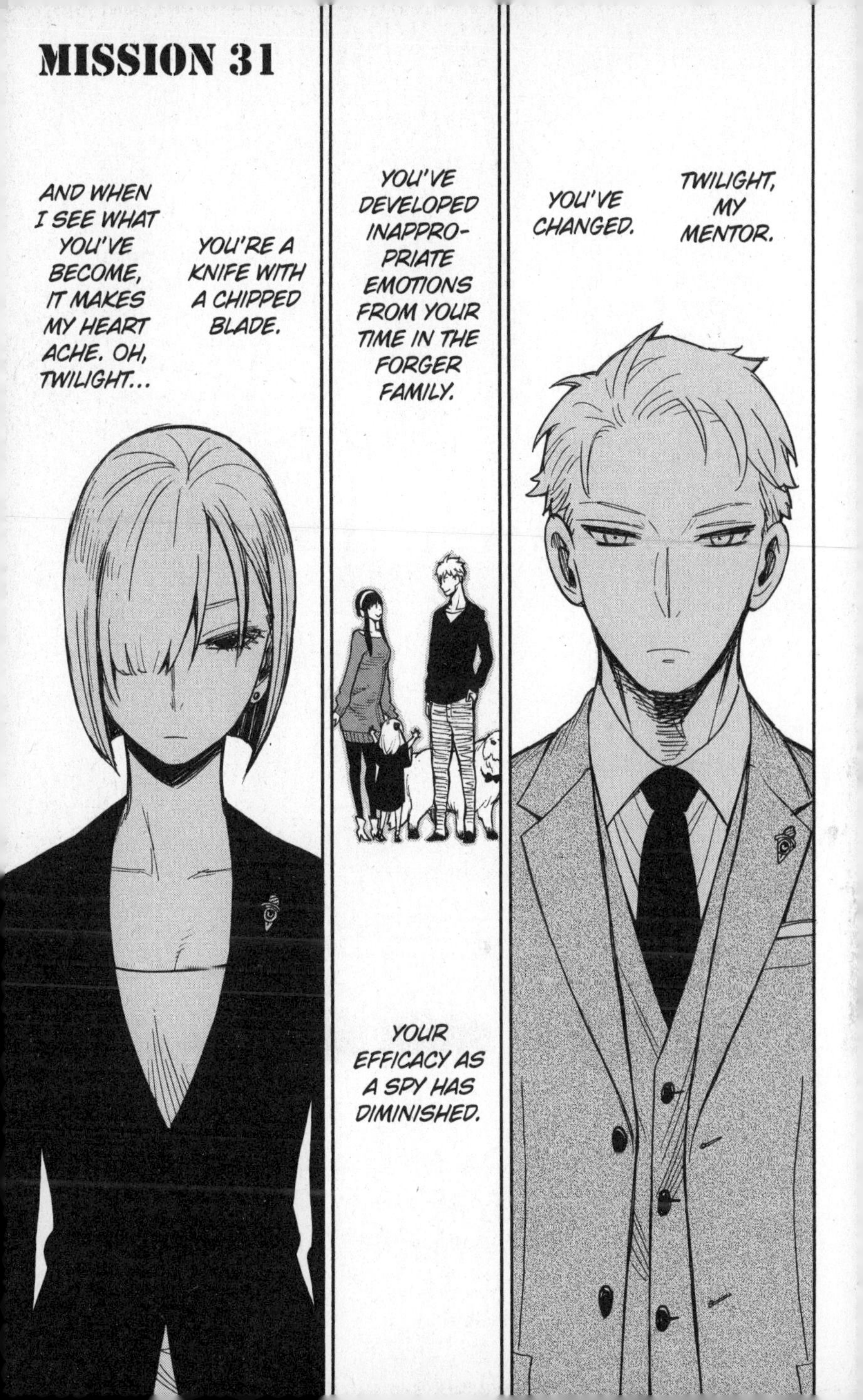
TWILIGHT, MY MENTOR.
YOU'VE CHANGED.
YOU'VE DEVELOPED INAPPRO-PRIATE EMOTIONS FROM YOUR TIME IN THE FORGER FAMILY.
YOUR EFFICACY AS A SPY HAS DIMINISHED.
YOU'RE A KNIFE WITH A CHIPPED BLADE.
AND WHEN I SEE WHAT YOU'VE BECOME, IT MAKES MY HEART ACHE. OH, TWILIGHT...

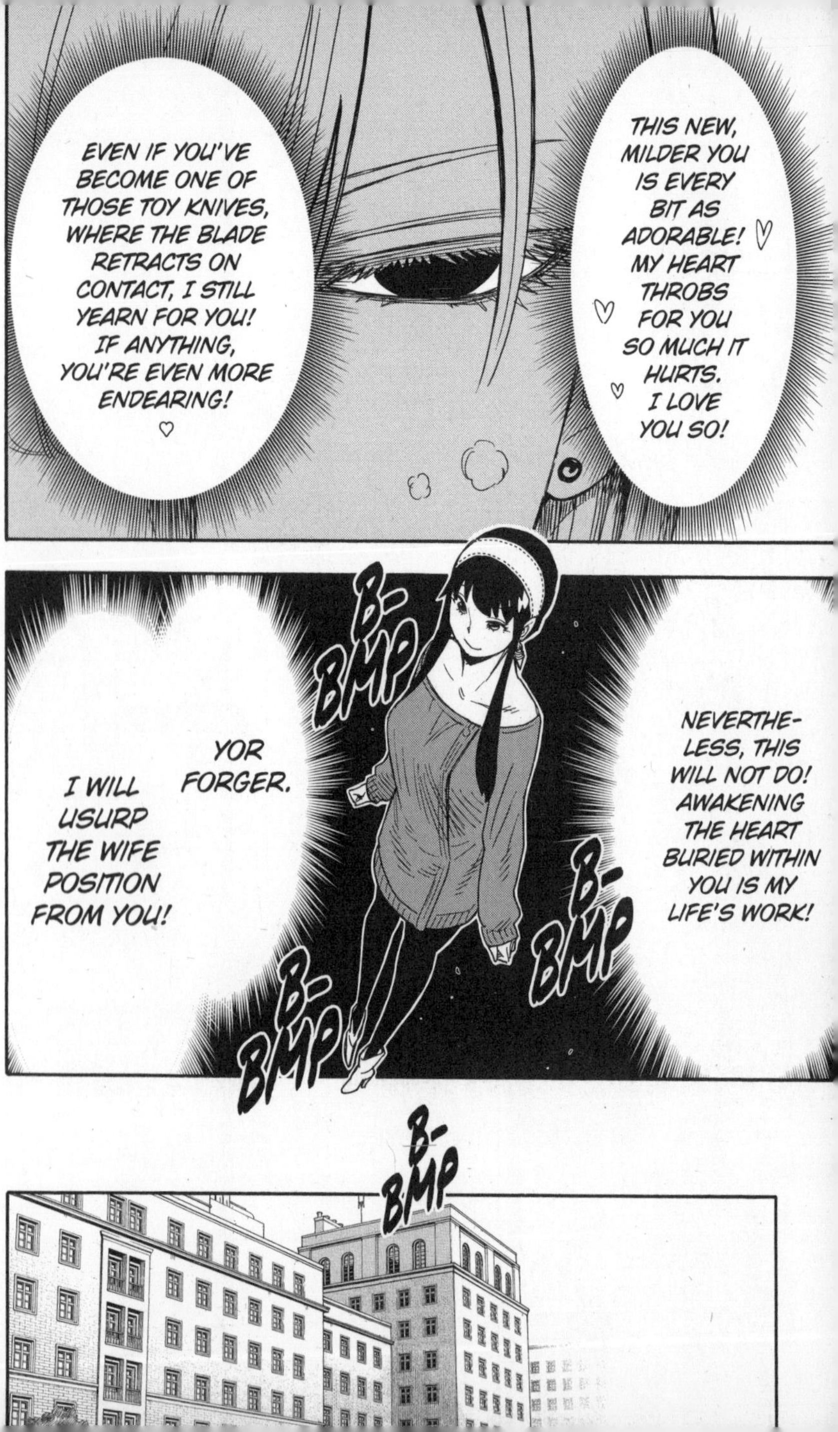

THIS NEW, MILDER YOU IS EVERY BIT AS ADORABLE! ♡ MY HEART THROBS ♡ FOR YOU SO MUCH IT ♡ HURTS. I LOVE YOU SO!
EVEN IF YOU'VE BECOME ONE OF THOSE TOY KNIVES, WHERE THE BLADE RETRACTS ON CONTACT, I STILL YEARN FOR YOU! IF ANYTHING, YOU'RE EVEN MORE ENDEARING! ♡
NEVERTHELESS, THIS WILL NOT DO! AWAKENING THE HEART BURIED WITHIN YOU IS MY LIFE'S WORK!
B-BMP
B-BMP
YOR FORGER.
I WILL USURP THE WIFE POSITION FROM YOU!
B-BMP
B-BMP

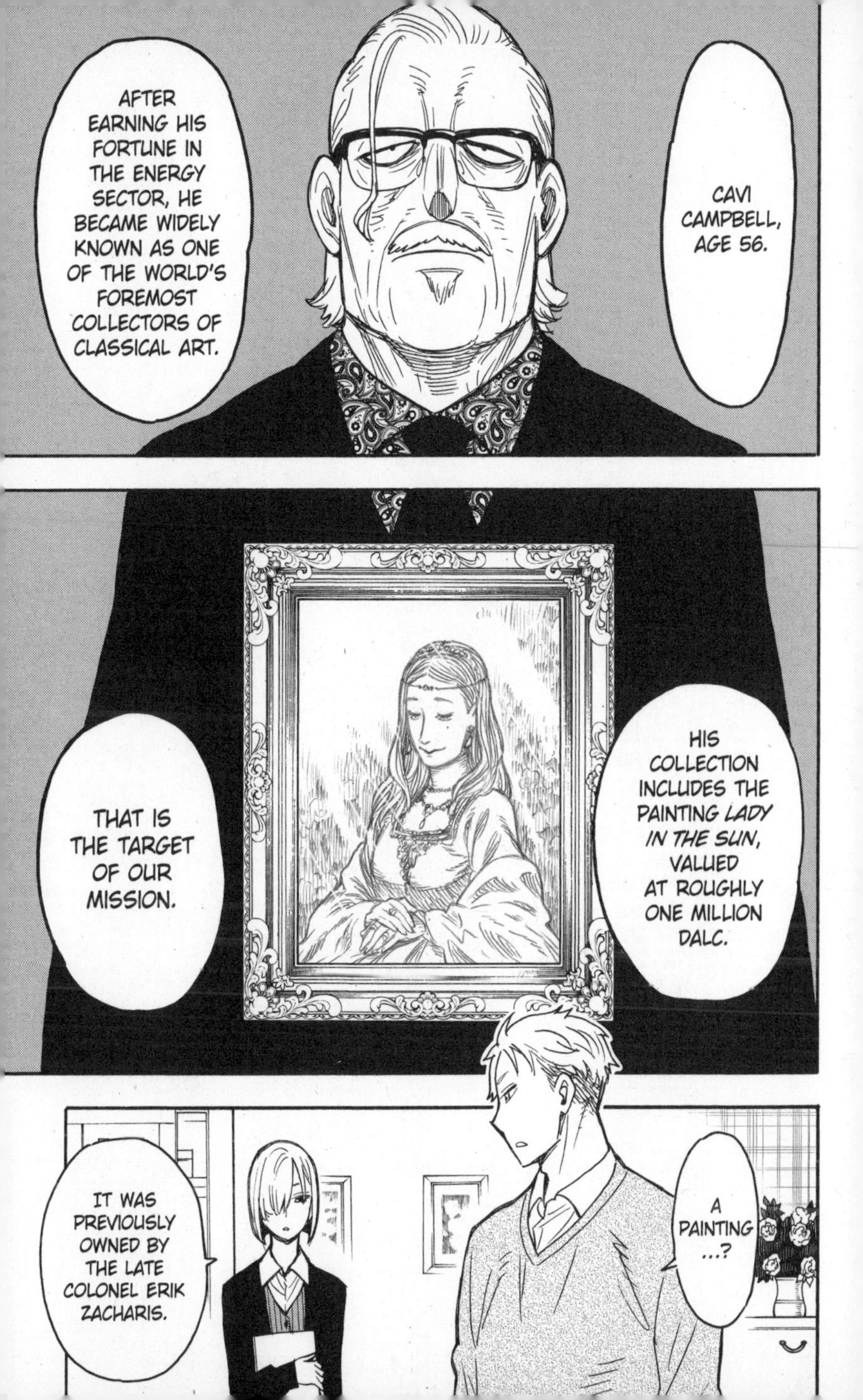
CAVI CAMPBELL, AGE 56.
AFTER EARNING HIS FORTUNE IN THE ENERGY SECTOR, HE BECAME WIDELY KNOWN AS ONE OF THE WORLD'S FOREMOST COLLECTORS OF CLASSICAL ART.
HIS COLLECTION INCLUDES THE PAINTING *LADY IN THE SUN*, VALUED AT ROUGHLY ONE MILLION DALC.
THAT IS THE TARGET OF OUR MISSION.
A PAINTING ...?
IT WAS PREVIOUSLY OWNED BY THE LATE COLONEL ERIK ZACHARIS.

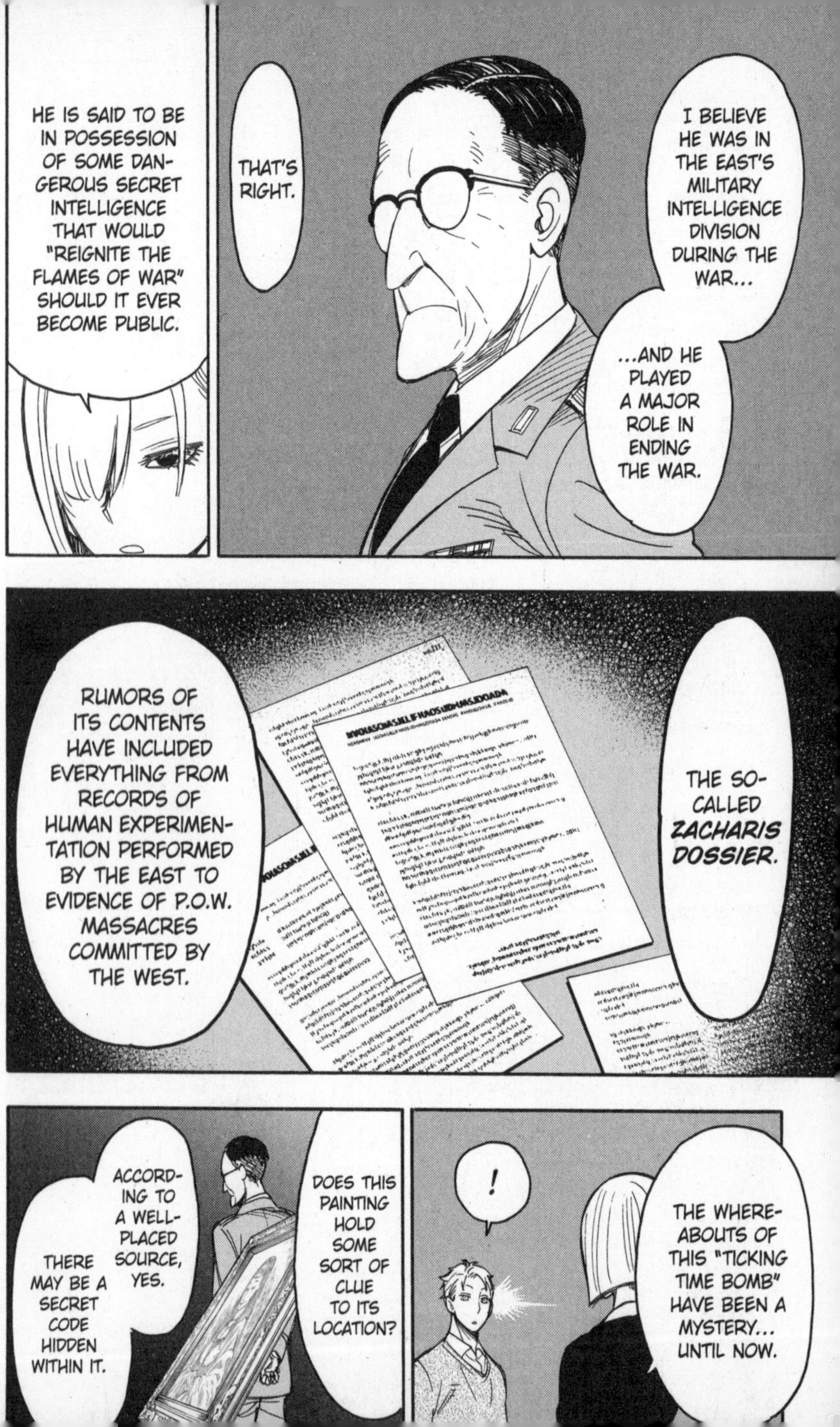
I BELIEVE HE WAS IN THE EAST'S MILITARY INTELLIGENCE DIVISION DURING THE WAR...
...AND HE PLAYED A MAJOR ROLE IN ENDING THE WAR.
THAT'S RIGHT.
HE IS SAID TO BE IN POSSESSION OF SOME DAN-GEROUS SECRET INTELLIGENCE THAT WOULD "REIGNITE THE FLAMES OF WAR" SHOULD IT EVER BECOME PUBLIC.
THE SO-CALLED *ZACHARIS DOSSIER*.
RUMORS OF ITS CONTENTS HAVE INCLUDED EVERYTHING FROM RECORDS OF HUMAN EXPERIMEN-TATION PERFORMED BY THE EAST TO EVIDENCE OF P.O.W. MASSACRES COMMITTED BY THE WEST.
!
THE WHERE-ABOUTS OF THIS "TICKING TIME BOMB" HAVE BEEN A MYSTERY... UNTIL NOW.
DOES THIS PAINTING HOLD SOME SORT OF CLUE TO ITS LOCATION?
ACCORD-ING TO A WELL-PLACED SOURCE, YES.
THERE MAY BE A SECRET CODE HIDDEN WITHIN IT.

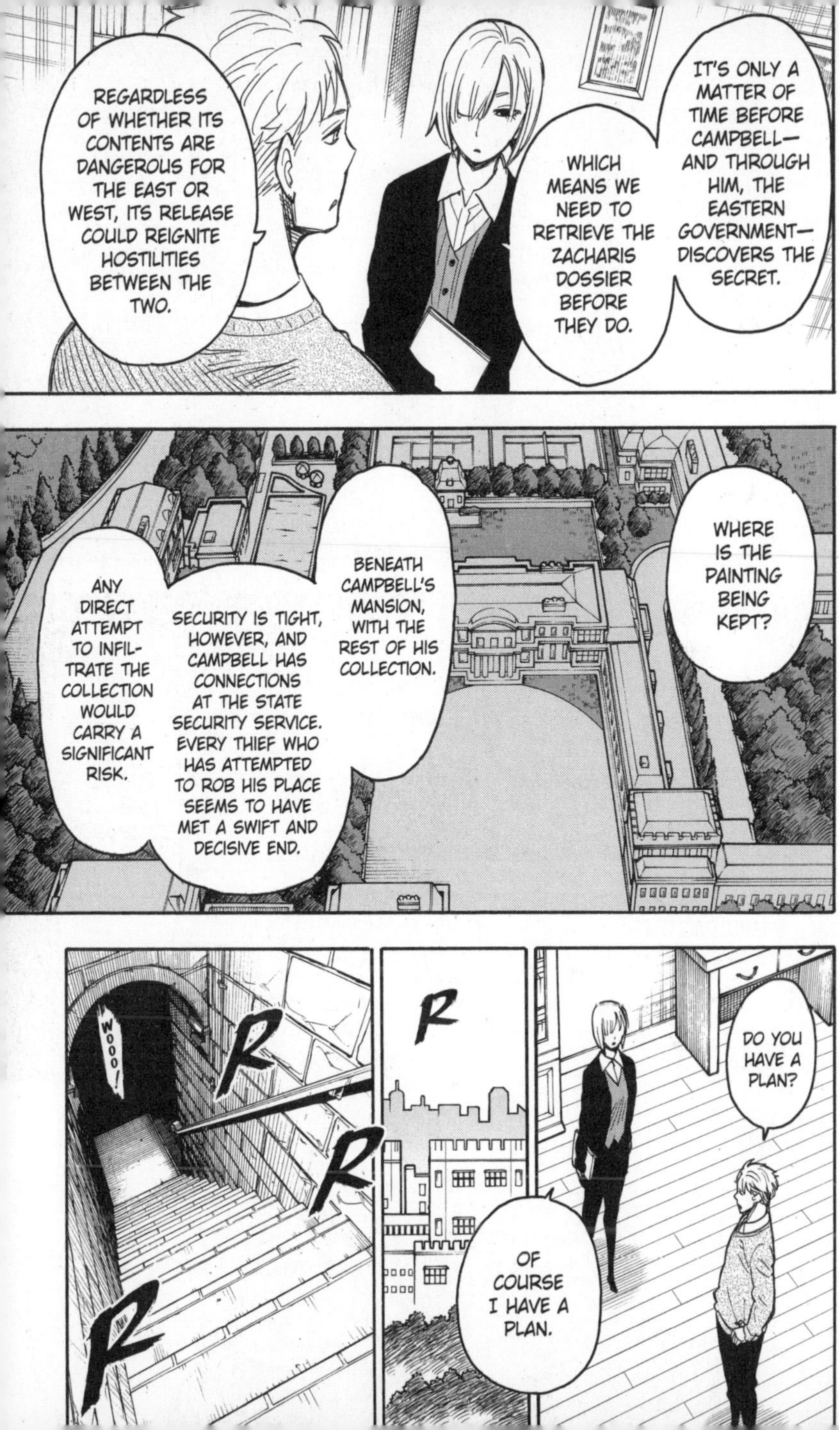
IT'S ONLY A MATTER OF TIME BEFORE CAMPBELL—AND THROUGH HIM, THE EASTERN GOVERNMENT—DISCOVERS THE SECRET.
WHICH MEANS WE NEED TO RETRIEVE THE ZACHARIS DOSSIER BEFORE THEY DO.
REGARDLESS OF WHETHER ITS CONTENTS ARE DANGEROUS FOR THE EAST OR WEST, ITS RELEASE COULD REIGNITE HOSTILITIES BETWEEN THE TWO.
WHERE IS THE PAINTING BEING KEPT?
BENEATH CAMPBELL'S MANSION, WITH THE REST OF HIS COLLECTION.
SECURITY IS TIGHT, HOWEVER, AND CAMPBELL HAS CONNECTIONS AT THE STATE SECURITY SERVICE. EVERY THIEF WHO HAS ATTEMPTED TO ROB HIS PLACE SEEMS TO HAVE MET A SWIFT AND DECISIVE END.
ANY DIRECT ATTEMPT TO INFIL-TRATE THE COLLECTION WOULD CARRY A SIGNIFICANT RISK.
DO YOU HAVE A PLAN?
OF COURSE I HAVE A PLAN.
R
R
R
R
WOOO!

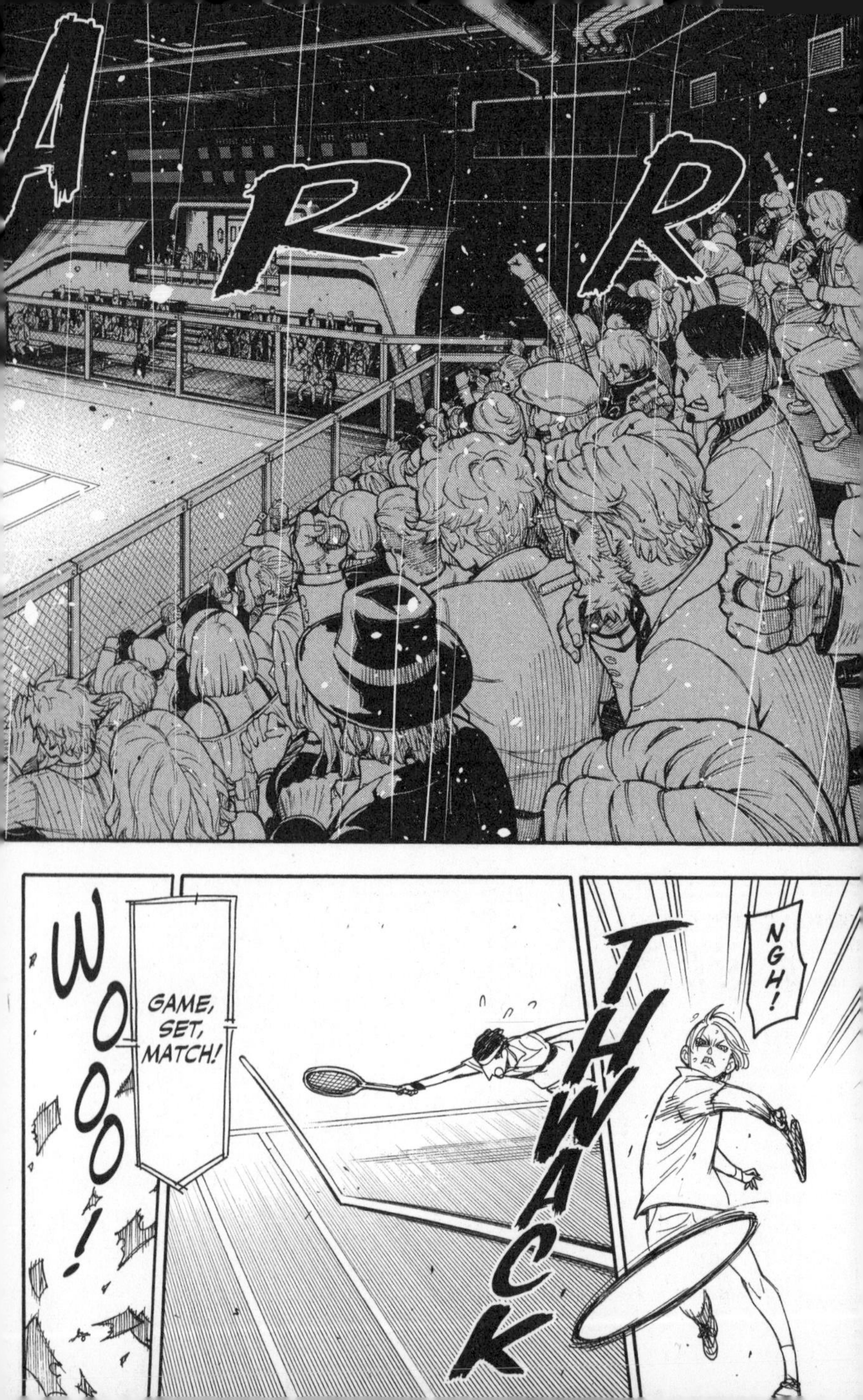
ARR
NGH!
THWACK
GAME, SET, MATCH!
WOOO!

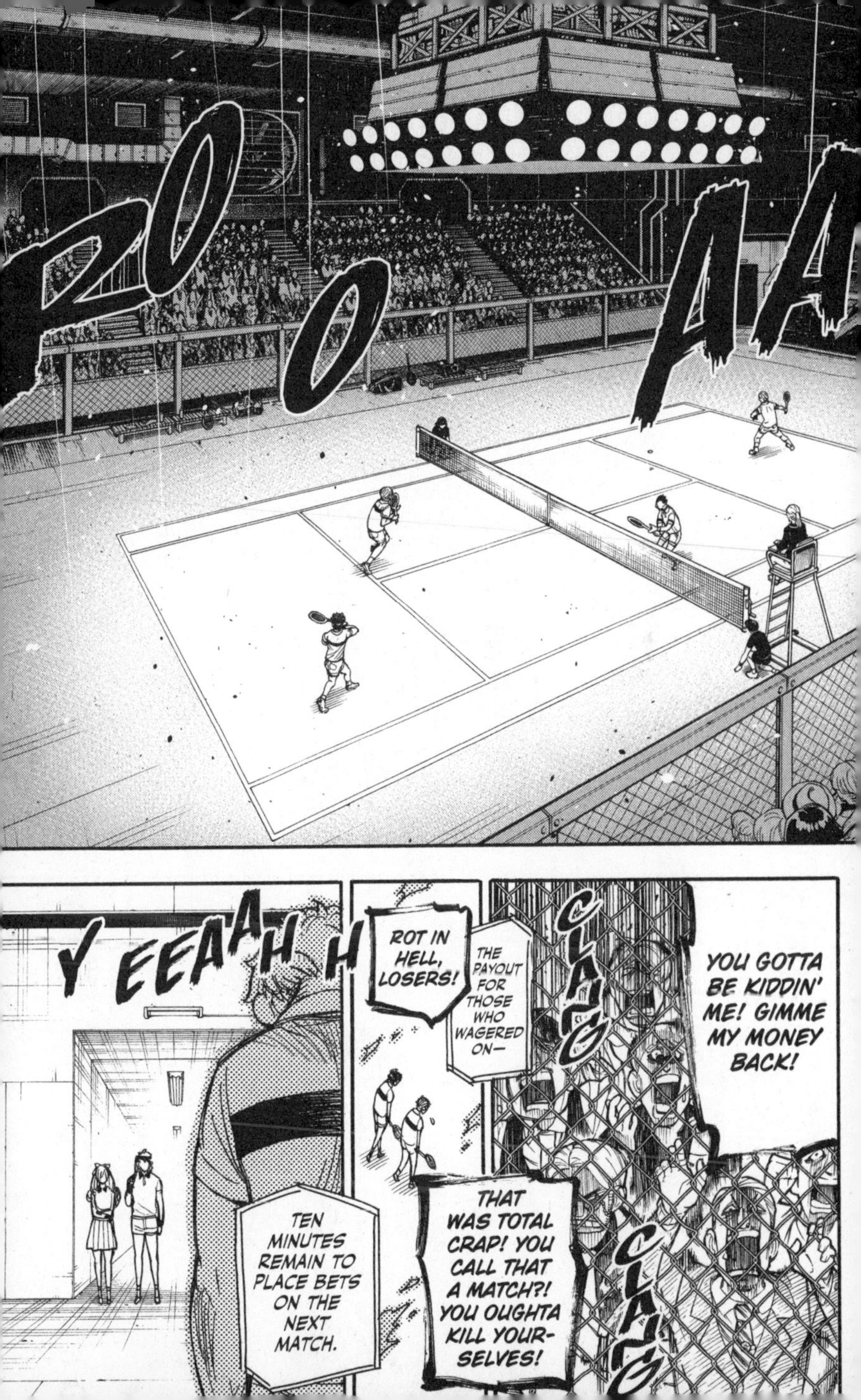
ROOOAA
YOU GOTTA BE KIDDIN' ME! GIMME MY MONEY BACK!
CLANG
CLANG
THAT WAS TOTAL CRAP! YOU CALL THAT A MATCH?! YOU OUGHTA KILL YOUR-SELVES!
THE PAYOUT FOR THOSE WHO WAGERED ON—
ROT IN HELL, LOSERS!
YEEAAHH
TEN MINUTES REMAIN TO PLACE BETS ON THE NEXT MATCH.

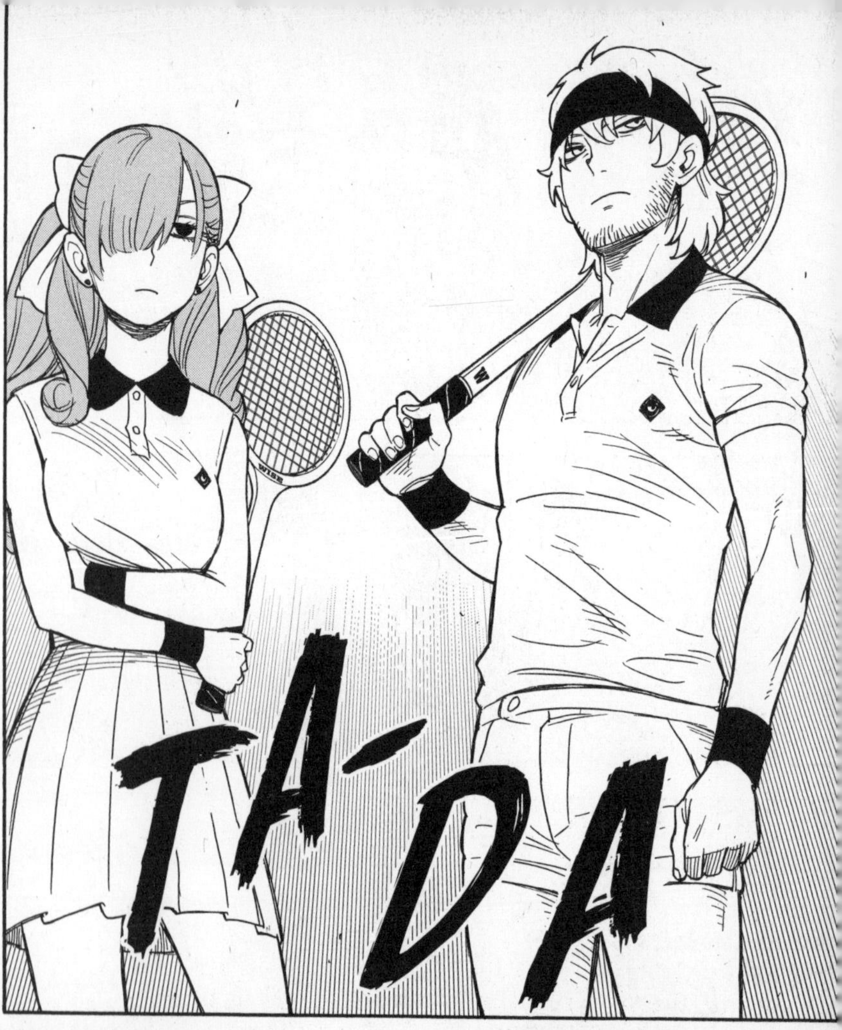
TA-DA

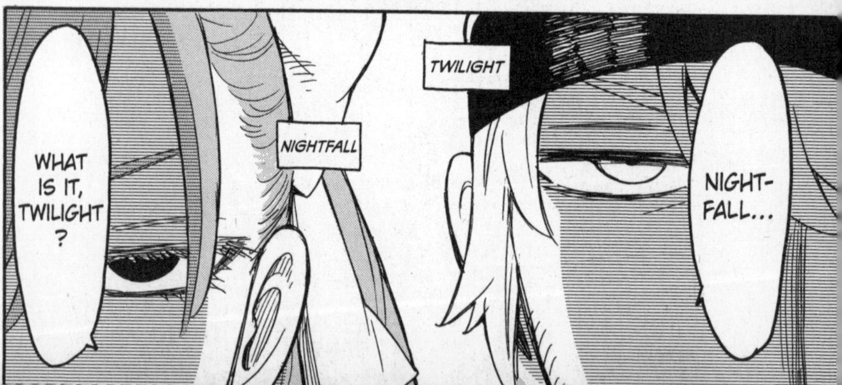
NIGHT-FALL...
TWILIGHT
NIGHTFALL
WHAT IS IT, TWILIGHT?

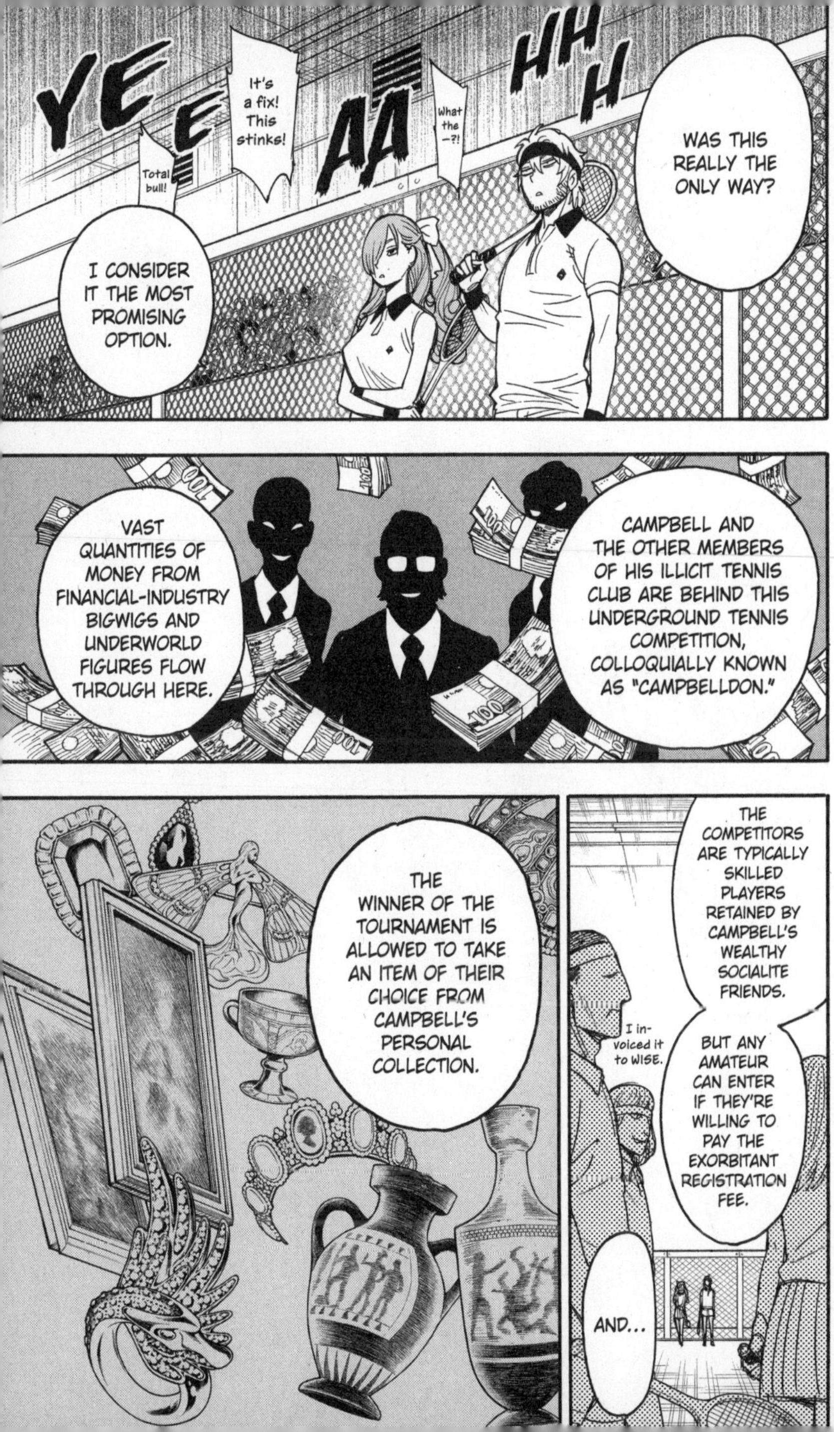
YEEAAHHH
WAS THIS REALLY THE ONLY WAY?
What the—?!
It's a fix! This stinks!
Total bull!
I CONSIDER IT THE MOST PROMISING OPTION.
CAMPBELL AND THE OTHER MEMBERS OF HIS ILLICIT TENNIS CLUB ARE BEHIND THIS UNDERGROUND TENNIS COMPETITION, COLLOQUIALLY KNOWN AS "CAMPBELLDON."
VAST QUANTITIES OF MONEY FROM FINANCIAL-INDUSTRY BIGWIGS AND UNDERWORLD FIGURES FLOW THROUGH HERE.
THE COMPETITORS ARE TYPICALLY SKILLED PLAYERS RETAINED BY CAMPBELL'S WEALTHY SOCIALITE FRIENDS.
I invoiced it to WISE.
BUT ANY AMATEUR CAN ENTER IF THEY'RE WILLING TO PAY THE EXORBITANT REGISTRATION FEE.
AND...
THE WINNER OF THE TOURNAMENT IS ALLOWED TO TAKE AN ITEM OF THEIR CHOICE FROM CAMPBELL'S PERSONAL COLLECTION.

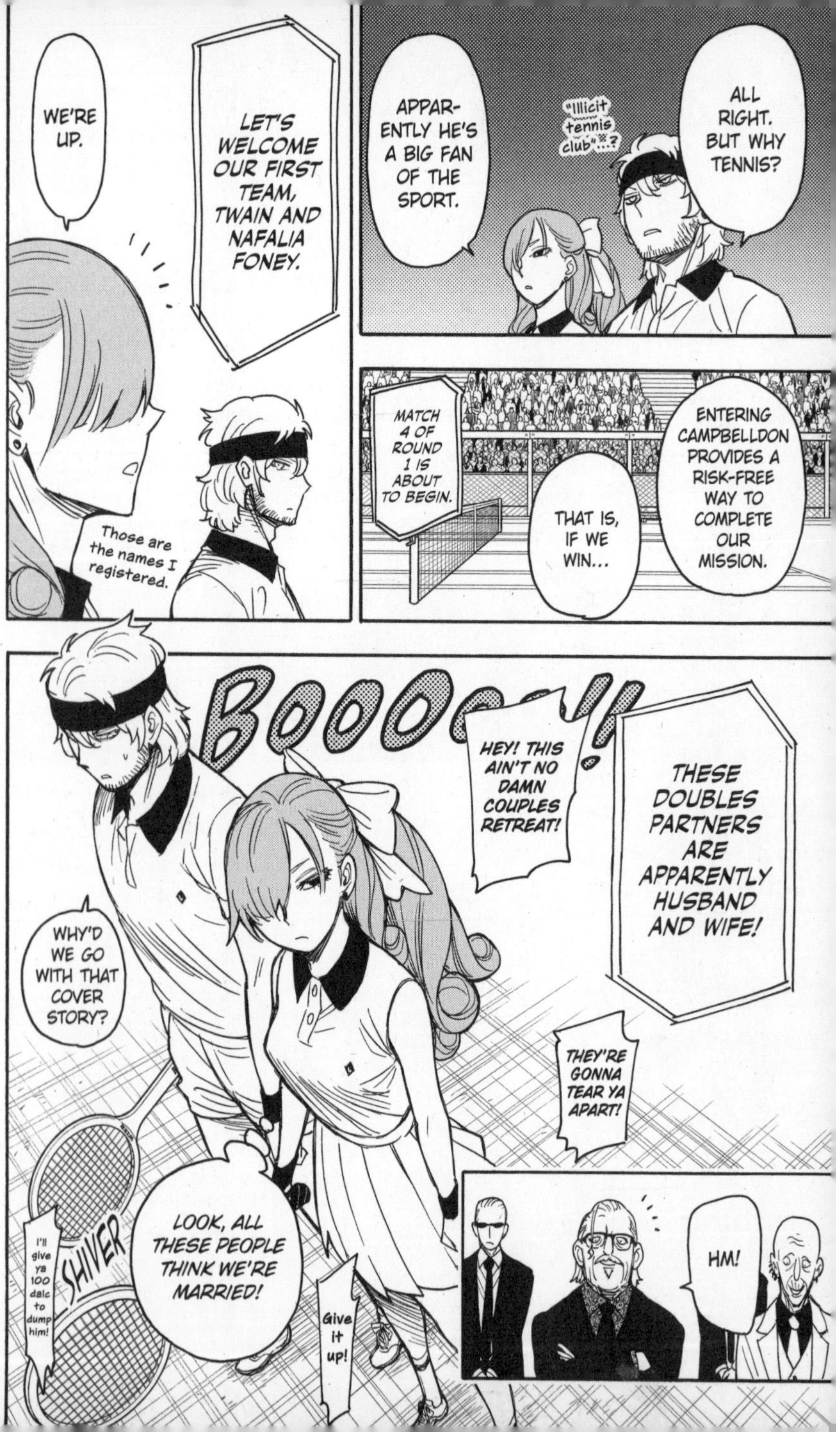
ALL RIGHT. BUT WHY TENNIS?
"Illicit tennis club"※...?
APPARENTLY HE'S A BIG FAN OF THE SPORT.
ENTERING CAMPBELLDON PROVIDES A RISK-FREE WAY TO COMPLETE OUR MISSION.
THAT IS, IF WE WIN...
MATCH 4 OF ROUND 1 IS ABOUT TO BEGIN.
LET'S WELCOME OUR FIRST TEAM, TWAIN AND NAFALIA FONEY.
WE'RE UP.
Those are the names I registered.
BOOOOO!!
THESE DOUBLES PARTNERS ARE APPARENTLY HUSBAND AND WIFE!
HEY! THIS AIN'T NO DAMN COUPLES RETREAT!
THEY'RE GONNA TEAR YA APART!
HM!
WHY'D WE GO WITH THAT COVER STORY?
LOOK, ALL THESE PEOPLE THINK WE'RE MARRIED!
Give it up!
SHIVER
I'll give ya 100 dalc to dump him!

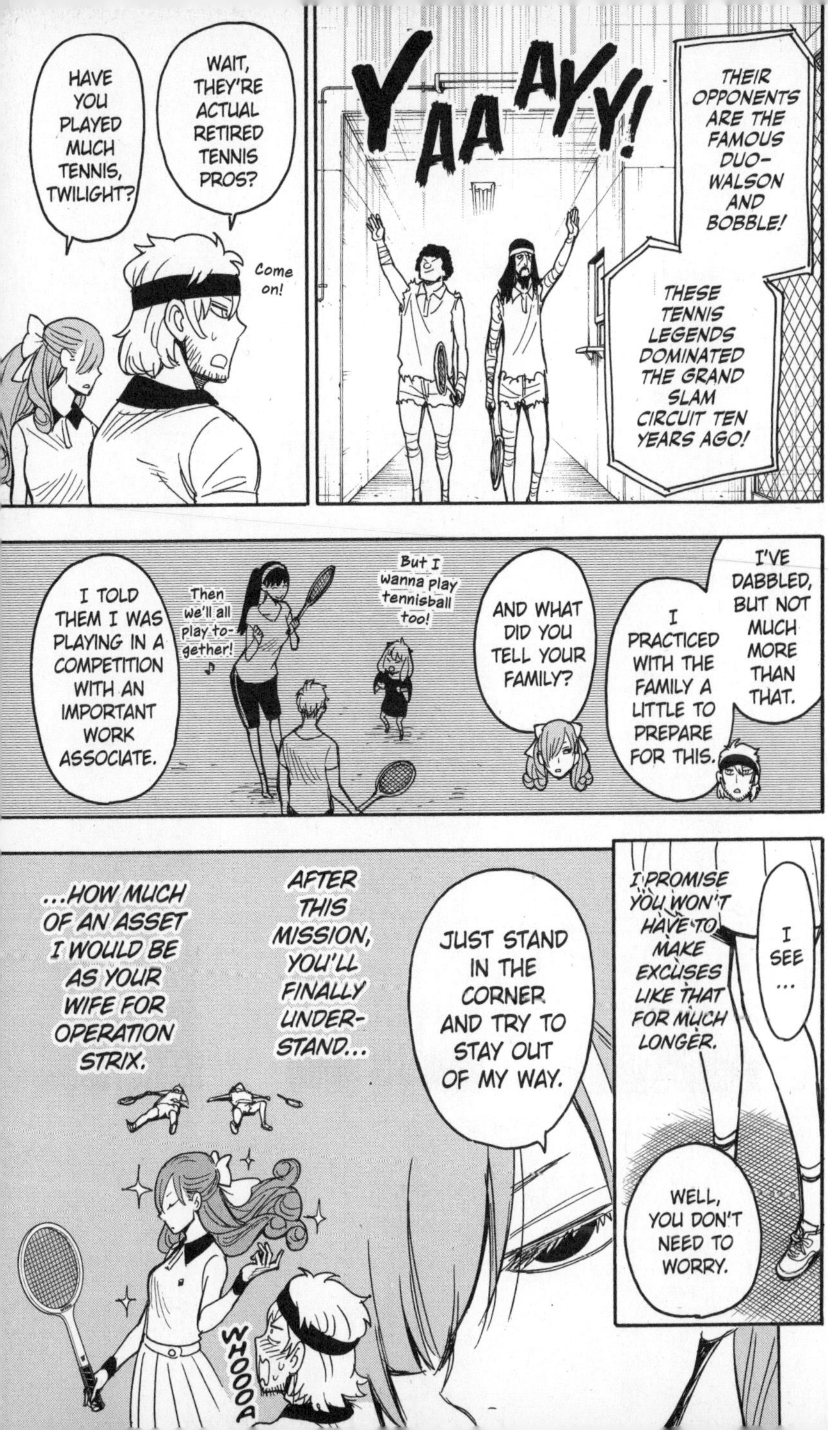
YAAAYY!
THEIR OPPONENTS ARE THE FAMOUS DUO—WALSON AND BOBBLE!
THESE TENNIS LEGENDS DOMINATED THE GRAND SLAM CIRCUIT TEN YEARS AGO!
WAIT, THEY'RE ACTUAL RETIRED TENNIS PROS?
Come on!
HAVE YOU PLAYED MUCH TENNIS, TWILIGHT?
I'VE DABBLED, BUT NOT MUCH MORE THAN THAT.
I PRACTICED WITH THE FAMILY A LITTLE TO PREPARE FOR THIS.
AND WHAT DID YOU TELL YOUR FAMILY?
I TOLD THEM I WAS PLAYING IN A COMPETITION WITH AN IMPORTANT WORK ASSOCIATE.
But I wanna play tennisball too!
Then we'll all play together! ♪
I SEE...
I PROMISE YOU WON'T HAVE TO MAKE EXCUSES LIKE THAT FOR MUCH LONGER.
WELL, YOU DON'T NEED TO WORRY.
JUST STAND IN THE CORNER AND TRY TO STAY OUT OF MY WAY.
AFTER THIS MISSION, YOU'LL FINALLY UNDERSTAND...
...HOW MUCH OF AN ASSET I WOULD BE AS YOUR WIFE FOR OPERATION STRIX.
WHOOOA

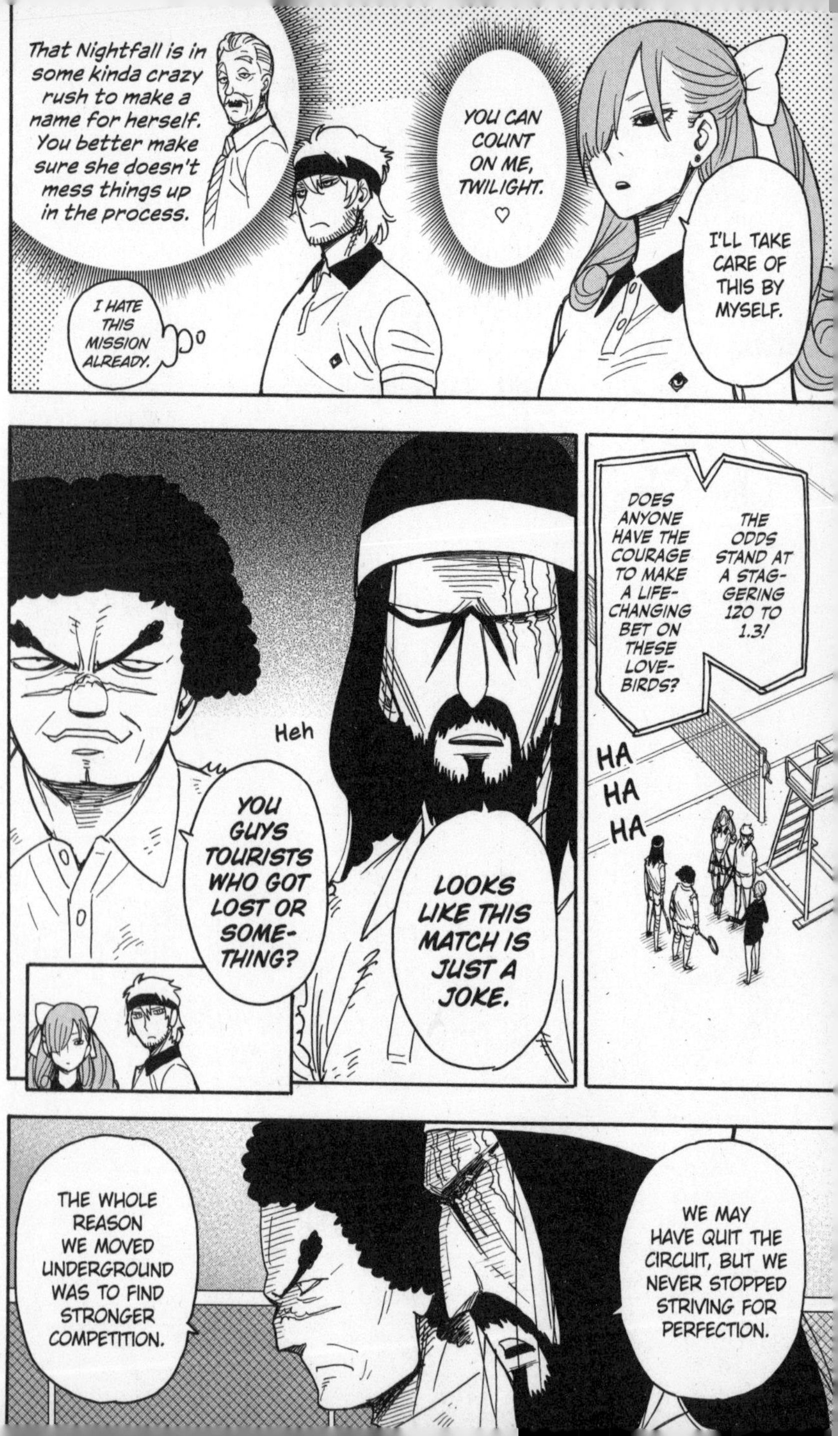
I'LL TAKE CARE OF THIS BY MYSELF.
YOU CAN COUNT ON ME, TWILIGHT. ♡
That Nightfall is in some kinda crazy rush to make a name for herself. You better make sure she doesn't mess things up in the process.
I HATE THIS MISSION ALREADY.
THE ODDS STAND AT A STAGGERING 120 TO 1.3!
DOES ANYONE HAVE THE COURAGE TO MAKE A LIFE-CHANGING BET ON THESE LOVEBIRDS?
HA HA HA
LOOKS LIKE THIS MATCH IS JUST A JOKE.
Heh
YOU GUYS TOURISTS WHO GOT LOST OR SOMETHING?
WE MAY HAVE QUIT THE CIRCUIT, BUT WE NEVER STOPPED STRIVING FOR PERFECTION.
THE WHOLE REASON WE MOVED UNDERGROUND WAS TO FIND STRONGER COMPETITION.

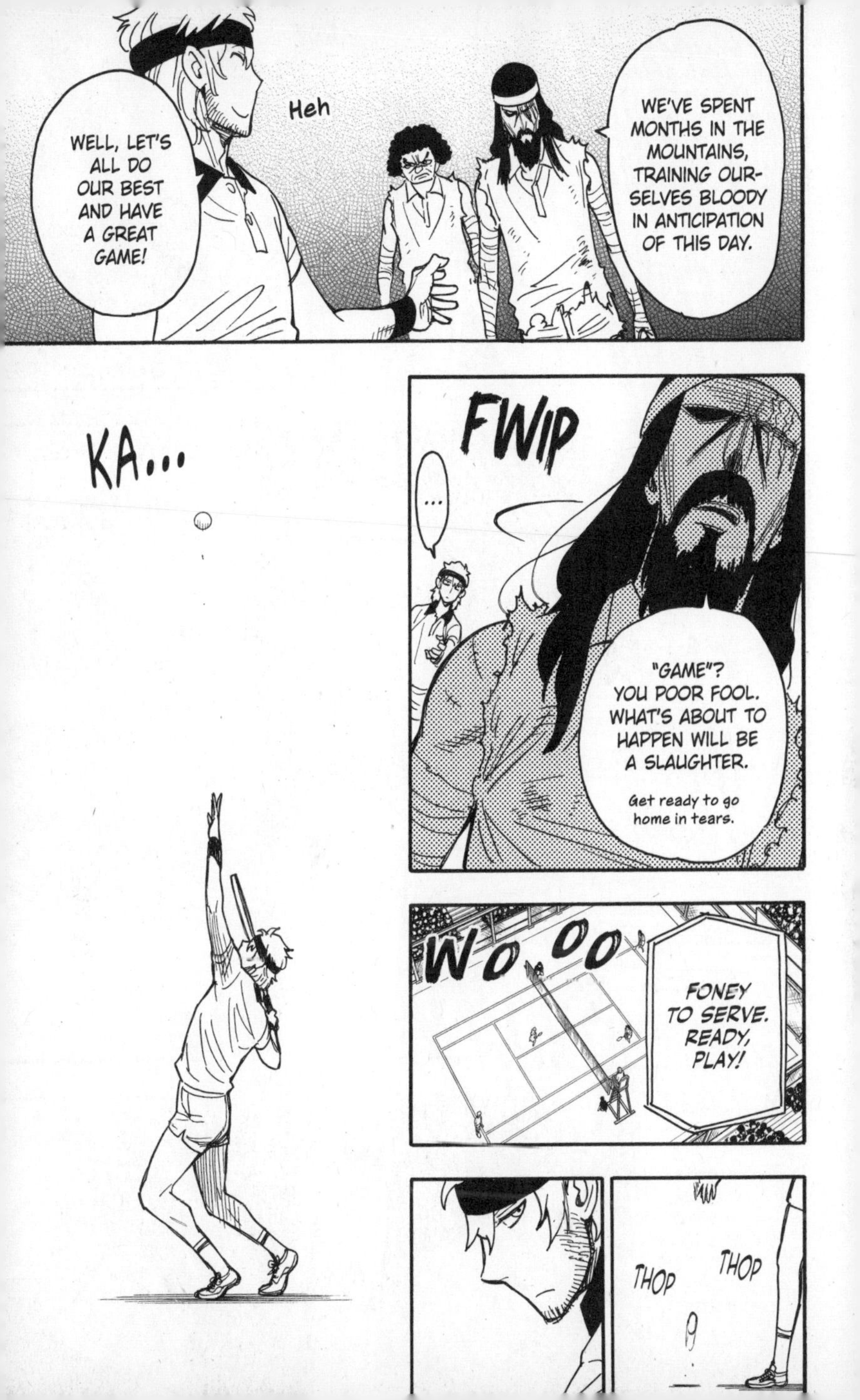
WE'VE SPENT MONTHS IN THE MOUNTAINS, TRAINING OUR-SELVES BLOODY IN ANTICIPATION OF THIS DAY.
Heh
WELL, LET'S ALL DO OUR BEST AND HAVE A GREAT GAME!
FWIP
...
"GAME"? YOU POOR FOOL. WHAT'S ABOUT TO HAPPEN WILL BE A SLAUGHTER.
Get ready to go home in tears.
WOOOO
FONEY TO SERVE. READY, PLAY!
THOP
THOP
KA...

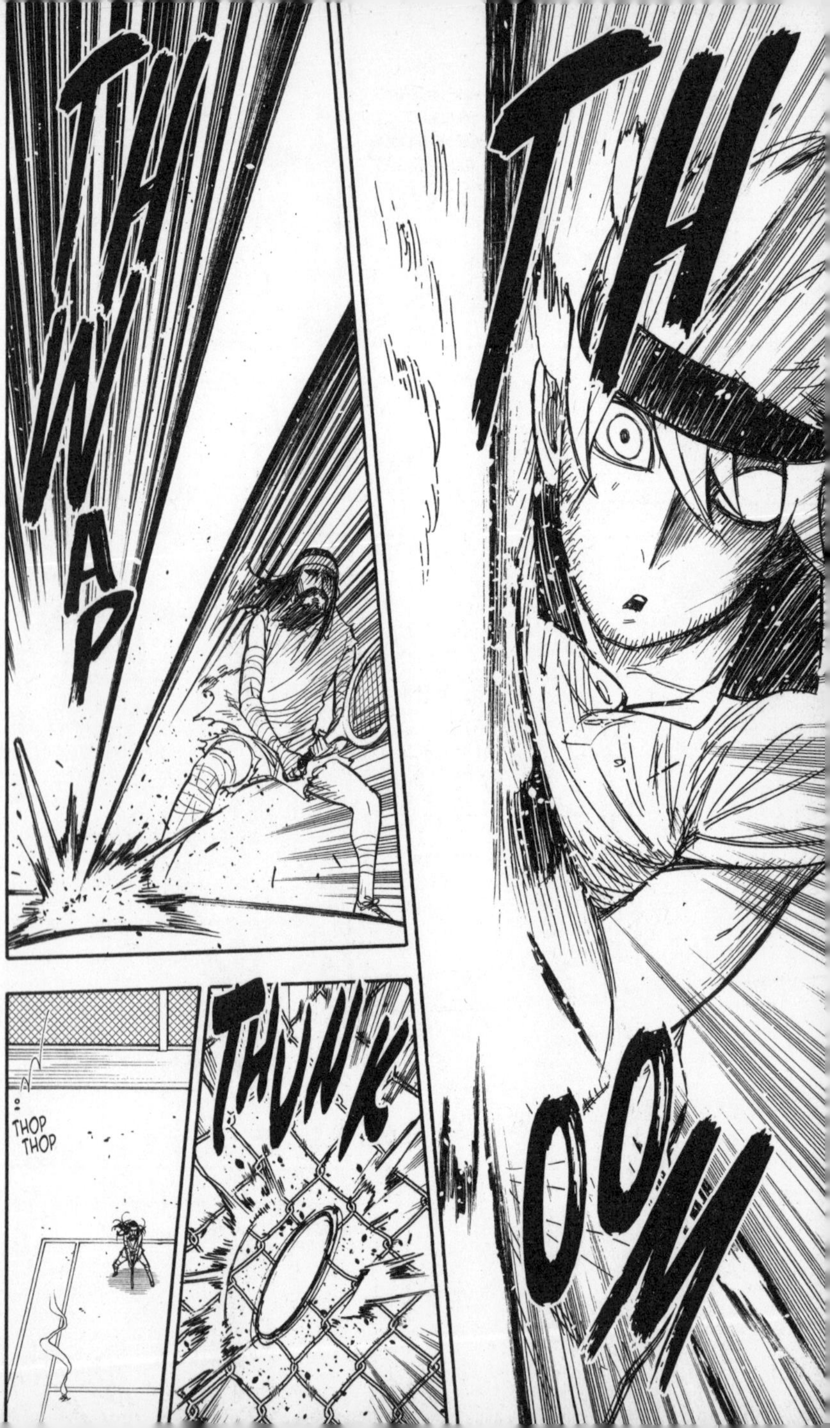
THOOM
THWAP
THUNK
THOP THOP

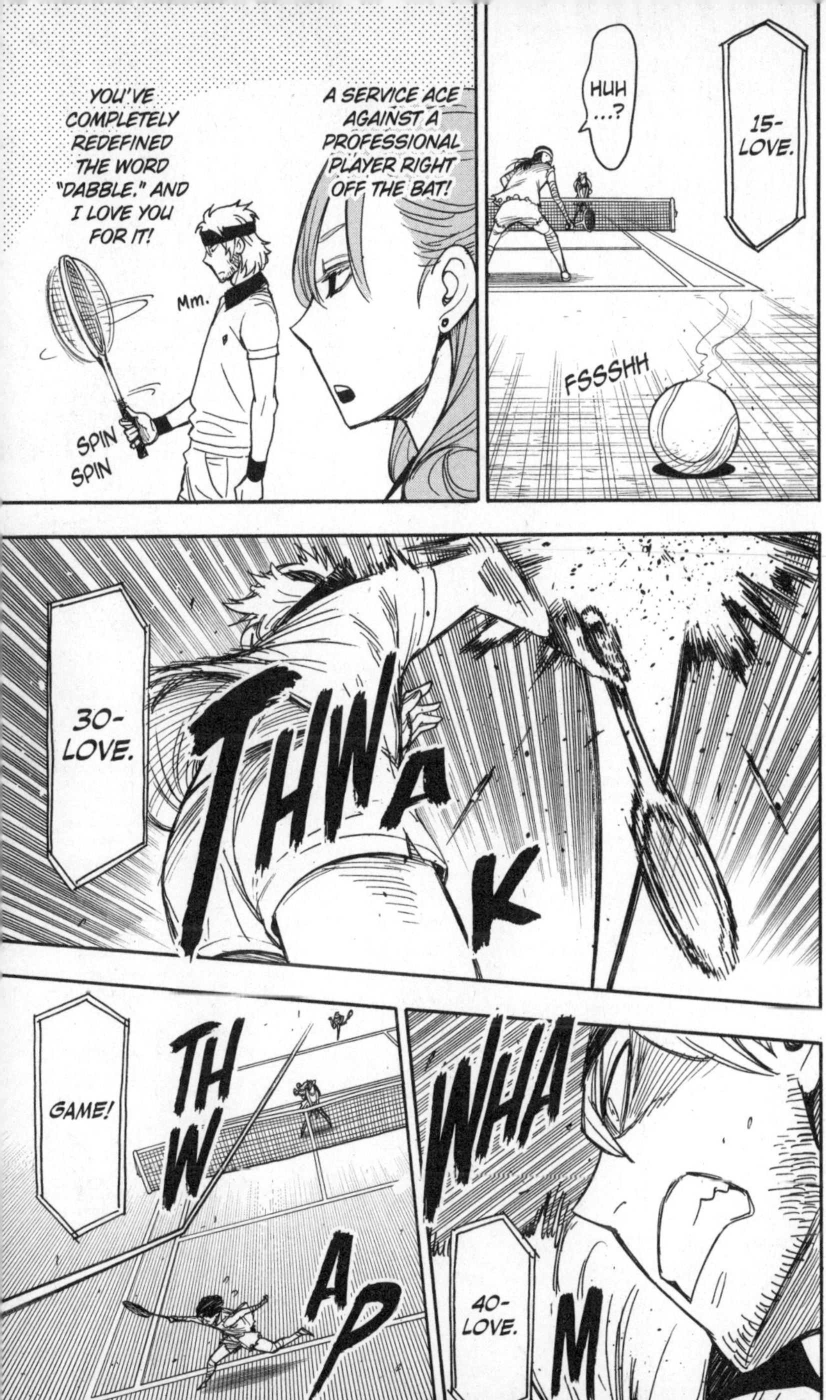
15-LOVE.
HUH ...?
FSSSHH
A SERVICE ACE AGAINST A PROFESSIONAL PLAYER RIGHT OFF THE BAT!
YOU'VE COMPLETELY REDEFINED THE WORD "DABBLE." AND I LOVE YOU FOR IT!
Mm.
SPIN SPIN
30-LOVE.
THWAK
WHAM
40-LOVE.
GAME!
THWAP

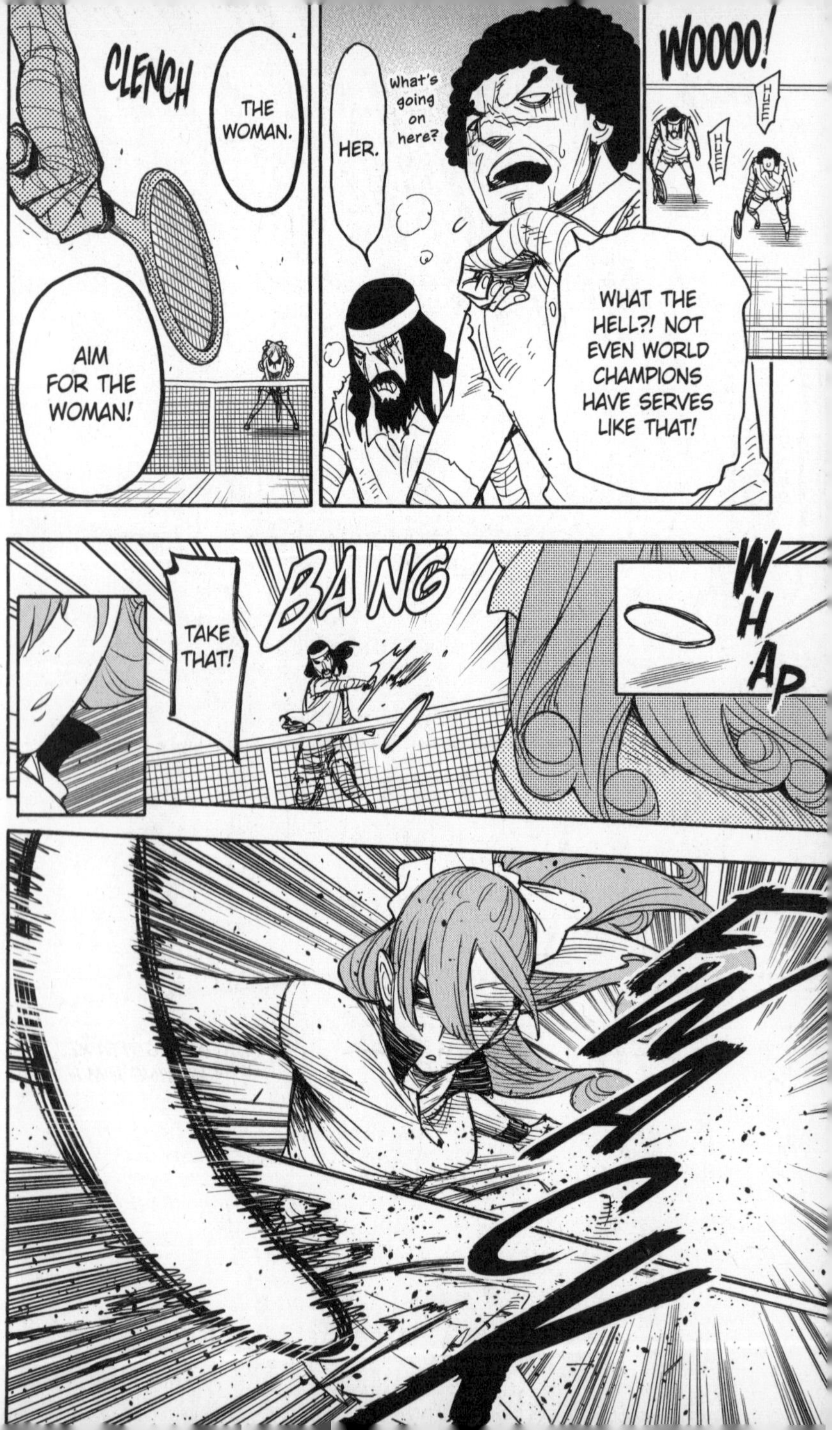
WOOOO!
HUFF
HUFF
WHAT THE HELL?! NOT EVEN WORLD CHAMPIONS HAVE SERVES LIKE THAT!
What's going on here?
HER.
THE WOMAN.
CLENCH
AIM FOR THE WOMAN!
WHAP
BANG
TAKE THAT!
WHACK

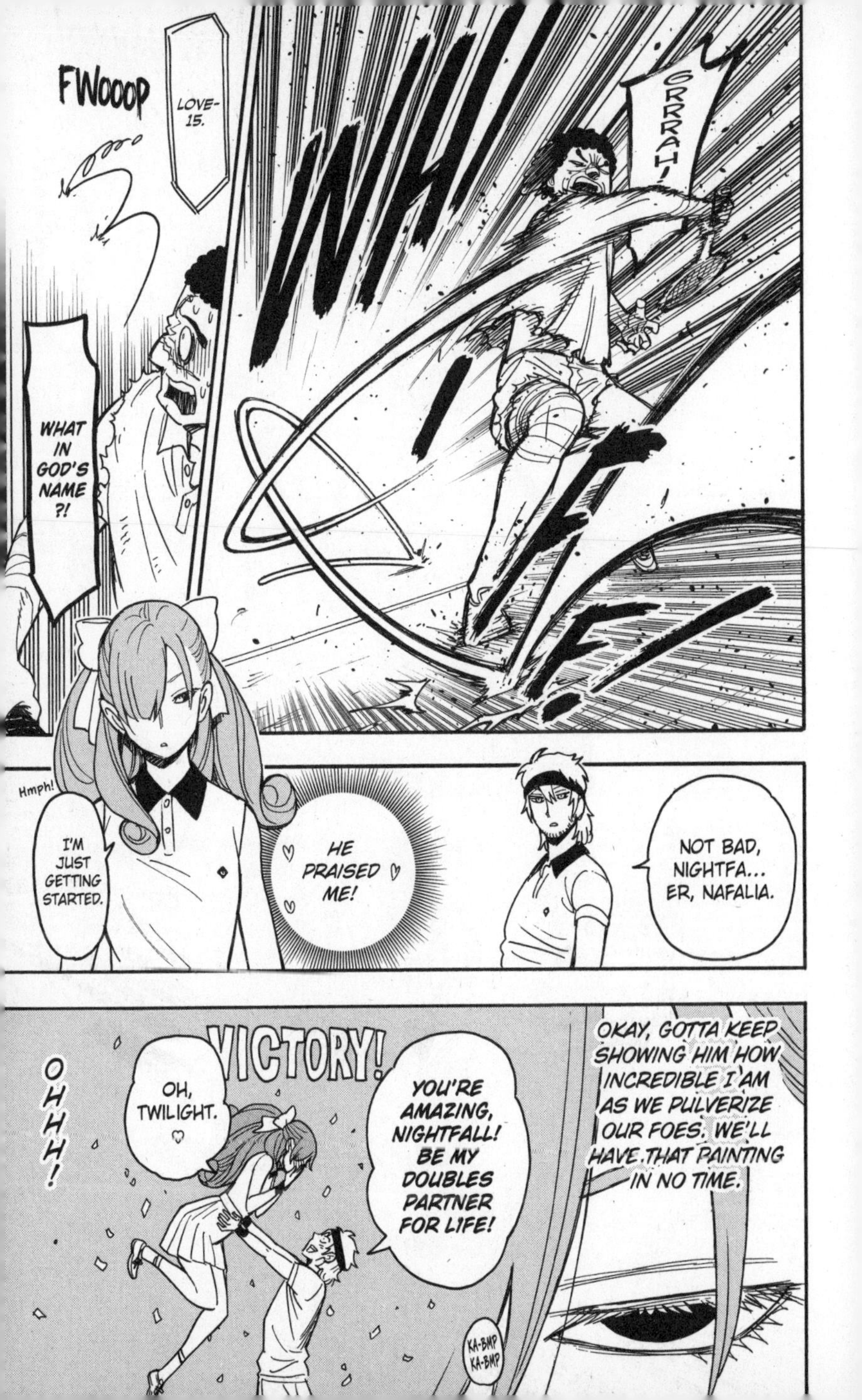
GRRRAH!
WHIFF!
LOVE-15.
FWOOOP
WHAT IN GOD'S NAME?!
NOT BAD, NIGHTFA... ER, NAFALIA.
HE PRAISED ME!
Hmph!
I'M JUST GETTING STARTED.
OKAY, GOTTA KEEP SHOWING HIM HOW INCREDIBLE I AM AS WE PULVERIZE OUR FOES. WE'LL HAVE THAT PAINTING IN NO TIME.
VICTORY!
YOU'RE AMAZING, NIGHTFALL! BE MY DOUBLES PARTNER FOR LIFE!
OH, TWILIGHT.
OHHH!
KA-BMP KA-BMP

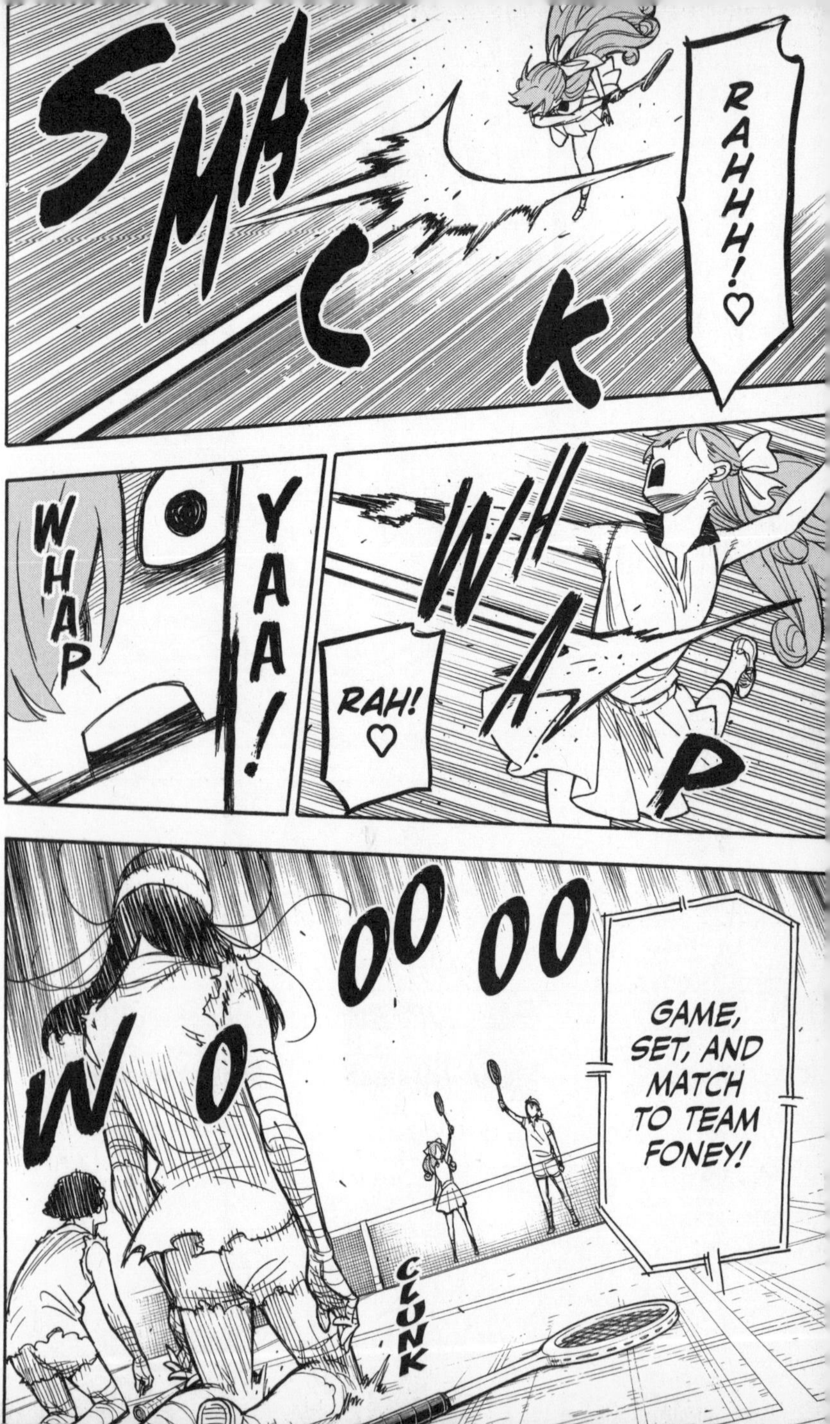
RAHHHH!♡
SMACK
WHAP
RAH!♡
YAA!
WHAP
GAME, SET, AND MATCH TO TEAM FONEY!
WOOOOO
CLUNK

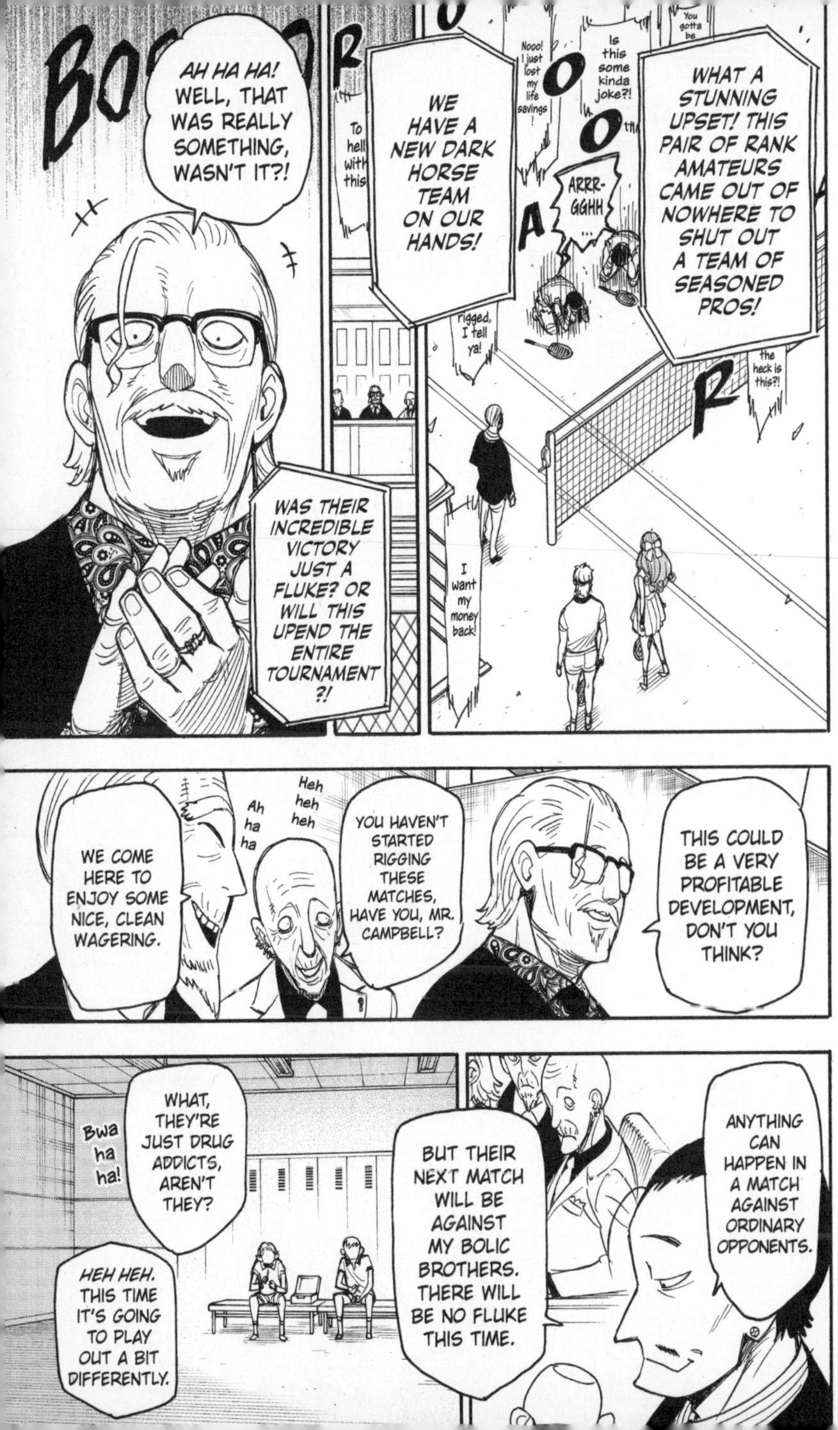
You gotta be
WHAT A STUNNING UPSET! THIS PAIR OF RANK AMATEURS CAME OUT OF NOWHERE TO SHUT OUT A TEAM OF SEASONED PROS!
Is this some kinda joke?!
Nooo! I just lost my life savings!
ARRR-GGHH...
WE HAVE A NEW DARK HORSE TEAM ON OUR HANDS!
To hell with this
the heck is this?!
rigged, I tell ya!
I want my money back!
AH HA HA! WELL, THAT WAS REALLY SOMETHING, WASN'T IT?!
WAS THEIR INCREDIBLE VICTORY JUST A FLUKE? OR WILL THIS UPEND THE ENTIRE TOURNAMENT?!
THIS COULD BE A VERY PROFITABLE DEVELOPMENT, DON'T YOU THINK?
YOU HAVEN'T STARTED RIGGING THESE MATCHES, HAVE YOU, MR. CAMPBELL?
Heh heh heh
Ah ha ha
WE COME HERE TO ENJOY SOME NICE, CLEAN WAGERING.
ANYTHING CAN HAPPEN IN A MATCH AGAINST ORDINARY OPPONENTS.
BUT THEIR NEXT MATCH WILL BE AGAINST MY BOLIC BROTHERS. THERE WILL BE NO FLUKE THIS TIME.
WHAT, THEY'RE JUST DRUG ADDICTS, AREN'T THEY?
Bwa ha ha!
HEH HEH. THIS TIME IT'S GOING TO PLAY OUT A BIT DIFFERENTLY.

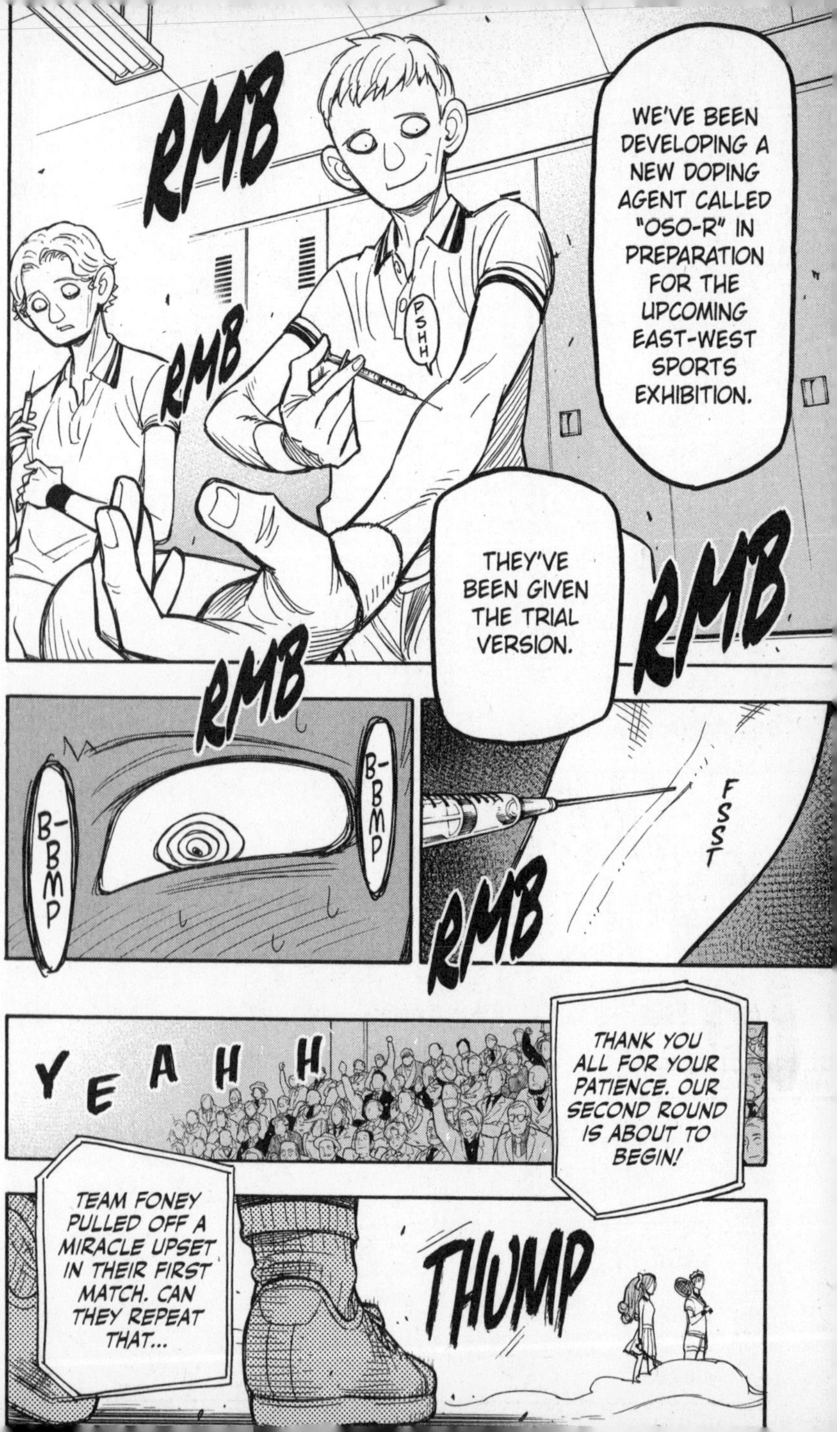
WE'VE BEEN DEVELOPING A NEW DOPING AGENT CALLED "OSO-R" IN PREPARATION FOR THE UPCOMING EAST-WEST SPORTS EXHIBITION.
RMB
PSHH
RMB
RMB
THEY'VE BEEN GIVEN THE TRIAL VERSION.
RMB
FSST
RMB
B-BBMP
B-BBMP
THANK YOU ALL FOR YOUR PATIENCE. OUR SECOND ROUND IS ABOUT TO BEGIN!
YEAHH
THUMP
TEAM FONEY PULLED OFF A MIRACLE UPSET IN THEIR FIRST MATCH. CAN THEY REPEAT THAT...

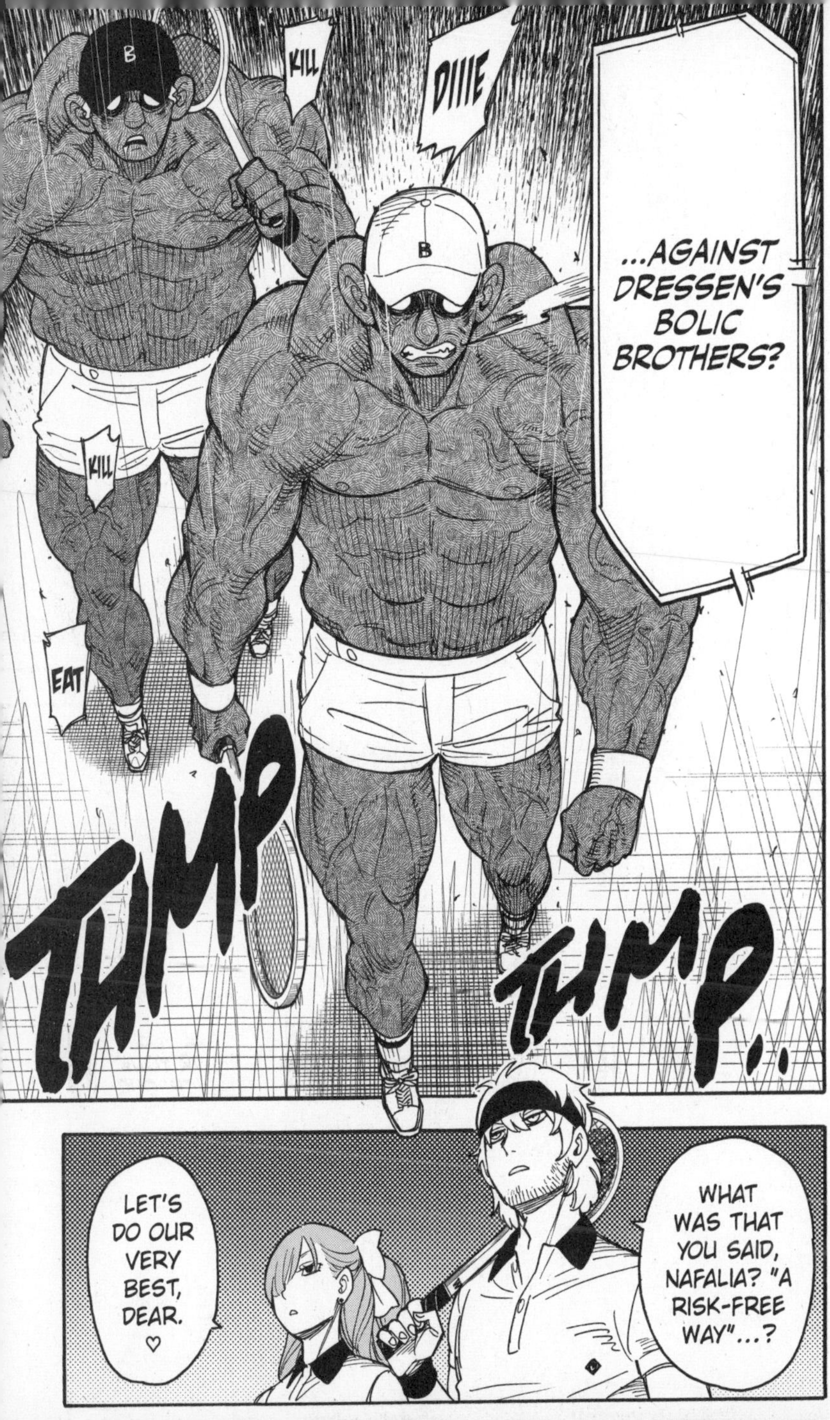
...AGAINST DRESSEN'S BOLIC BROTHERS?
DIIIE
KILL
KILL
EAT
THMP
THMP..
WHAT WAS THAT YOU SAID, NAFALIA? "A RISK-FREE WAY"...?
LET'S DO OUR VERY BEST, DEAR. ♡

SPY×FAMILY

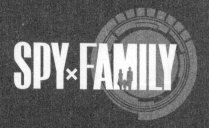

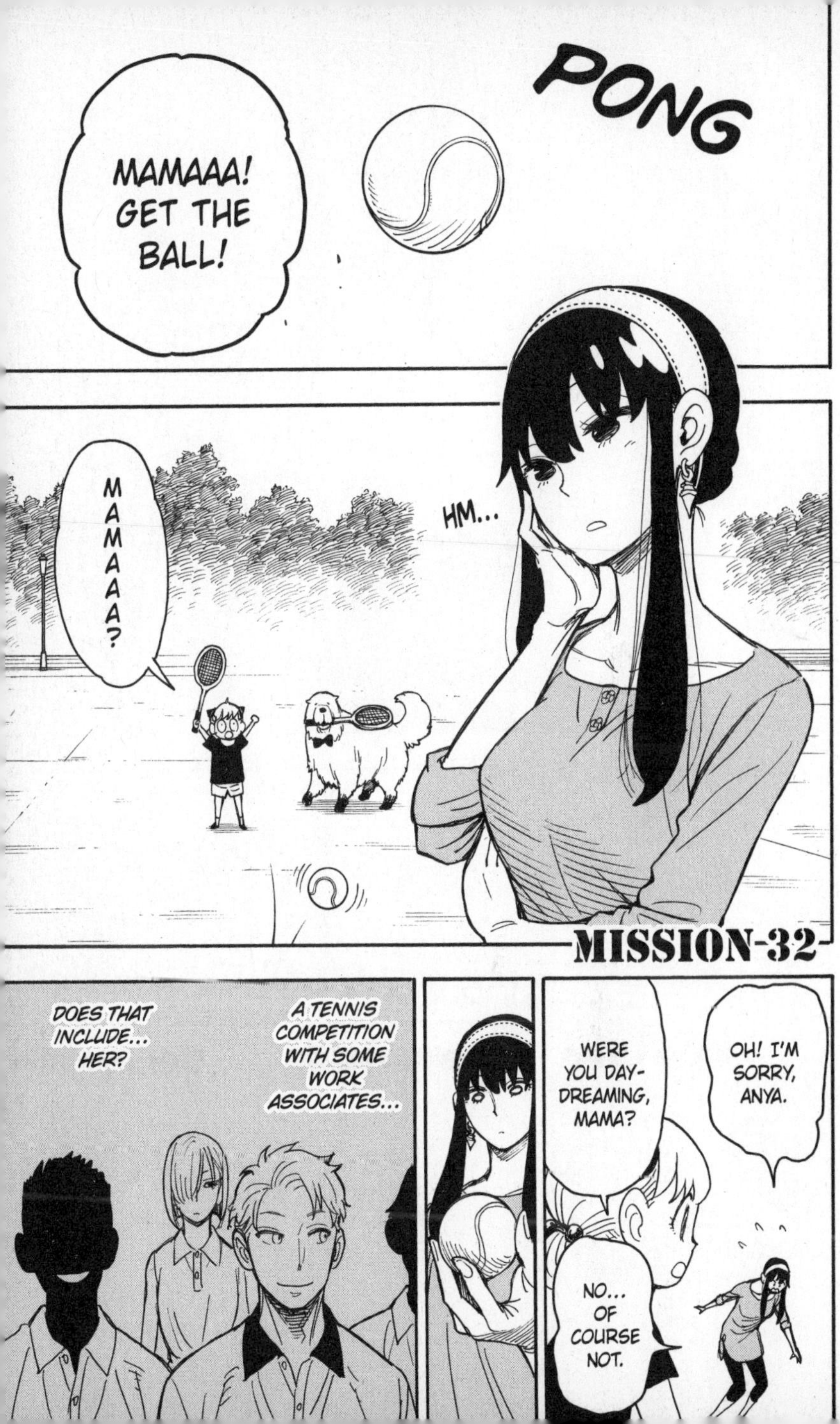
PONG
MAMAAA! GET THE BALL!
HM...
MAMAAAA?
MISSION-32
OH! I'M SORRY, ANYA.
WERE YOU DAY-DREAMING, MAMA?
NO... OF COURSE NOT.
A TENNIS COMPETITION WITH SOME WORK ASSOCIATES...
DOES THAT INCLUDE... HER?

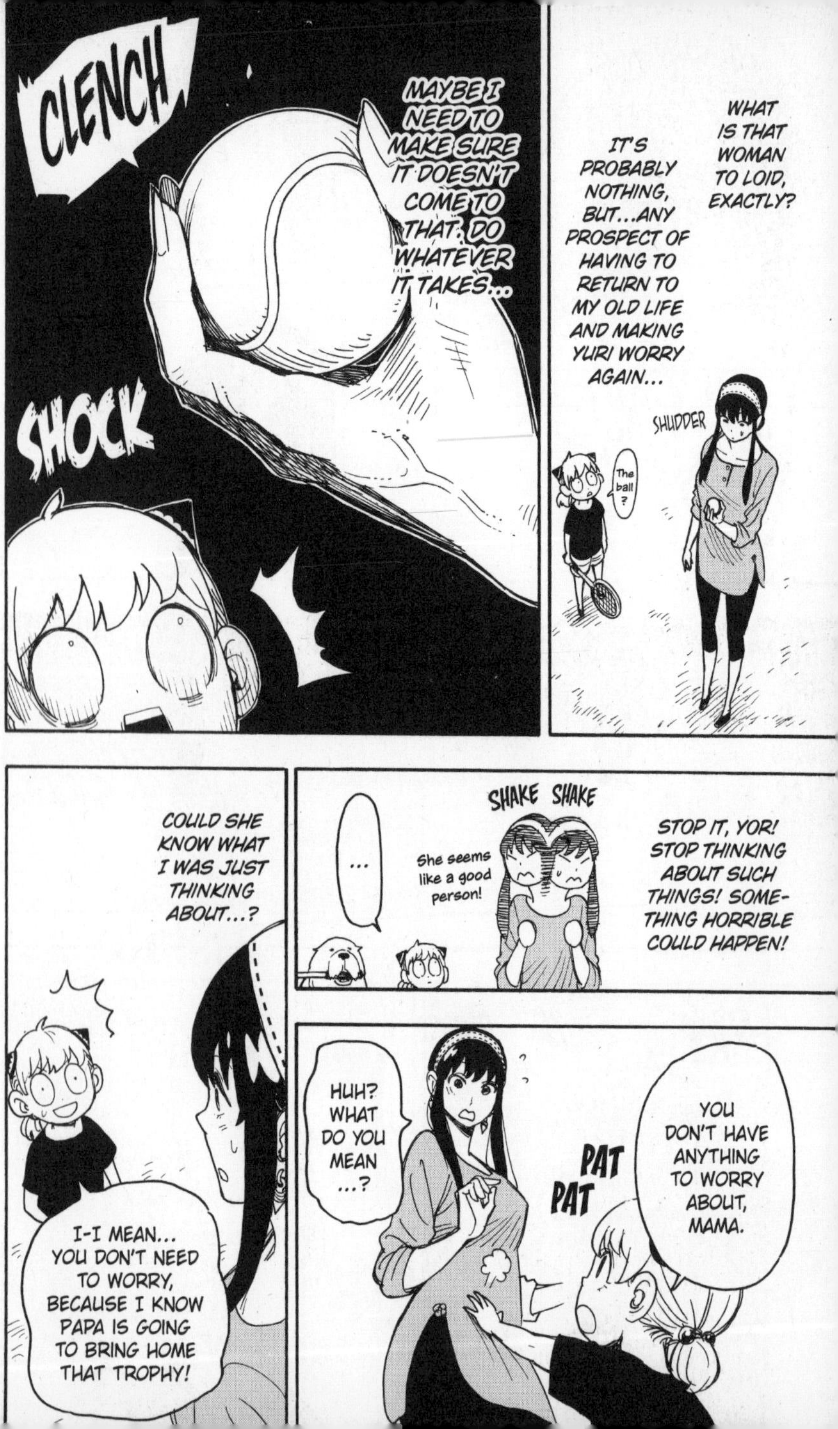
WHAT IS THAT WOMAN TO LOID, EXACTLY?
IT'S PROBABLY NOTHING, BUT...ANY PROSPECT OF HAVING TO RETURN TO MY OLD LIFE AND MAKING YURI WORRY AGAIN...
SHUDDER
The ball?
MAYBE I NEED TO MAKE SURE IT DOESN'T COME TO THAT. DO WHATEVER IT TAKES...
CLENCH
SHOCK
STOP IT, YOR! STOP THINKING ABOUT SUCH THINGS! SOMETHING HORRIBLE COULD HAPPEN!
SHAKE SHAKE
She seems like a good person!
...
YOU DON'T HAVE ANYTHING TO WORRY ABOUT, MAMA.
PAT PAT
HUH? WHAT DO YOU MEAN...?
COULD SHE KNOW WHAT I WAS JUST THINKING ABOUT...?
I-I MEAN... YOU DON'T NEED TO WORRY, BECAUSE I KNOW PAPA IS GOING TO BRING HOME THAT TROPHY!

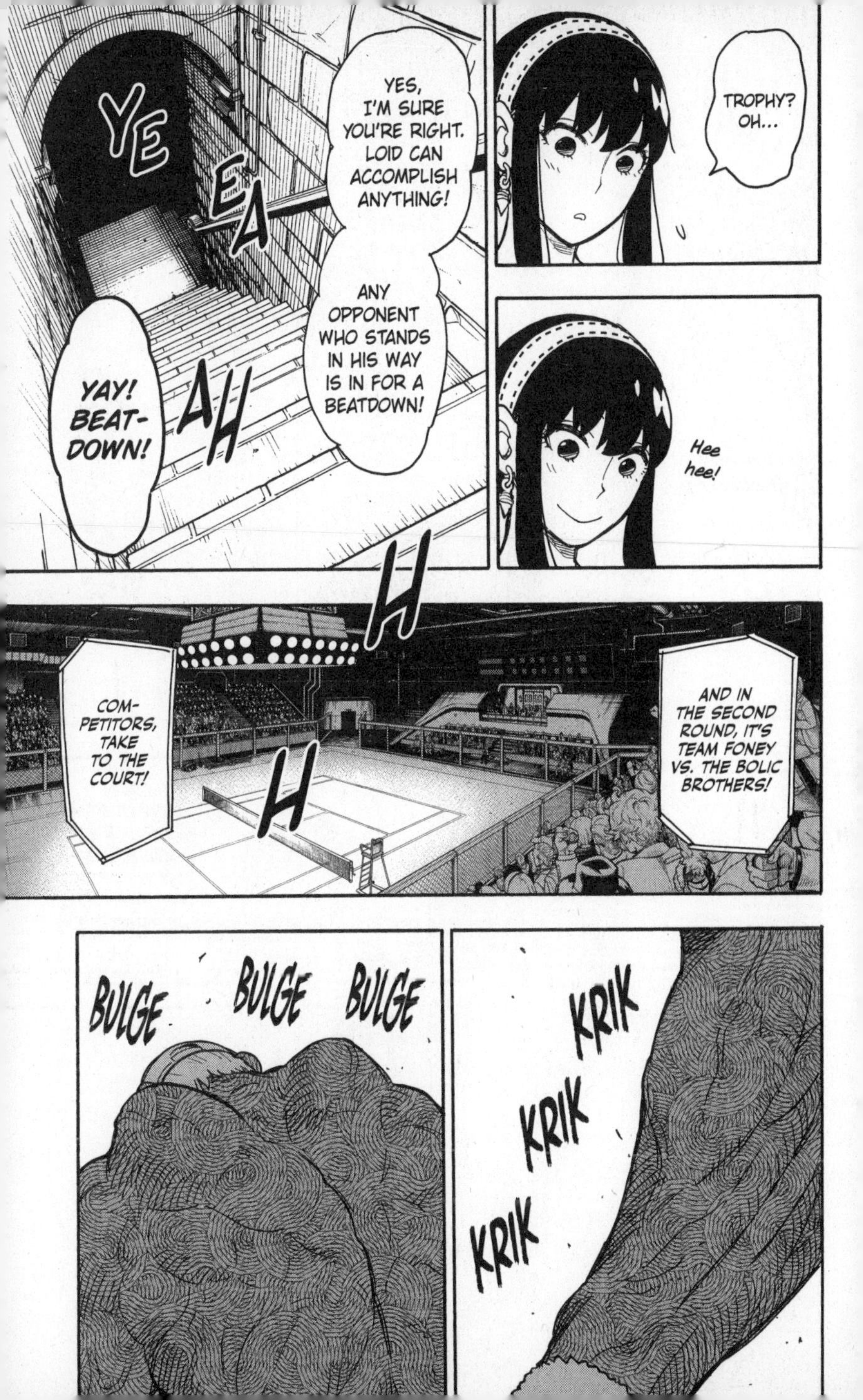
TROPHY? OH...
Hee hee!
YES, I'M SURE YOU'RE RIGHT. LOID CAN ACCOMPLISH ANYTHING!
ANY OPPONENT WHO STANDS IN HIS WAY IS IN FOR A BEATDOWN!
YAY! BEAT-DOWN!
YEEAAHHHH
AND IN THE SECOND ROUND, IT'S TEAM FONEY VS. THE BOLIC BROTHERS!
COM-PETITORS, TAKE TO THE COURT!
KRIK KRIK KRIK
BULGE BULGE BULGE

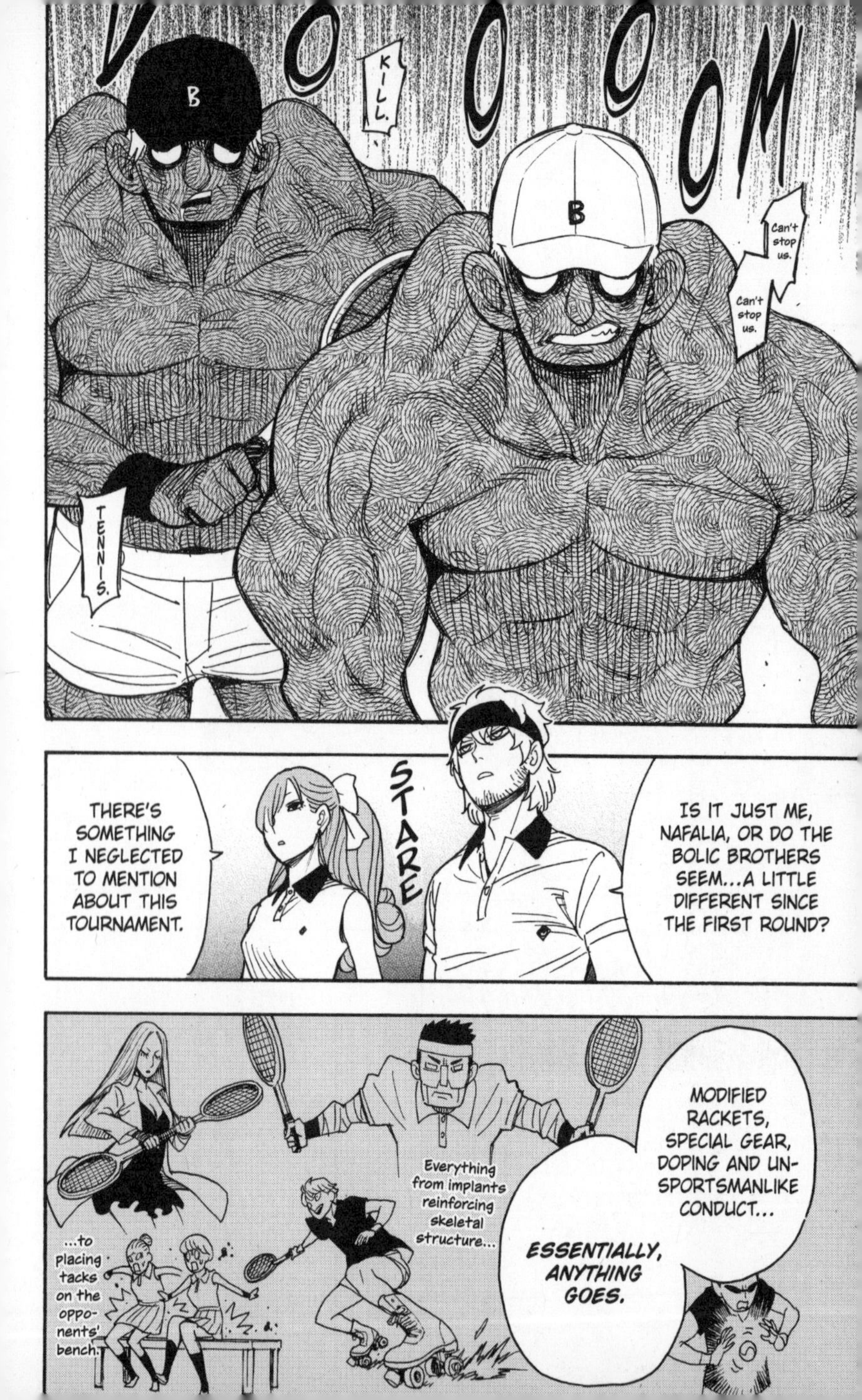
VOOOOOM
Can't stop us.
Can't stop us.
KILL.
TENNIS.
IS IT JUST ME, NAFALIA, OR DO THE BOLIC BROTHERS SEEM...A LITTLE DIFFERENT SINCE THE FIRST ROUND?
STARE
THERE'S SOMETHING I NEGLECTED TO MENTION ABOUT THIS TOURNAMENT.
MODIFIED RACKETS, SPECIAL GEAR, DOPING AND UN-SPORTSMANLIKE CONDUCT...
ESSENTIALLY, ANYTHING GOES.
Everything from implants reinforcing skeletal structure...
...to placing tacks on the oppo-nents' bench.

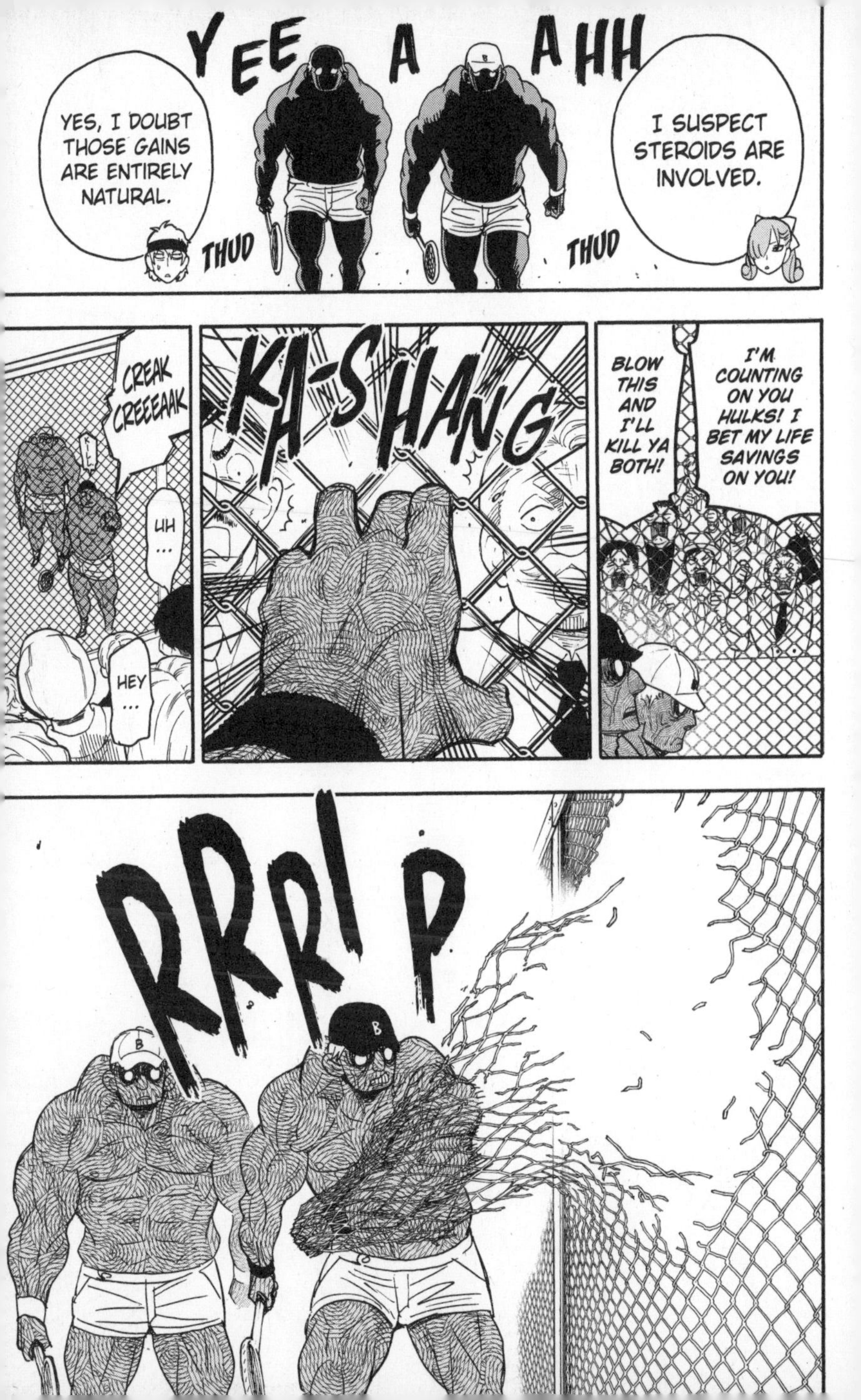
YEE A AHH
I SUSPECT STEROIDS ARE INVOLVED.
THUD
THUD
YES, I DOUBT THOSE GAINS ARE ENTIRELY NATURAL.
I'M COUNTING ON YOU HULKS! I BET MY LIFE SAVINGS ON YOU!
BLOW THIS AND I'LL KILL YA BOTH!
KA-SHANG
CREAK CREEEAAK
UH...
HEY...
RRRIP

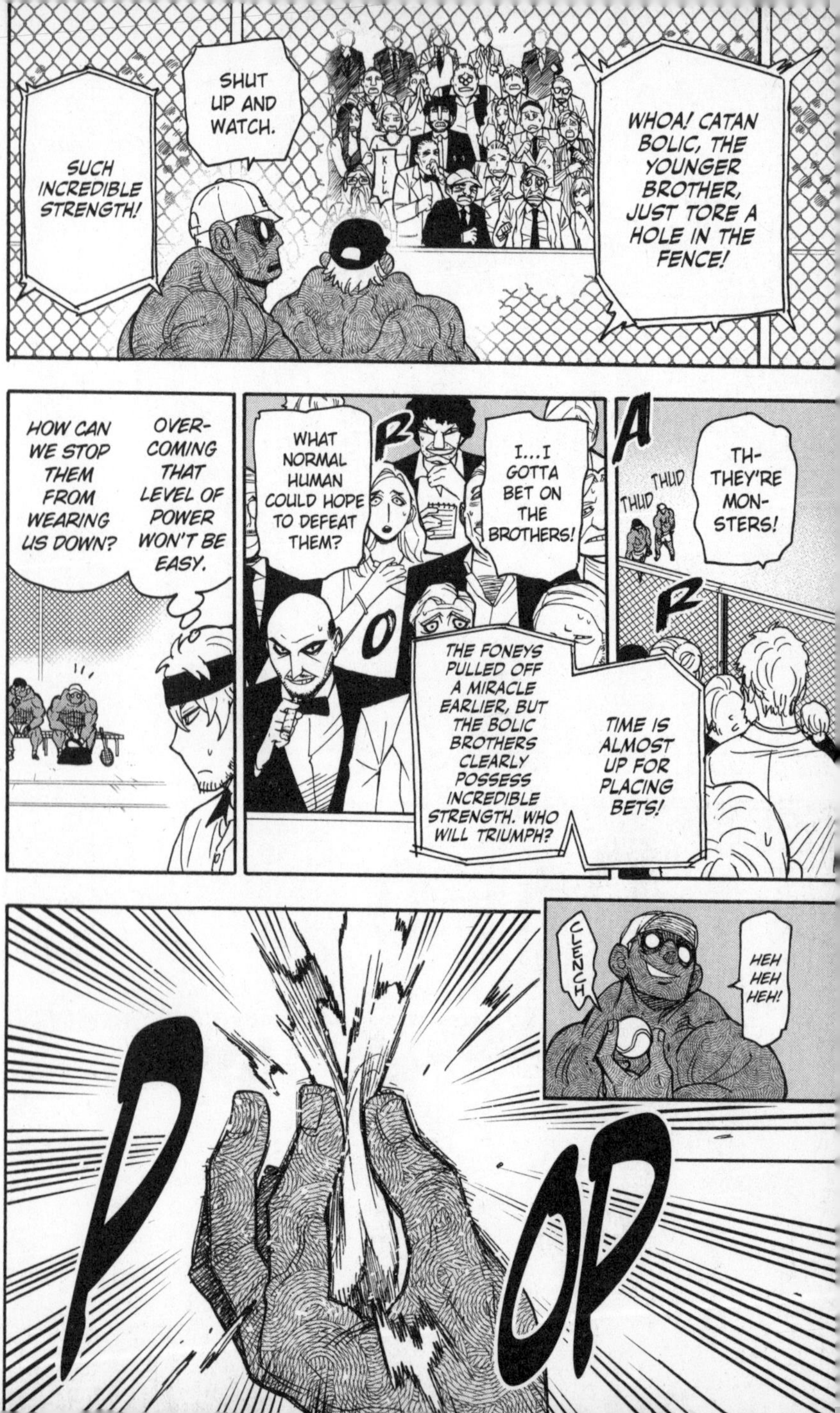
WHOA! CATAN BOLIC, THE YOUNGER BROTHER, JUST TORE A HOLE IN THE FENCE!
SHUT UP AND WATCH.
SUCH INCREDIBLE STRENGTH!
KILL
THUD THUD
TH-THEY'RE MONSTERS!
R
A
I...I GOTTA BET ON THE BROTHERS!
R
WHAT NORMAL HUMAN COULD HOPE TO DEFEAT THEM?
O
THE FONEYS PULLED OFF A MIRACLE EARLIER, BUT THE BOLIC BROTHERS CLEARLY POSSESS INCREDIBLE STRENGTH. WHO WILL TRIUMPH?
TIME IS ALMOST UP FOR PLACING BETS!
OVER-COMING THAT LEVEL OF POWER WON'T BE EASY.
HOW CAN WE STOP THEM FROM WEARING US DOWN?
CLENCH
HEH HEH HEH!
D
OP

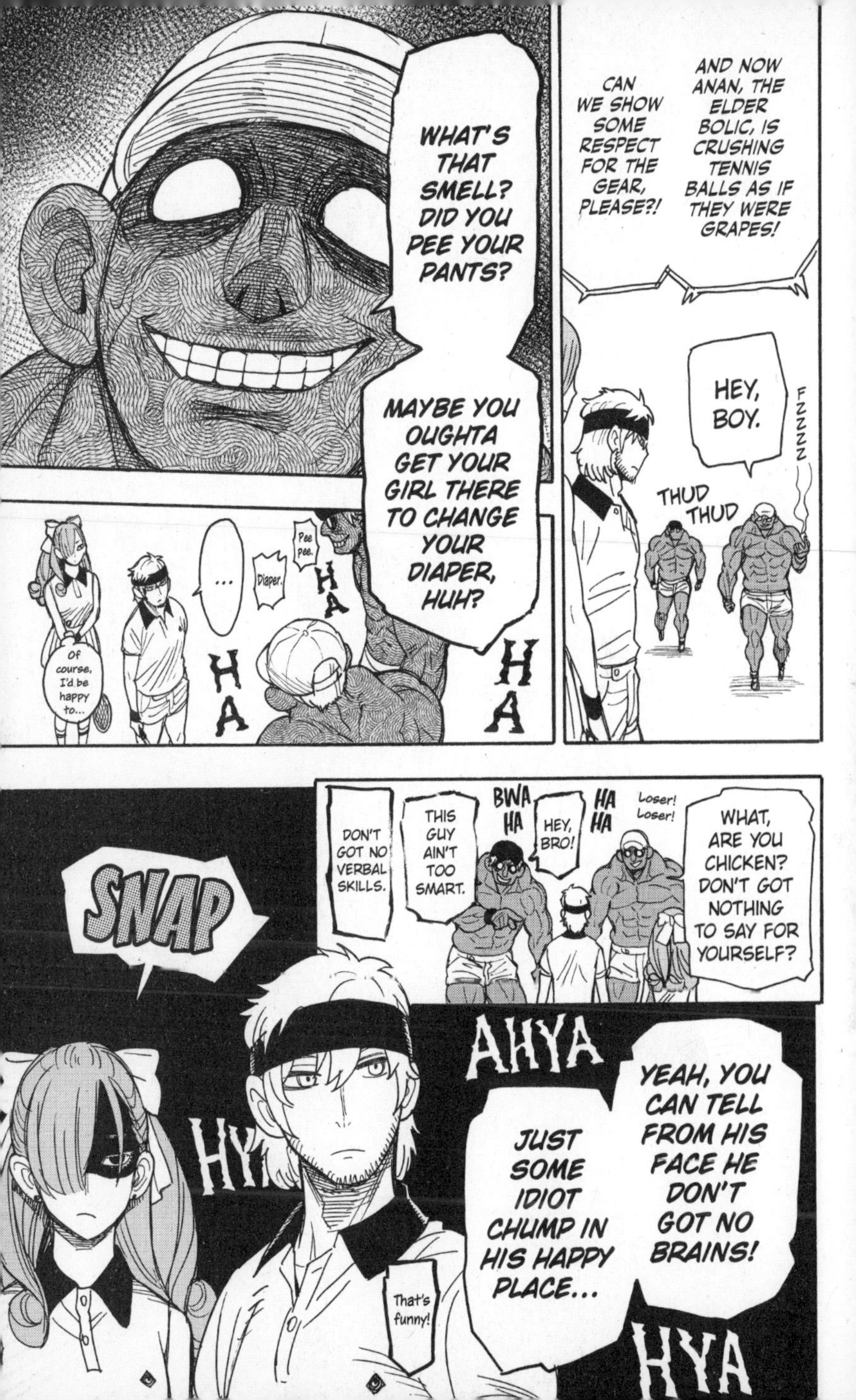
AND NOW ANAN, THE ELDER BOLIC, IS CRUSHING TENNIS BALLS AS IF THEY WERE GRAPES!
CAN WE SHOW SOME RESPECT FOR THE GEAR, PLEASE?!
WHAT'S THAT SMELL? DID YOU PEE YOUR PANTS?
MAYBE YOU OUGHTA GET YOUR GIRL THERE TO CHANGE YOUR DIAPER, HUH?
HEY, BOY.
FZZZZ
THUD
THUD
HA
HA
Pee pee.
Diaper.
...
HA
Of course, I'd be happy to...
WHAT, ARE YOU CHICKEN? DON'T GOT NOTHING TO SAY FOR YOURSELF?
Loser! Loser!
HA HA
HEY, BRO!
BWA HA
THIS GUY AIN'T TOO SMART.
DON'T GOT NO VERBAL SKILLS.
SNAP
AHYA
YEAH, YOU CAN TELL FROM HIS FACE HE DON'T GOT NO BRAINS!
JUST SOME IDIOT CHUMP IN HIS HAPPY PLACE...
HYA
HYA
That's funny!

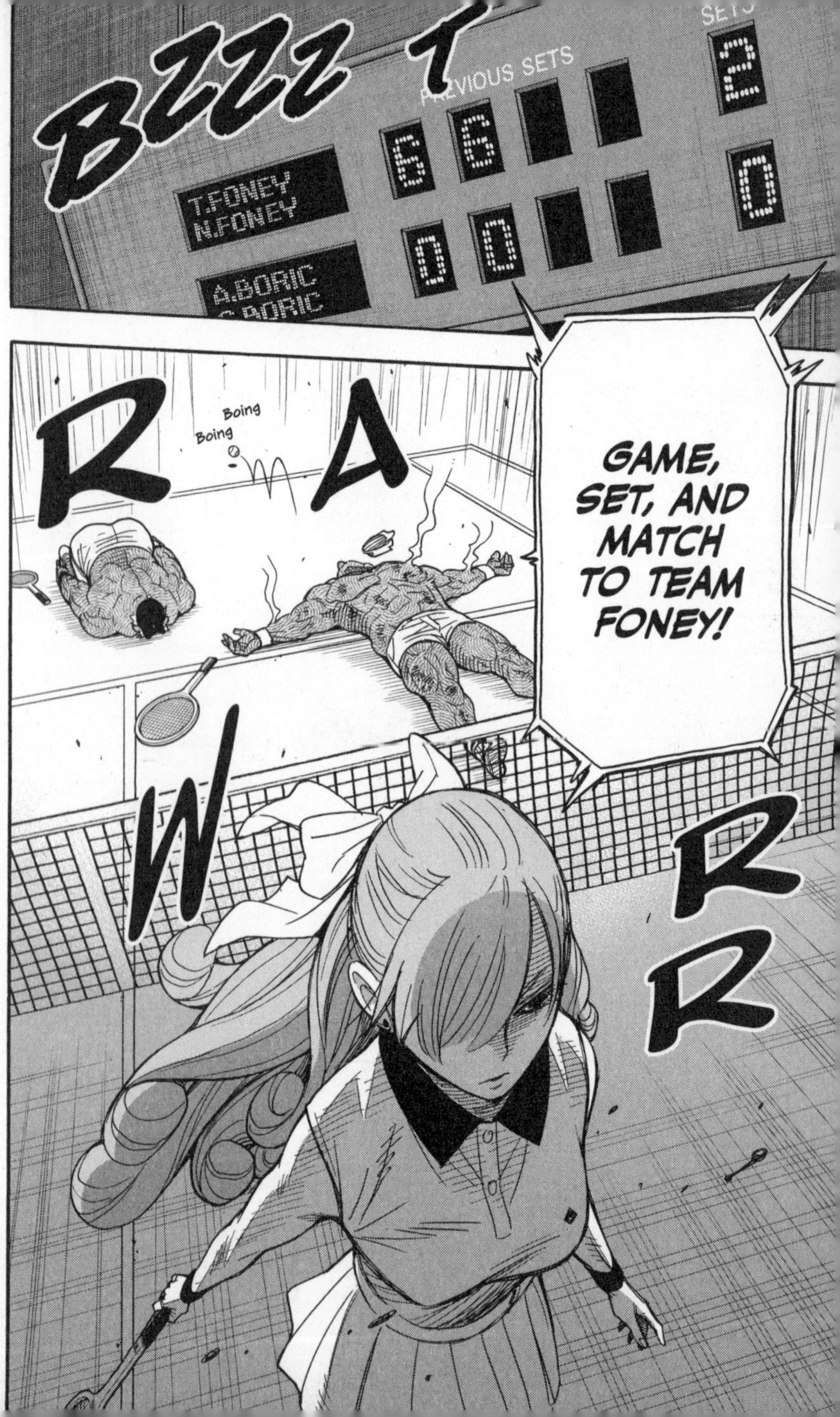
BZZZ T
SETS
PREVIOUS SETS
T.FONEY
N.FONEY
6 6 2
A.BORIC
0 0 0
GAME, SET, AND MATCH TO TEAM FONEY!
Boing
Boing
RAWRR

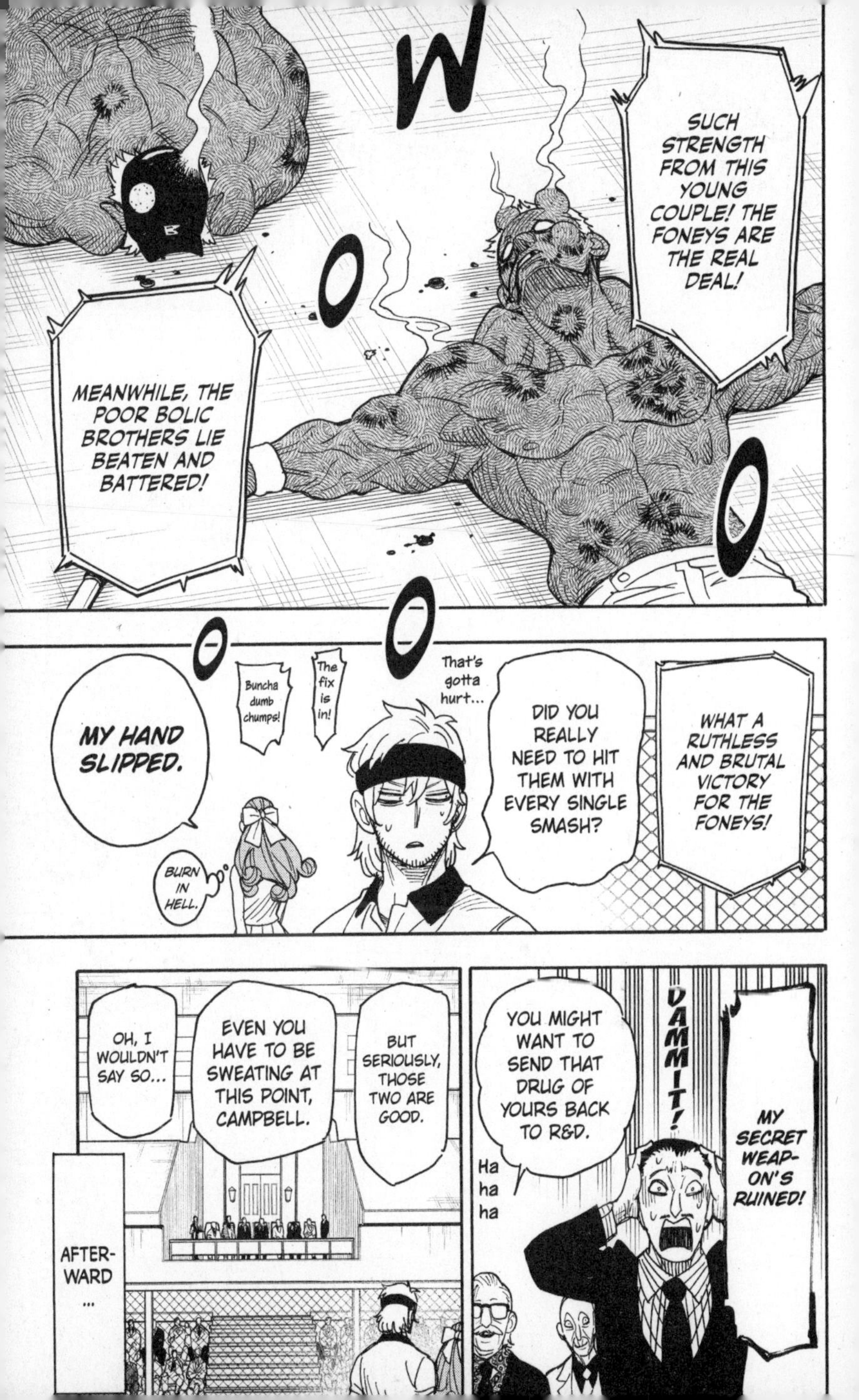

SUCH STRENGTH FROM THIS YOUNG COUPLE! THE FONEYS ARE THE REAL DEAL!
WOOOO
MEANWHILE, THE POOR BOLIC BROTHERS LIE BEATEN AND BATTERED!
WHAT A RUTHLESS AND BRUTAL VICTORY FOR THE FONEYS!
DID YOU REALLY NEED TO HIT THEM WITH EVERY SINGLE SMASH?
That's gotta hurt...
The fix is in!
Buncha dumb chumps!
MY HAND SLIPPED.
BURN IN HELL.
MY SECRET WEAP-ON'S RUINED!
DAMMIT!
YOU MIGHT WANT TO SEND THAT DRUG OF YOURS BACK TO R&D.
Ha ha ha
BUT SERIOUSLY, THOSE TWO ARE GOOD.
EVEN YOU HAVE TO BE SWEATING AT THIS POINT, CAMPBELL.
OH, I WOULDN'T SAY SO...
AFTER-WARD...

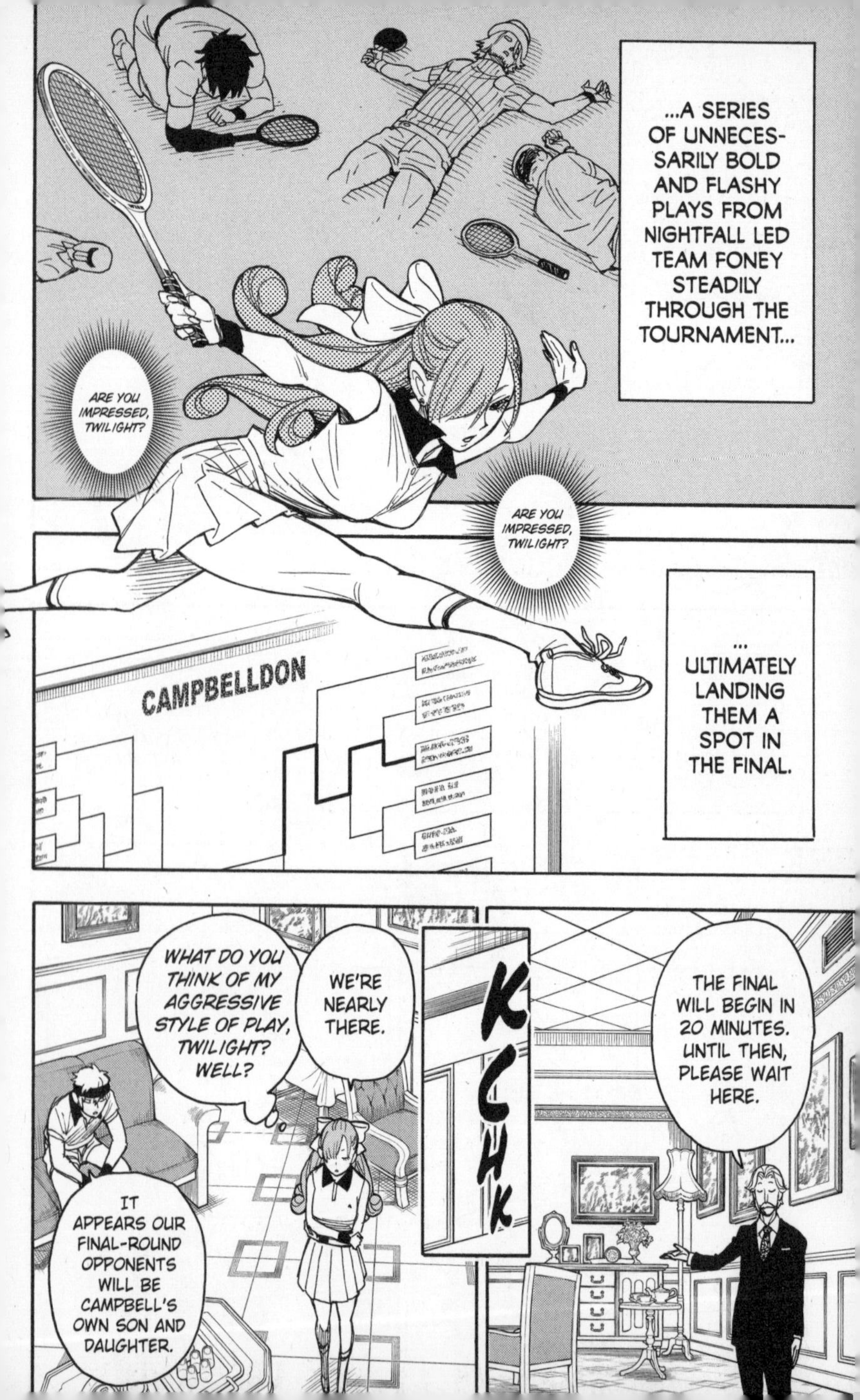
...A SERIES OF UNNECESSARILY BOLD AND FLASHY PLAYS FROM NIGHTFALL LED TEAM FONEY STEADILY THROUGH THE TOURNAMENT...
ARE YOU IMPRESSED, TWILIGHT?
ARE YOU IMPRESSED, TWILIGHT?
... ULTIMATELY LANDING THEM A SPOT IN THE FINAL.
CAMPBELLDON
THE FINAL WILL BEGIN IN 20 MINUTES. UNTIL THEN, PLEASE WAIT HERE.
KCHK
WE'RE NEARLY THERE.
WHAT DO YOU THINK OF MY AGGRESSIVE STYLE OF PLAY, TWILIGHT? WELL?
IT APPEARS OUR FINAL-ROUND OPPONENTS WILL BE CAMPBELL'S OWN SON AND DAUGHTER.

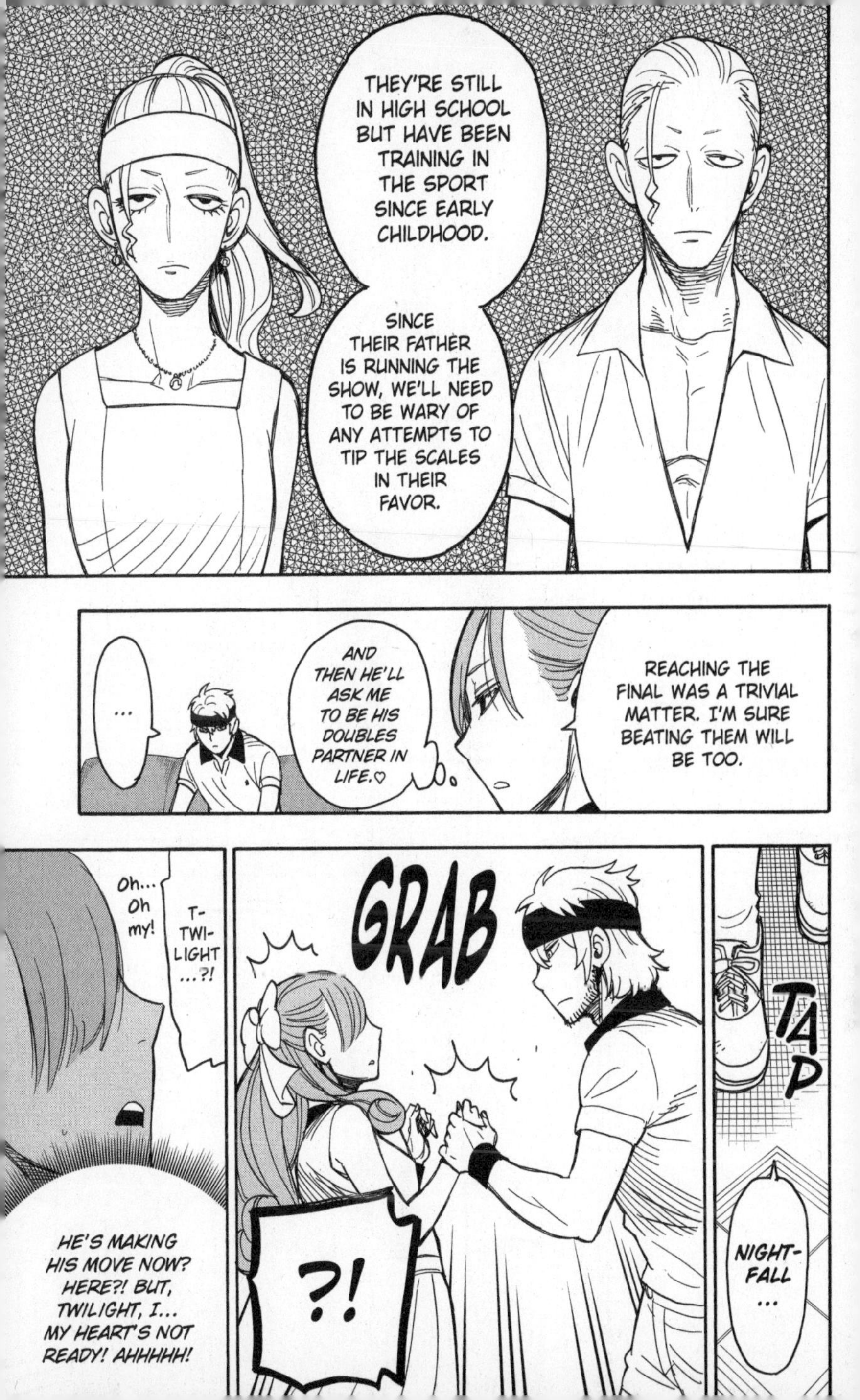
THEY'RE STILL IN HIGH SCHOOL BUT HAVE BEEN TRAINING IN THE SPORT SINCE EARLY CHILDHOOD.
SINCE THEIR FATHER IS RUNNING THE SHOW, WE'LL NEED TO BE WARY OF ANY ATTEMPTS TO TIP THE SCALES IN THEIR FAVOR.
REACHING THE FINAL WAS A TRIVIAL MATTER. I'M SURE BEATING THEM WILL BE TOO.
AND THEN HE'LL ASK ME TO BE HIS DOUBLES PARTNER IN LIFE.♡
...
TAP
TAP
NIGHT-FALL...
GRAB
?!
T-TWI-LIGHT...?!
Oh... Oh my!
HE'S MAKING HIS MOVE NOW? HERE?! BUT, TWILIGHT, I... MY HEART'S NOT READY! AHHHHH!

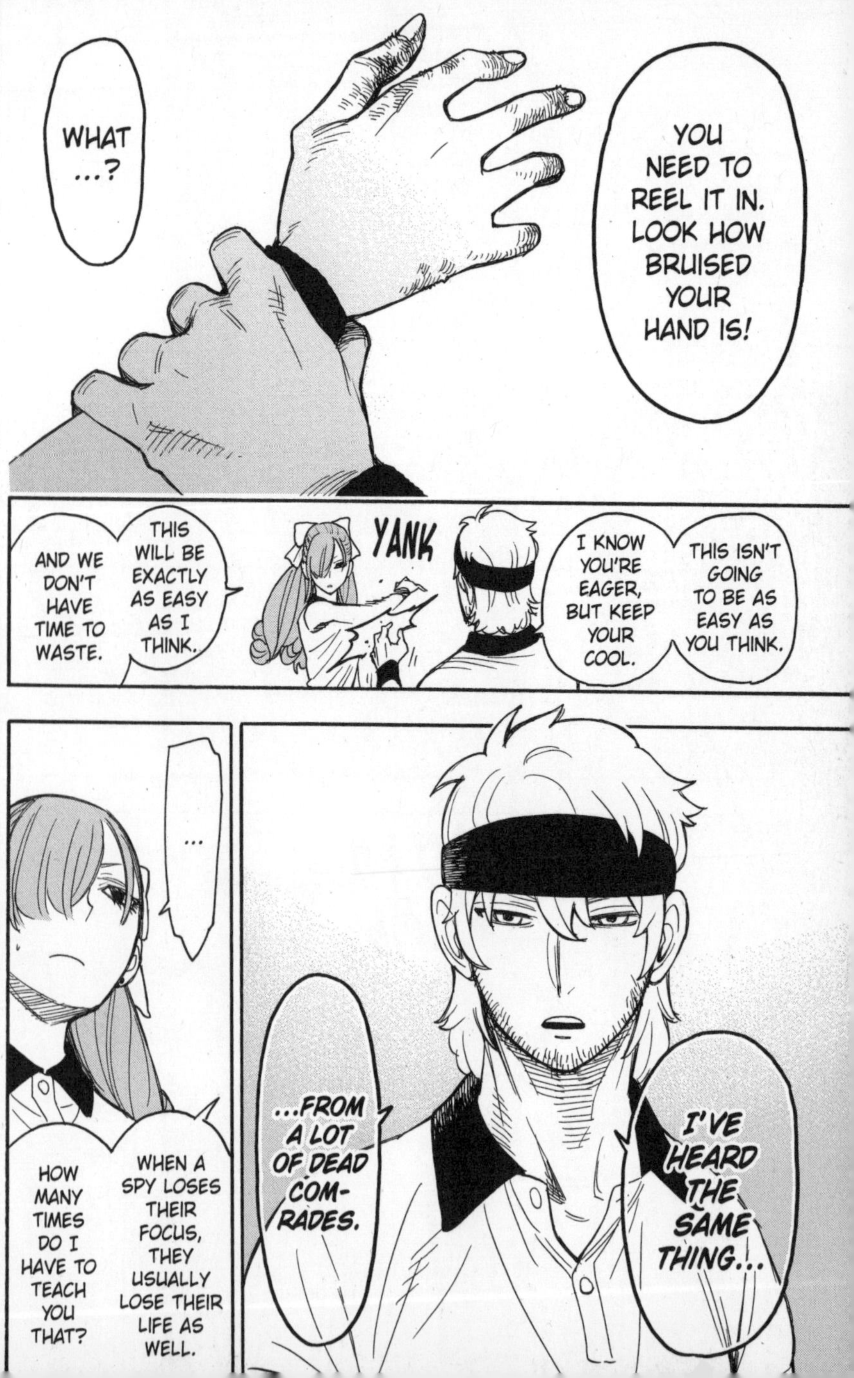
YOU NEED TO REEL IT IN. LOOK HOW BRUISED YOUR HAND IS!
WHAT ...?
THIS ISN'T GOING TO BE AS EASY AS YOU THINK.
I KNOW YOU'RE EAGER, BUT KEEP YOUR COOL.
YANK
THIS WILL BE EXACTLY AS EASY AS I THINK.
AND WE DON'T HAVE TIME TO WASTE.
I'VE HEARD THE SAME THING...
...FROM A LOT OF DEAD COM-RADES.
...
WHEN A SPY LOSES THEIR FOCUS, THEY USUALLY LOSE THEIR LIFE AS WELL.
HOW MANY TIMES DO I HAVE TO TEACH YOU THAT?

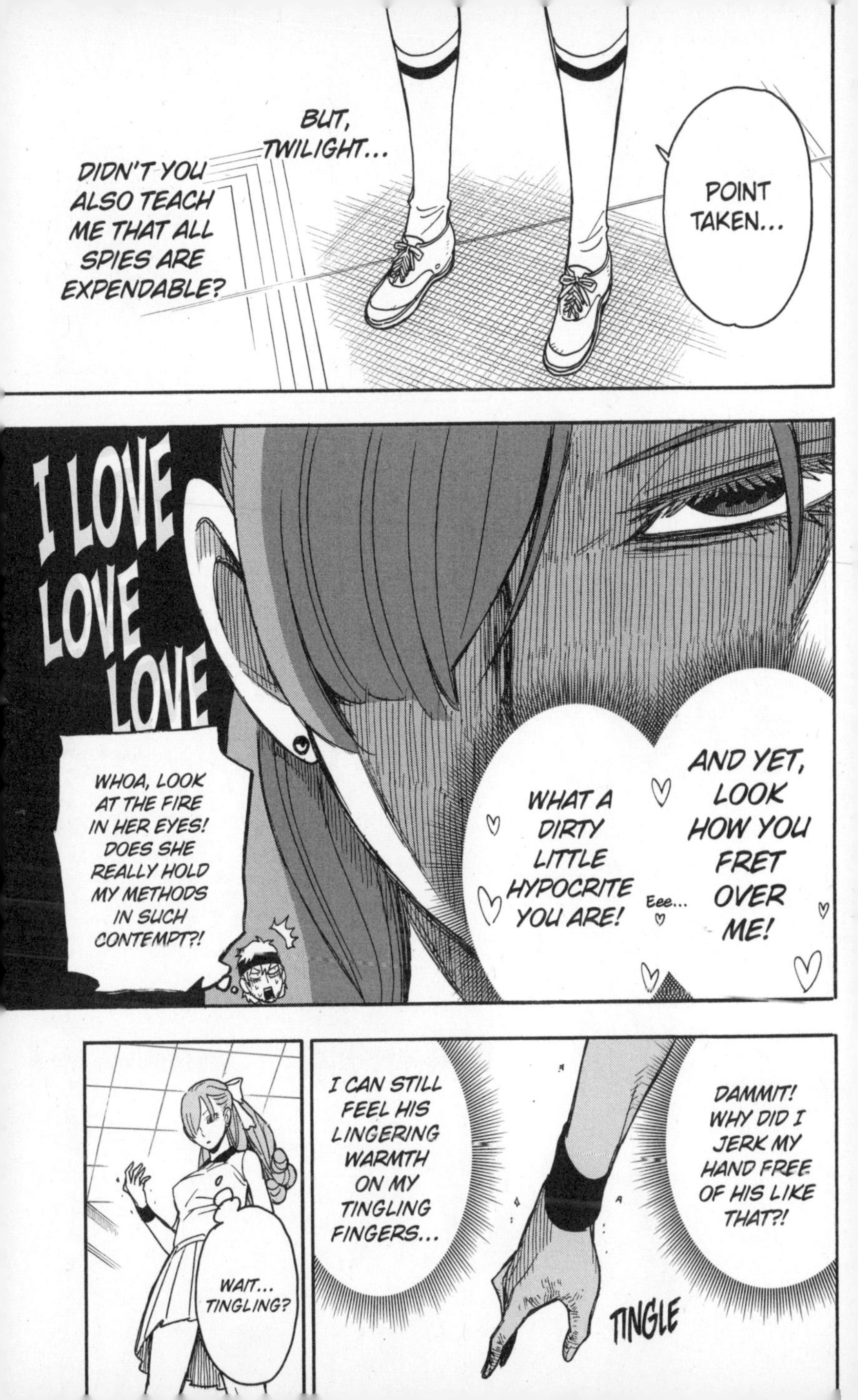
POINT TAKEN...
BUT, TWILIGHT...
DIDN'T YOU ALSO TEACH ME THAT ALL SPIES ARE EXPENDABLE?
AND YET, LOOK HOW YOU FRET OVER ME!
Eee...
WHAT A DIRTY LITTLE HYPOCRITE YOU ARE!
I LOVE LOVE LOVE
WHOA, LOOK AT THE FIRE IN HER EYES! DOES SHE REALLY HOLD MY METHODS IN SUCH CONTEMPT?!
DAMMIT! WHY DID I JERK MY HAND FREE OF HIS LIKE THAT?!
I CAN STILL FEEL HIS LINGERING WARMTH ON MY TINGLING FINGERS...
TINGLE
WAIT... TINGLING?

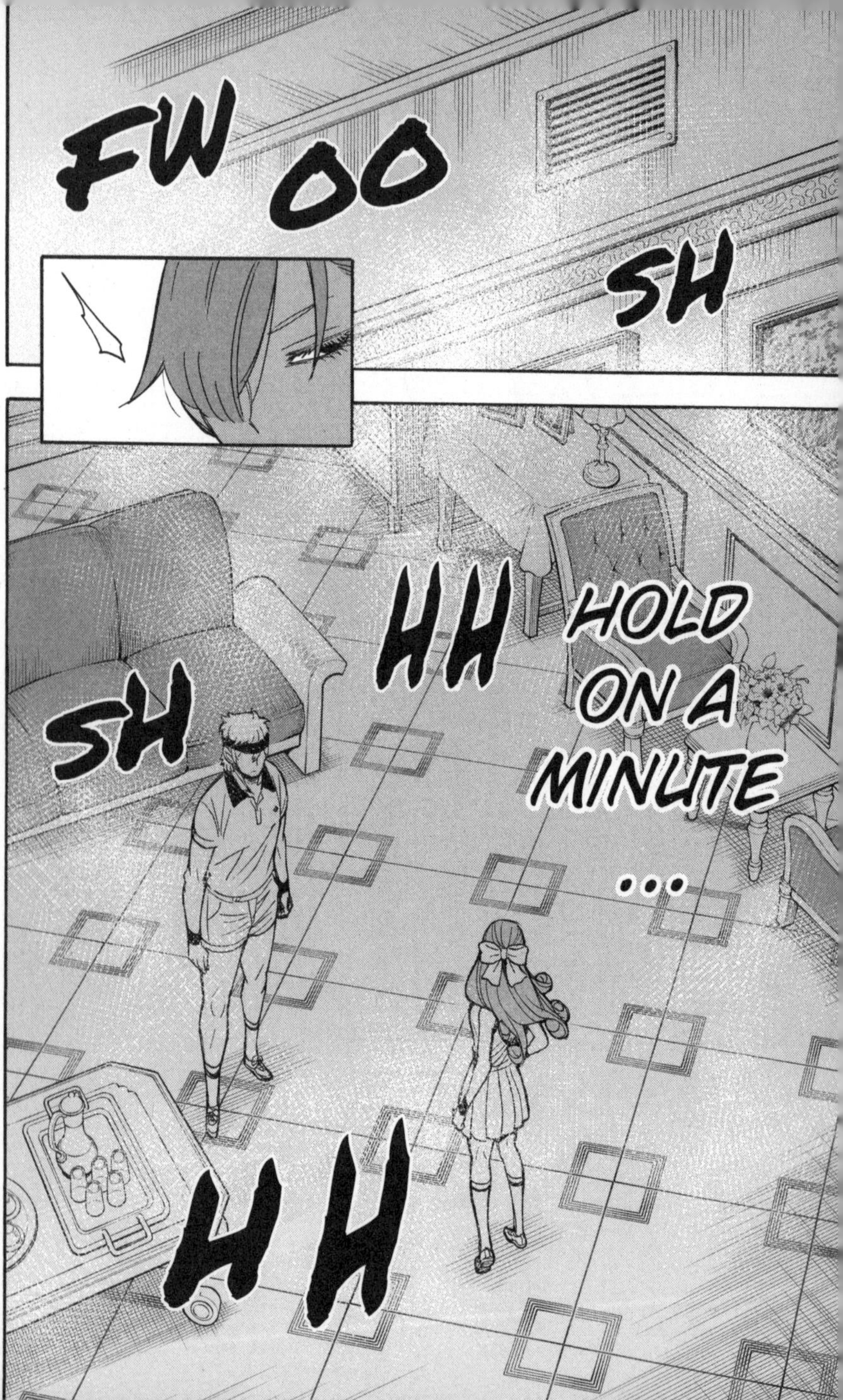
FWOOSHSHHHHH
HOLD ON A MINUTE...

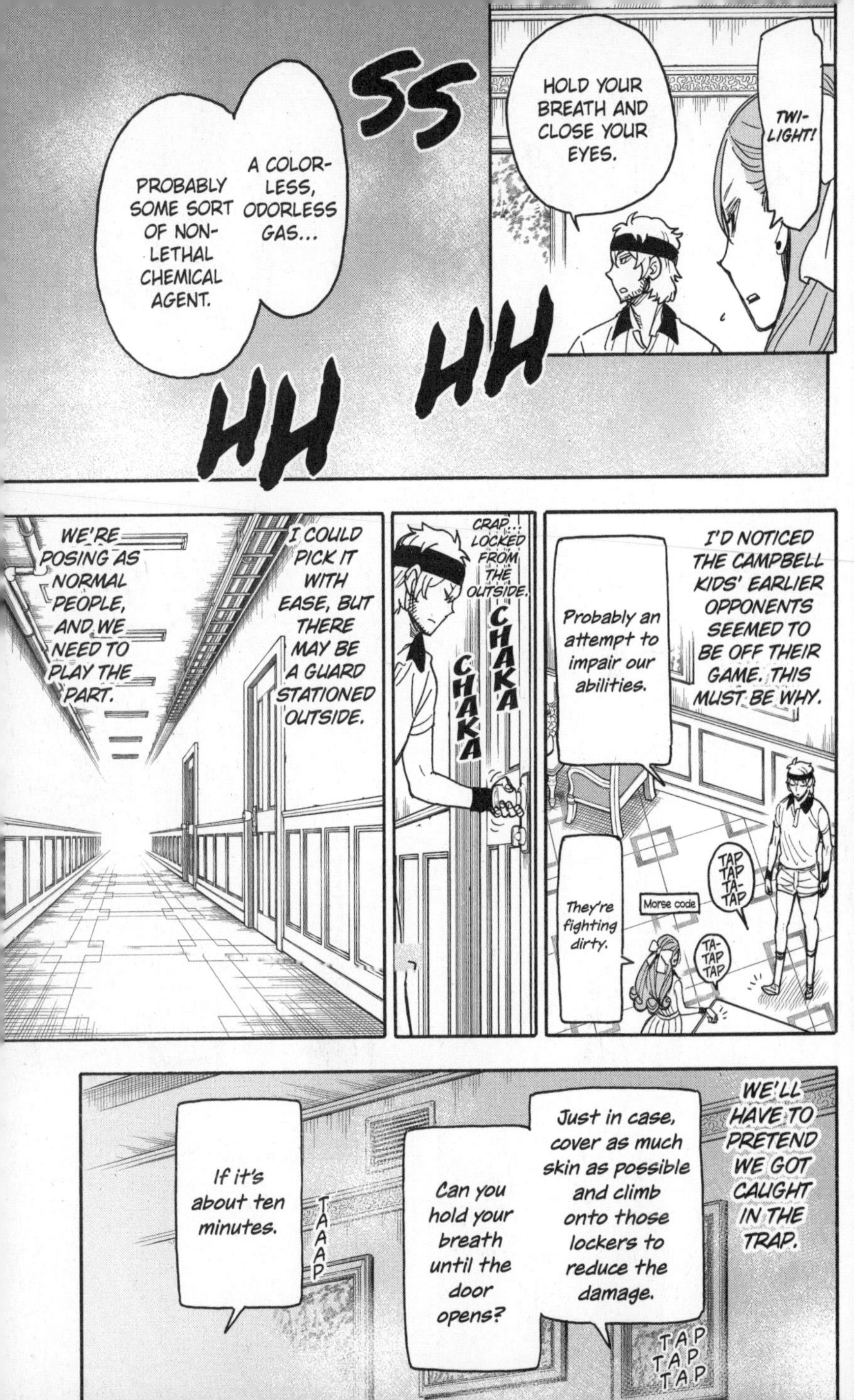
TWI-LIGHT!
HOLD YOUR BREATH AND CLOSE YOUR EYES.
SS
HH
HH
A COLOR-LESS, ODORLESS GAS...
PROBABLY SOME SORT OF NON-LETHAL CHEMICAL AGENT.
I'D NOTICED THE CAMPBELL KIDS' EARLIER OPPONENTS SEEMED TO BE OFF THEIR GAME. THIS MUST BE WHY.
Probably an attempt to impair our abilities.
TAP TAP TA-TAP
Morse code
They're fighting dirty.
TA-TAP TAP
CRAP... LOCKED FROM THE OUTSIDE.
CHAKA
CHAKA
I COULD PICK IT WITH EASE, BUT THERE MAY BE A GUARD STATIONED OUTSIDE.
WE'RE POSING AS NORMAL PEOPLE, AND WE NEED TO PLAY THE PART.
WE'LL HAVE TO PRETEND WE GOT CAUGHT IN THE TRAP.
Just in case, cover as much skin as possible and climb onto those lockers to reduce the damage.
TAP TAP TAP
Can you hold your breath until the door opens?
TAAAAP
If it's about ten minutes.

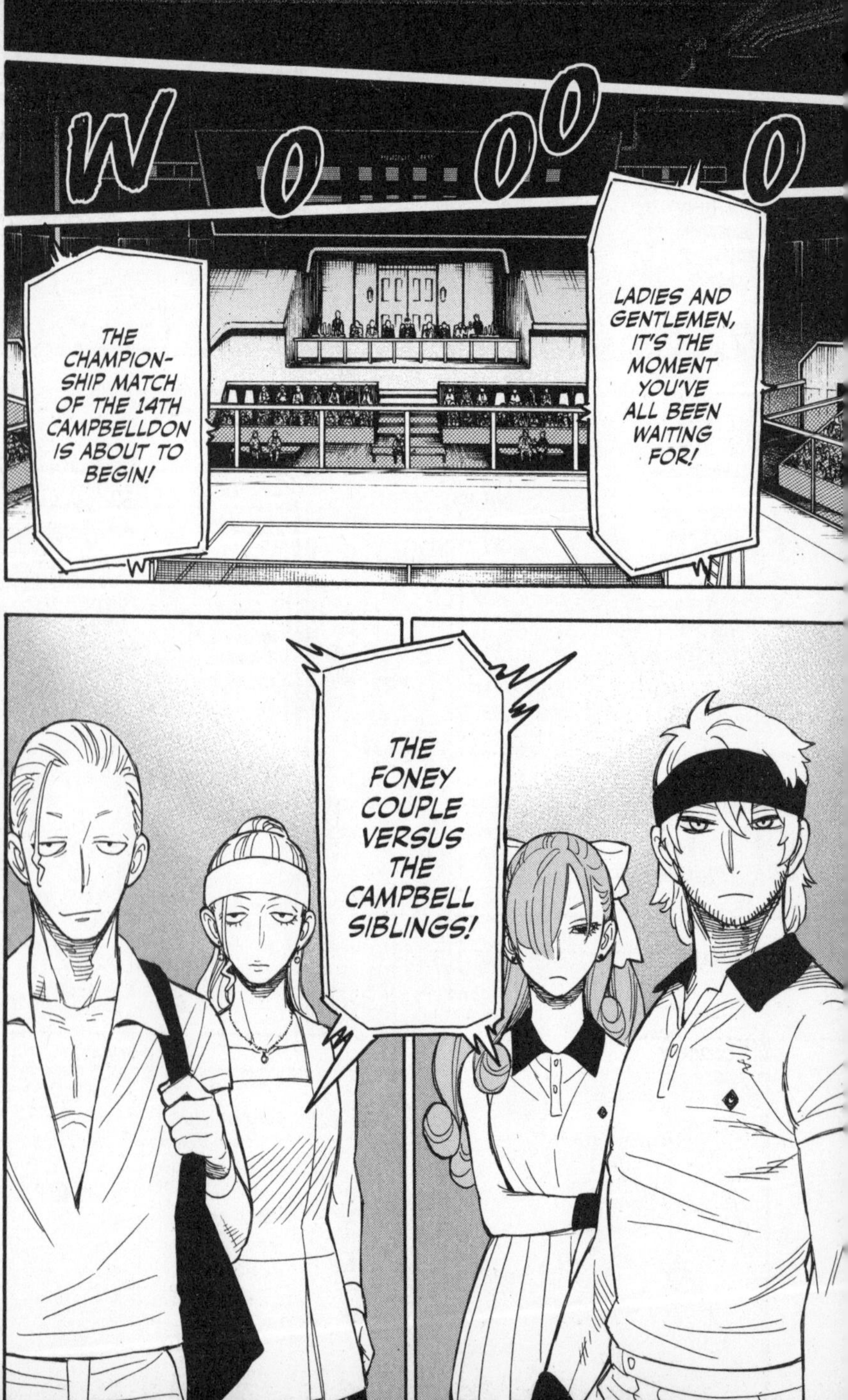
WOOOO
LADIES AND GENTLEMEN, IT'S THE MOMENT YOU'VE ALL BEEN WAITING FOR!
THE CHAMPIONSHIP MATCH OF THE 14TH CAMPBELLDON IS ABOUT TO BEGIN!
THE FONEY COUPLE VERSUS THE CAMPBELL SIBLINGS!

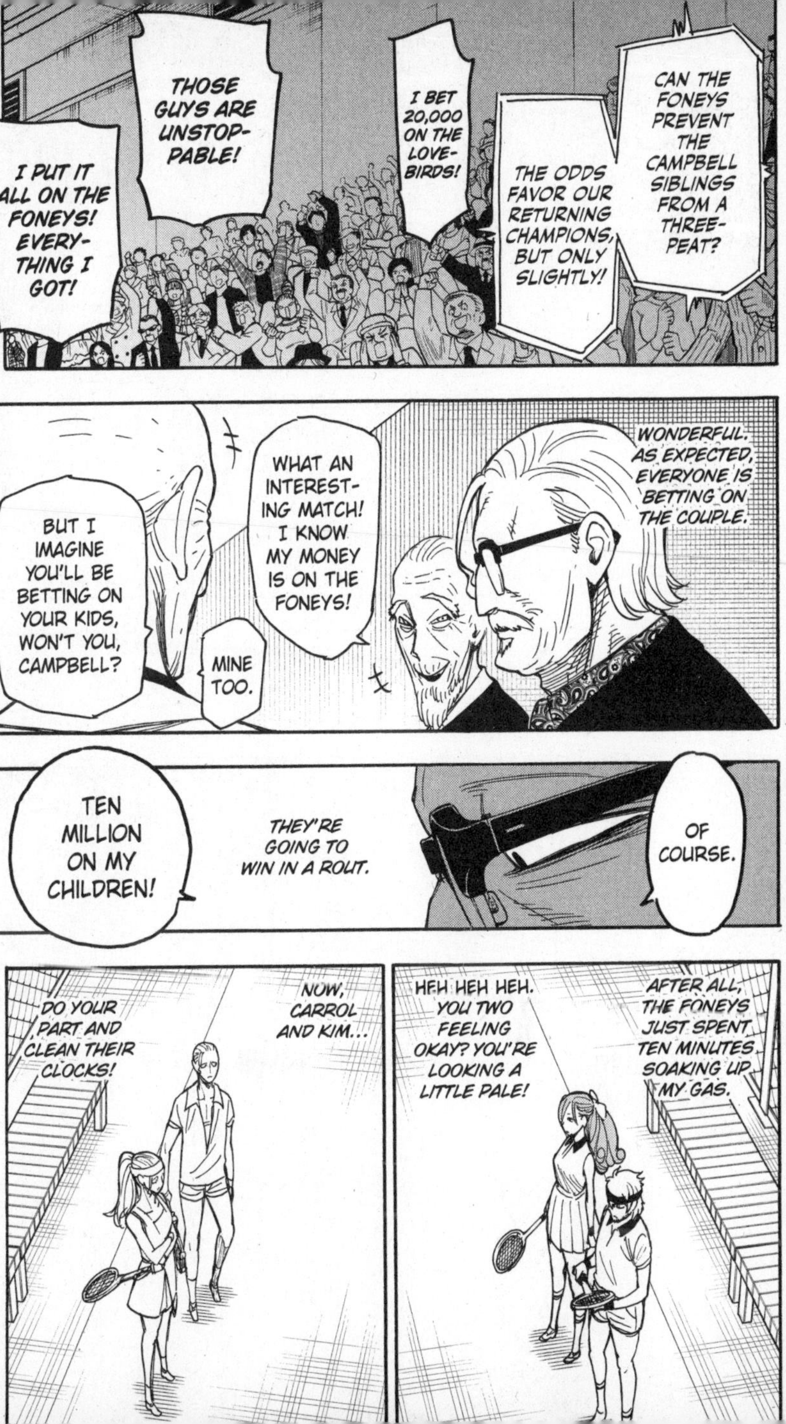
CAN THE FONEYS PREVENT THE CAMPBELL SIBLINGS FROM A THREE-PEAT?
THE ODDS FAVOR OUR RETURNING CHAMPIONS, BUT ONLY SLIGHTLY!
I BET 20,000 ON THE LOVE-BIRDS!
THOSE GUYS ARE UNSTOP-PABLE!
I PUT IT ALL ON THE FONEYS! EVERY-THING I GOT!
WONDERFUL. AS EXPECTED, EVERYONE IS BETTING ON THE COUPLE.
WHAT AN INTEREST-ING MATCH! I KNOW MY MONEY IS ON THE FONEYS!
MINE TOO.
BUT I IMAGINE YOU'LL BE BETTING ON YOUR KIDS, WON'T YOU, CAMPBELL?
OF COURSE.
THEY'RE GOING TO WIN IN A ROUT.
TEN MILLION ON MY CHILDREN!
AFTER ALL, THE FONEYS JUST SPENT TEN MINUTES SOAKING UP MY GAS.
HEH HEH HEH. YOU TWO FEELING OKAY? YOU'RE LOOKING A LITTLE PALE!
NOW, CARROL AND KIM...
DO YOUR PART AND CLEAN THEIR CLOCKS!

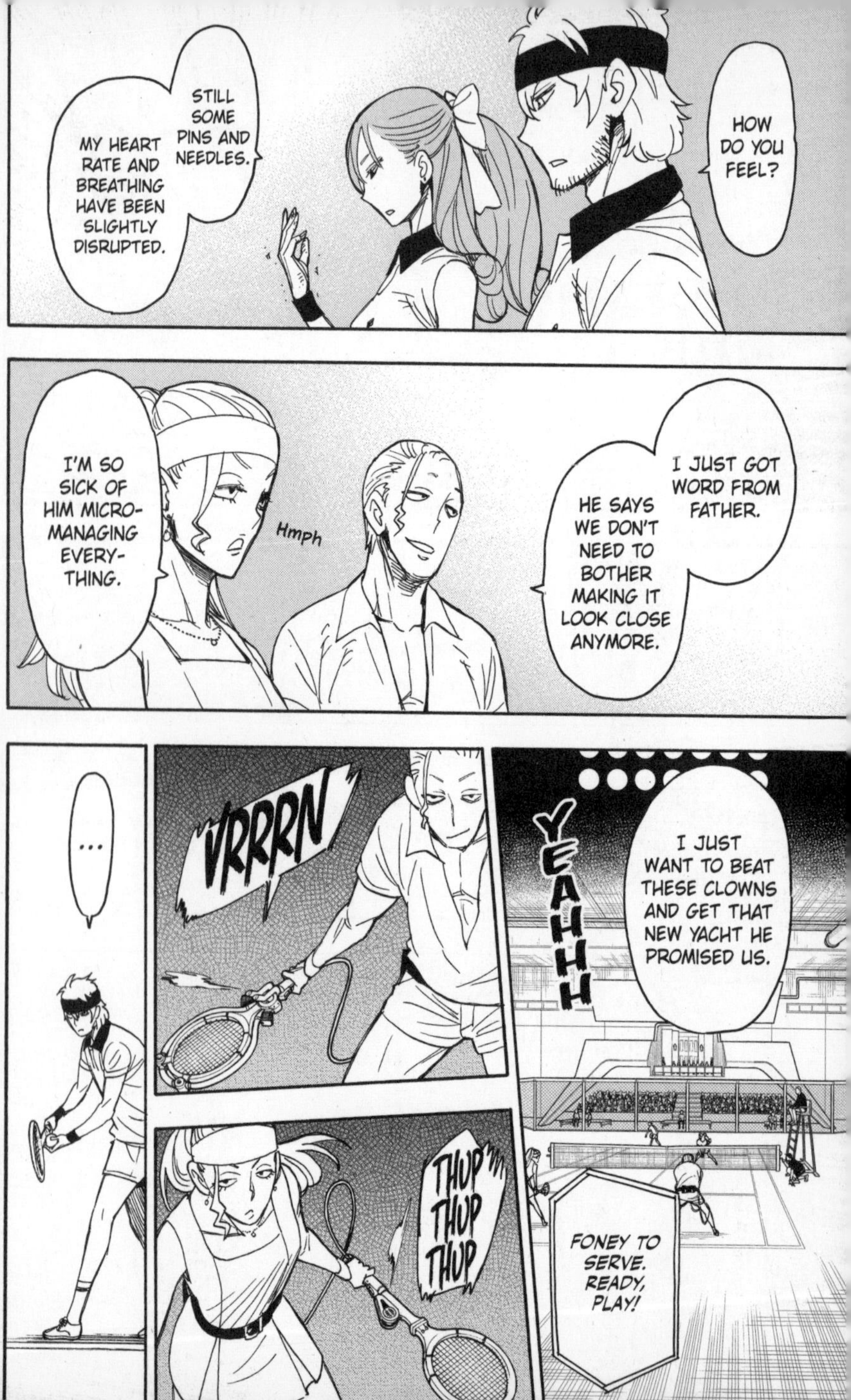
HOW DO YOU FEEL?
STILL SOME PINS AND NEEDLES.
MY HEART RATE AND BREATHING HAVE BEEN SLIGHTLY DISRUPTED.
I JUST GOT WORD FROM FATHER.
HE SAYS WE DON'T NEED TO BOTHER MAKING IT LOOK CLOSE ANYMORE.
Hmph
I'M SO SICK OF HIM MICRO-MANAGING EVERY-THING.
YEAHHH
I JUST WANT TO BEAT THESE CLOWNS AND GET THAT NEW YACHT HE PROMISED US.
FONEY TO SERVE. READY, PLAY!
VRRRN
THUP THUP THUP
...

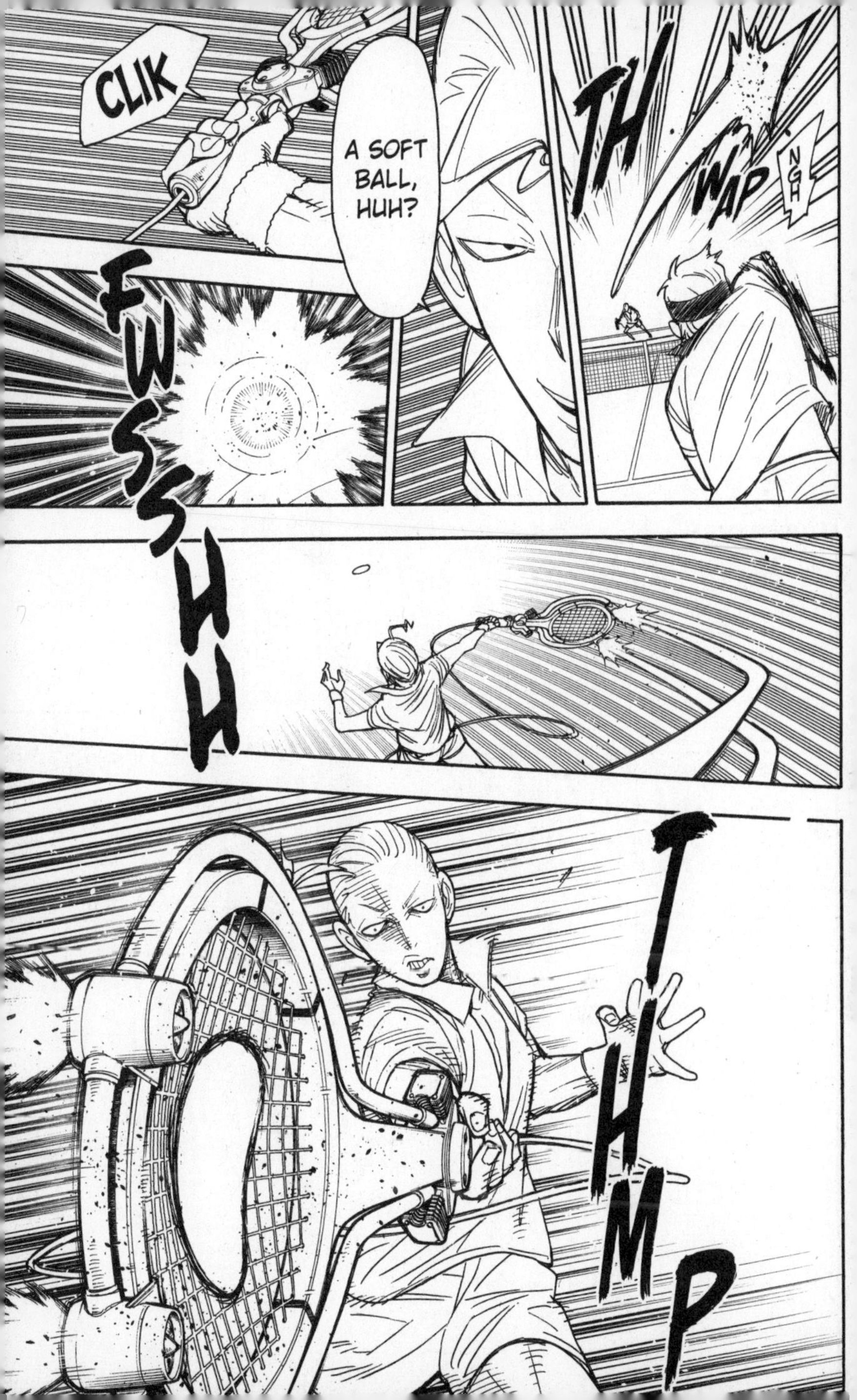
THWAP
NGH
A SOFT BALL, HUH?
CLIK
FWSSHHH
THMP

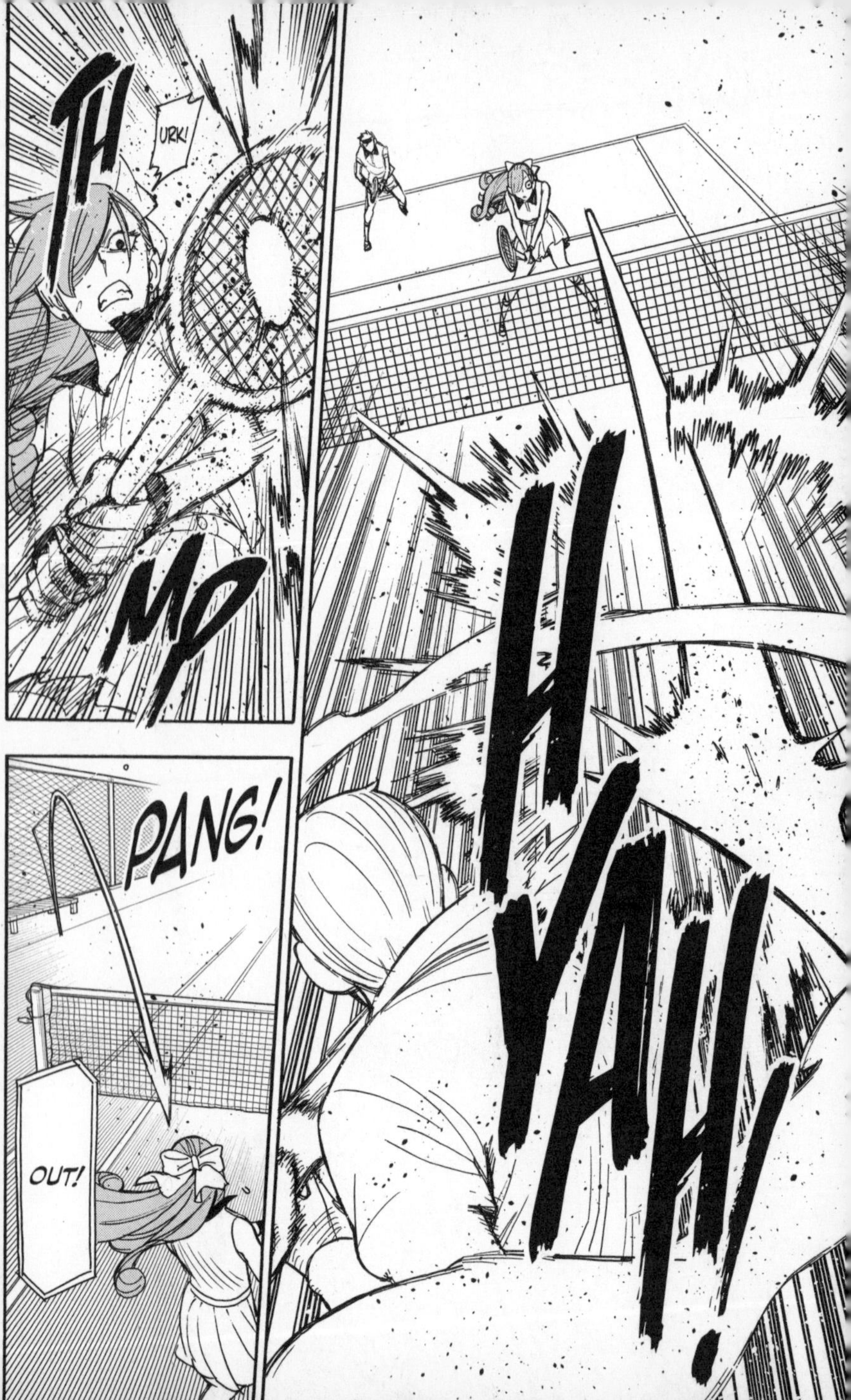
HYAH!
URK!
THMP
PANG!
OUT!

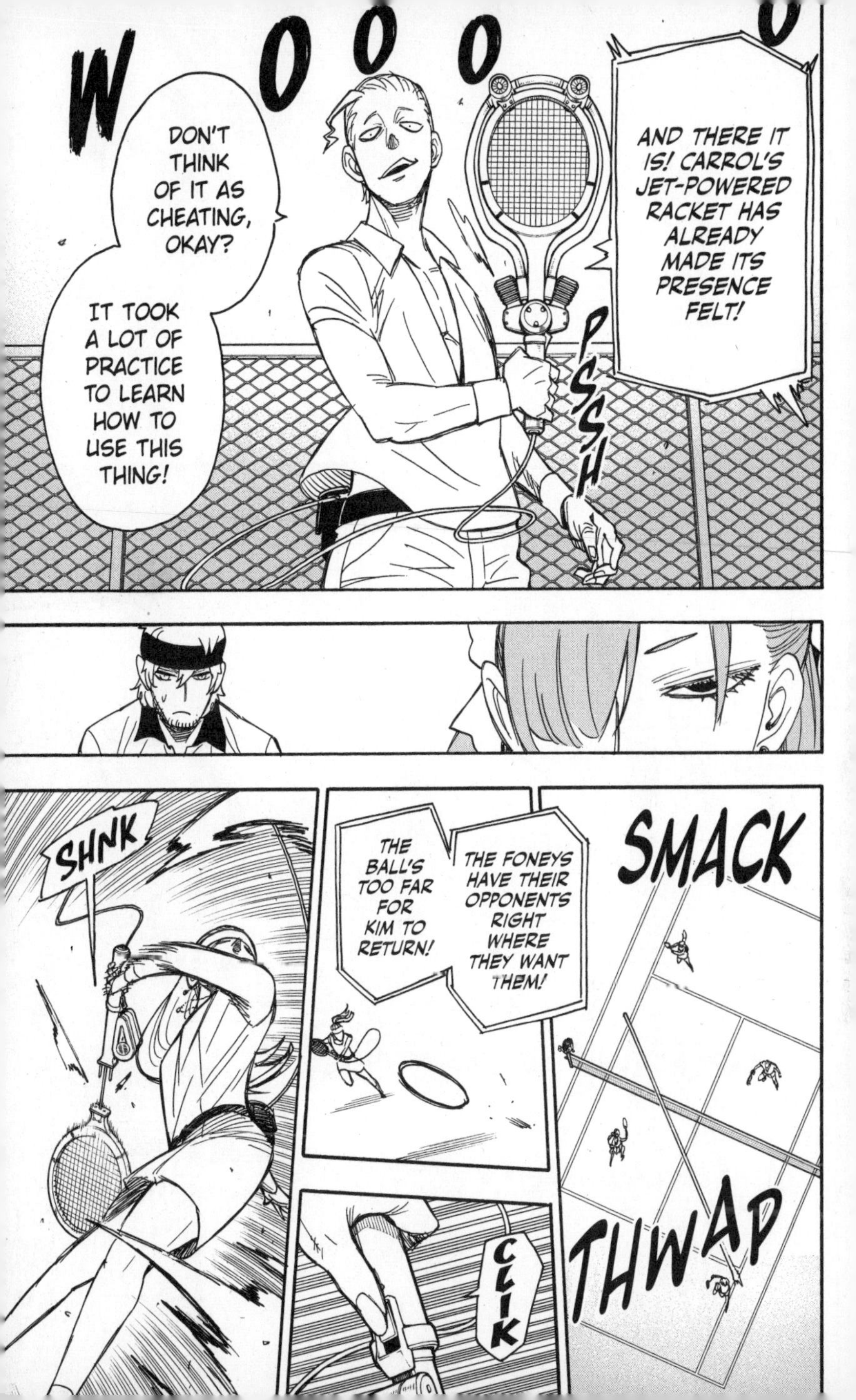
WOOOO
AND THERE IT IS! CARROL'S JET-POWERED RACKET HAS ALREADY MADE ITS PRESENCE FELT!
PSSH
DON'T THINK OF IT AS CHEATING, OKAY?
IT TOOK A LOT OF PRACTICE TO LEARN HOW TO USE THIS THING!
SMACK
THWAP
THE FONEYS HAVE THEIR OPPONENTS RIGHT WHERE THEY WANT THEM!
THE BALL'S TOO FAR FOR KIM TO RETURN!
CLIK
SHNK

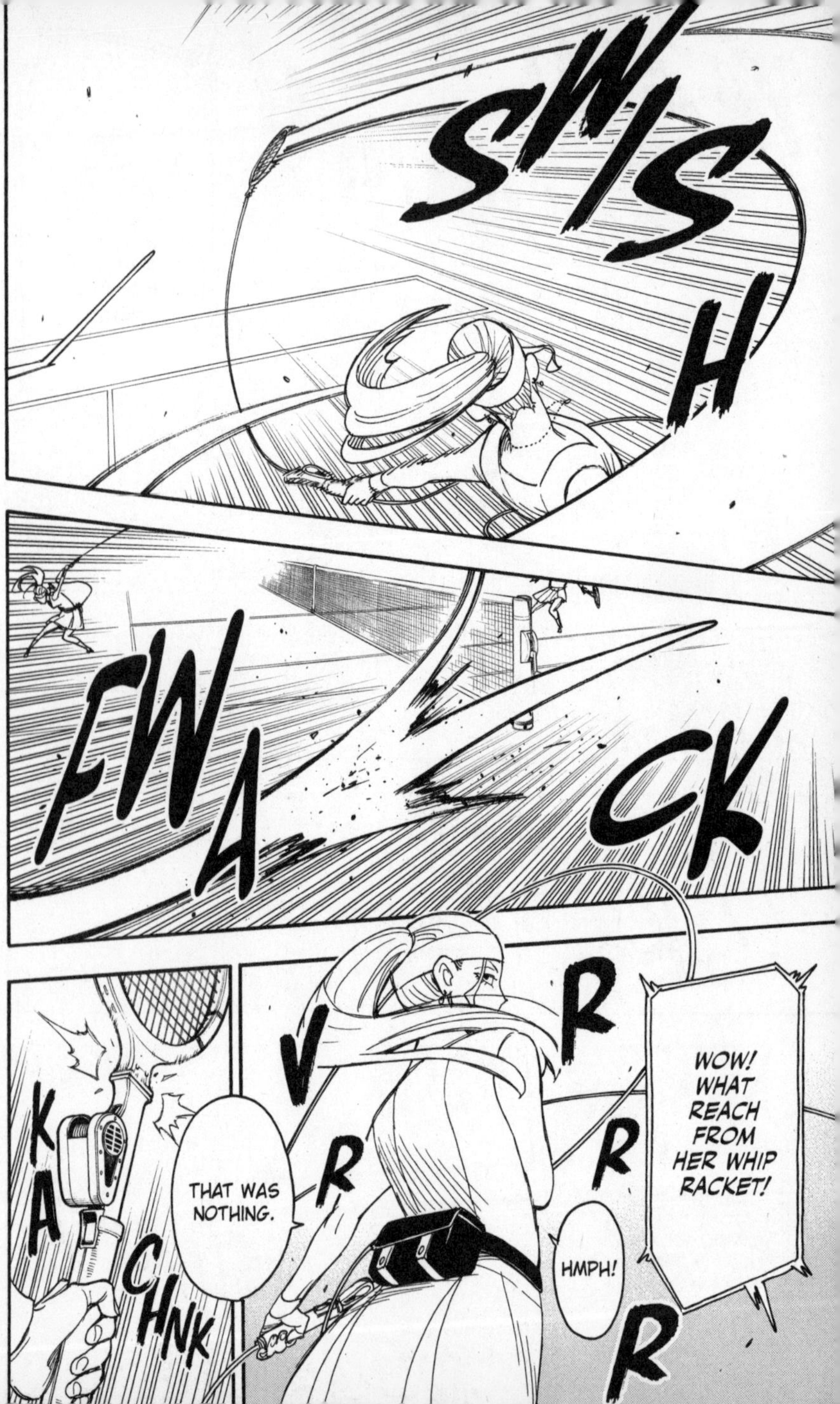
SWISH
FWACK
WOW! WHAT REACH FROM HER WHIP RACKET!
VRRRR
HMPH!
THAT WAS NOTHING.
KACHNK

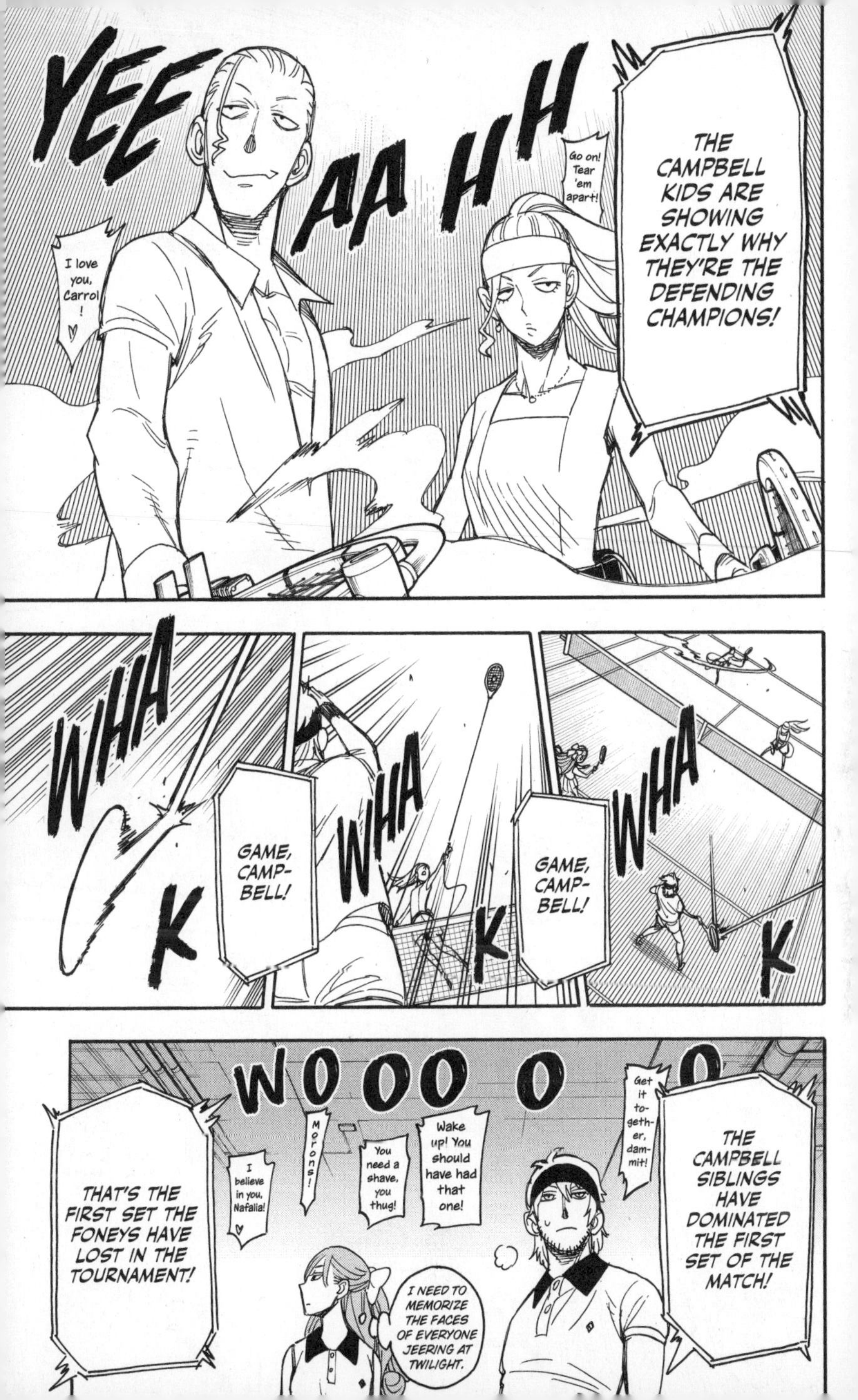
THE CAMPBELL KIDS ARE SHOWING EXACTLY WHY THEY'RE THE DEFENDING CHAMPIONS!
Go on! Tear 'em apart!
YEEAAHH
I love you, Carrol! ♡
WHAK
GAME, CAMP-BELL!
WHAK
GAME, CAMP-BELL!
WHAK
THE CAMPBELL SIBLINGS HAVE DOMINATED THE FIRST SET OF THE MATCH!
Get it to-geth-er, dam-mit!
WOOOOO
Wake up! You should have had that one!
You need a shave, you thug!
Morons!
I believe in you, Nafalia! ♡
THAT'S THE FIRST SET THE FONEYS HAVE LOST IN THE TOURNAMENT!
I NEED TO MEMORIZE THE FACES OF EVERYONE JEERING AT TWILIGHT.

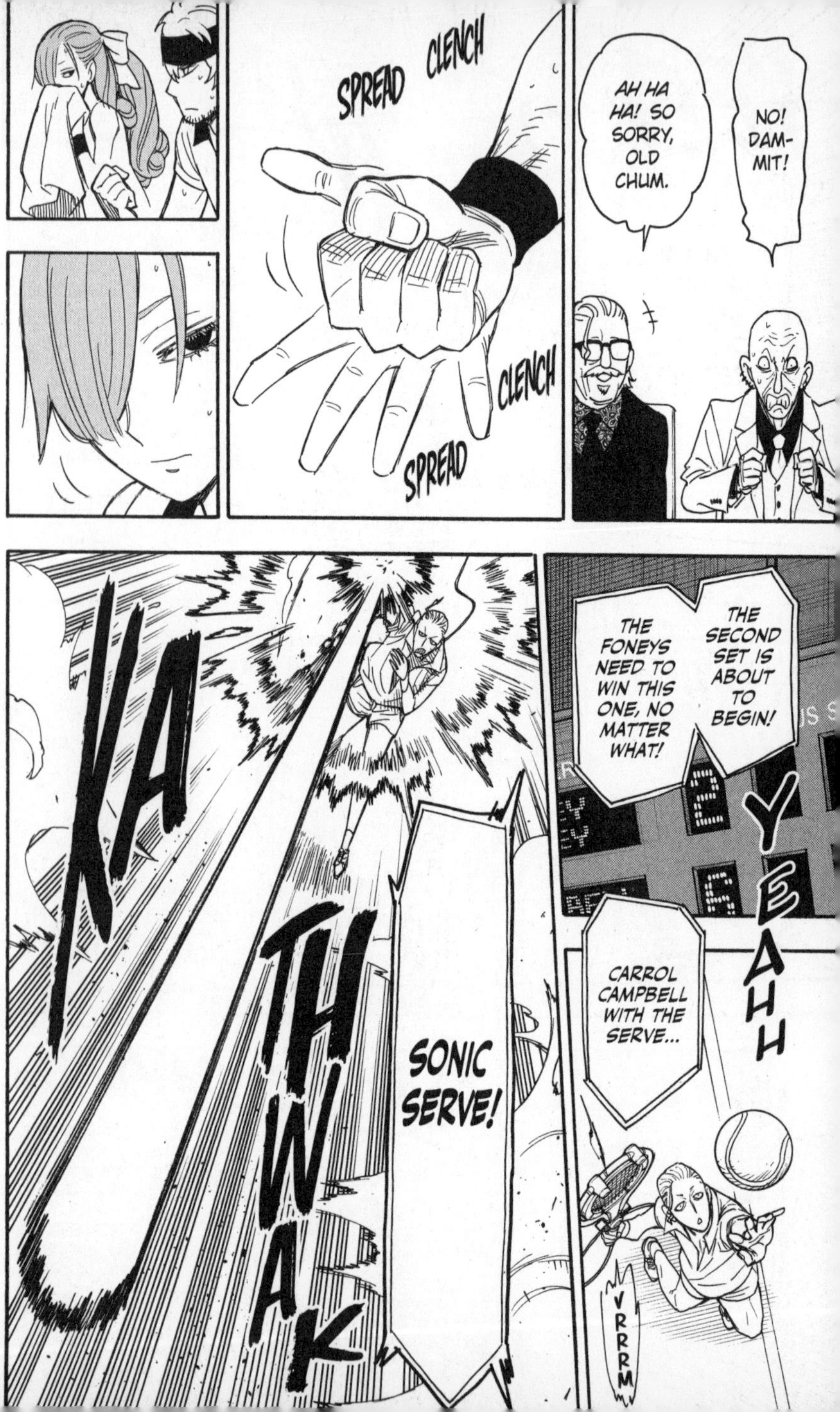
NO! DAM-MIT!
AH HA HA! SO SORRY, OLD CHUM.
CLENCH
SPREAD
CLENCH
SPREAD
THE SECOND SET IS ABOUT TO BEGIN!
THE FONEYS NEED TO WIN THIS ONE, NO MATTER WHAT!
YEAHH
CARROL CAMPBELL WITH THE SERVE...
VRRRM
SONIC SERVE!
KA
THWAK

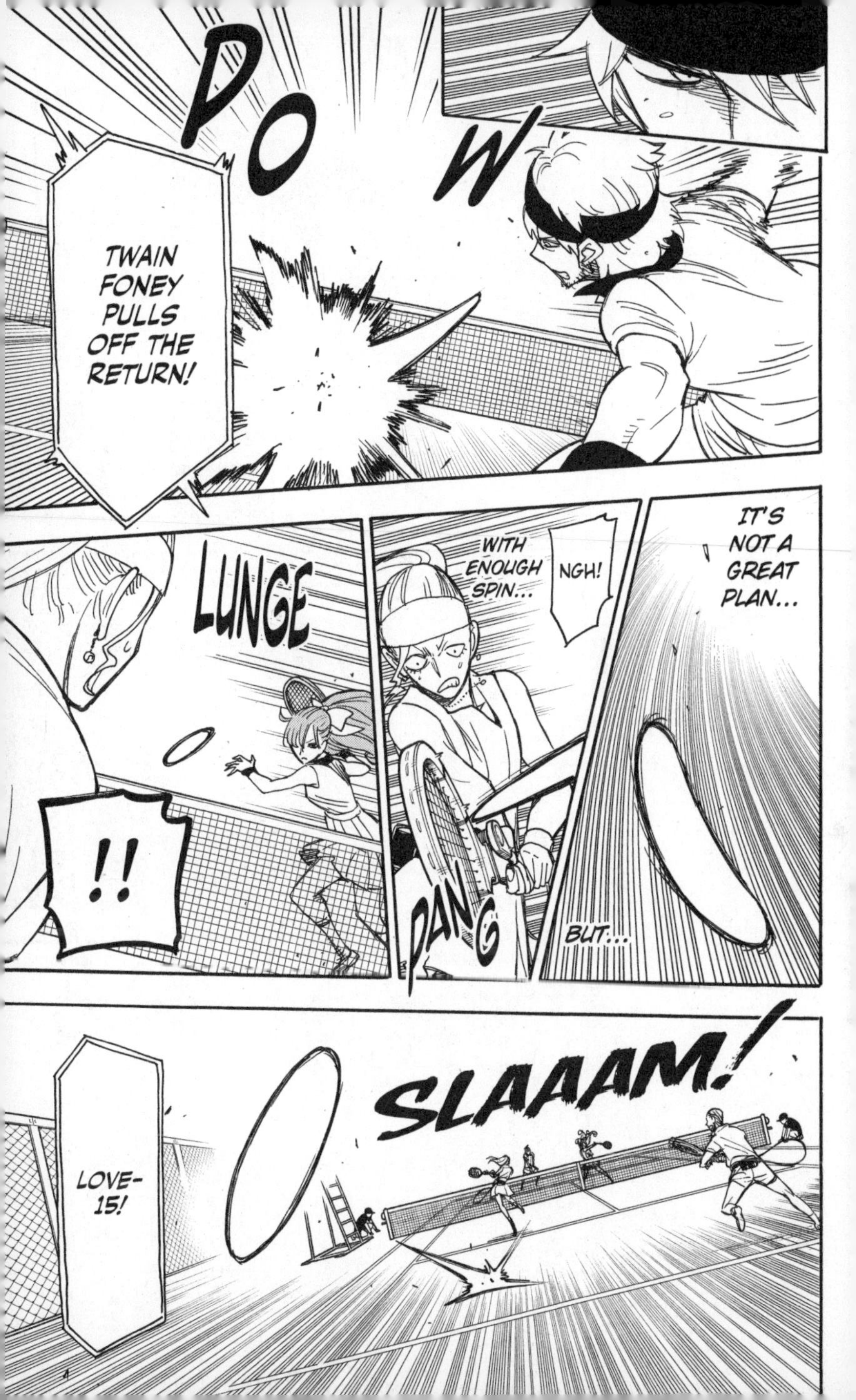
POW
TWAIN FONEY PULLS OFF THE RETURN!
IT'S NOT A GREAT PLAN...
BUT...
NGH!
WITH ENOUGH SPIN...
DANG
LUNGE
!!
SLAAAM!
LOVE-15!

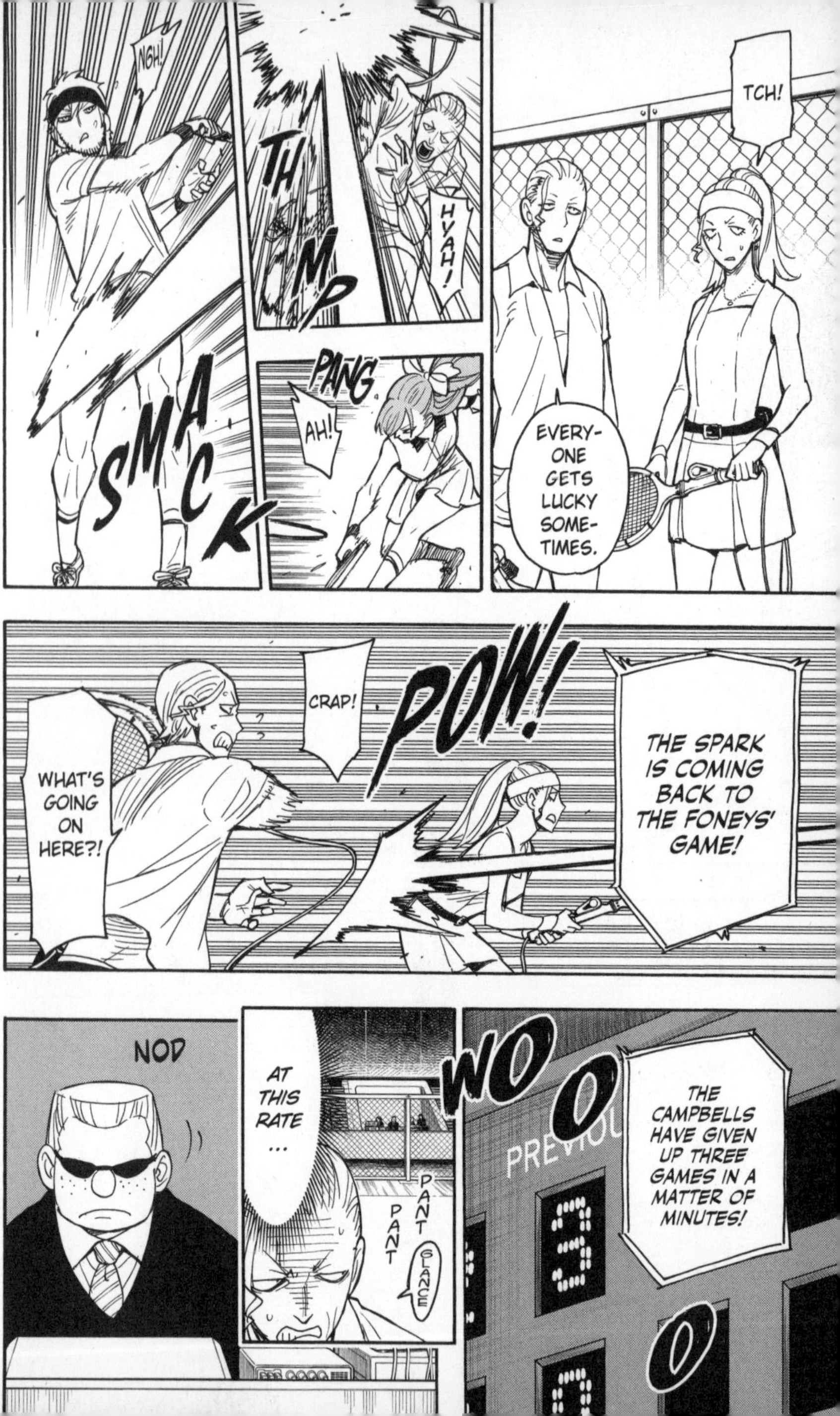

TCH!
EVERY-ONE GETS LUCKY SOME-TIMES.
THUMP
HYAH!
PANG
AH!
NGH!
SMACK
THE SPARK IS COMING BACK TO THE FONEYS' GAME!
POW!
CRAP!
WHAT'S GOING ON HERE?!
WOOO
THE CAMPBELLS HAVE GIVEN UP THREE GAMES IN A MATTER OF MINUTES!
AT THIS RATE...
PANT
PANT
GLANCE
NOD

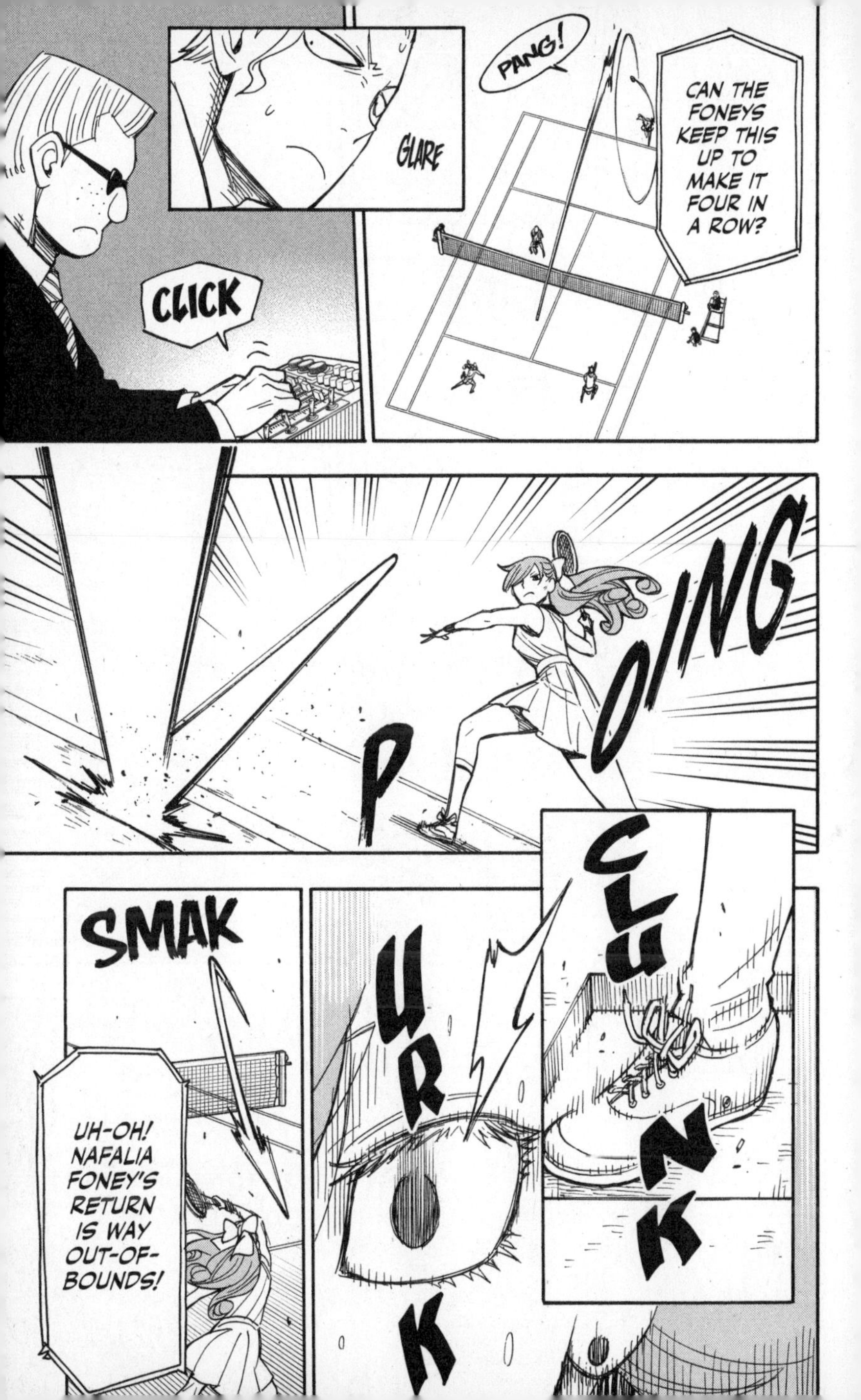
PANG!
CAN THE FONEYS KEEP THIS UP TO MAKE IT FOUR IN A ROW?
GLARE
CLICK
POING
CLUNK
URK
SMAK
UH-OH! NAFALIA FONEY'S RETURN IS WAY OUT-OF-BOUNDS!

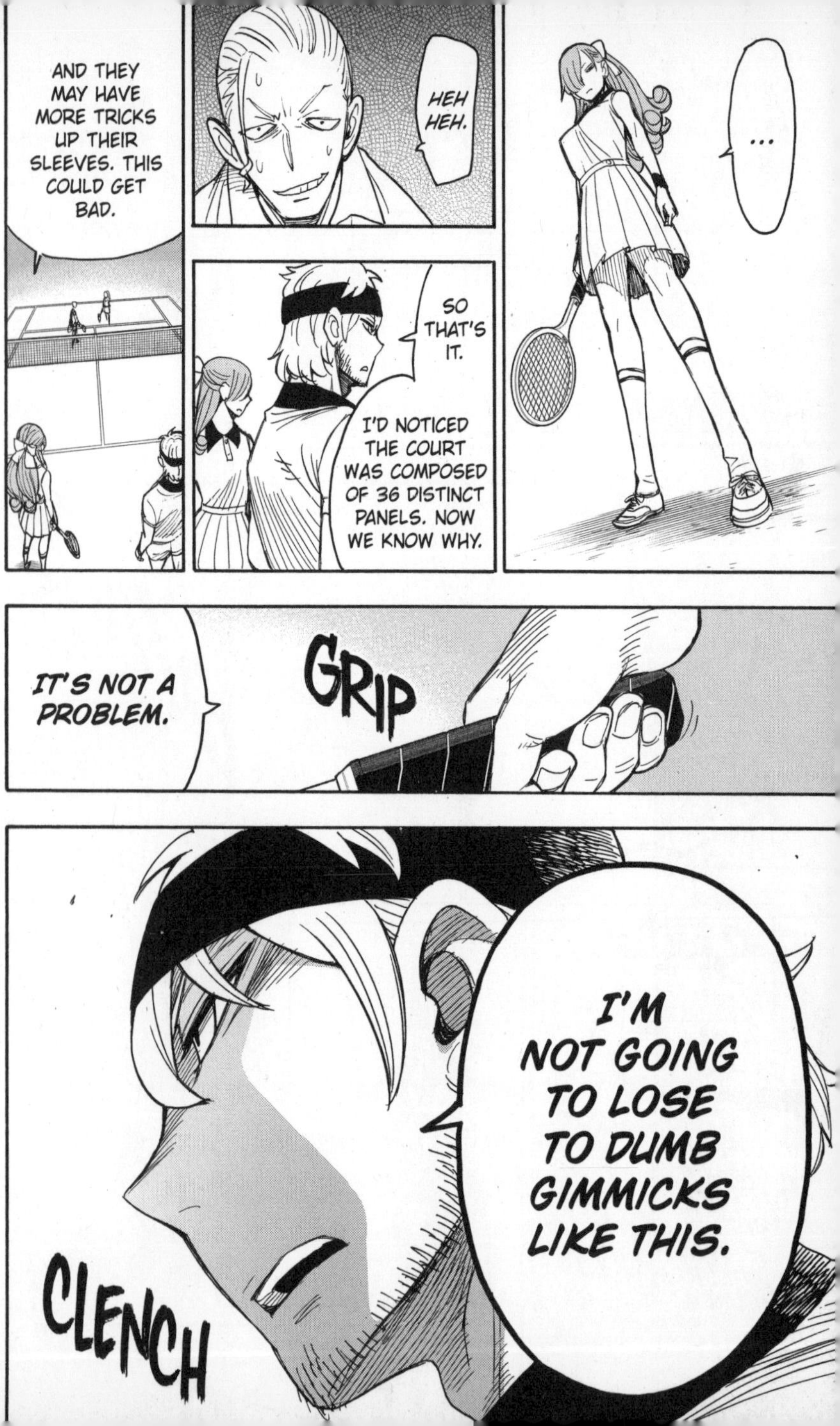
...
HEH HEH.
SO THAT'S IT.
I'D NOTICED THE COURT WAS COMPOSED OF 36 DISTINCT PANELS. NOW WE KNOW WHY.
AND THEY MAY HAVE MORE TRICKS UP THEIR SLEEVES. THIS COULD GET BAD.
GRIP
IT'S NOT A PROBLEM.
I'M NOT GOING TO LOSE TO DUMB GIMMICKS LIKE THIS.
CLENCH

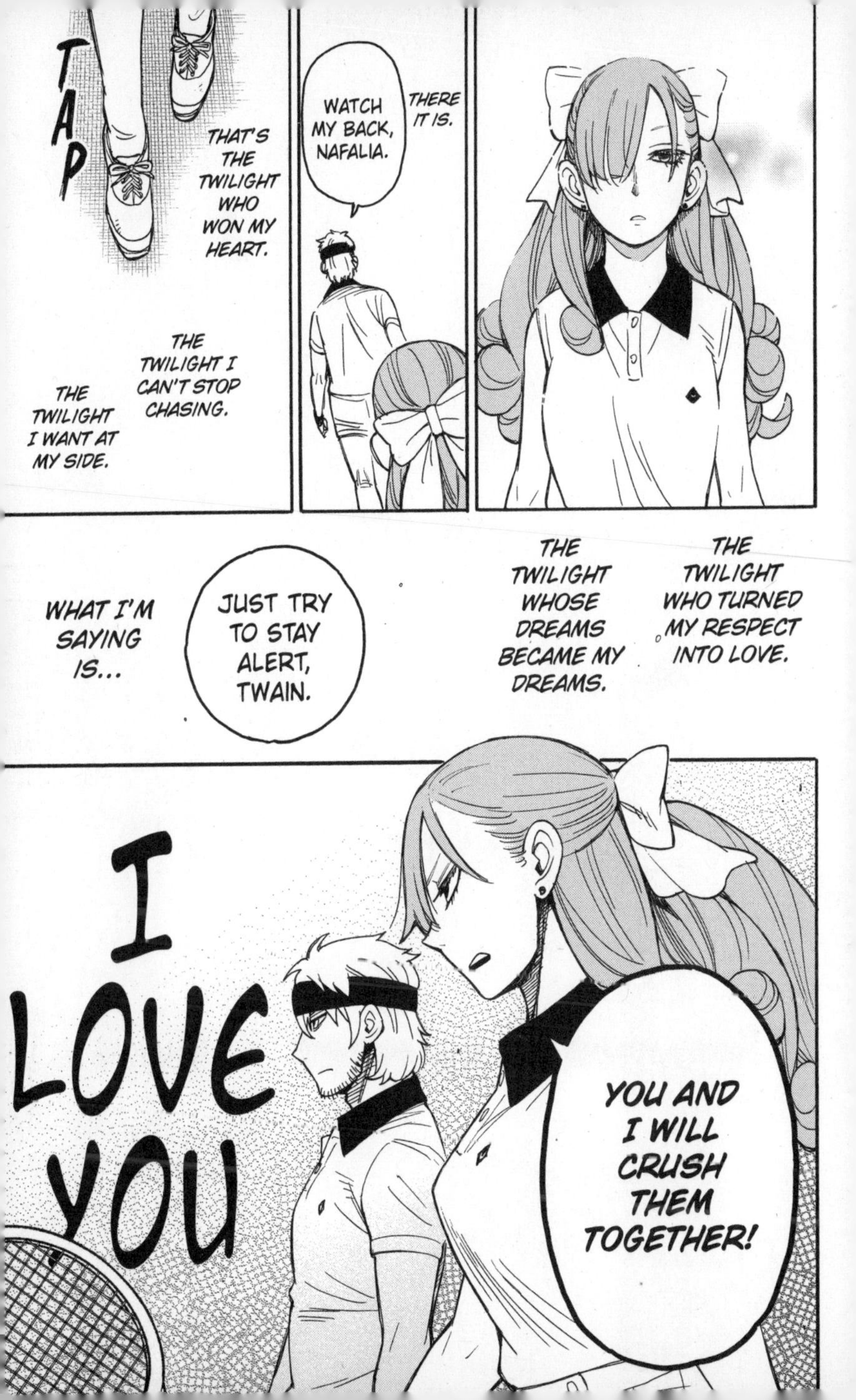
THERE IT IS.
WATCH MY BACK, NAFALIA.
TAP
THAT'S THE TWILIGHT WHO WON MY HEART.
THE TWILIGHT I CAN'T STOP CHASING.
THE TWILIGHT I WANT AT MY SIDE.
THE TWILIGHT WHO TURNED MY RESPECT INTO LOVE.
THE TWILIGHT WHOSE DREAMS BECAME MY DREAMS.
JUST TRY TO STAY ALERT, TWAIN.
WHAT I'M SAYING IS...
YOU AND I WILL CRUSH THEM TOGETHER!
I LOVE YOU

SPY×FAMILY

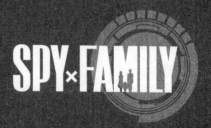

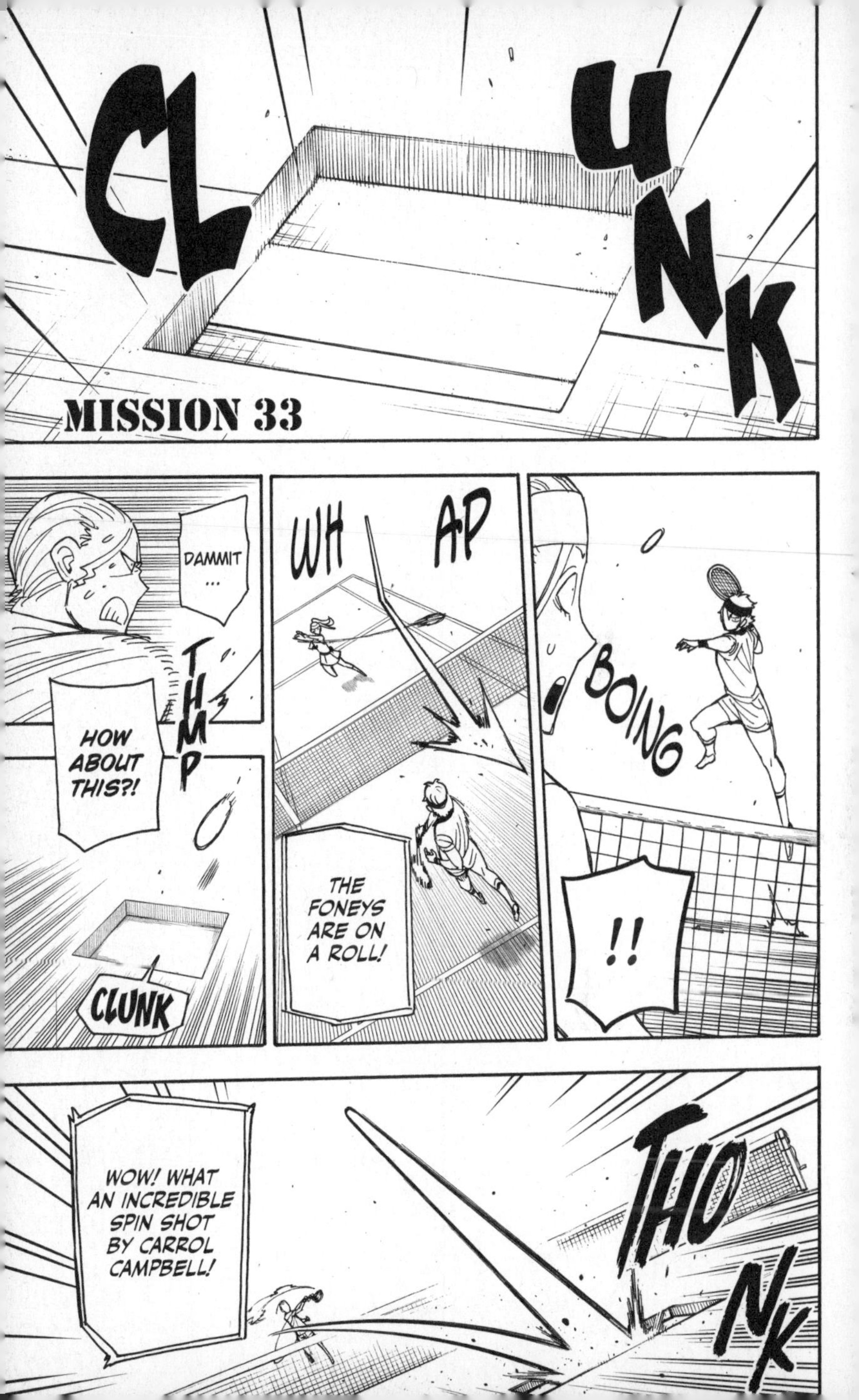
CLUNK
MISSION 33
BOING
!!
WHAP
THE FONEYS ARE ON A ROLL!
DAMMIT ...
THUMP
HOW ABOUT THIS?!
CLUNK
THONK
WOW! WHAT AN INCREDIBLE SPIN SHOT BY CARROL CAMPBELL!

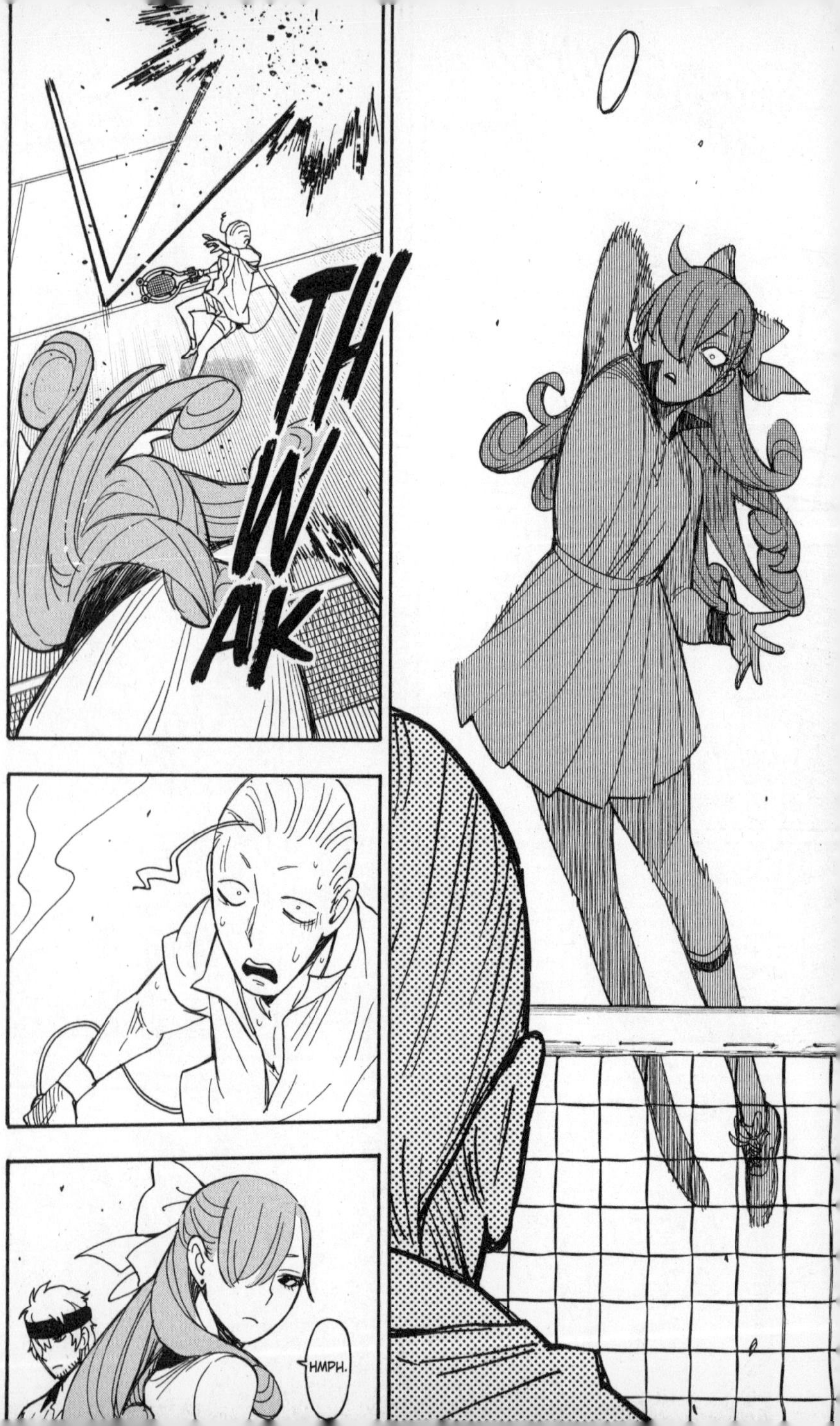
THWAK
HMPH.

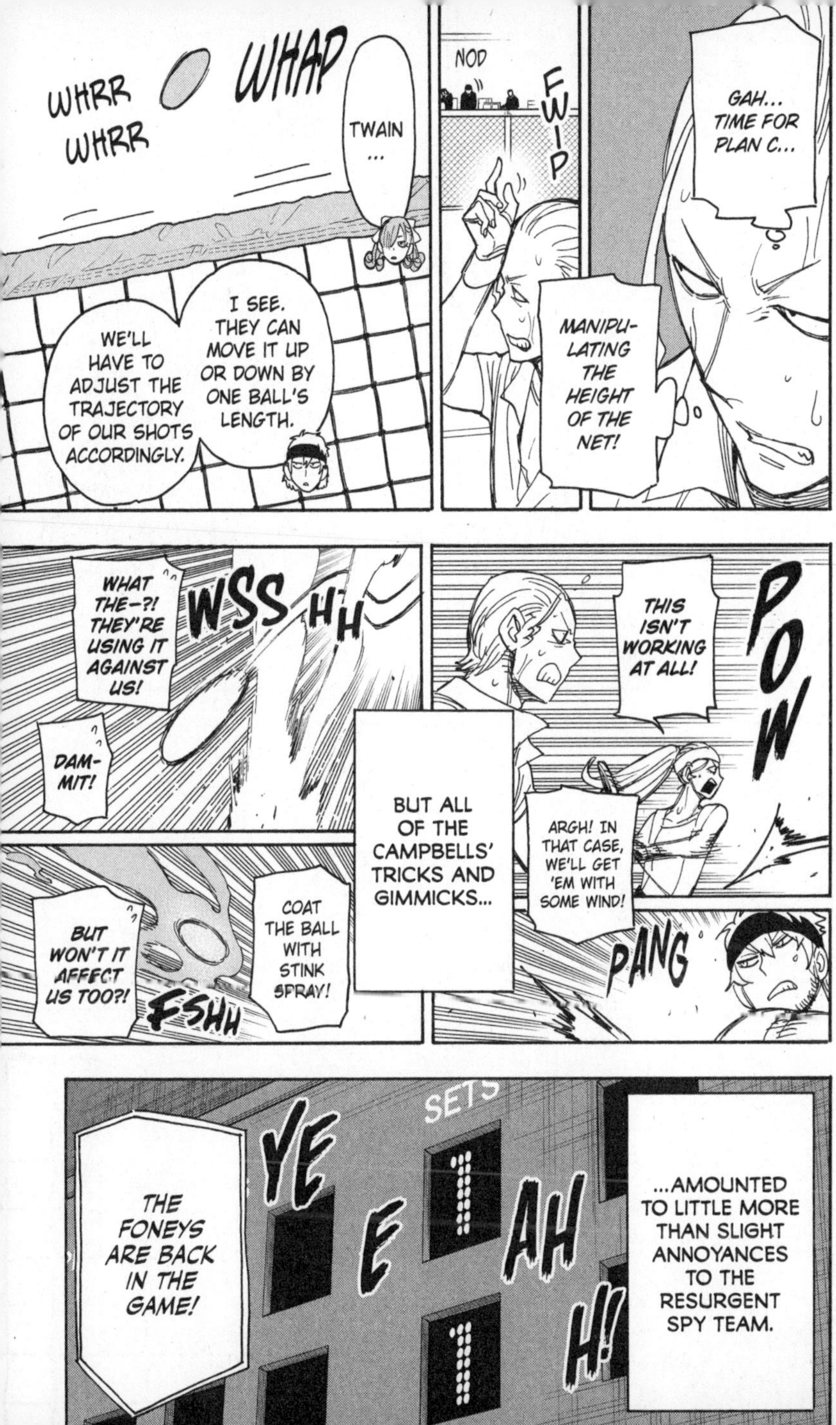
GAH... TIME FOR PLAN C...
NOD
FWIP
MANIPULATING THE HEIGHT OF THE NET!
WHRR WHRR
WHAP
TWAIN ...
I SEE. THEY CAN MOVE IT UP OR DOWN BY ONE BALL'S LENGTH.
WE'LL HAVE TO ADJUST THE TRAJECTORY OF OUR SHOTS ACCORDINGLY.
THIS ISN'T WORKING AT ALL!
POW
ARGH! IN THAT CASE, WE'LL GET 'EM WITH SOME WIND!
PANG
WHAT THE-?! THEY'RE USING IT AGAINST US!
WSSHH
DAMMIT!
COAT THE BALL WITH STINK SPRAY!
BUT WON'T IT AFFECT US TOO?!
FSHH
BUT ALL OF THE CAMPBELLS' TRICKS AND GIMMICKS...
...AMOUNTED TO LITTLE MORE THAN SLIGHT ANNOYANCES TO THE RESURGENT SPY TEAM.
SETS
YEEAHH!
THE FONEYS ARE BACK IN THE GAME!

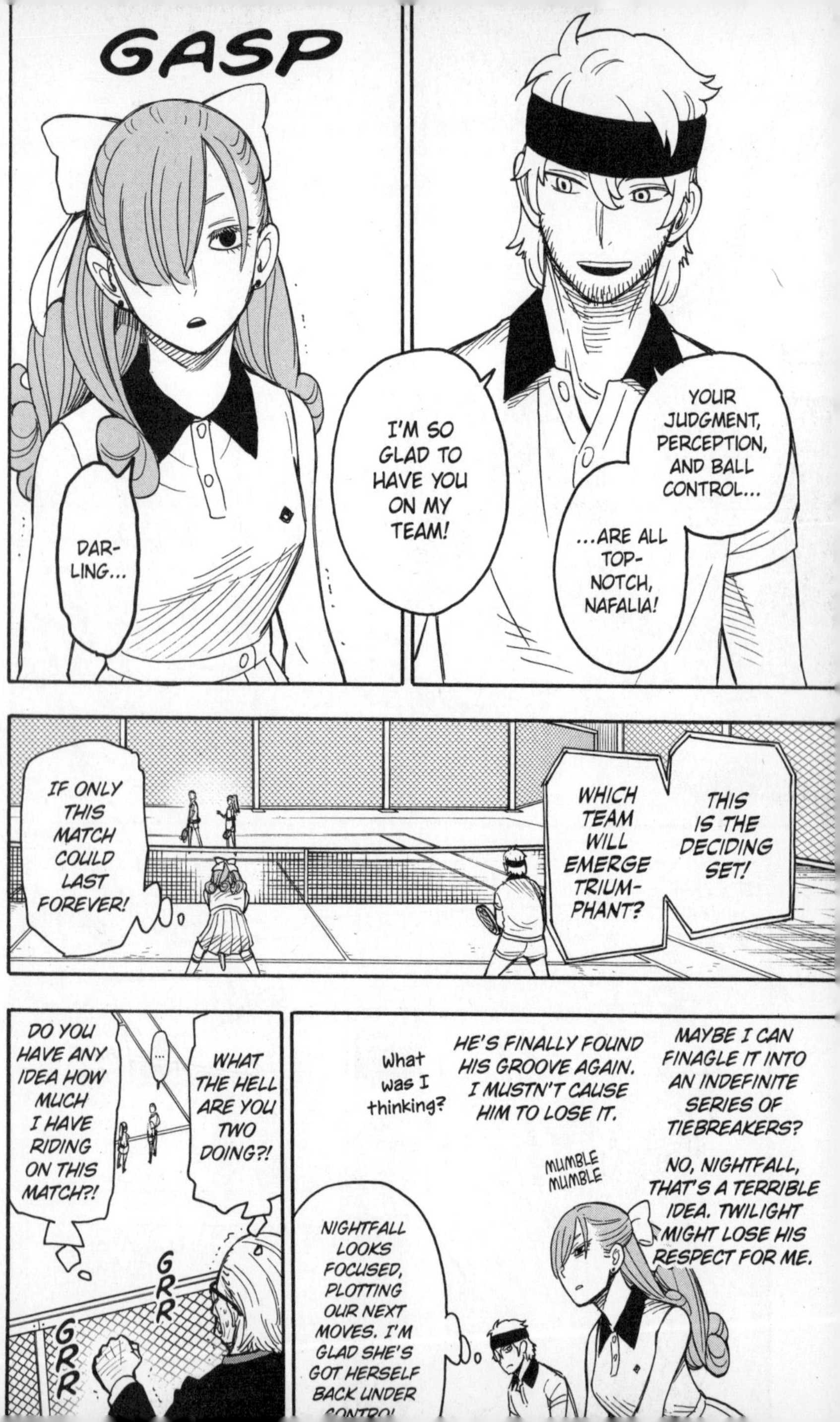
YOUR JUDGMENT, PERCEPTION, AND BALL CONTROL...
...ARE ALL TOP-NOTCH, NAFALIA!
I'M SO GLAD TO HAVE YOU ON MY TEAM!
GASP
DAR-LING...
THIS IS THE DECIDING SET!
WHICH TEAM WILL EMERGE TRIUMPHANT?
IF ONLY THIS MATCH COULD LAST FOREVER!
MAYBE I CAN FINAGLE IT INTO AN INDEFINITE SERIES OF TIEBREAKERS?
NO, NIGHTFALL, THAT'S A TERRIBLE IDEA. TWILIGHT MIGHT LOSE HIS RESPECT FOR ME.
HE'S FINALLY FOUND HIS GROOVE AGAIN. I MUSTN'T CAUSE HIM TO LOSE IT.
What was I thinking?
MUMBLE MUMBLE
NIGHTFALL LOOKS FOCUSED, PLOTTING OUR NEXT MOVES. I'M GLAD SHE'S GOT HERSELF BACK UNDER
WHAT THE HELL ARE YOU TWO DOING?!
...
DO YOU HAVE ANY IDEA HOW MUCH I HAVE RIDING ON THIS MATCH?!
GRR
GRR

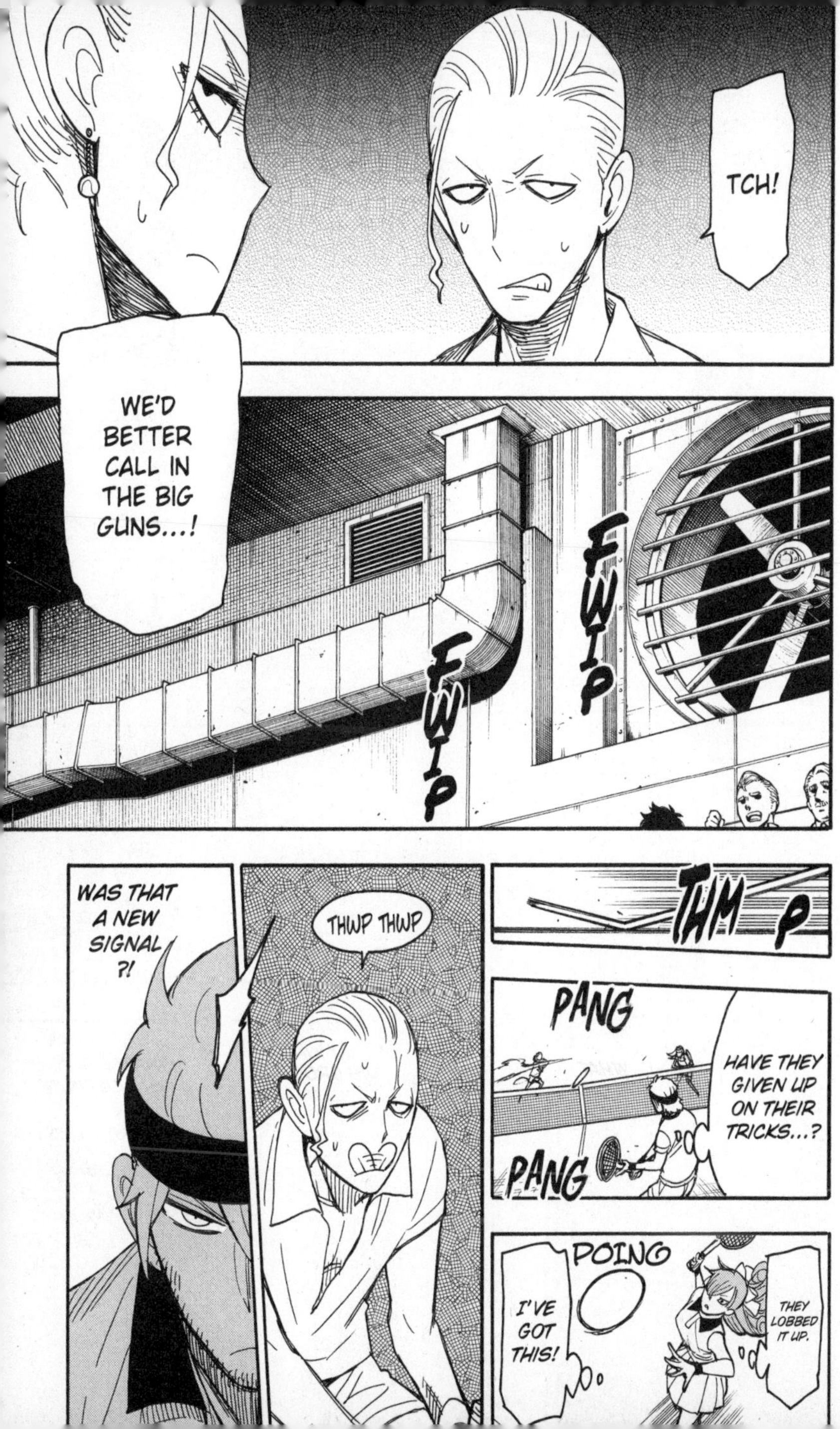
TCH!
WE'D BETTER CALL IN THE BIG GUNS...!
FWIP
FWIP
THMP
PANG
HAVE THEY GIVEN UP ON THEIR TRICKS...?
PANG
THEY LOBBED IT UP.
POING
I'VE GOT THIS!
THWP THWP
WAS THAT A NEW SIGNAL?!

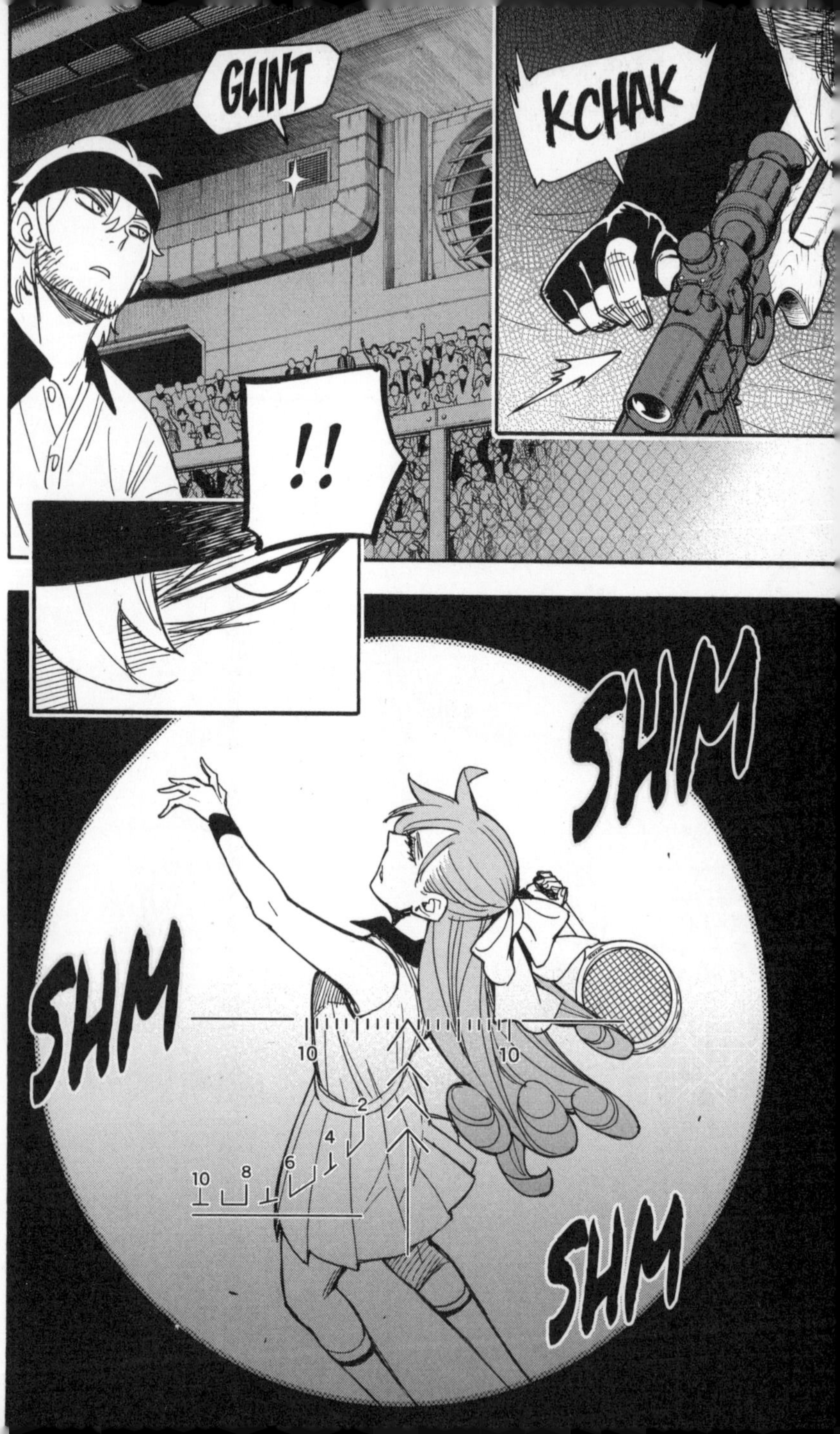
KCHAK
GLINT
!!
SHM
SHM
10 10
2 4 6 8 10
SHM

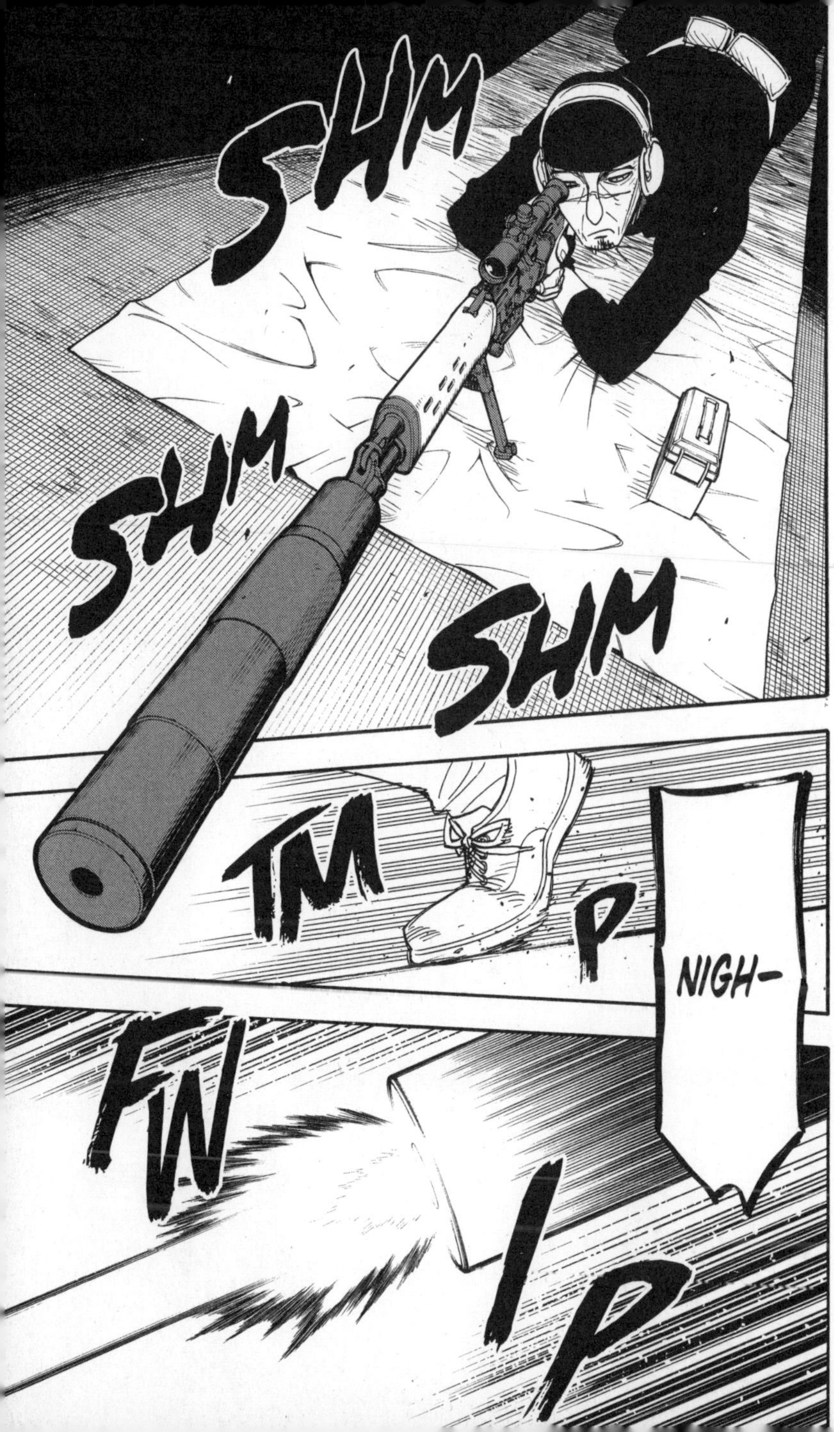
SHM
SHM
SHM
NIGH-
TMP
FWIP

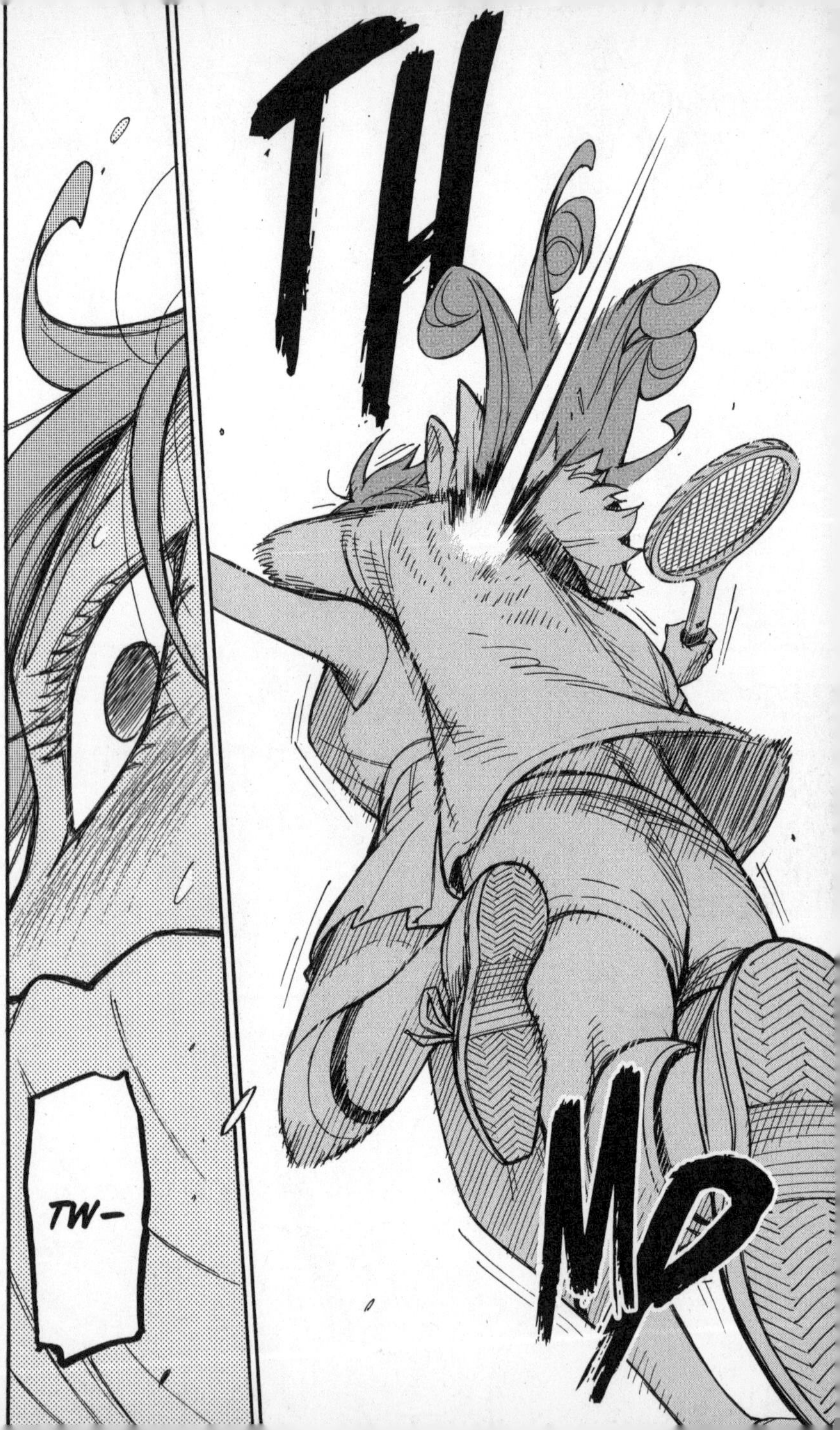
TH
MP
TW—

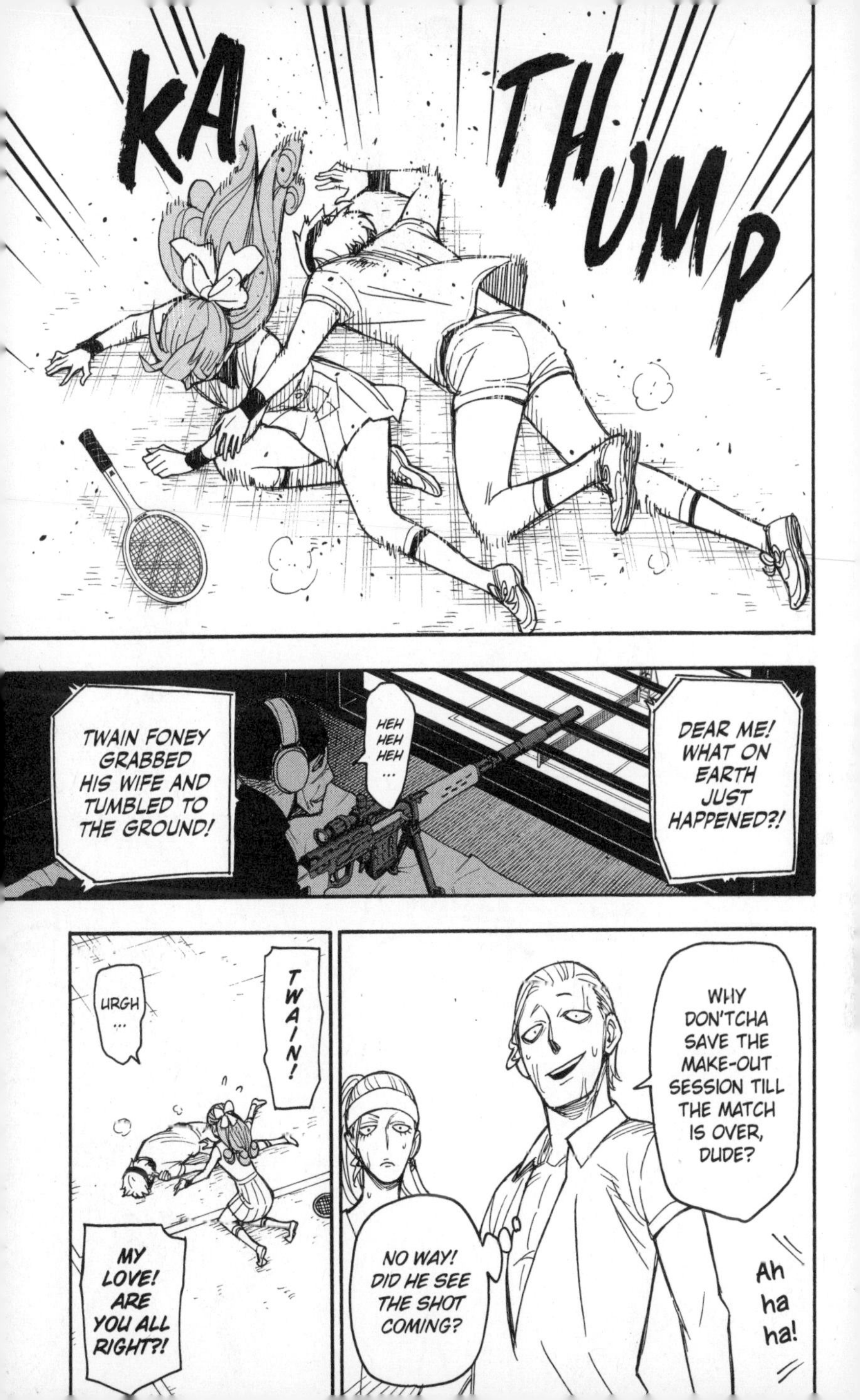
KA THUMP
DEAR ME! WHAT ON EARTH JUST HAPPENED?!
HEH HEH HEH ...
TWAIN FONEY GRABBED HIS WIFE AND TUMBLED TO THE GROUND!
WHY DON'TCHA SAVE THE MAKE-OUT SESSION TILL THE MATCH IS OVER, DUDE?
Ah ha ha!
NO WAY! DID HE SEE THE SHOT COMING?
TWAIN!
URGH ...
MY LOVE! ARE YOU ALL RIGHT?!

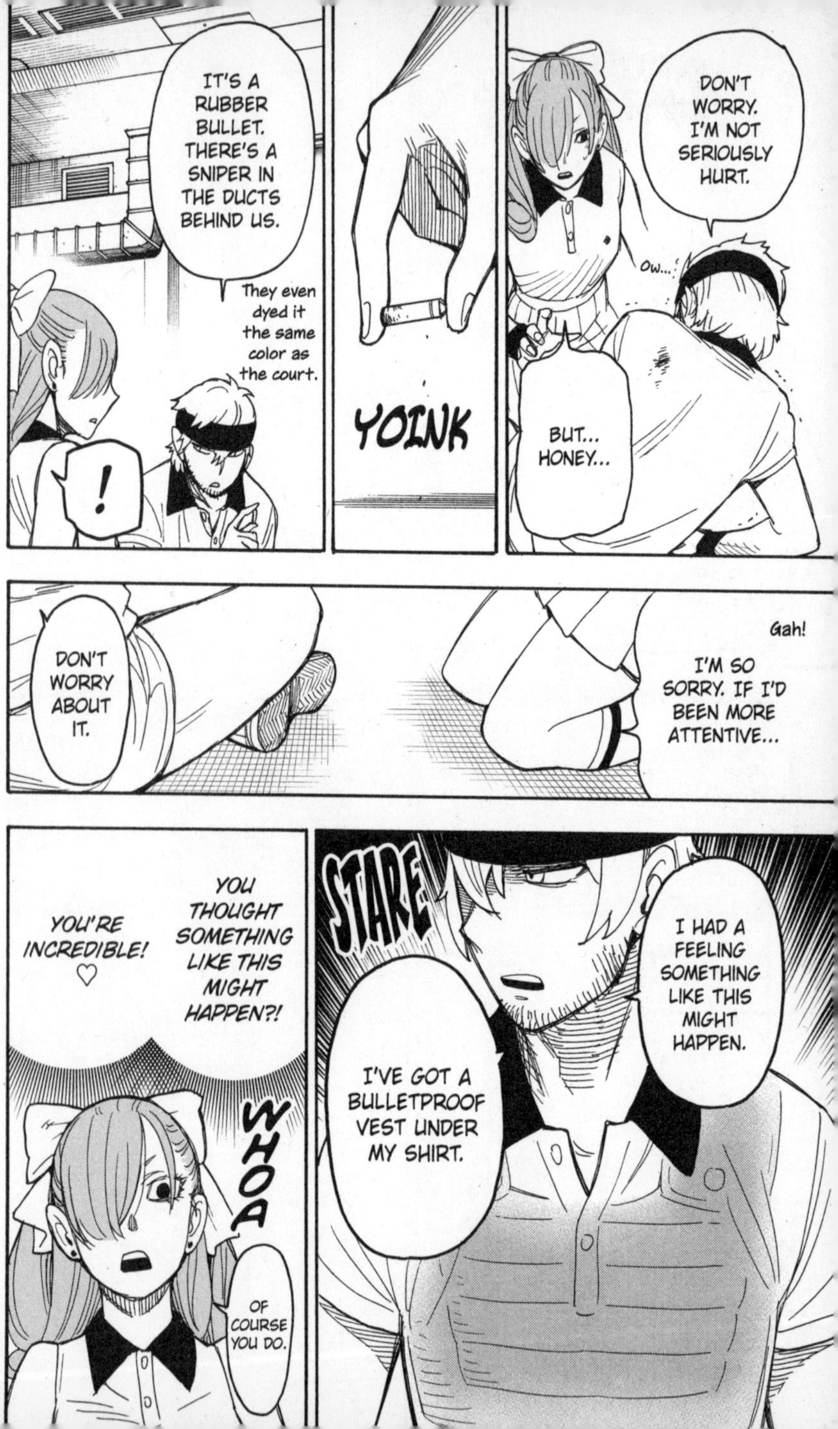
DON'T WORRY. I'M NOT SERIOUSLY HURT.
Ow...
BUT... HONEY...
YOINK
IT'S A RUBBER BULLET. THERE'S A SNIPER IN THE DUCTS BEHIND US.
They even dyed it the same color as the court.
!
Gah!
I'M SO SORRY. IF I'D BEEN MORE ATTENTIVE...
DON'T WORRY ABOUT IT.
STARE
I HAD A FEELING SOMETHING LIKE THIS MIGHT HAPPEN.
I'VE GOT A BULLETPROOF VEST UNDER MY SHIRT.
YOU THOUGHT SOMETHING LIKE THIS MIGHT HAPPEN?!
YOU'RE INCREDIBLE! ♡
WHOA
OF COURSE YOU DO.

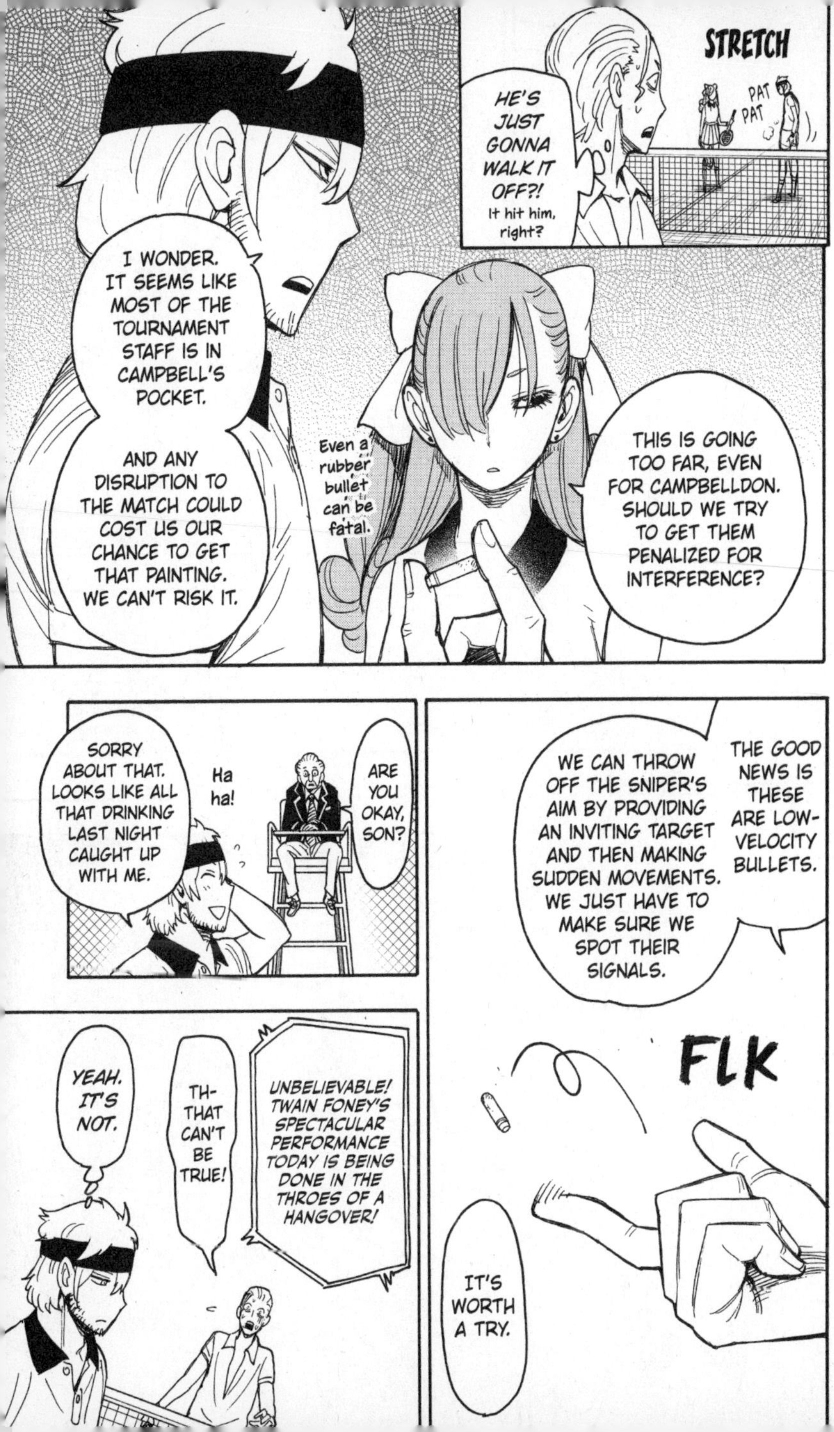
STRETCH
PAT PAT
HE'S JUST GONNA WALK IT OFF?!
It hit him, right?
THIS IS GOING TOO FAR, EVEN FOR CAMPBELLDON. SHOULD WE TRY TO GET THEM PENALIZED FOR INTERFERENCE?
Even a rubber bullet can be fatal.
I WONDER. IT SEEMS LIKE MOST OF THE TOURNAMENT STAFF IS IN CAMPBELL'S POCKET.
AND ANY DISRUPTION TO THE MATCH COULD COST US OUR CHANCE TO GET THAT PAINTING. WE CAN'T RISK IT.
THE GOOD NEWS IS THESE ARE LOW-VELOCITY BULLETS.
WE CAN THROW OFF THE SNIPER'S AIM BY PROVIDING AN INVITING TARGET AND THEN MAKING SUDDEN MOVEMENTS. WE JUST HAVE TO MAKE SURE WE SPOT THEIR SIGNALS.
FLK
IT'S WORTH A TRY.
ARE YOU OKAY, SON?
Ha ha!
SORRY ABOUT THAT. LOOKS LIKE ALL THAT DRINKING LAST NIGHT CAUGHT UP WITH ME.
UNBELIEVABLE! TWAIN FONEY'S SPECTACULAR PERFORMANCE TODAY IS BEING DONE IN THE THROES OF A HANGOVER!
TH-THAT CAN'T BE TRUE!
YEAH. IT'S NOT.

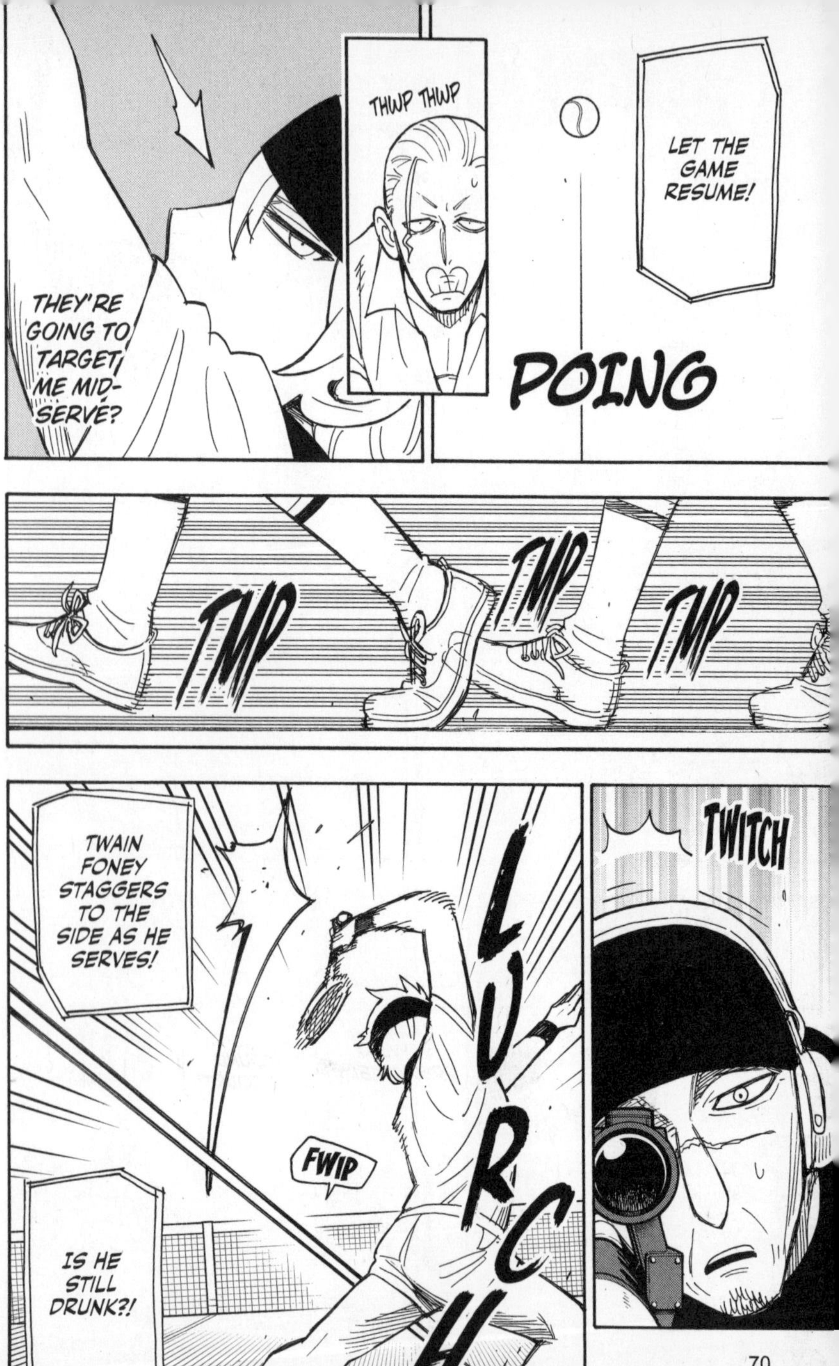
LET THE GAME RESUME!
POING
THWP THWP
THEY'RE GOING TO TARGET ME MID-SERVE?
TMP
TMP
TMP
TWITCH
TWAIN FONEY STAGGERS TO THE SIDE AS HE SERVES!
LURCH
FWIP
IS HE STILL DRUNK?!

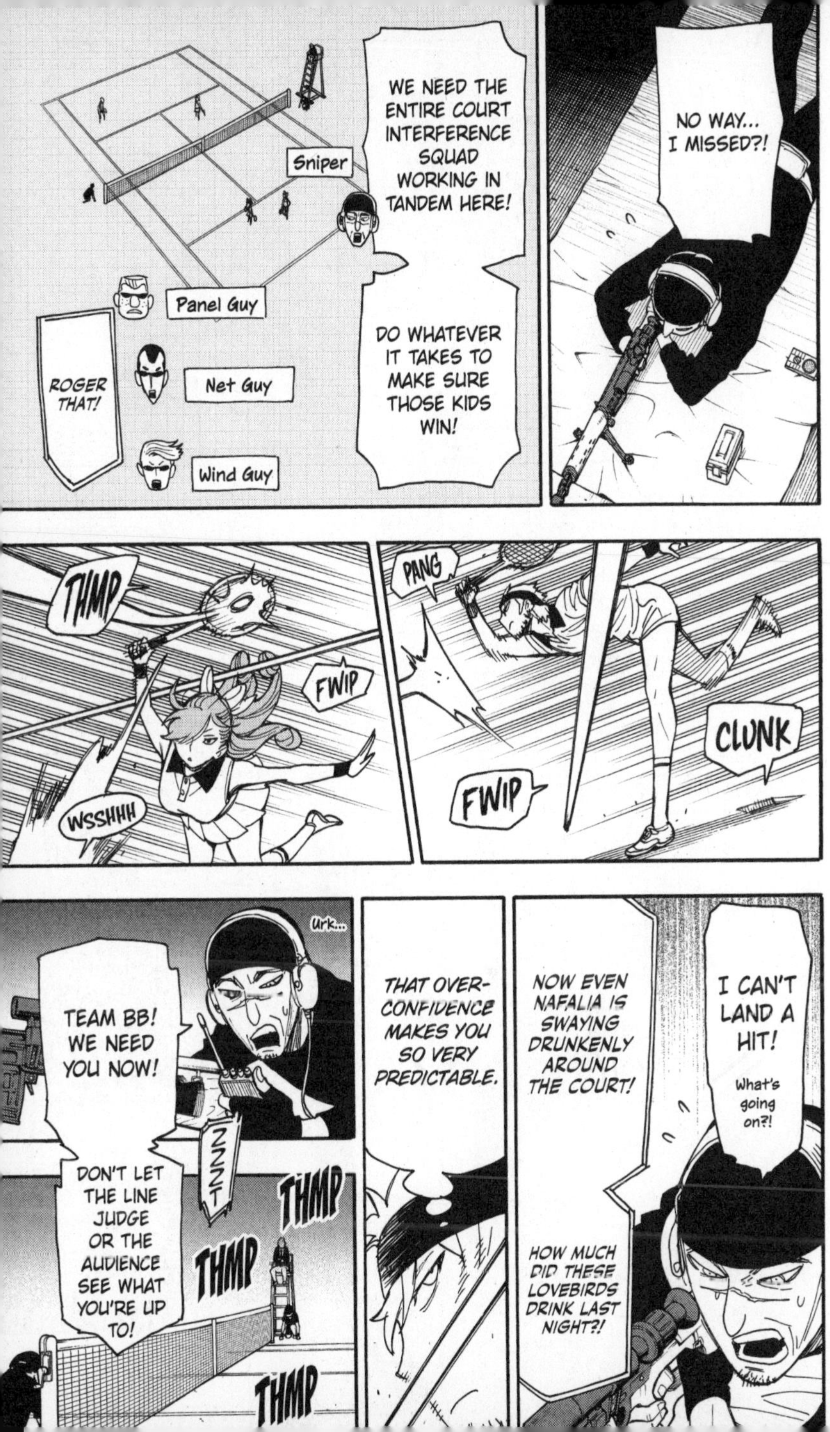
NO WAY... I MISSED?!
WE NEED THE ENTIRE COURT INTERFERENCE SQUAD WORKING IN TANDEM HERE!
Sniper
DO WHATEVER IT TAKES TO MAKE SURE THOSE KIDS WIN!
Panel Guy
Net Guy
Wind Guy
ROGER THAT!
PANG
CLUNK
FWIP
THMP
FWIP
WSSHHH
I CAN'T LAND A HIT!
What's going on?!
NOW EVEN NAFALIA IS SWAYING DRUNKENLY AROUND THE COURT!
HOW MUCH DID THESE LOVEBIRDS DRINK LAST NIGHT?!
THAT OVER-CONFIDENCE MAKES YOU SO VERY PREDICTABLE.
Urk...
TEAM BB! WE NEED YOU NOW!
ZZZT
DON'T LET THE LINE JUDGE OR THE AUDIENCE SEE WHAT YOU'RE UP TO!
THMP
THMP
THMP

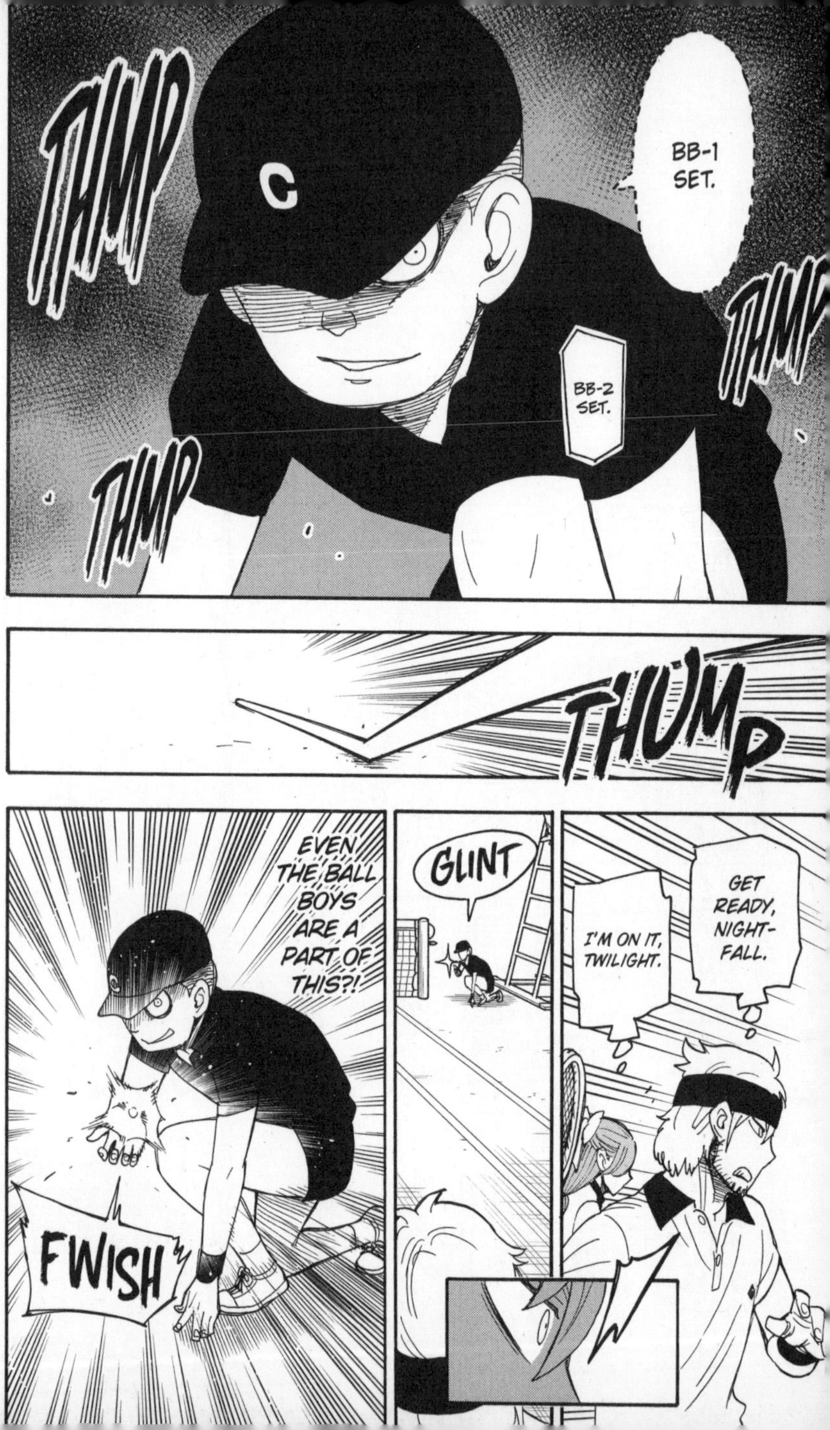
BB-1 SET.
THMP
BB-2 SET.
THMP
THMP
THUMP
GET READY, NIGHT-FALL.
I'M ON IT, TWILIGHT.
GLINT
EVEN THE BALL BOYS ARE A PART OF THIS?!
FWISH

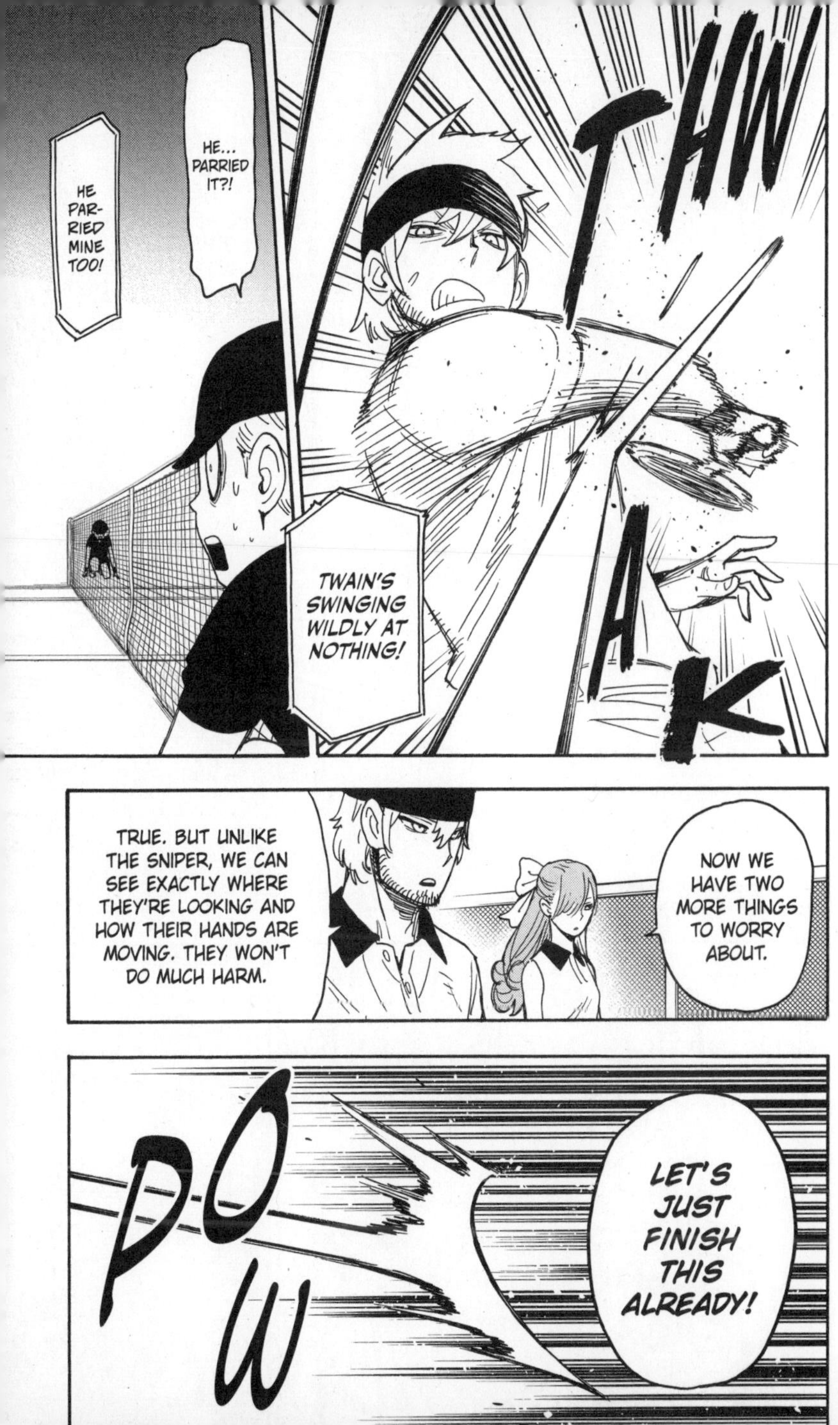
THWAK
HE... PARRIED IT?!
HE PAR-RIED MINE TOO!
TWAIN'S SWINGING WILDLY AT NOTHING!
NOW WE HAVE TWO MORE THINGS TO WORRY ABOUT.
TRUE. BUT UNLIKE THE SNIPER, WE CAN SEE EXACTLY WHERE THEY'RE LOOKING AND HOW THEIR HANDS ARE MOVING. THEY WON'T DO MUCH HARM.
LET'S JUST FINISH THIS ALREADY!
POW

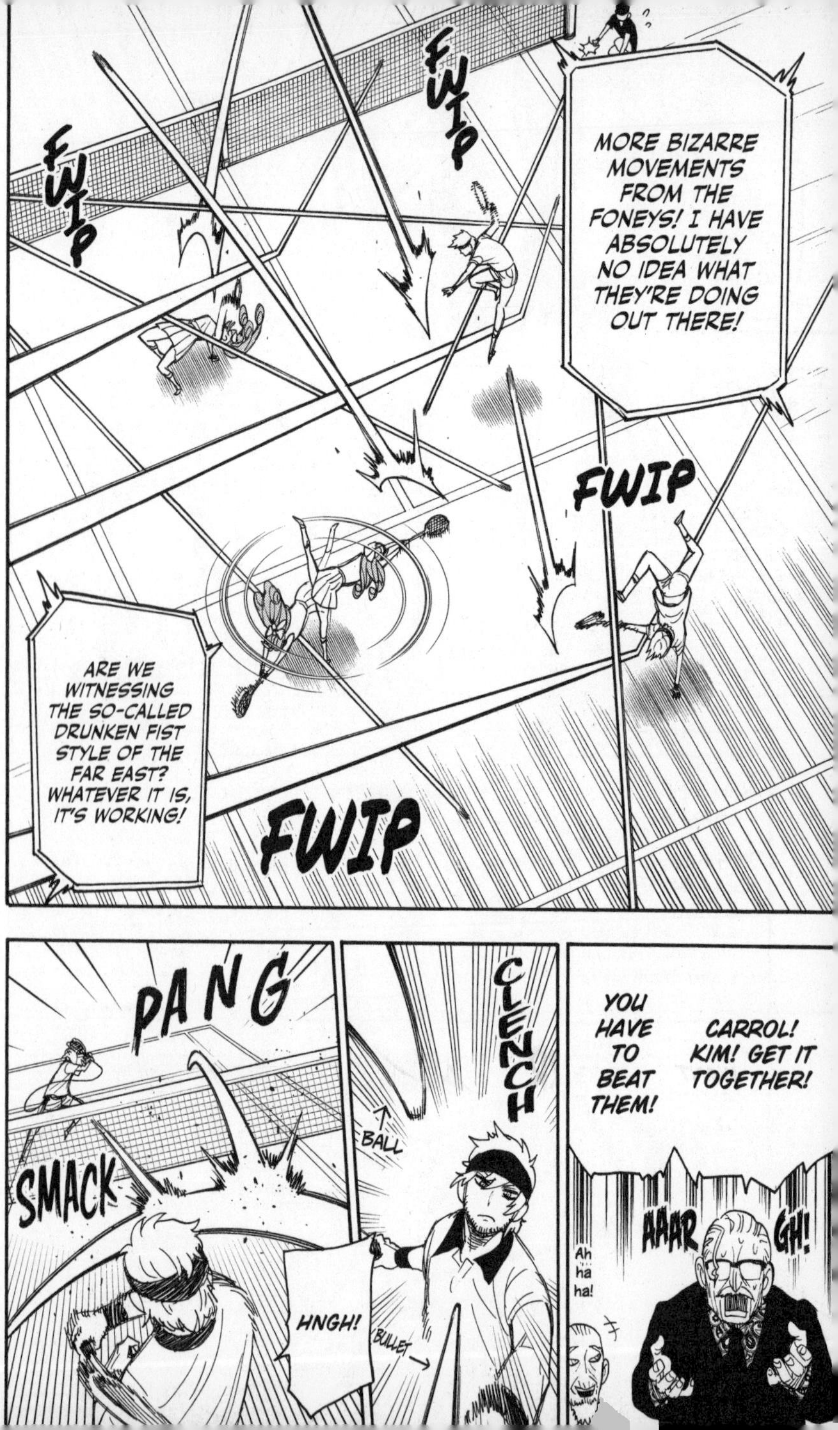
MORE BIZARRE MOVEMENTS FROM THE FONEYS! I HAVE ABSOLUTELY NO IDEA WHAT THEY'RE DOING OUT THERE!
FWIP
FWIP
FWIP
ARE WE WITNESSING THE SO-CALLED DRUNKEN FIST STYLE OF THE FAR EAST? WHATEVER IT IS, IT'S WORKING!
FWIP
CARROL! KIM! GET IT TOGETHER!
YOU HAVE TO BEAT THEM!
AAARGH!
Ah ha ha!
CLENCH
BALL
HNGH!
BULLET
PANG
SMACK

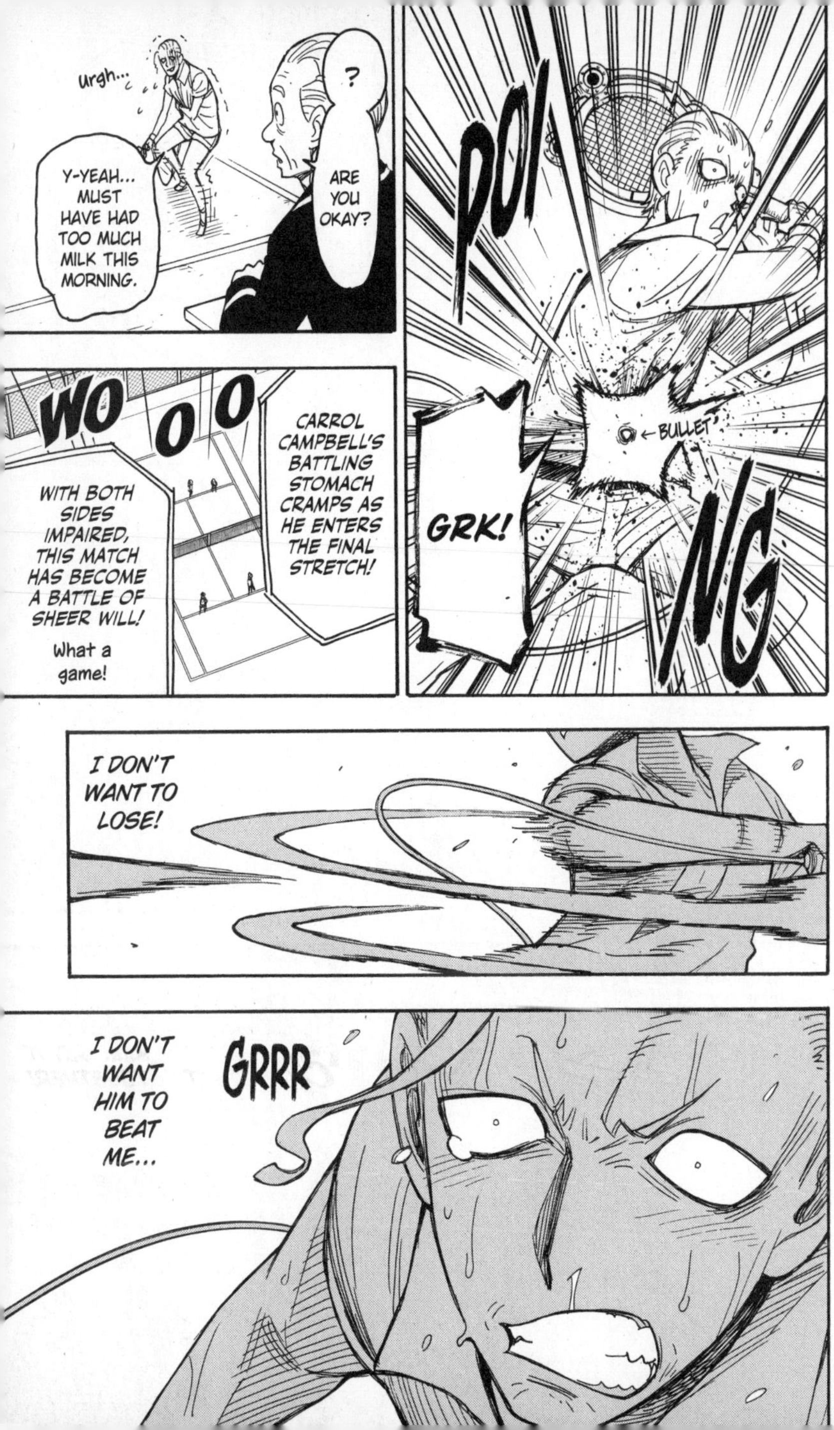
POI
←BULLET
GRK!
NG
?
ARE YOU OKAY?
Urgh...
Y-YEAH... MUST HAVE HAD TOO MUCH MILK THIS MORNING.
WOOO
CARROL CAMPBELL'S BATTLING STOMACH CRAMPS AS HE ENTERS THE FINAL STRETCH!
WITH BOTH SIDES IMPAIRED, THIS MATCH HAS BECOME A BATTLE OF SHEER WILL!
What a game!
I DON'T WANT TO LOSE!
GRRR
I DON'T WANT HIM TO BEAT ME...

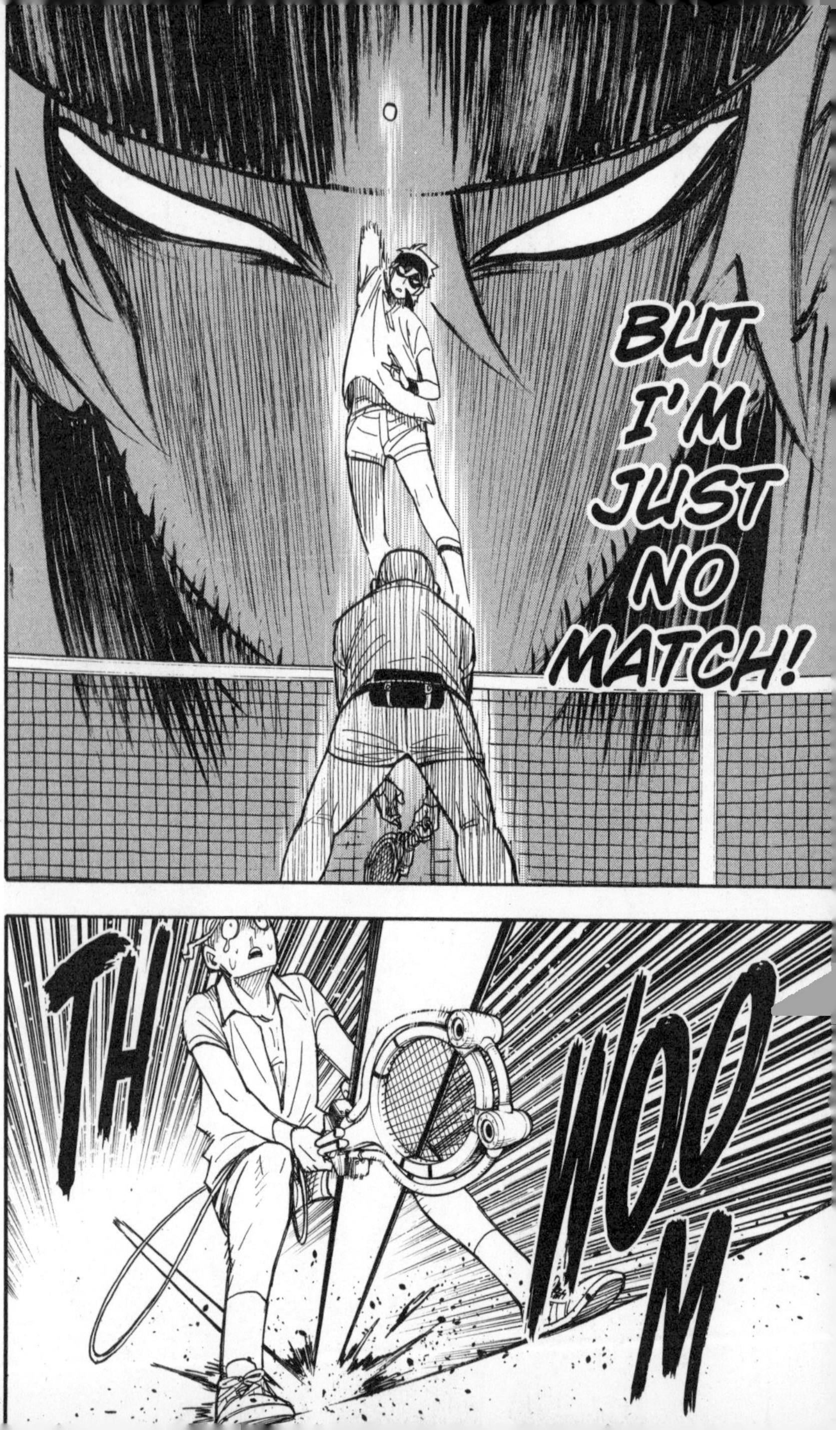
BUT I'M JUST NO MATCH!
THWOOM

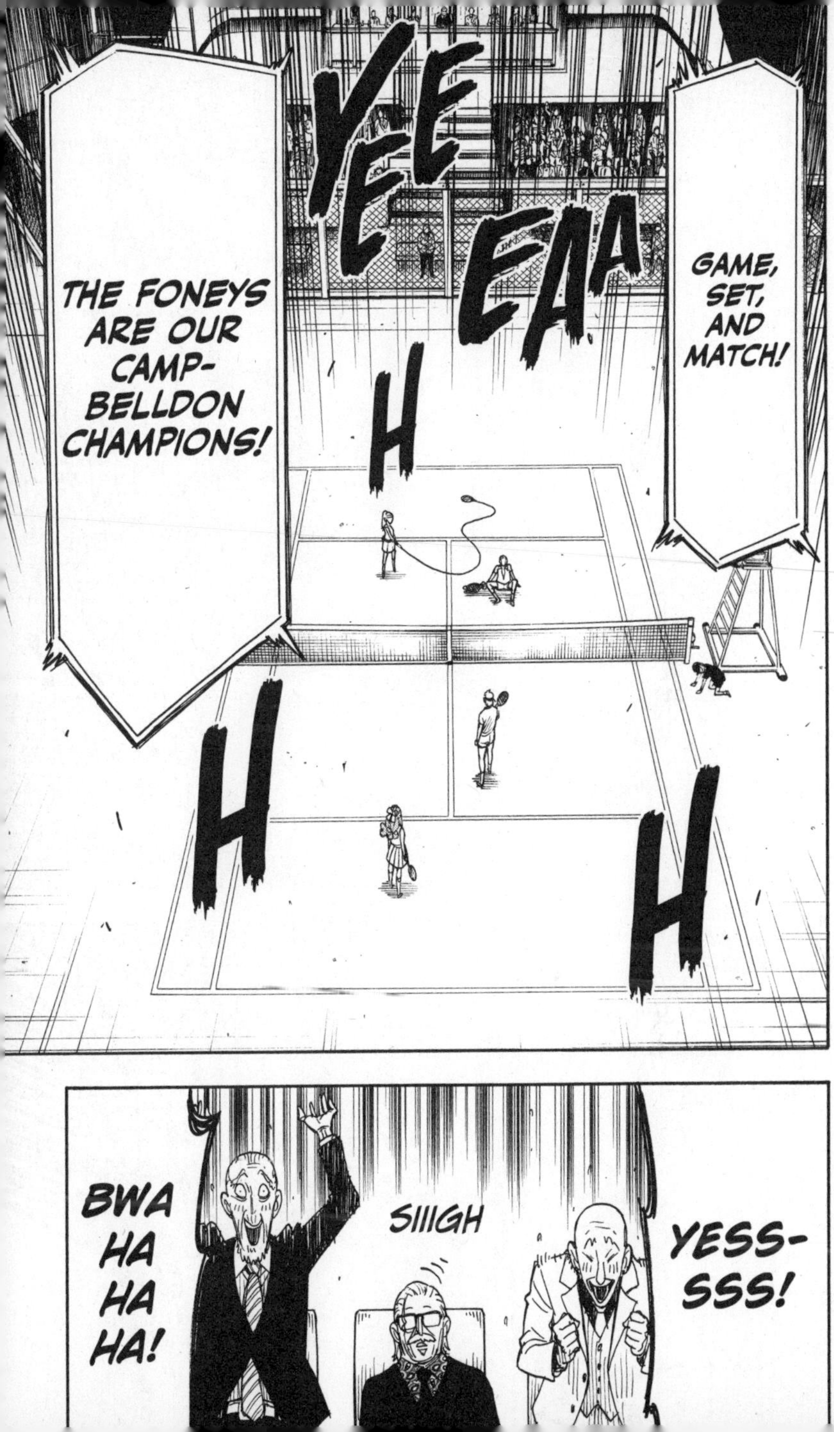
GAME, SET, AND MATCH!
THE FONEYS ARE OUR CAMP-BELLDON CHAMPIONS!
YEEEAAHHHH
YESS-SSS!
SIIIGH
BWA HA HA HA!

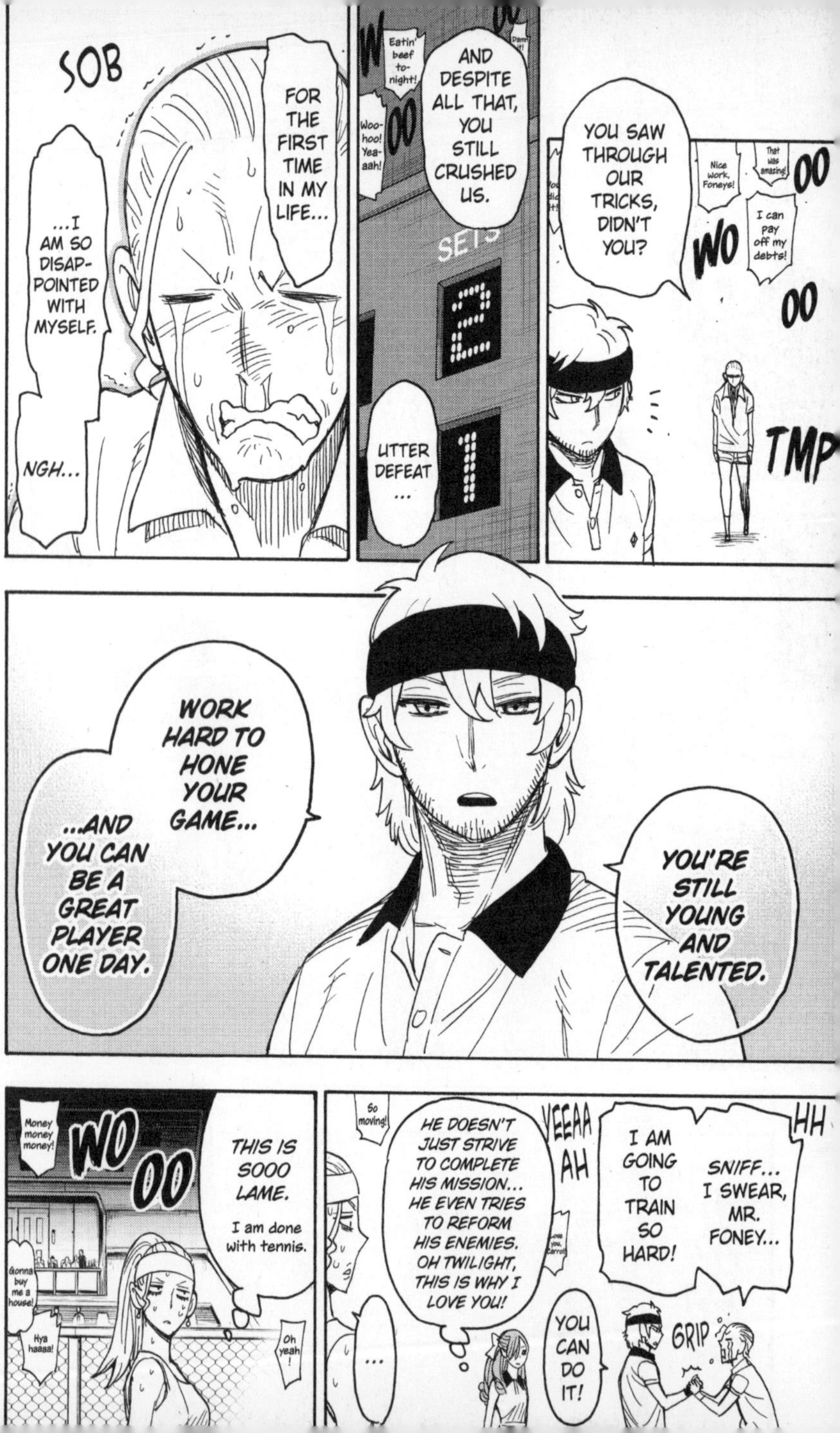
YOU SAW THROUGH OUR TRICKS, DIDN'T YOU?
That was amazing!
Nice work, Foneys!
I can pay off my debts!
WOOOO
TMP
Damn it!
Eatin' beef to-night!
AND DESPITE ALL THAT, YOU STILL CRUSHED US.
Woo-hoo! Yea-aah!
W OO
SETS
2
1
UTTER DEFEAT...
FOR THE FIRST TIME IN MY LIFE...
SOB
...I AM SO DISAP-POINTED WITH MYSELF.
NGH...
YOU'RE STILL YOUNG AND TALENTED.
WORK HARD TO HONE YOUR GAME...
...AND YOU CAN BE A GREAT PLAYER ONE DAY.
YEEAAAAHH
SNIFF... I SWEAR, MR. FONEY...
I AM GOING TO TRAIN SO HARD!
Love you, Carrot!
HE DOESN'T JUST STRIVE TO COMPLETE HIS MISSION... HE EVEN TRIES TO REFORM HIS ENEMIES. OH TWILIGHT, THIS IS WHY I LOVE YOU!
So moving!
YOU CAN DO IT!
GRIP
...
Money money money!
WOOO
THIS IS SOOO LAME.
I am done with tennis.
Gonna buy me a house!
Hya haaa!
Oh yeah!

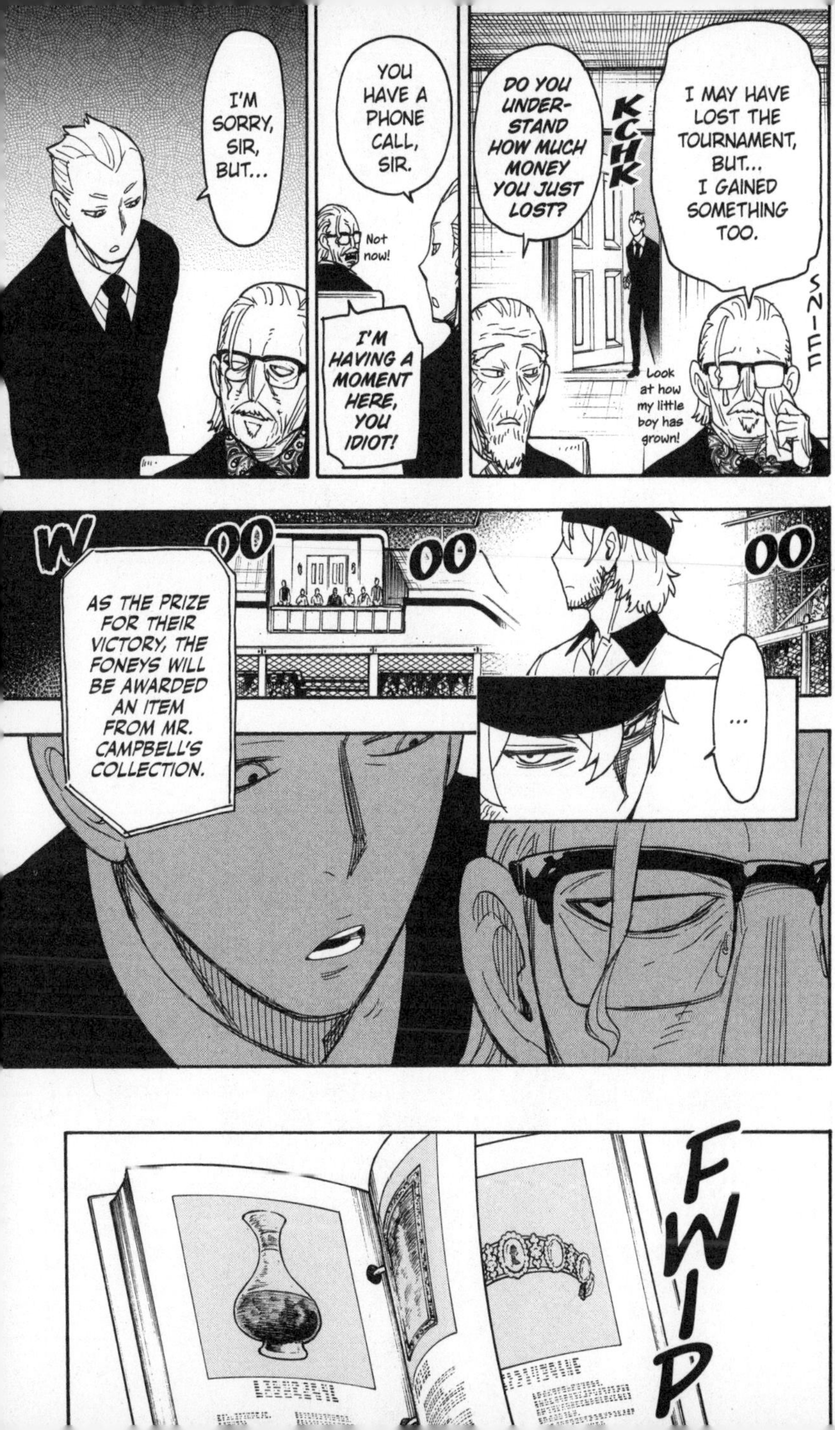
I MAY HAVE LOST THE TOURNAMENT, BUT... I GAINED SOMETHING TOO.
KCHK
DO YOU UNDERSTAND HOW MUCH MONEY YOU JUST LOST?
SNIFF
Look at how my little boy has grown!
YOU HAVE A PHONE CALL, SIR.
Not now!
I'M HAVING A MOMENT HERE, YOU IDIOT!
I'M SORRY, SIR, BUT...
WOOOOOO
...
AS THE PRIZE FOR THEIR VICTORY, THE FONEYS WILL BE AWARDED AN ITEM FROM MR. CAMPBELL'S COLLECTION.
FWIP

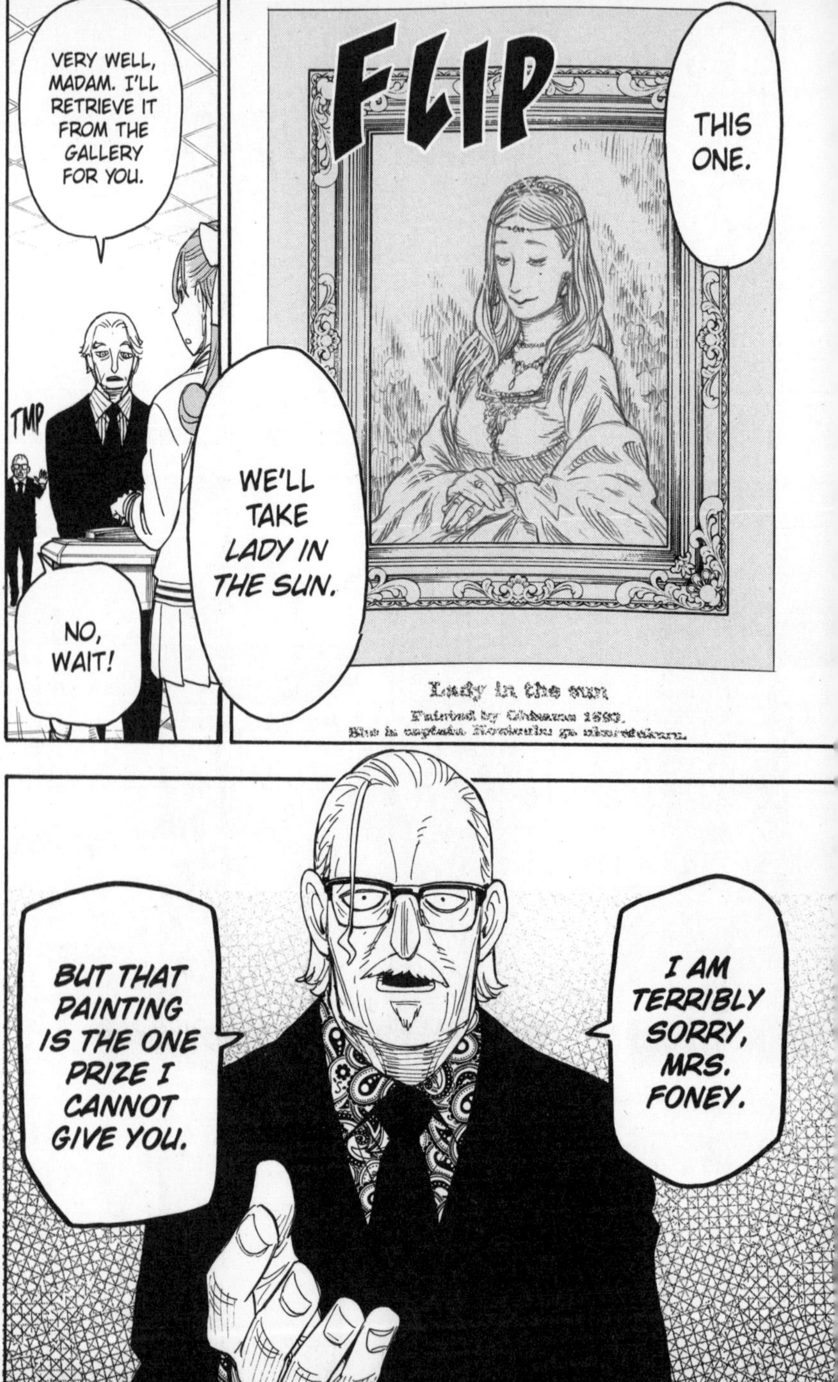
THIS ONE.
FLIP
WE'LL TAKE LADY IN THE SUN.
Lady in the sun
VERY WELL, MADAM. I'LL RETRIEVE IT FROM THE GALLERY FOR YOU.
TMP
NO, WAIT!
I AM TERRIBLY SORRY, MRS. FONEY.
BUT THAT PAINTING IS THE ONE PRIZE I CANNOT GIVE YOU.

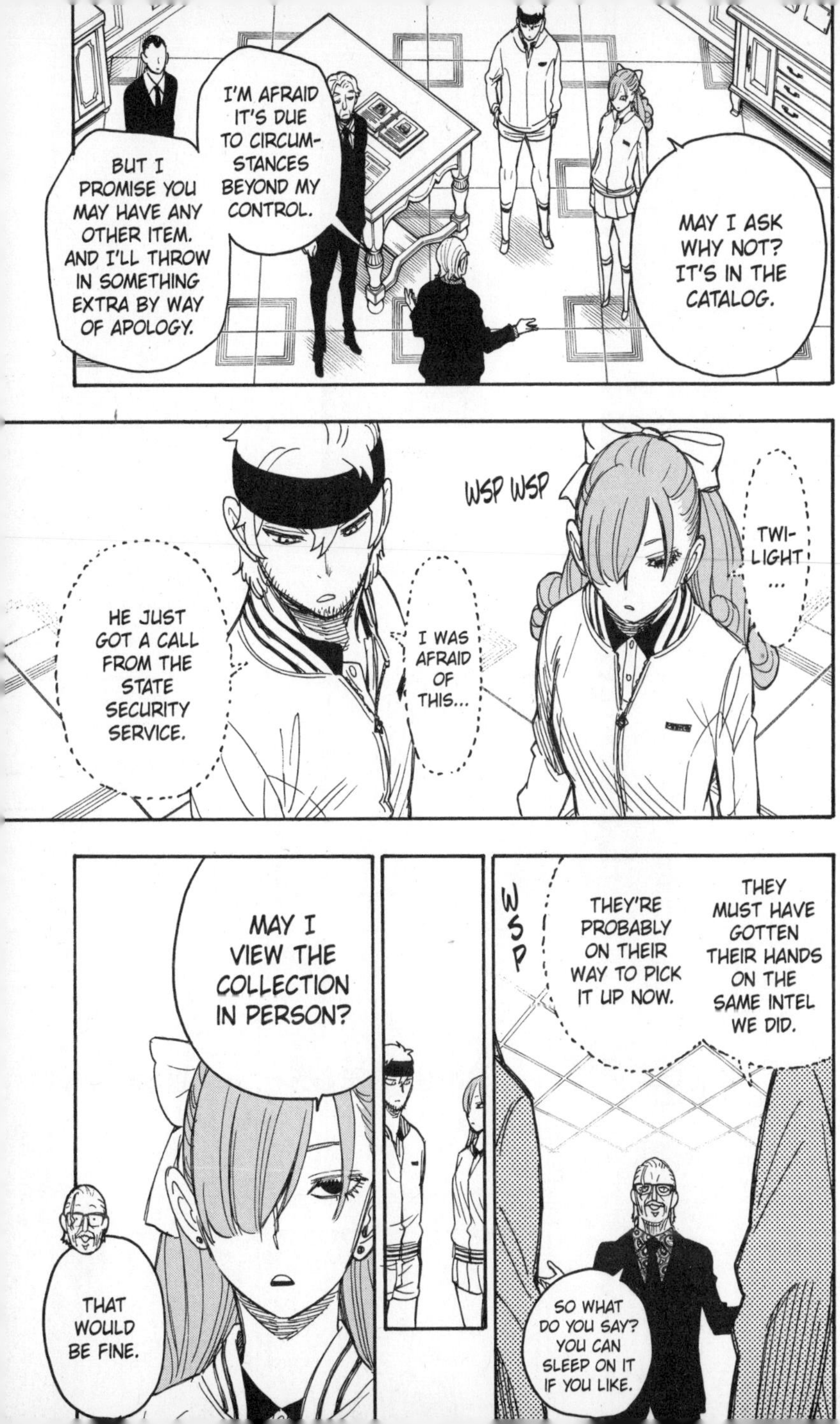
MAY I ASK WHY NOT? IT'S IN THE CATALOG.
I'M AFRAID IT'S DUE TO CIRCUM-STANCES BEYOND MY CONTROL.
BUT I PROMISE YOU MAY HAVE ANY OTHER ITEM. AND I'LL THROW IN SOMETHING EXTRA BY WAY OF APOLOGY.
WSP WSP
TWI-LIGHT...
I WAS AFRAID OF THIS...
HE JUST GOT A CALL FROM THE STATE SECURITY SERVICE.
WSP
THEY MUST HAVE GOTTEN THEIR HANDS ON THE SAME INTEL WE DID.
THEY'RE PROBABLY ON THEIR WAY TO PICK IT UP NOW.
SO WHAT DO YOU SAY? YOU CAN SLEEP ON IT IF YOU LIKE.
MAY I VIEW THE COLLECTION IN PERSON?
THAT WOULD BE FINE.

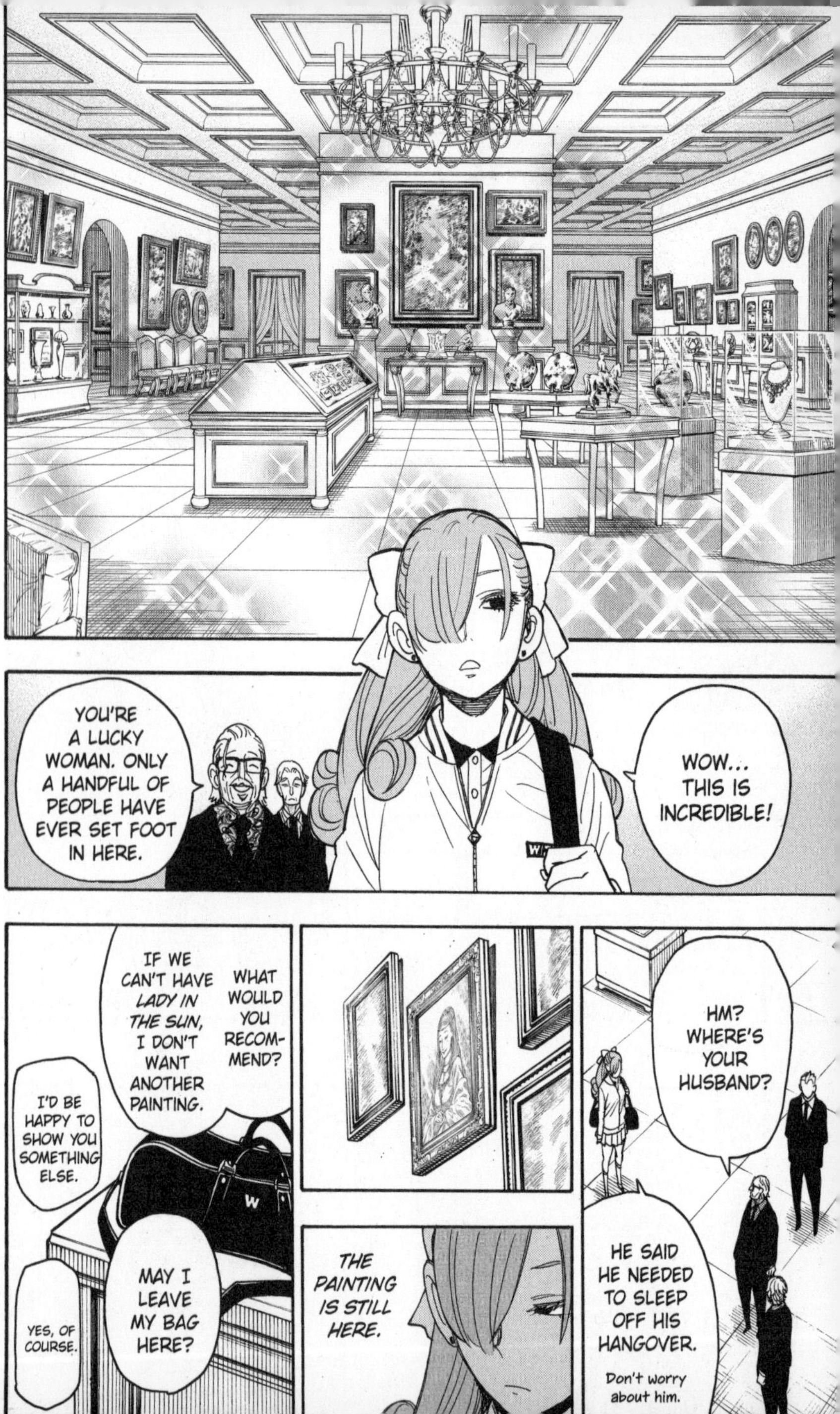
WOW... THIS IS INCREDIBLE!
YOU'RE A LUCKY WOMAN. ONLY A HANDFUL OF PEOPLE HAVE EVER SET FOOT IN HERE.
HM? WHERE'S YOUR HUSBAND?
HE SAID HE NEEDED TO SLEEP OFF HIS HANGOVER.
Don't worry about him.
THE PAINTING IS STILL HERE.
IF WE CAN'T HAVE *LADY IN THE SUN*, I DON'T WANT ANOTHER PAINTING.
WHAT WOULD YOU RECOMMEND?
I'D BE HAPPY TO SHOW YOU SOMETHING ELSE.
MAY I LEAVE MY BAG HERE?
YES, OF COURSE.

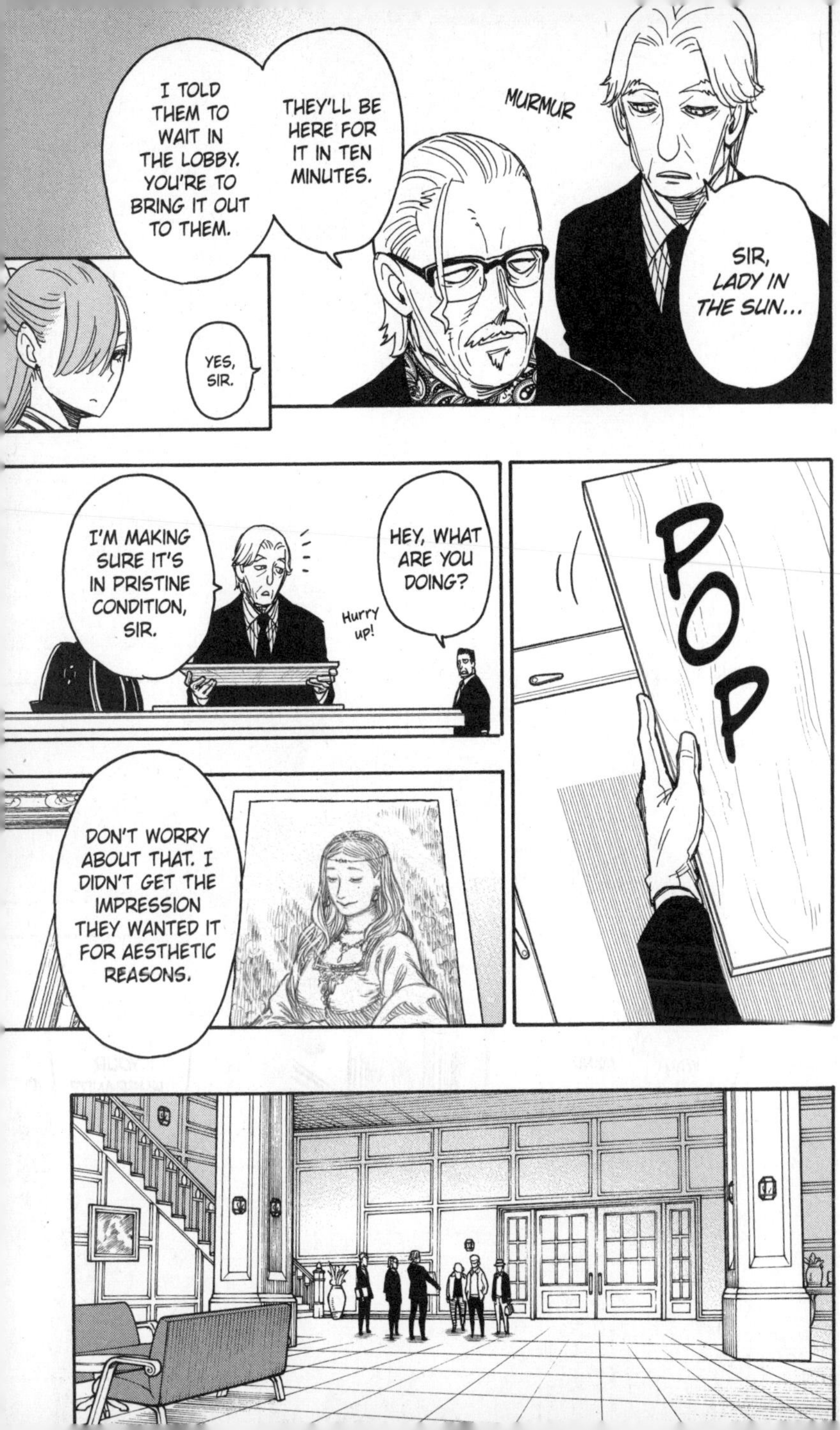
MURMUR
SIR, LADY IN THE SUN...
THEY'LL BE HERE FOR IT IN TEN MINUTES.
I TOLD THEM TO WAIT IN THE LOBBY. YOU'RE TO BRING IT OUT TO THEM.
YES, SIR.
POP
HEY, WHAT ARE YOU DOING?
Hurry up!
I'M MAKING SURE IT'S IN PRISTINE CONDITION, SIR.
DON'T WORRY ABOUT THAT. I DIDN'T GET THE IMPRESSION THEY WANTED IT FOR AESTHETIC REASONS.

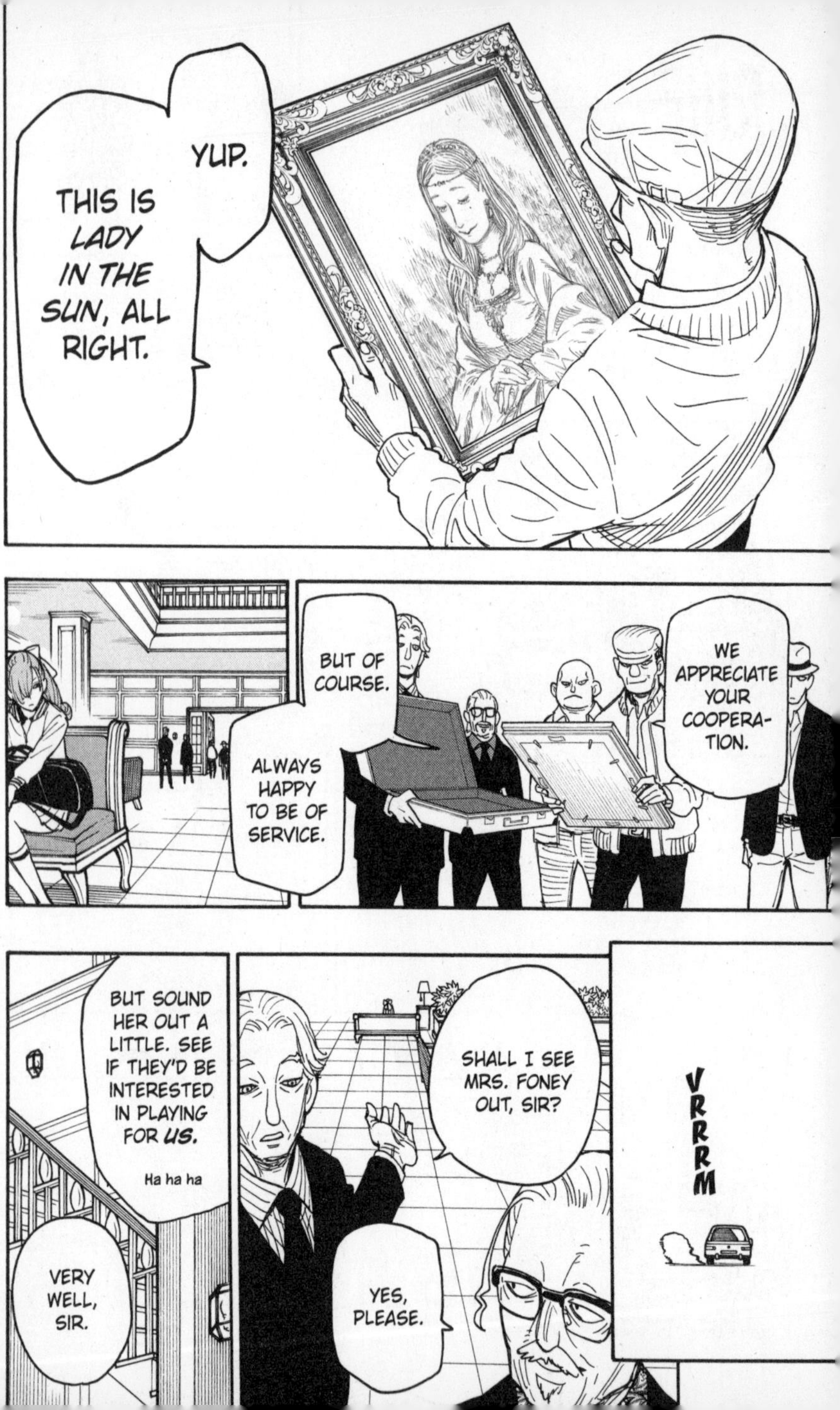
YUP.
THIS IS *LADY IN THE SUN*, ALL RIGHT.
WE APPRECIATE YOUR COOPERATION.
BUT OF COURSE.
ALWAYS HAPPY TO BE OF SERVICE.
VRRRM
SHALL I SEE MRS. FONEY OUT, SIR?
YES, PLEASE.
BUT SOUND HER OUT A LITTLE. SEE IF THEY'D BE INTERESTED IN PLAYING FOR *US*.
Ha ha ha
VERY WELL, SIR.

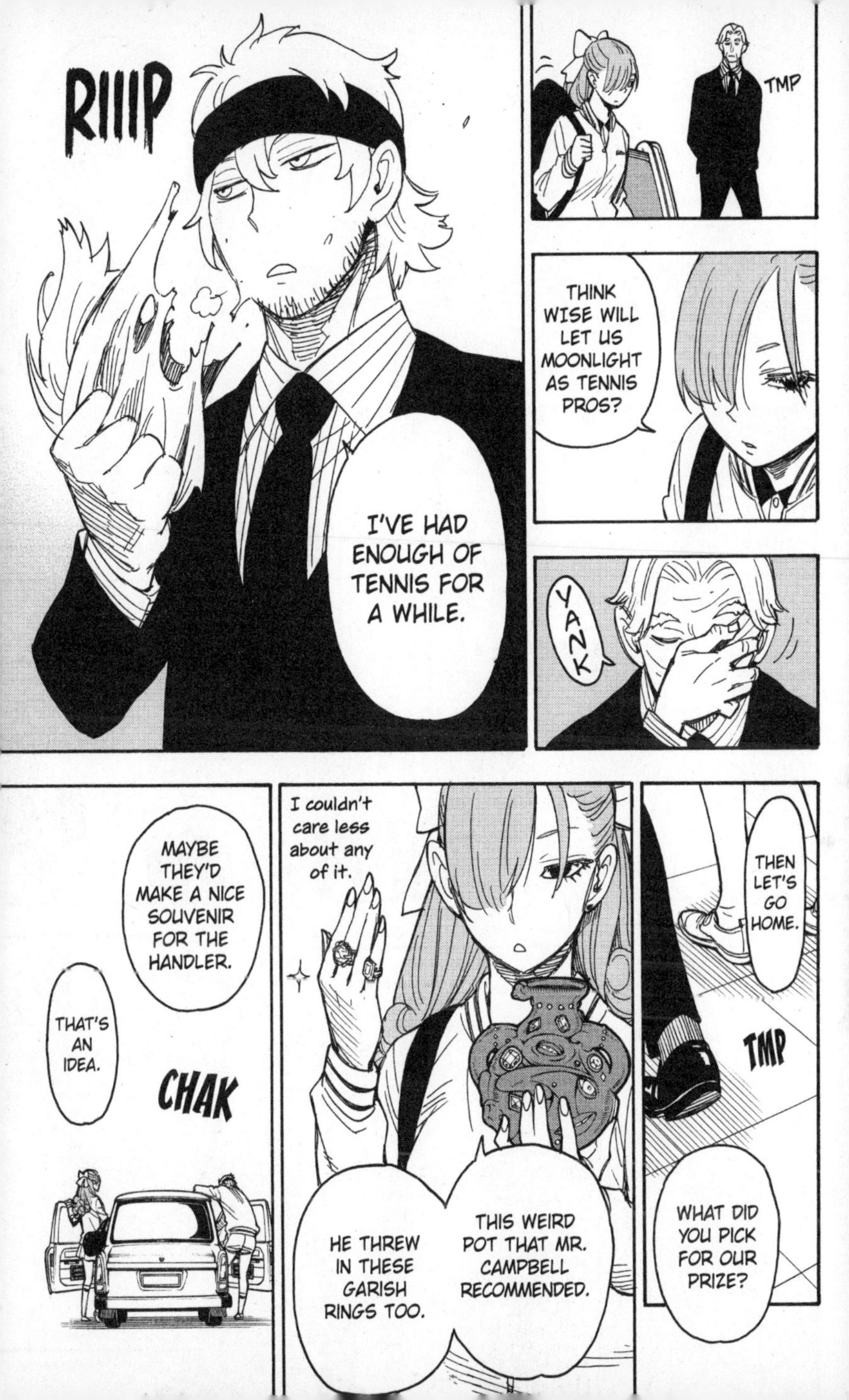
TMP
THINK WISE WILL LET US MOONLIGHT AS TENNIS PROS?
YANK
RIIIP
I'VE HAD ENOUGH OF TENNIS FOR A WHILE.
THEN LET'S GO HOME.
TMP
WHAT DID YOU PICK FOR OUR PRIZE?
THIS WEIRD POT THAT MR. CAMPBELL RECOMMENDED.
HE THREW IN THESE GARISH RINGS TOO.
I couldn't care less about any of it.
MAYBE THEY'D MAKE A NICE SOUVENIR FOR THE HANDLER.
THAT'S AN IDEA.
CHAK

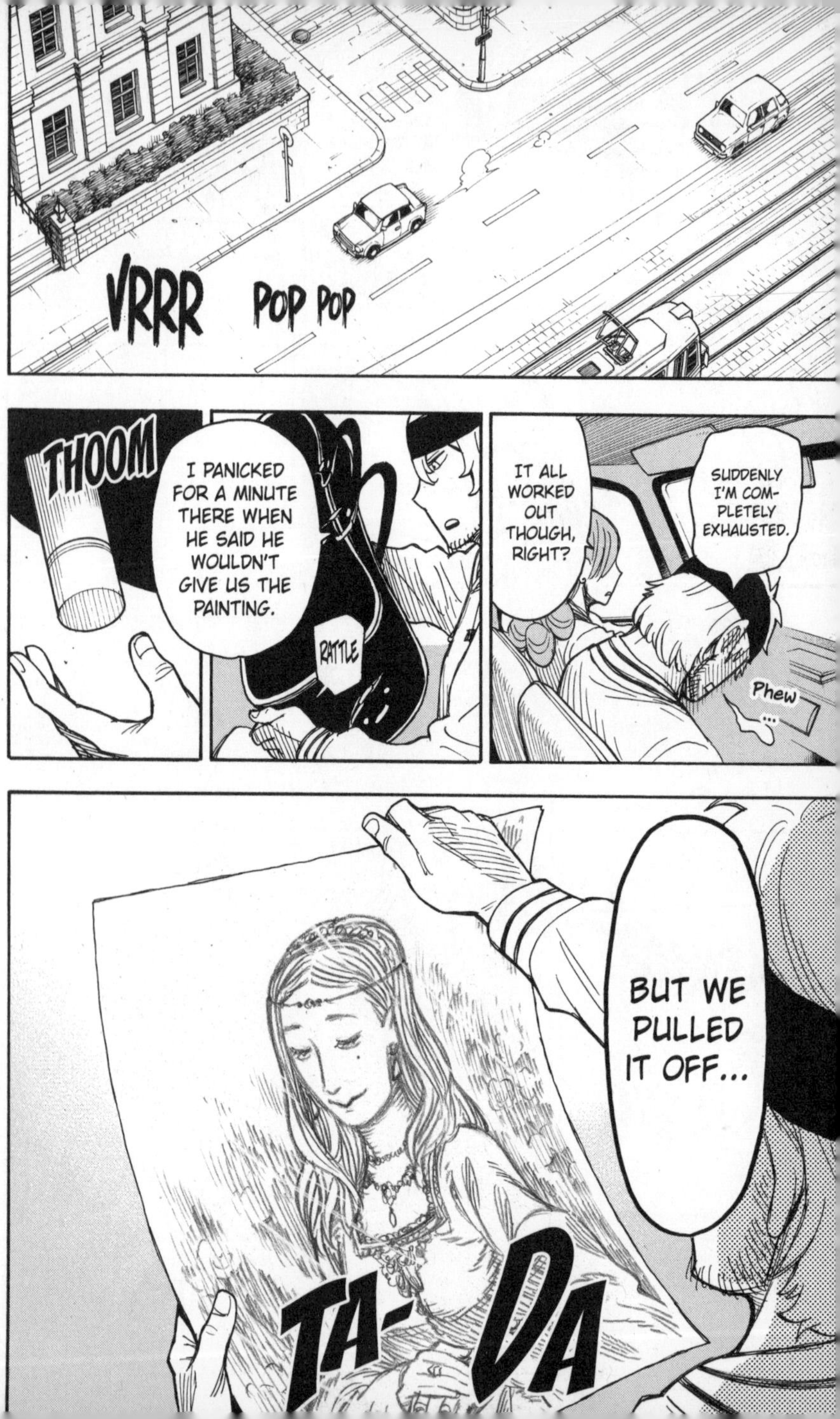
POP POP
VRRR
SUDDENLY I'M COMPLETELY EXHAUSTED.
IT ALL WORKED OUT THOUGH, RIGHT?
Phew...
I PANICKED FOR A MINUTE THERE WHEN HE SAID HE WOULDN'T GIVE US THE PAINTING.
RATTLE
THOOM
BUT WE PULLED IT OFF...
TA-DA

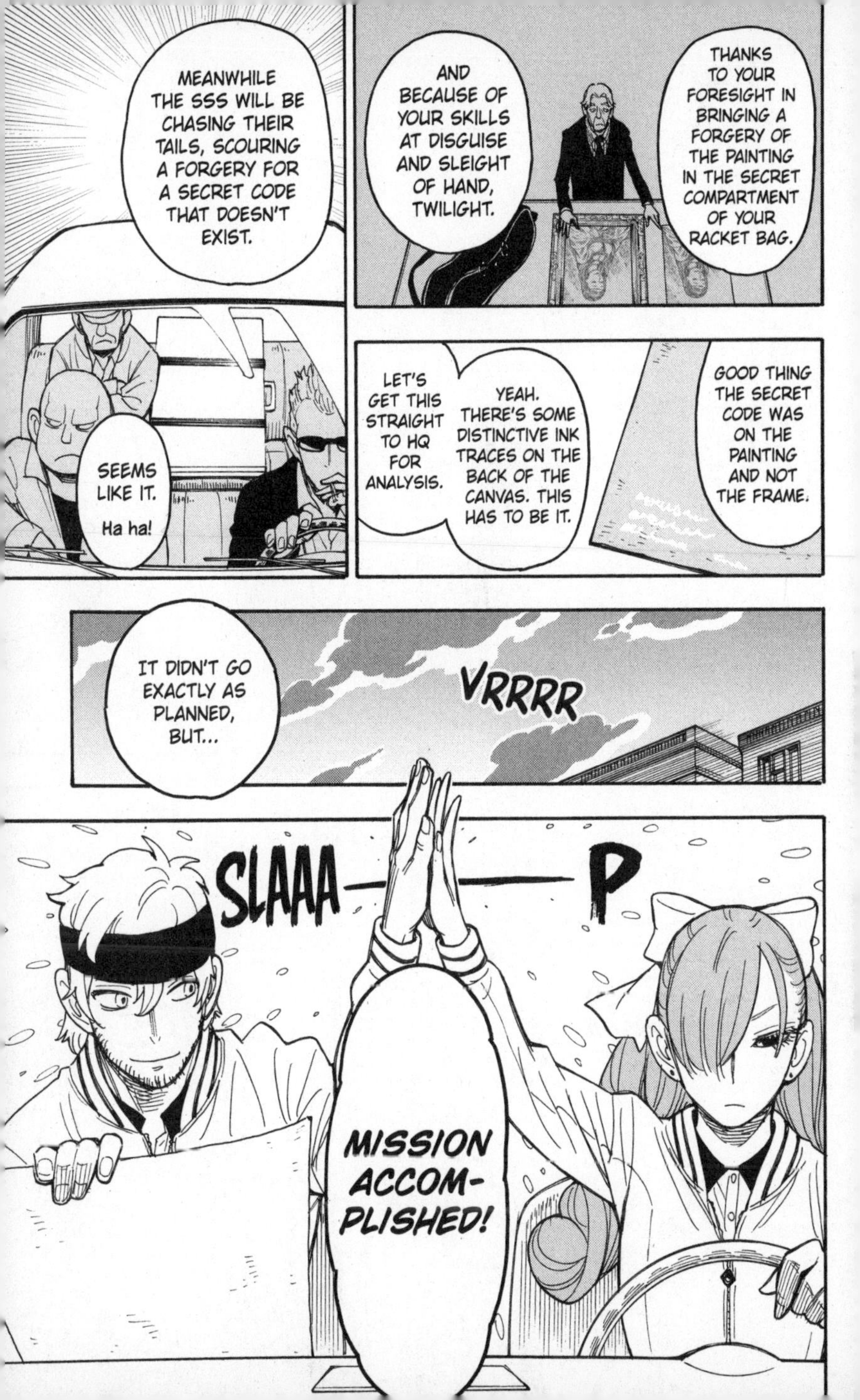
THANKS TO YOUR FORESIGHT IN BRINGING A FORGERY OF THE PAINTING IN THE SECRET COMPARTMENT OF YOUR RACKET BAG.
AND BECAUSE OF YOUR SKILLS AT DISGUISE AND SLEIGHT OF HAND, TWILIGHT.
MEANWHILE THE SSS WILL BE CHASING THEIR TAILS, SCOURING A FORGERY FOR A SECRET CODE THAT DOESN'T EXIST.
GOOD THING THE SECRET CODE WAS ON THE PAINTING AND NOT THE FRAME.
YEAH. THERE'S SOME DISTINCTIVE INK TRACES ON THE BACK OF THE CANVAS. THIS HAS TO BE IT.
LET'S GET THIS STRAIGHT TO HQ FOR ANALYSIS.
SEEMS LIKE IT.
Ha ha!
IT DIDN'T GO EXACTLY AS PLANNED, BUT...
VRRRR
SLAAA——P
MISSION ACCOM-PLISHED!

SPY×FAMILY

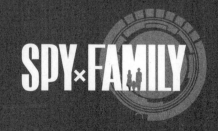

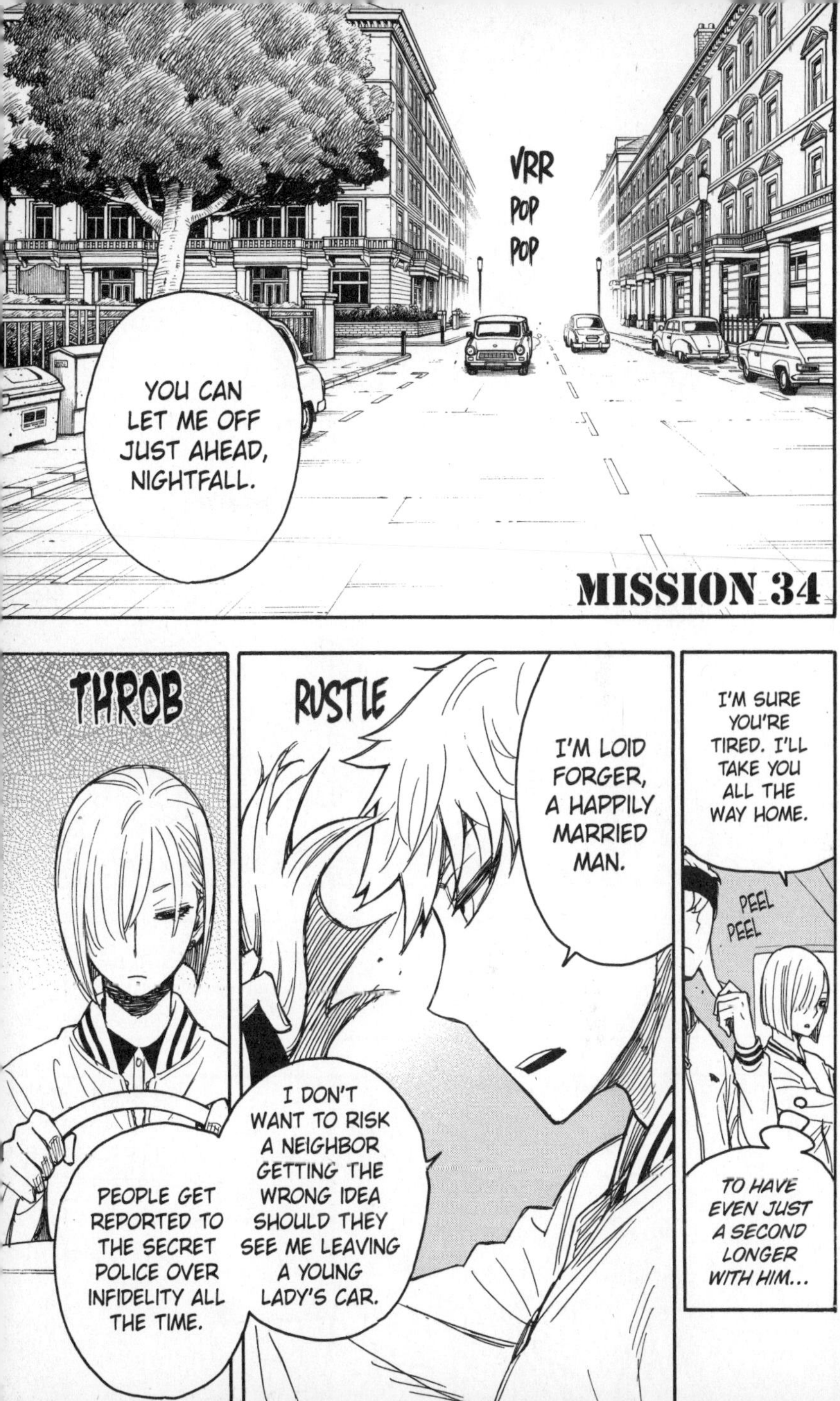
MISSION 34
VRR POP POP
YOU CAN LET ME OFF JUST AHEAD, NIGHTFALL.
I'M SURE YOU'RE TIRED. I'LL TAKE YOU ALL THE WAY HOME.
PEEL PEEL
TO HAVE EVEN JUST A SECOND LONGER WITH HIM...
RUSTLE
I'M LOID FORGER, A HAPPILY MARRIED MAN.
I DON'T WANT TO RISK A NEIGHBOR GETTING THE WRONG IDEA SHOULD THEY SEE ME LEAVING A YOUNG LADY'S CAR.
THROB
PEOPLE GET REPORTED TO THE SECRET POLICE OVER INFIDELITY ALL THE TIME.

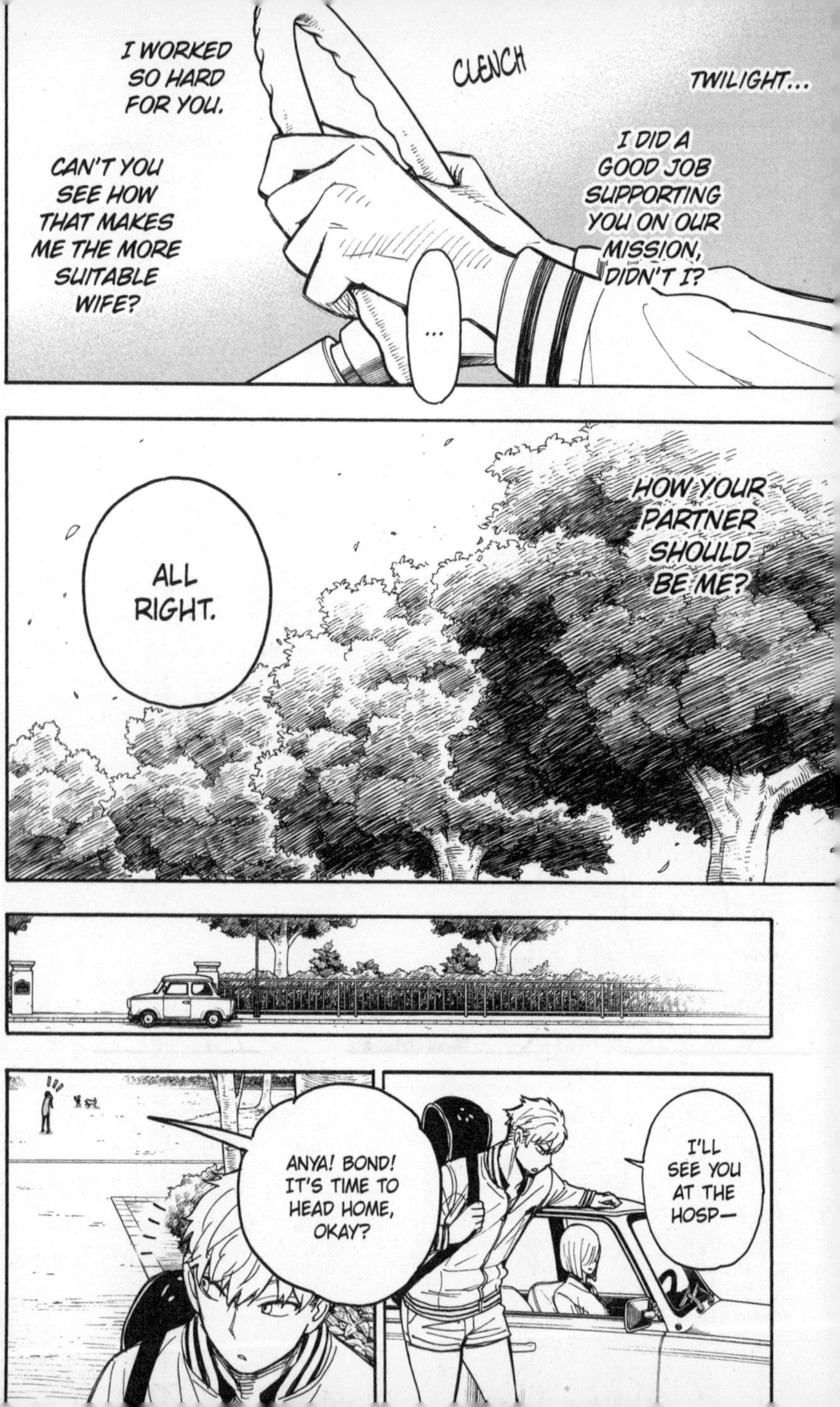
TWILIGHT...
I DID A GOOD JOB SUPPORTING YOU ON OUR MISSION, DIDN'T I?
CLENCH
I WORKED SO HARD FOR YOU.
CAN'T YOU SEE HOW THAT MAKES ME THE MORE SUITABLE WIFE?
...
HOW YOUR PARTNER SHOULD BE ME?
ALL RIGHT.
I'LL SEE YOU AT THE HOSP—
ANYA! BOND! IT'S TIME TO HEAD HOME, OKAY?

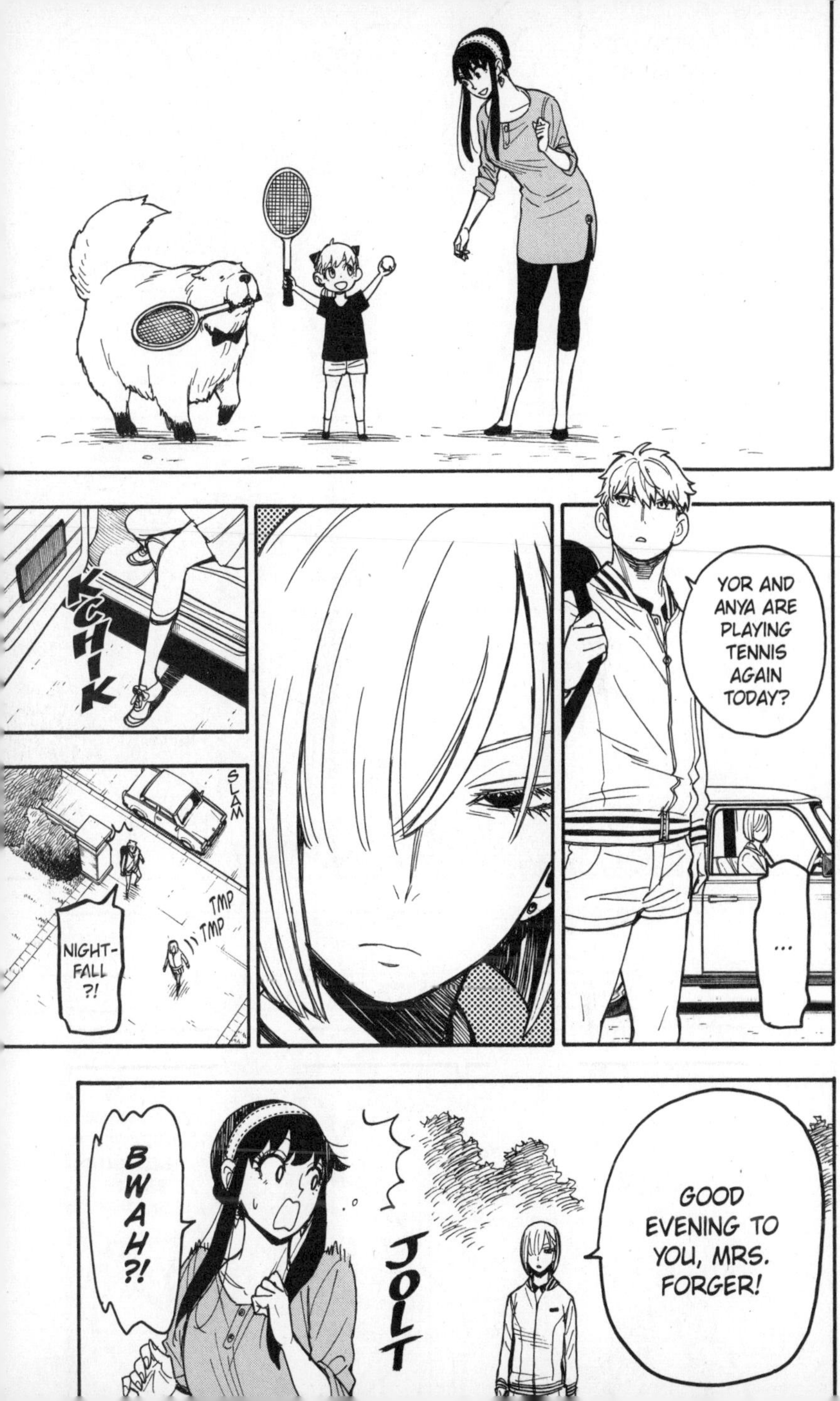
YOR AND ANYA ARE PLAYING TENNIS AGAIN TODAY?
...
KCHIK
SLAM
TMP TMP
NIGHT-FALL ?!
GOOD EVENING TO YOU, MRS. FORGER!
JOLT
BWAH?!

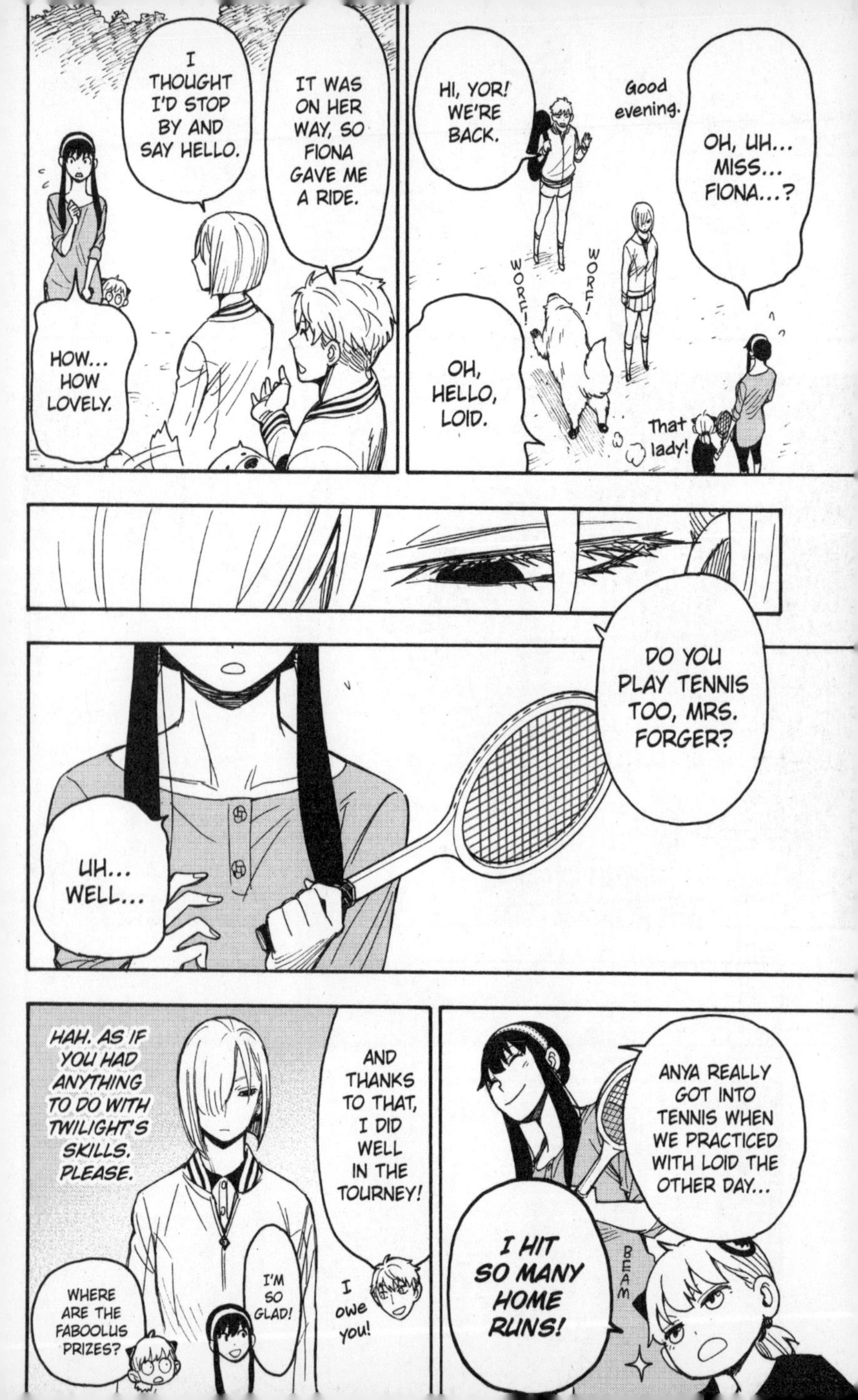
Good evening.
OH, UH... MISS... FIONA...?
HI, YOR! WE'RE BACK.
WORF!
WORF!
That lady!
OH, HELLO, LOID.
IT WAS ON HER WAY, SO FIONA GAVE ME A RIDE.
I THOUGHT I'D STOP BY AND SAY HELLO.
HOW... HOW LOVELY.
DO YOU PLAY TENNIS TOO, MRS. FORGER?
UH... WELL...
ANYA REALLY GOT INTO TENNIS WHEN WE PRACTICED WITH LOID THE OTHER DAY...
BEAM
I HIT SO MANY HOME RUNS!
AND THANKS TO THAT, I DID WELL IN THE TOURNEY!
HAH. AS IF YOU HAD ANYTHING TO DO WITH TWILIGHT'S SKILLS. PLEASE.
I owe you!
I'M SO GLAD!
WHERE ARE THE FABOOLUS PRIZES?

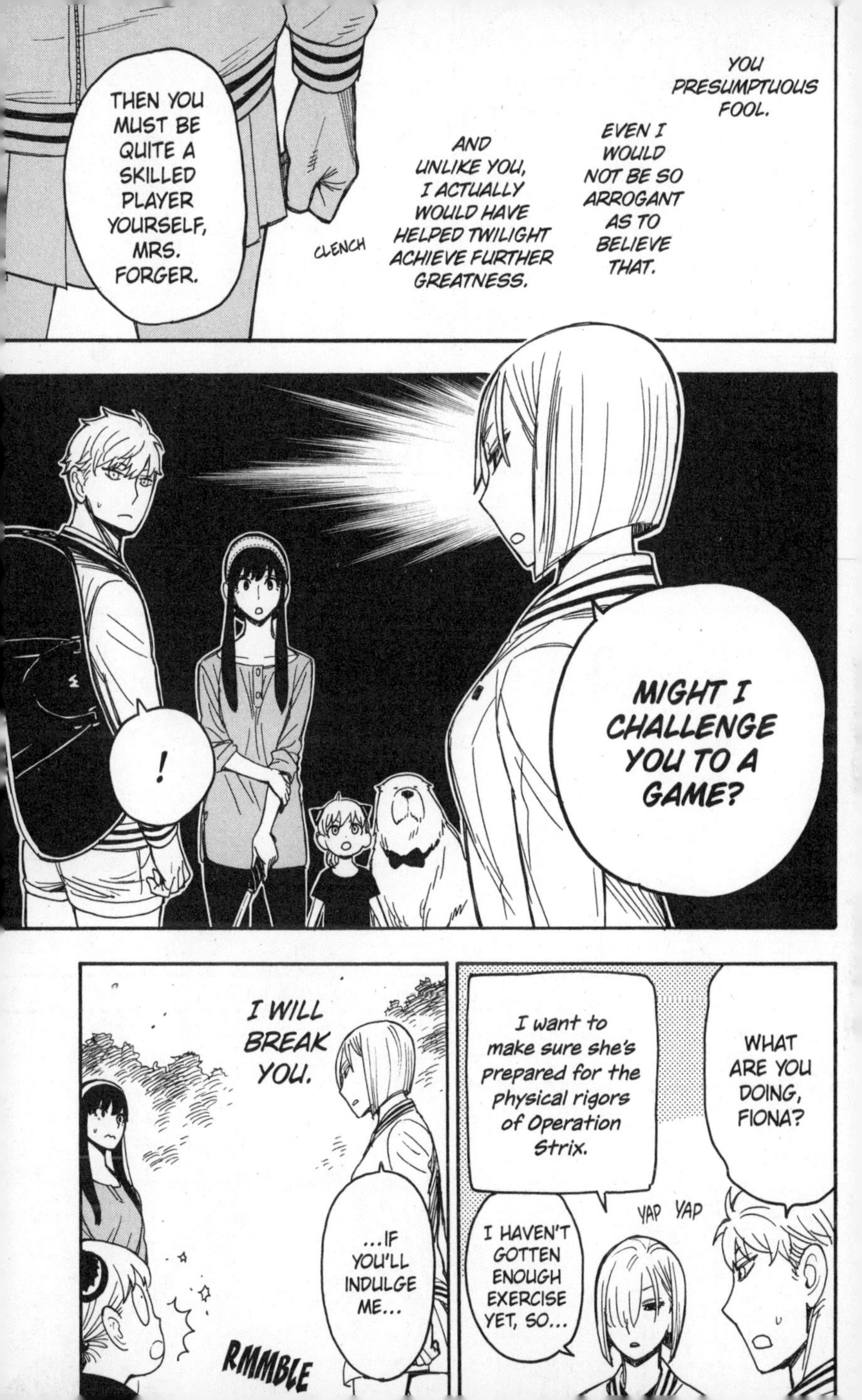
YOU PRESUMPTUOUS FOOL.
EVEN I WOULD NOT BE SO ARROGANT AS TO BELIEVE THAT.
AND UNLIKE YOU, I ACTUALLY WOULD HAVE HELPED TWILIGHT ACHIEVE FURTHER GREATNESS.
CLENCH
THEN YOU MUST BE QUITE A SKILLED PLAYER YOURSELF, MRS. FORGER.
MIGHT I CHALLENGE YOU TO A GAME?
!
WHAT ARE YOU DOING, FIONA?
I want to make sure she's prepared for the physical rigors of Operation Strix.
YAP YAP
I HAVEN'T GOTTEN ENOUGH EXERCISE YET, SO...
I WILL BREAK YOU.
...IF YOU'LL INDULGE ME...
RMMBLE

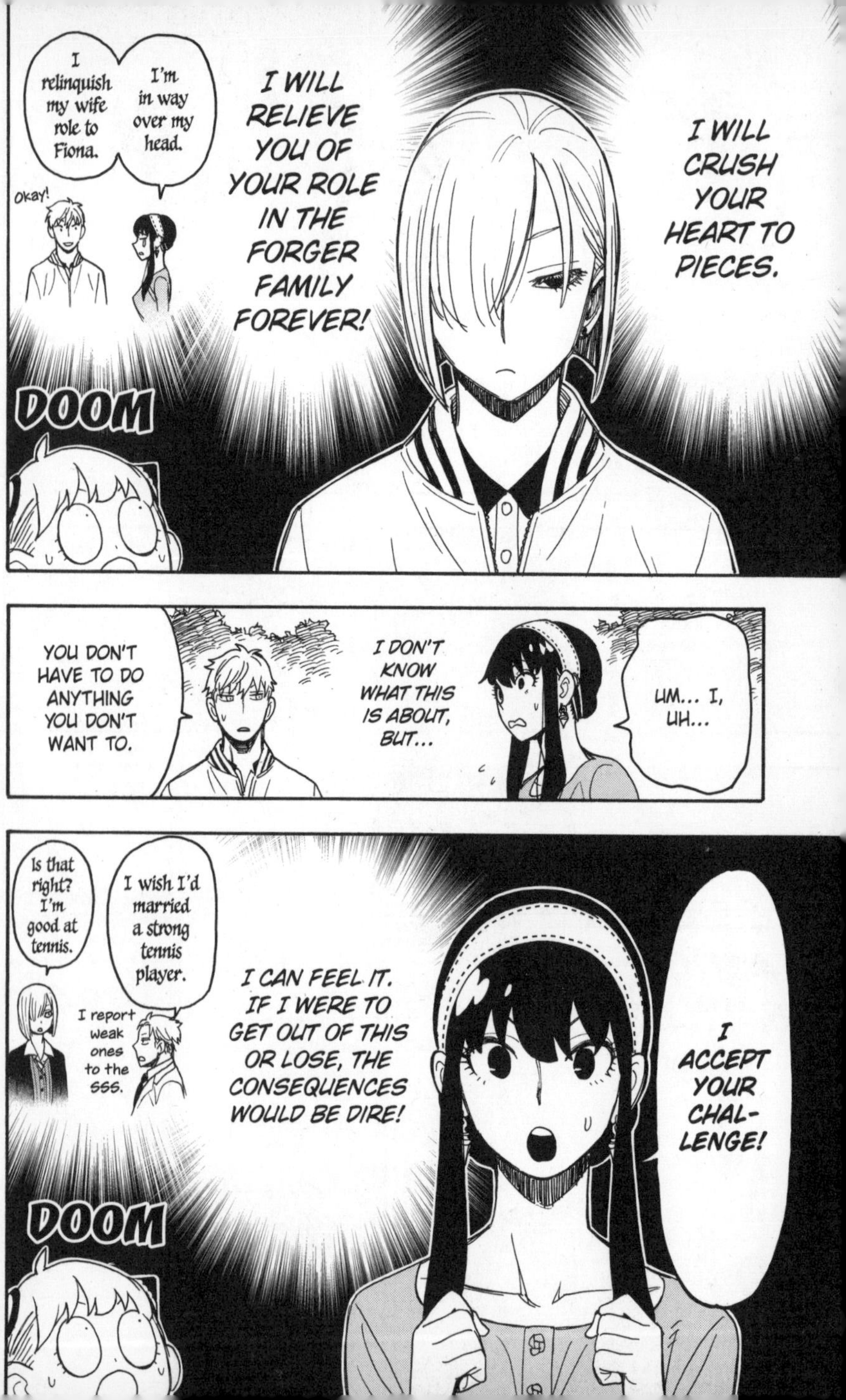
I WILL CRUSH YOUR HEART TO PIECES.
I WILL RELIEVE YOU OF YOUR ROLE IN THE FORGER FAMILY FOREVER!
I'm in way over my head.
I relinquish my wife role to Fiona.
Okay!
DOOM
UM... I, UH...
I DON'T KNOW WHAT THIS IS ABOUT, BUT...
YOU DON'T HAVE TO DO ANYTHING YOU DON'T WANT TO.
I ACCEPT YOUR CHAL-LENGE!
I CAN FEEL IT. IF I WERE TO GET OUT OF THIS OR LOSE, THE CONSEQUENCES WOULD BE DIRE!
I wish I'd married a strong tennis player.
Is that right? I'm good at tennis.
I report weak ones to the SSS.
DOOM

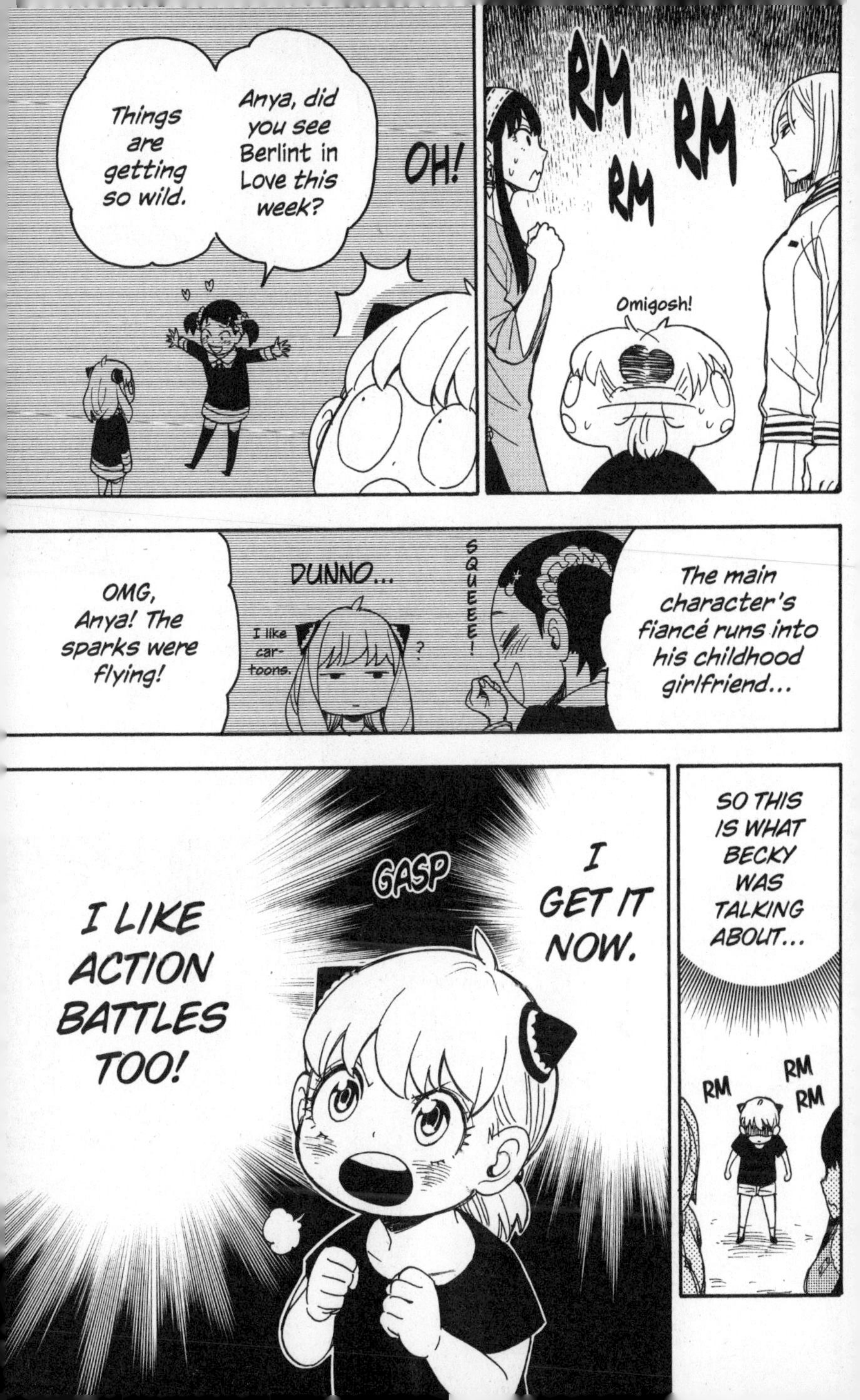
RM RM RM
Omigosh!
OH!
Anya, did you see Berlint in Love this week?
Things are getting so wild.
The main character's fiancé runs into his childhood girlfriend...
SQUEEEE!
?
I like cartoons.
DUNNO...
OMG, Anya! The sparks were flying!
SO THIS IS WHAT BECKY WAS TALKING ABOUT...
RM RM RM
I GET IT NOW.
GASP
I LIKE ACTION BATTLES TOO!

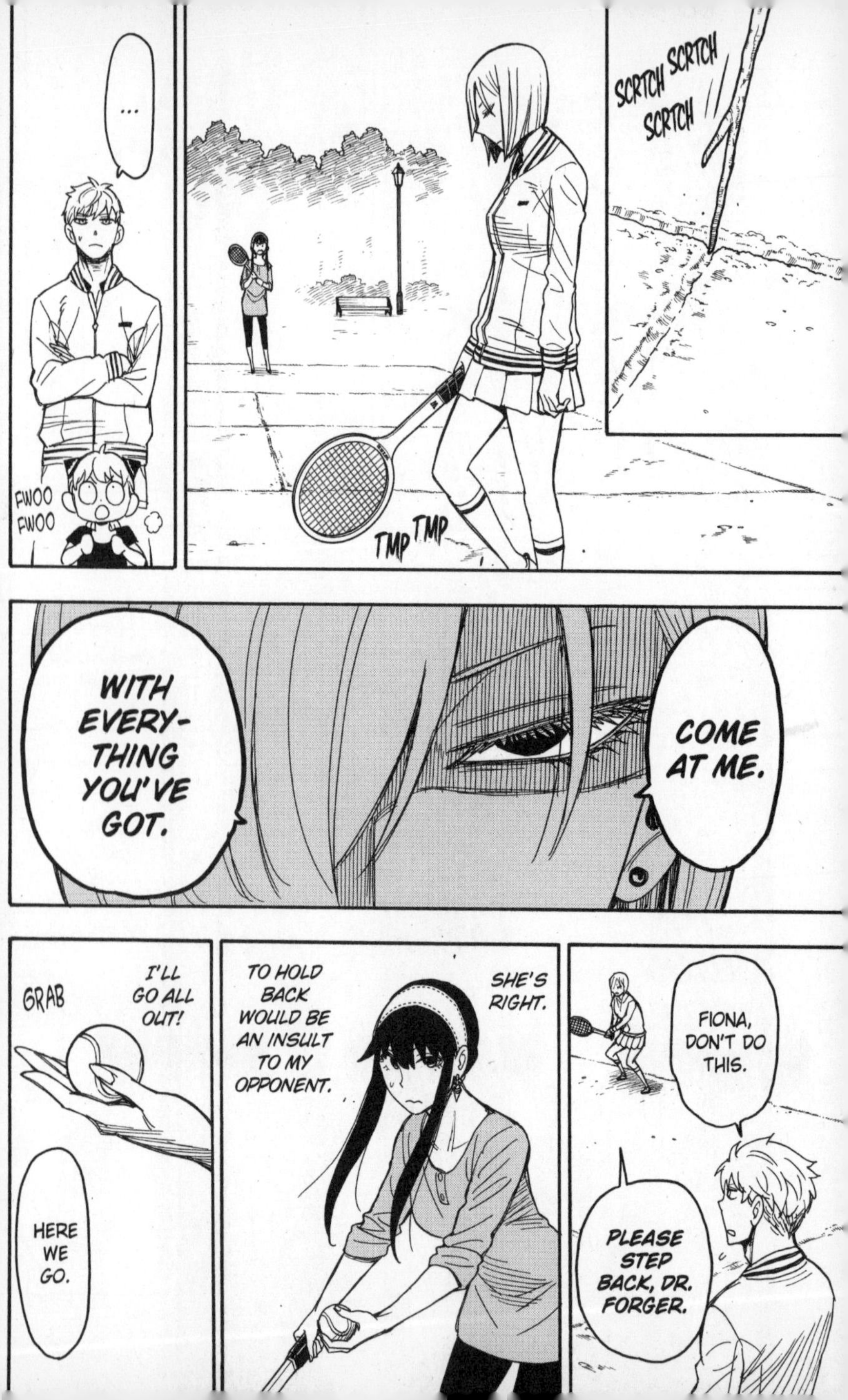
SCRTCH SCRTCH SCRTCH
TMP TMP
...
FWOO FWOO
COME AT ME.
WITH EVERY-THING YOU'VE GOT.
FIONA, DON'T DO THIS.
PLEASE STEP BACK, DR. FORGER.
SHE'S RIGHT.
TO HOLD BACK WOULD BE AN INSULT TO MY OPPONENT.
I'LL GO ALL OUT!
GRAB
HERE WE GO.

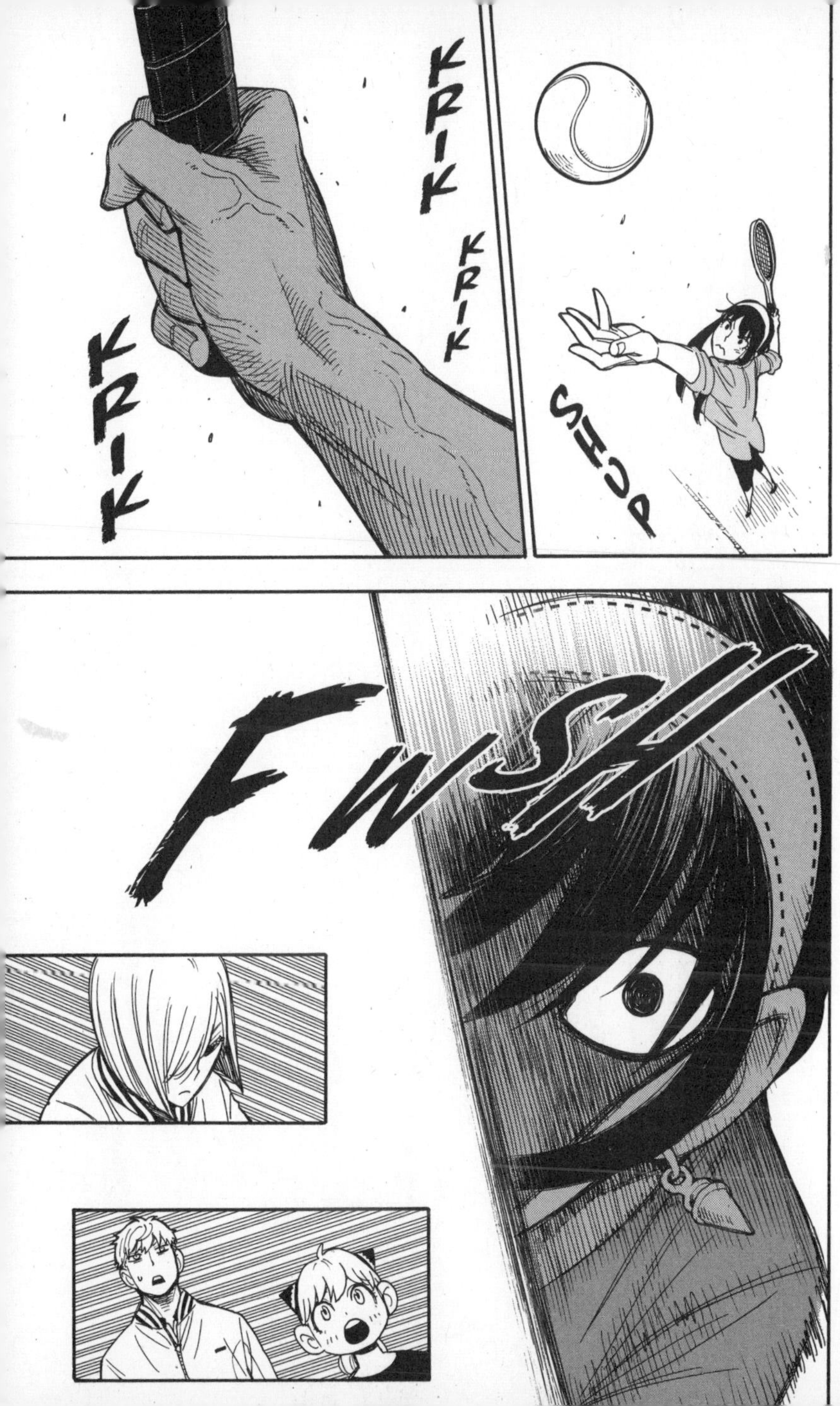
SHOOP
KRIK
KRIK
KRIK
FWSH

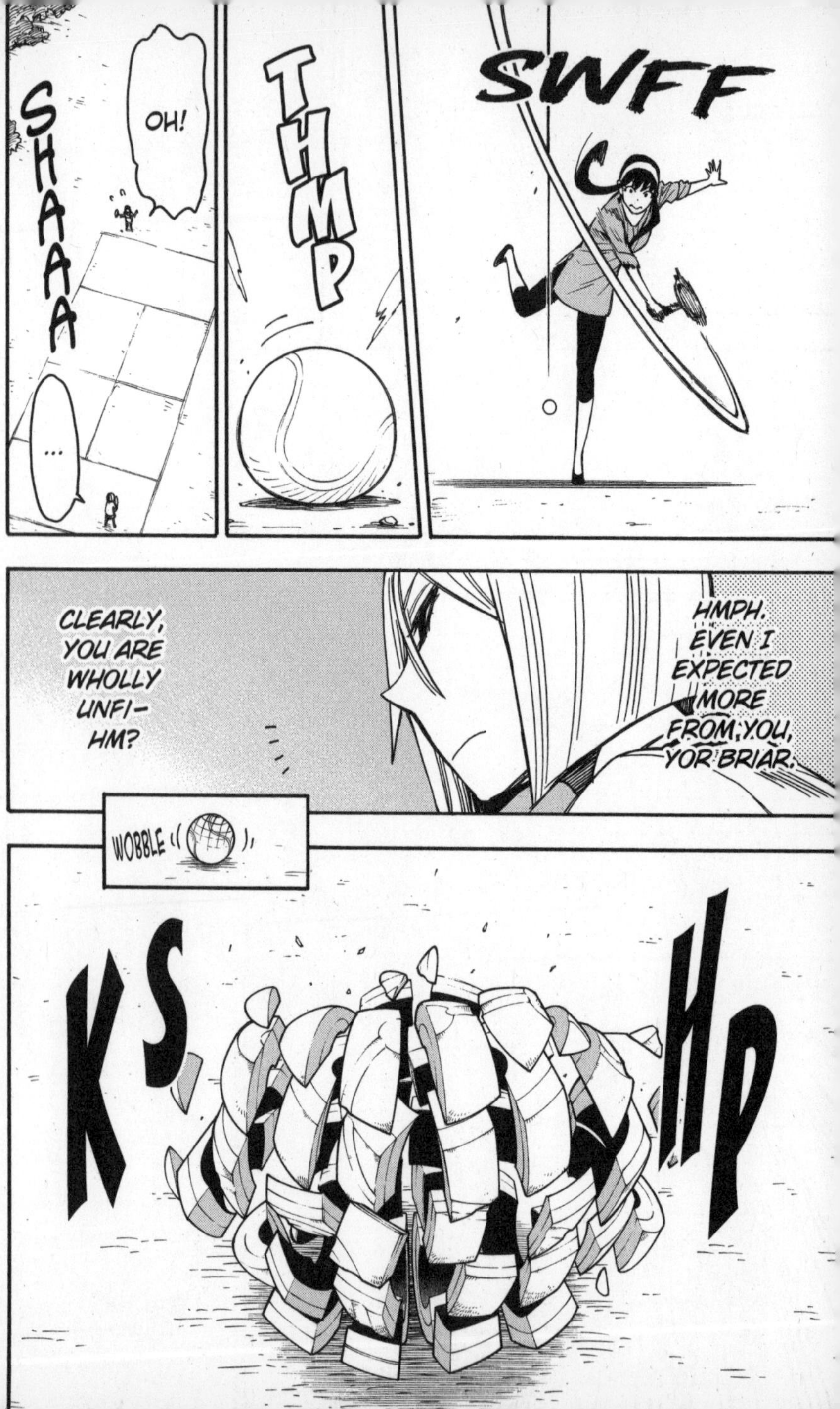
SWFF
THMP
OH!
SHAAA
...
HMPH. EVEN I EXPECTED MORE FROM YOU, YOR BRIAR.
CLEARLY, YOU ARE WHOLLY UNFI- HM?
WOBBLE
KSHP

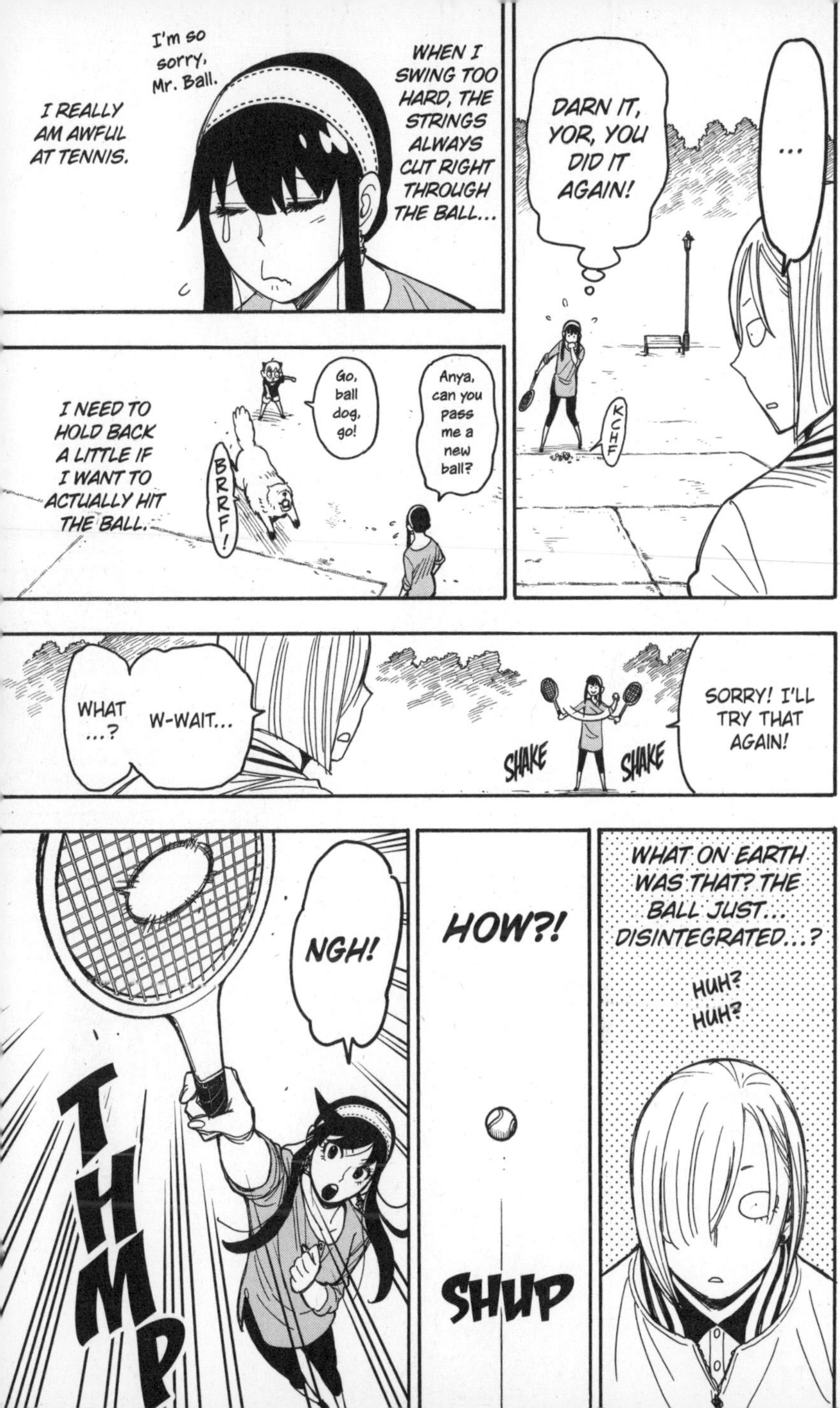
...
DARN IT, YOR, YOU DID IT AGAIN!
KCHF
WHEN I SWING TOO HARD, THE STRINGS ALWAYS CUT RIGHT THROUGH THE BALL...
I'm so sorry, Mr. Ball.
I REALLY AM AWFUL AT TENNIS.
Anya, can you pass me a new ball?
Go, ball dog, go!
BRRF!
I NEED TO HOLD BACK A LITTLE IF I WANT TO ACTUALLY HIT THE BALL.
SORRY! I'LL TRY THAT AGAIN!
SHAKE
SHAKE
W-WAIT...
WHAT ...?
WHAT ON EARTH WAS THAT? THE BALL JUST... DISINTEGRATED...?
HUH? HUH?
HOW?!
SHUP
NGH!
THMP

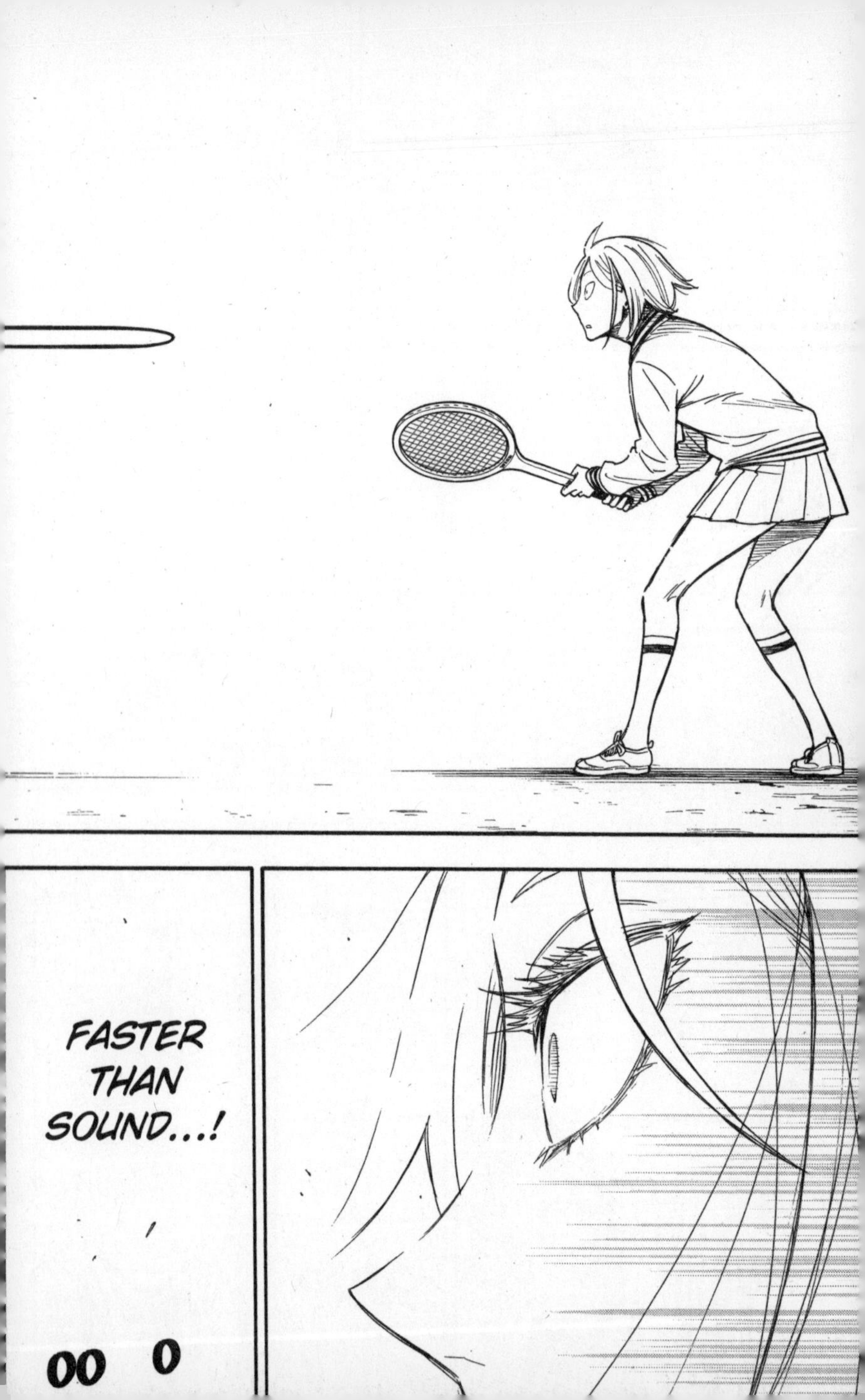
FASTER THAN SOUND...!
OO O

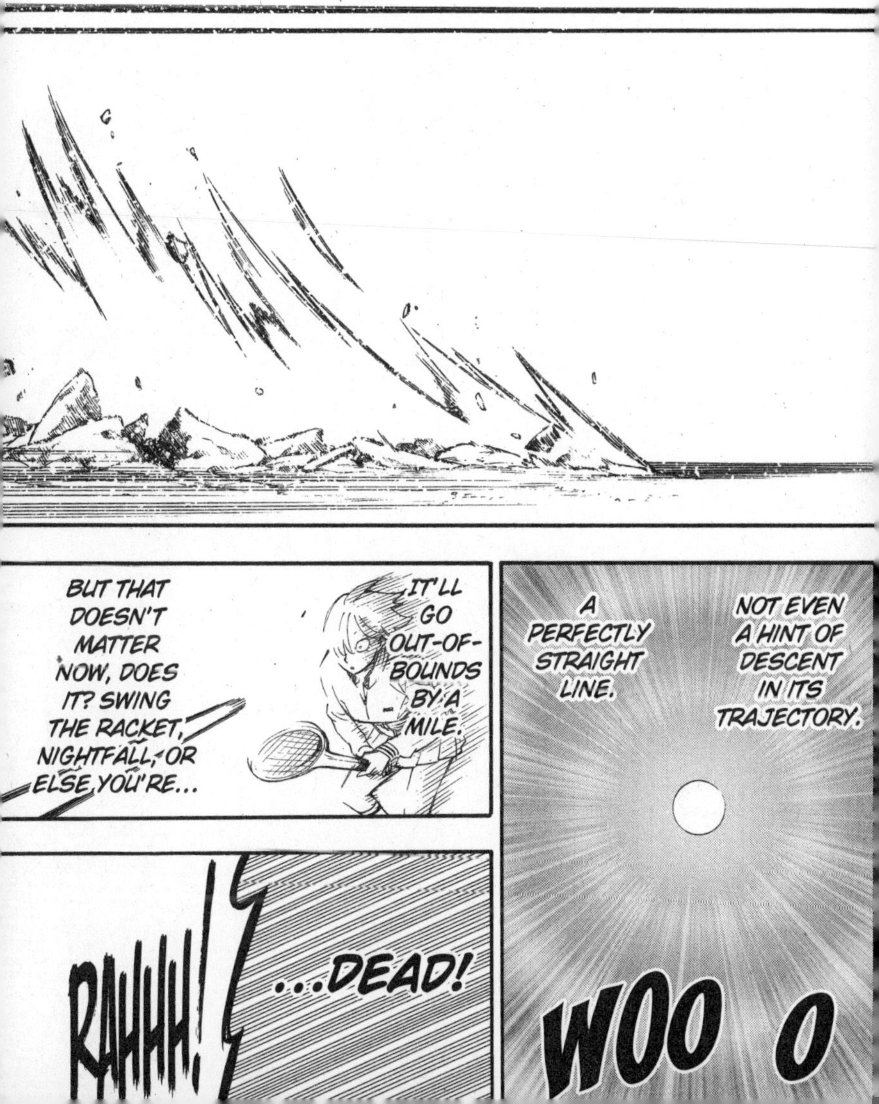
NOT EVEN A HINT OF DESCENT IN ITS TRAJECTORY.
A PERFECTLY STRAIGHT LINE.
WOO O
IT'LL GO OUT-OF-BOUNDS BY A MILE.
BUT THAT DOESN'T MATTER NOW, DOES IT? SWING THE RACKET, NIGHTFALL, OR ELSE YOU'RE...
...DEAD!
RAHHH!

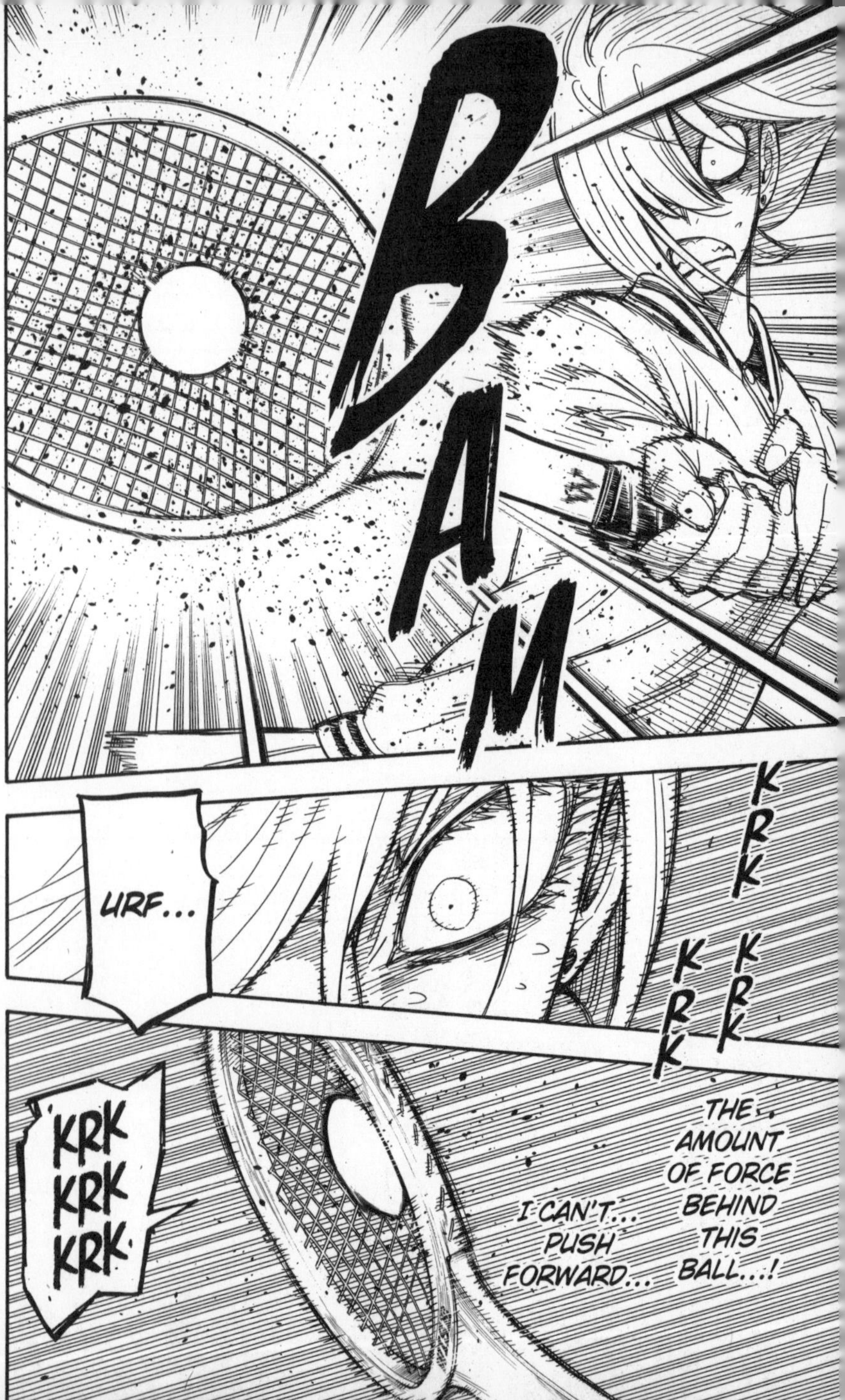
BAM
KRK
KRK KRK
KRK KRK
URF...
THE AMOUNT OF FORCE BEHIND THIS BALL...!
I CAN'T... PUSH FORWARD...
KRK KRK KRK

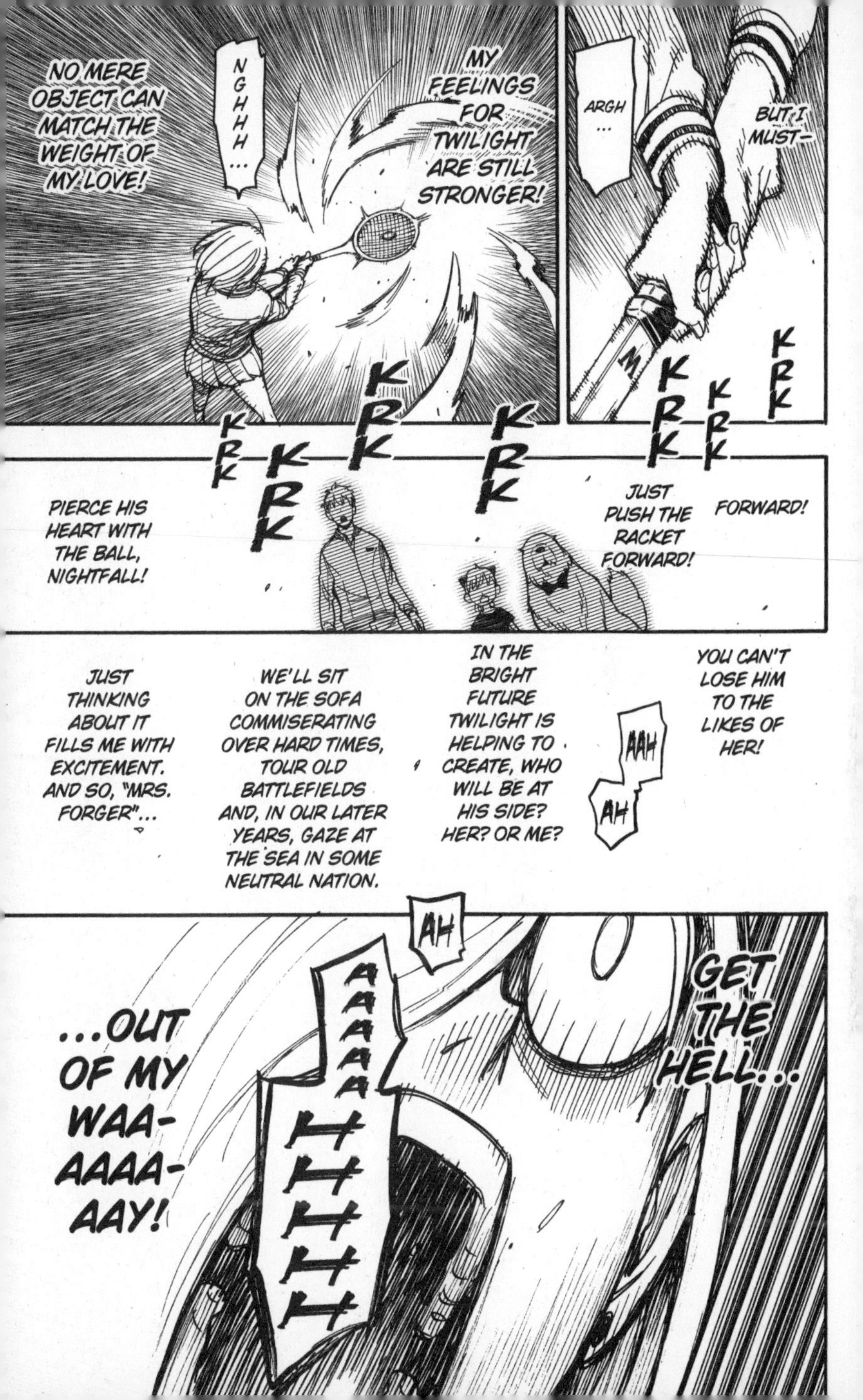

BUT I MUST-
ARGH...
KRK
KRK
KRK
MY FEELINGS FOR TWILIGHT ARE STILL STRONGER!
NGHHH...
NO MERE OBJECT CAN MATCH THE WEIGHT OF MY LOVE!
KRK
KRK
KRK
KRK
FORWARD!
JUST PUSH THE RACKET FORWARD!
PIERCE HIS HEART WITH THE BALL, NIGHTFALL!
YOU CAN'T LOSE HIM TO THE LIKES OF HER!
AAH
AH
IN THE BRIGHT FUTURE TWILIGHT IS HELPING TO CREATE, WHO WILL BE AT HIS SIDE? HER? OR ME?
WE'LL SIT ON THE SOFA COMMISERATING OVER HARD TIMES, TOUR OLD BATTLEFIELDS AND, IN OUR LATER YEARS, GAZE AT THE SEA IN SOME NEUTRAL NATION.
JUST THINKING ABOUT IT FILLS ME WITH EXCITEMENT. AND SO, "MRS. FORGER"...
AH
GET THE HELL...
AAAAAAHHHHHH
...OUT OF MY WAA-AAAA-AAY!

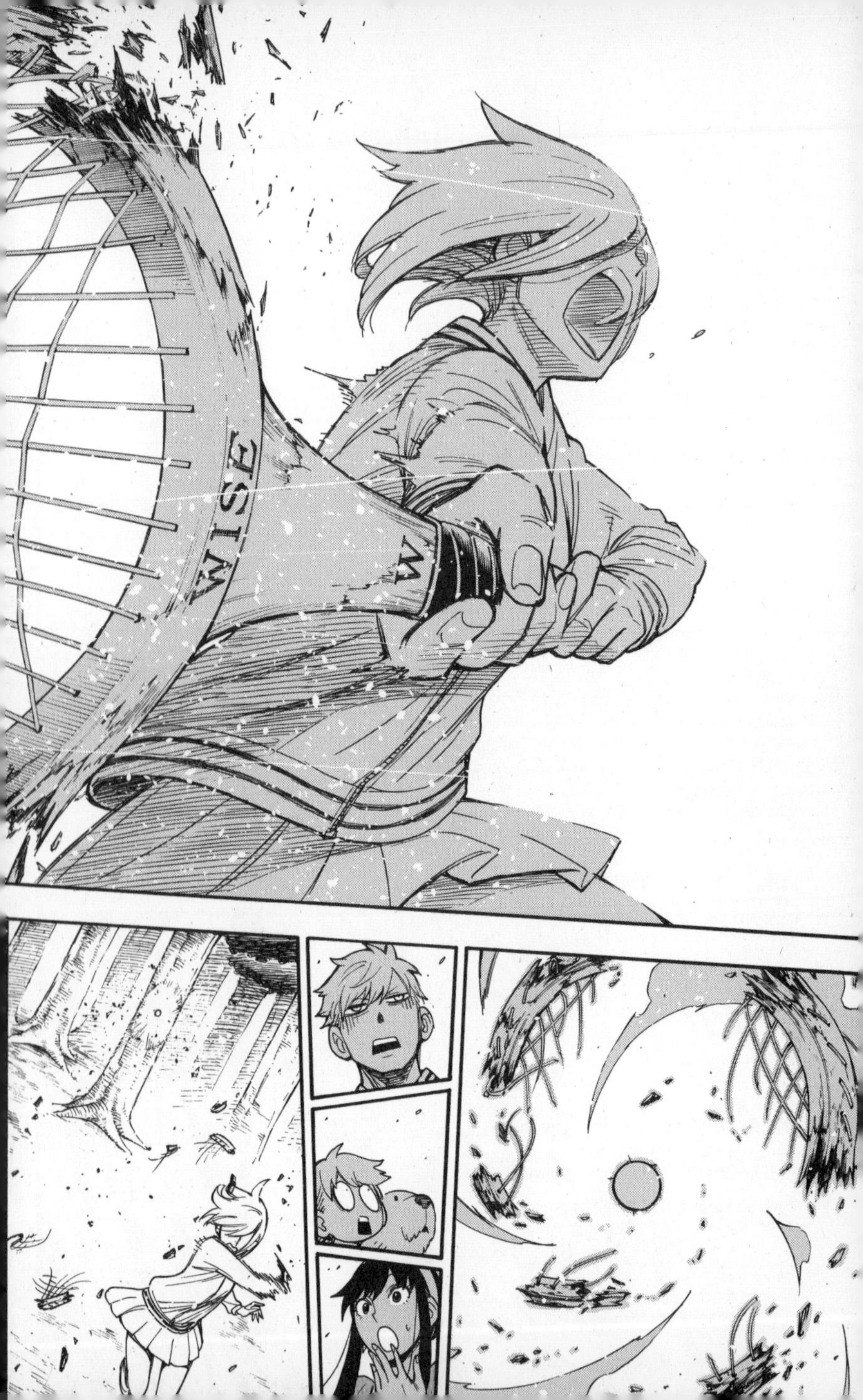
WISE

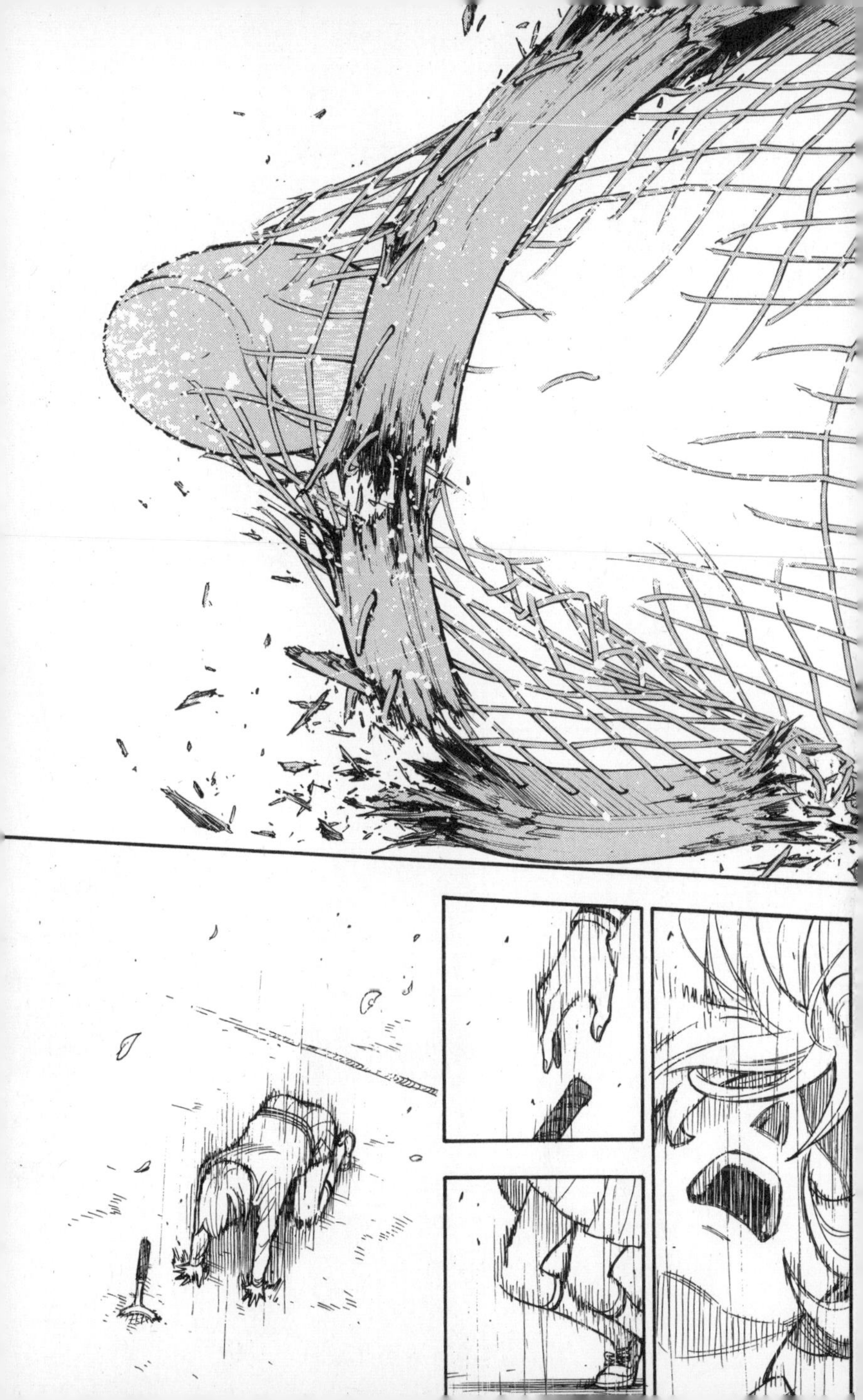

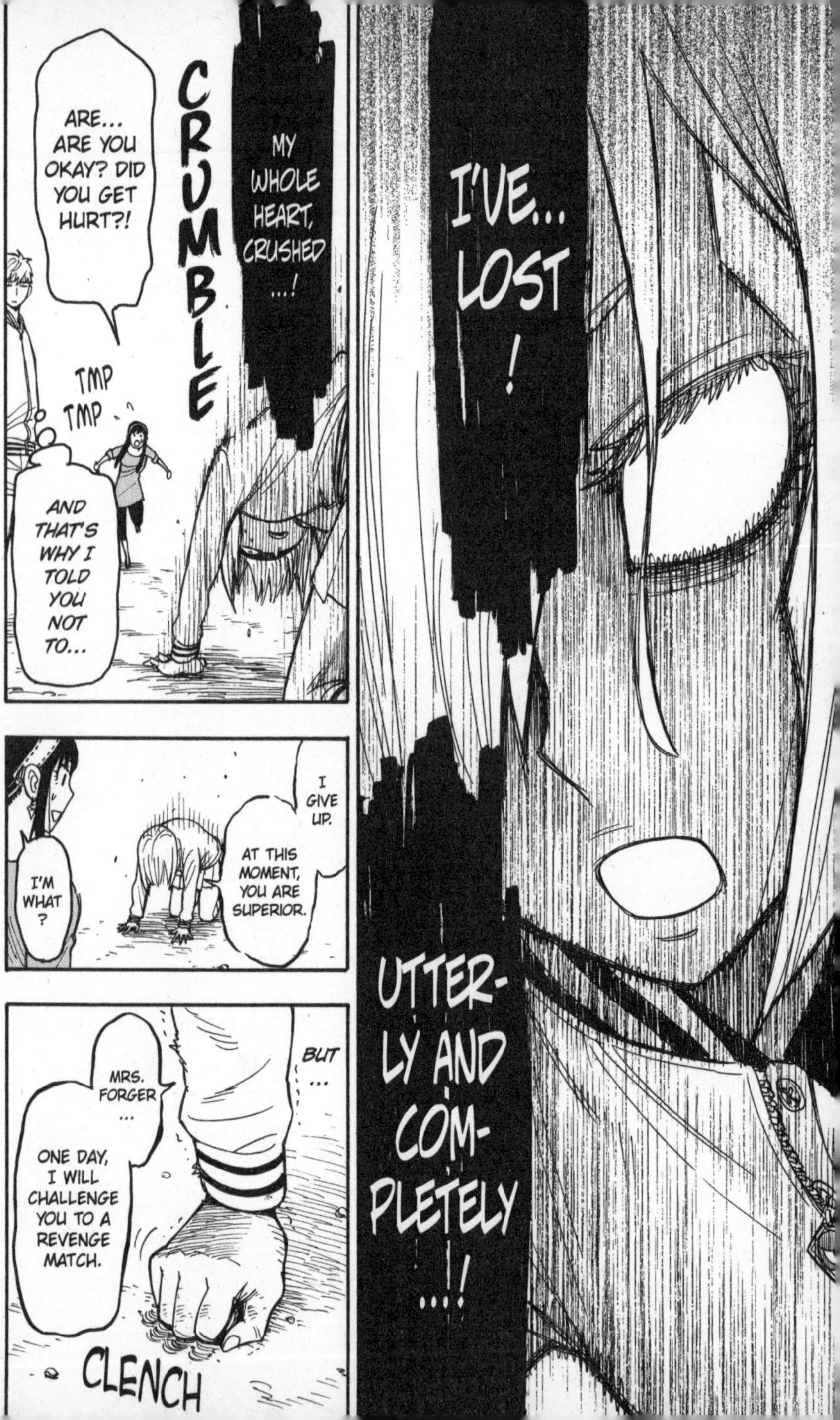
I'VE... LOST!
UTTERLY AND COMPLETELY...!!
CRUMBLE
MY WHOLE HEART, CRUSHED...!
ARE... ARE YOU OKAY? DID YOU GET HURT?!
TMP TMP
AND THAT'S WHY I TOLD YOU NOT TO...
I GIVE UP.
AT THIS MOMENT, YOU ARE SUPERIOR.
I'M WHAT?
BUT...
MRS. FORGER...
ONE DAY, I WILL CHALLENGE YOU TO A REVENGE MATCH.
CLENCH

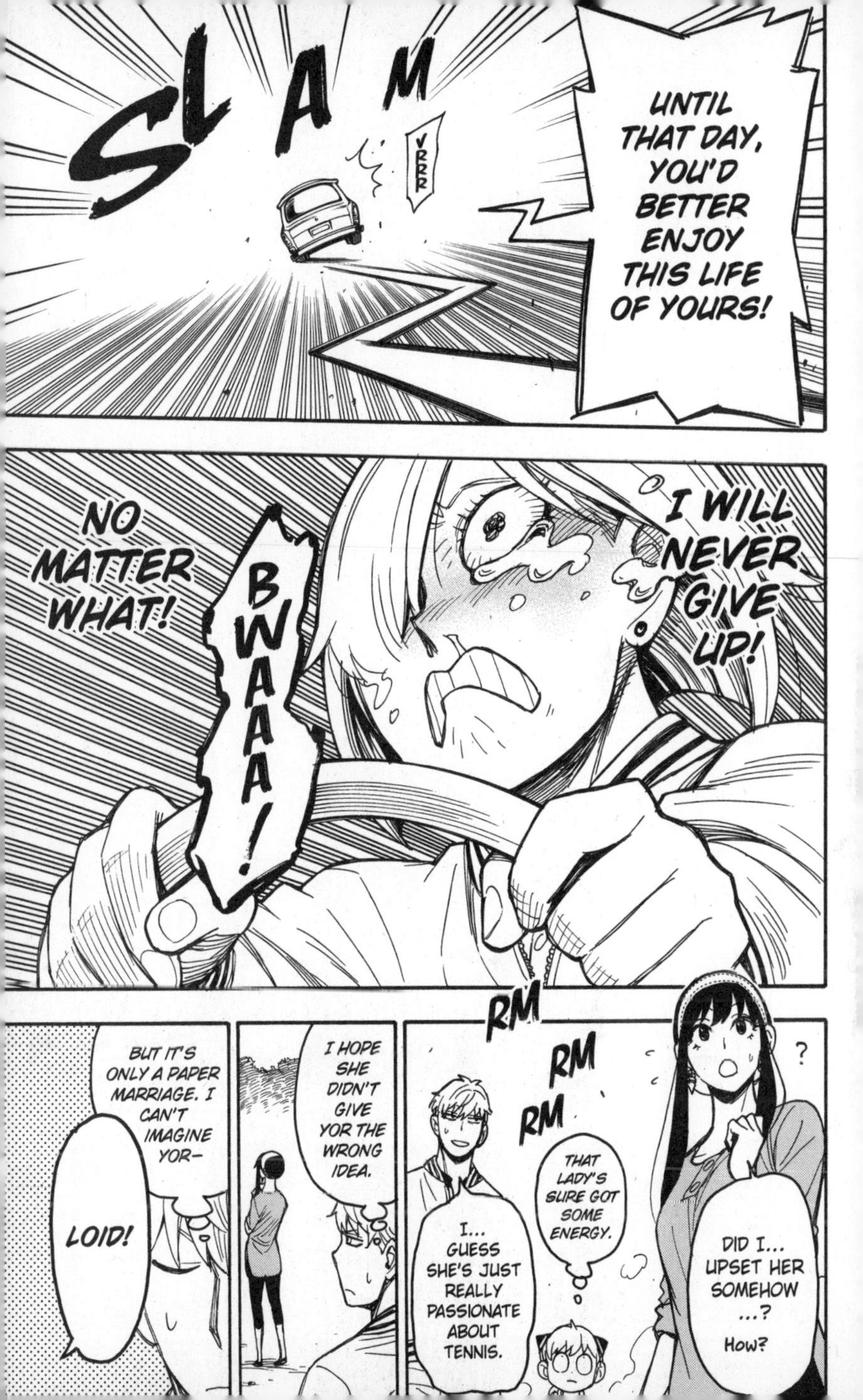

UNTIL THAT DAY, YOU'D BETTER ENJOY THIS LIFE OF YOURS!
SLAM
VRRR
I WILL NEVER GIVE UP!
BWAAAA!
NO MATTER WHAT!
?
DID I... UPSET HER SOMEHOW ...?
How?
RM
RM
RM
THAT LADY'S SURE GOT SOME ENERGY.
I... GUESS SHE'S JUST REALLY PASSIONATE ABOUT TENNIS.
I HOPE SHE DIDN'T GIVE YOR THE WRONG IDEA.
BUT IT'S ONLY A PAPER MARRIAGE. I CAN'T IMAGINE YOR—
LOID!

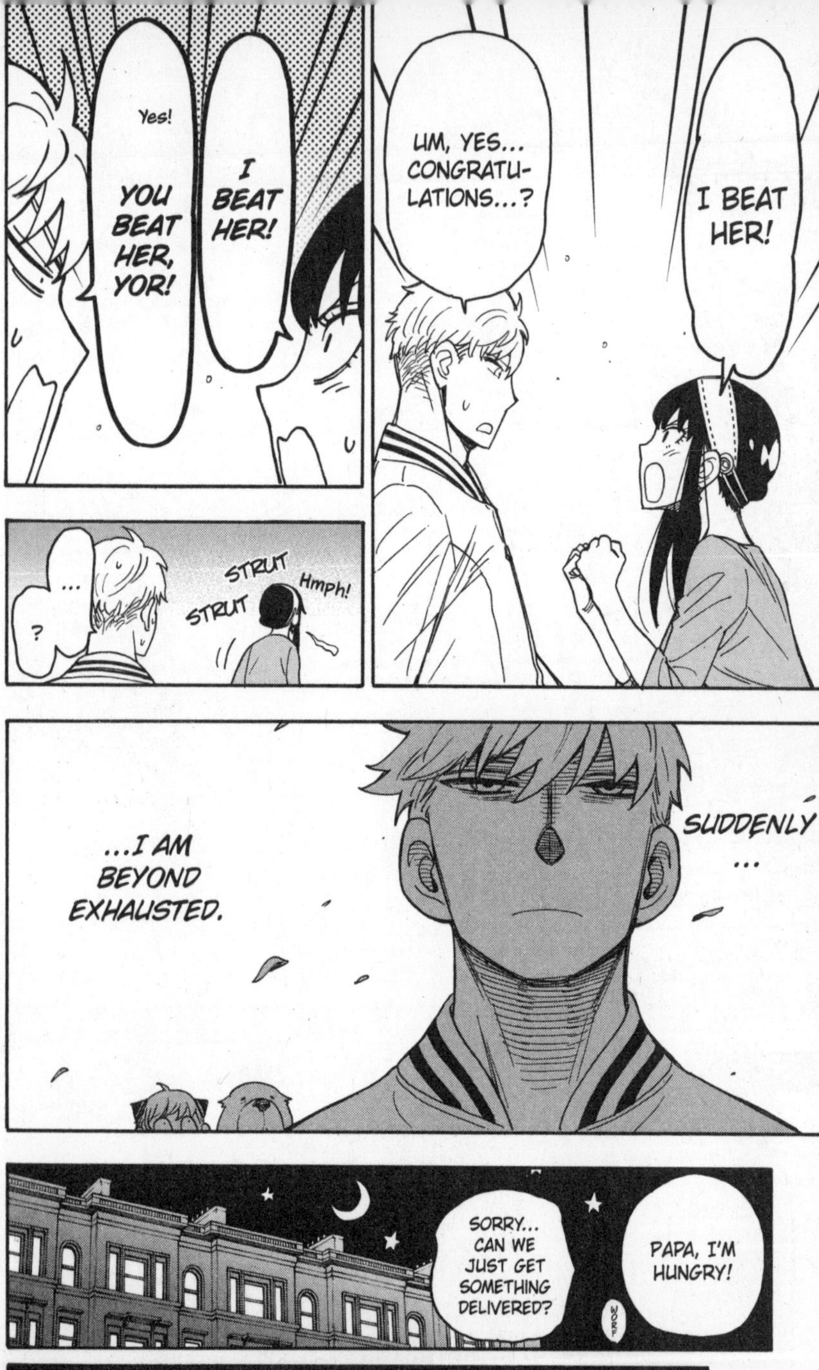
I BEAT HER!
UM, YES... CONGRATU-LATIONS...?
I BEAT HER!
Yes! YOU BEAT HER, YOR!
Hmph!
STRUT STRUT
... ?
SUDDENLY...
...I AM BEYOND EXHAUSTED.
PAPA, I'M HUNGRY!
WORF
SORRY... CAN WE JUST GET SOMETHING DELIVERED?

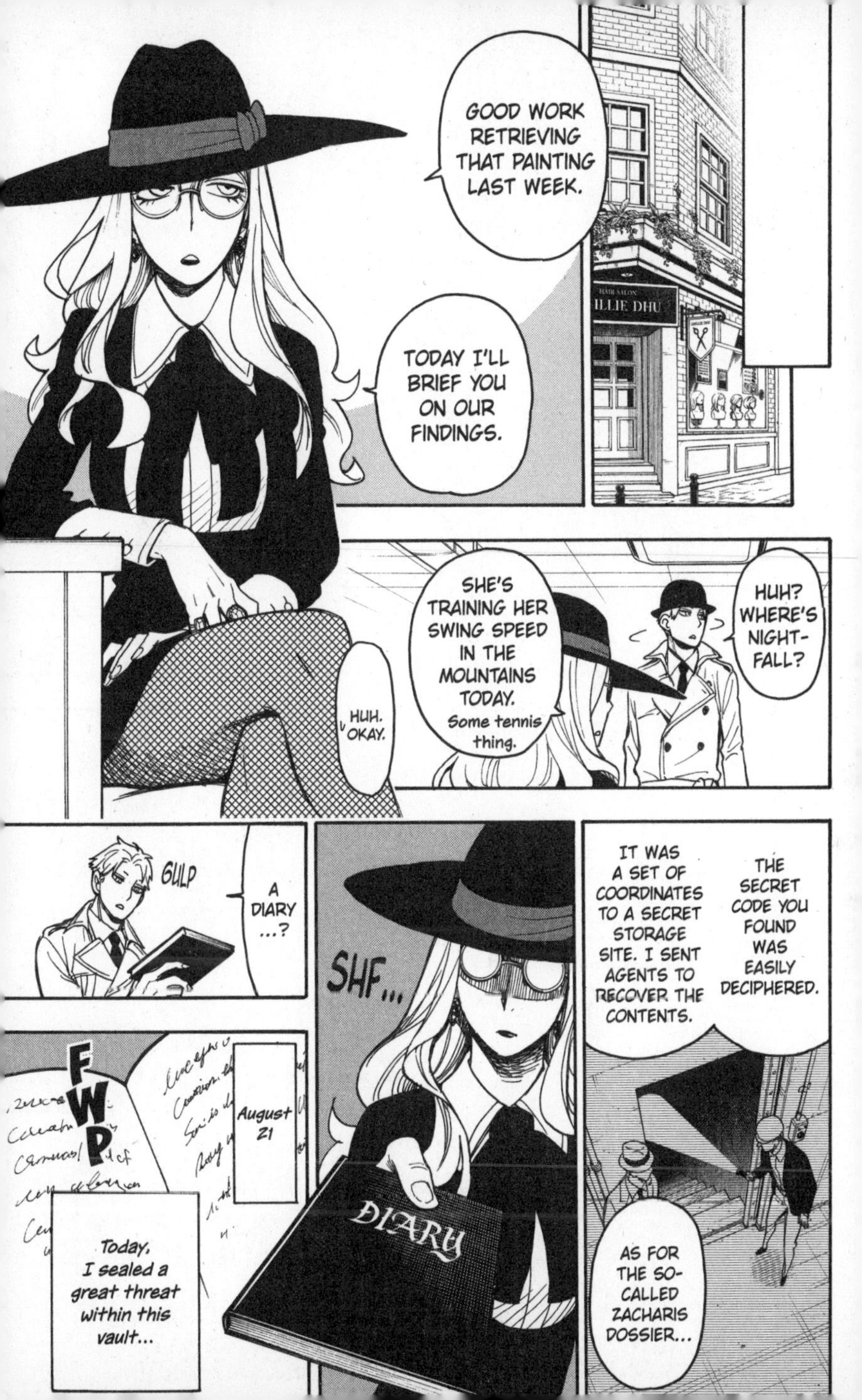
HAIR SALON
ILLIE DHU
GOOD WORK RETRIEVING THAT PAINTING LAST WEEK.
TODAY I'LL BRIEF YOU ON OUR FINDINGS.
HUH? WHERE'S NIGHT-FALL?
SHE'S TRAINING HER SWING SPEED IN THE MOUNTAINS TODAY. Some tennis thing.
HUH. OKAY.
THE SECRET CODE YOU FOUND WAS EASILY DECIPHERED.
IT WAS A SET OF COORDINATES TO A SECRET STORAGE SITE. I SENT AGENTS TO RECOVER THE CONTENTS.
AS FOR THE SO-CALLED ZACHARIS DOSSIER...
SHF...
A DIARY ...?
GULP
FWP
August 21
Today, I sealed a great threat within this vault...
DIARY

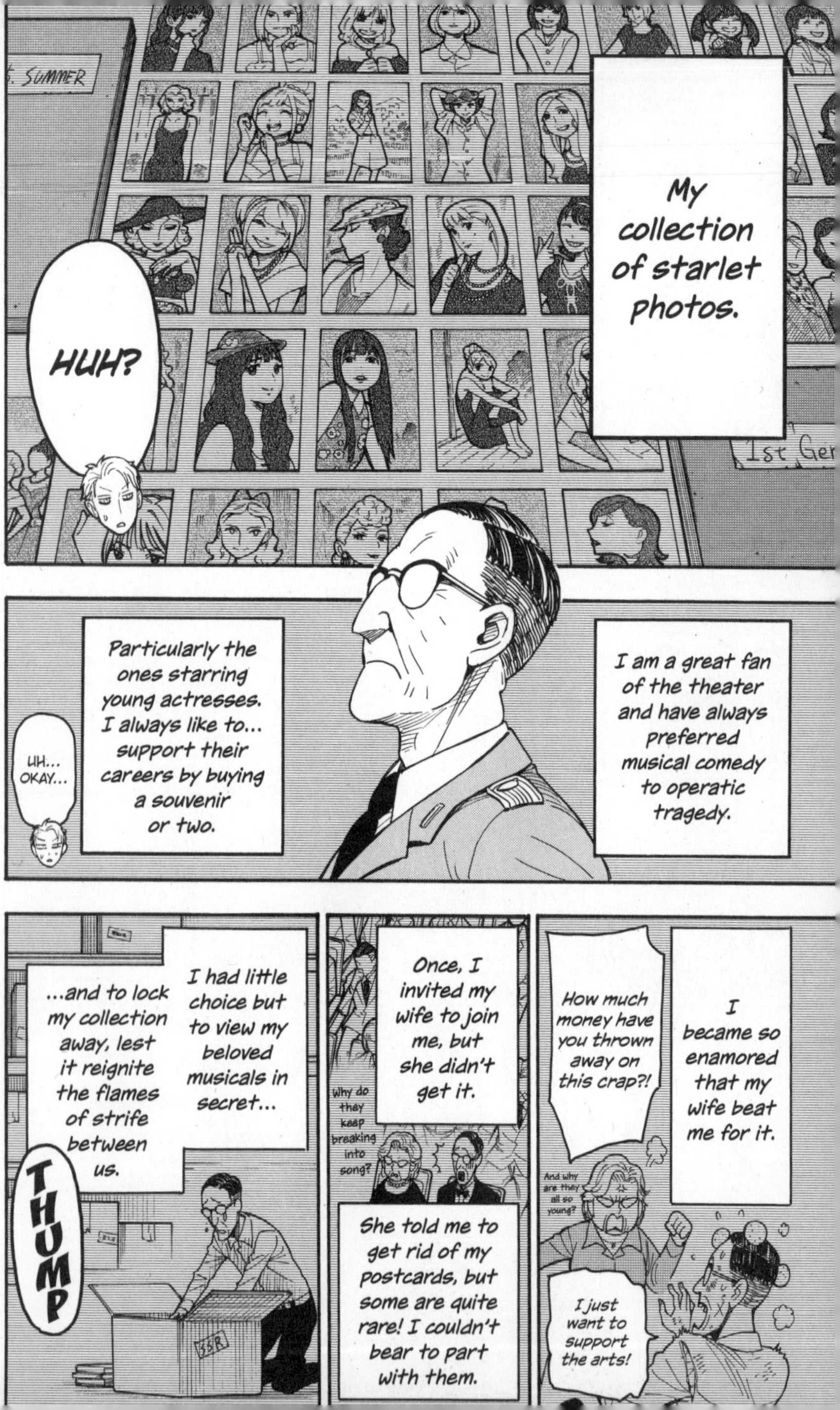
My collection of starlet photos.
HUH?
I am a great fan of the theater and have always preferred musical comedy to operatic tragedy.
Particularly the ones starring young actresses. I always like to... support their careers by buying a souvenir or two.
UH... OKAY...
I became so enamored that my wife beat me for it.
How much money have you thrown away on this crap?!
And why are they all so young?
I just want to support the arts!
Once, I invited my wife to join me, but she didn't get it.
Why do they keep breaking into song?
She told me to get rid of my postcards, but some are quite rare! I couldn't bear to part with them.
I had little choice but to view my beloved musicals in secret...
...and to lock my collection away, lest it reignite the flames of strife between us.
THUMP

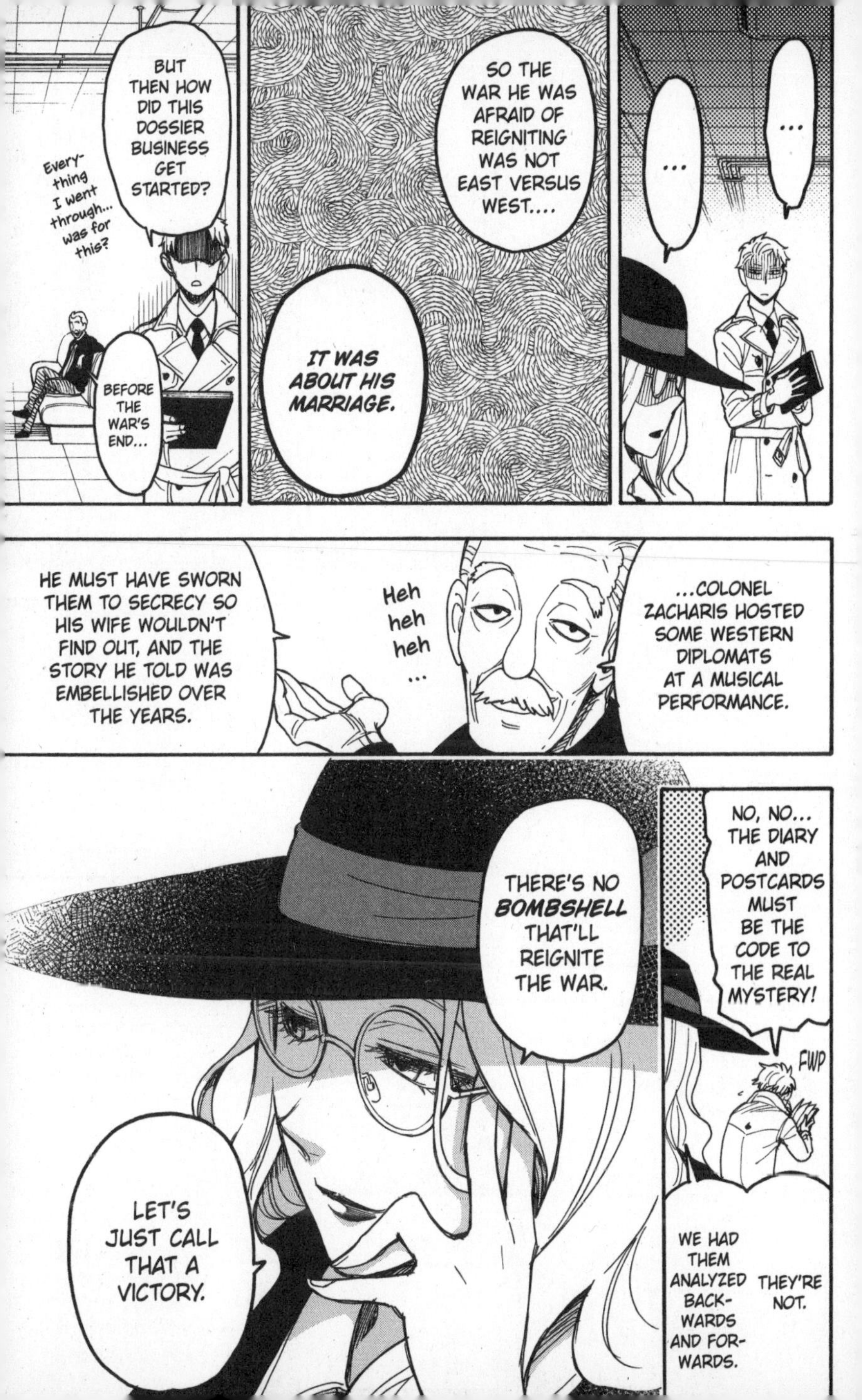
...
...
SO THE WAR HE WAS AFRAID OF REIGNITING WAS NOT EAST VERSUS WEST....
IT WAS ABOUT HIS MARRIAGE.
BUT THEN HOW DID THIS DOSSIER BUSINESS GET STARTED?
Everything I went through... was for this?
BEFORE THE WAR'S END...
...COLONEL ZACHARIS HOSTED SOME WESTERN DIPLOMATS AT A MUSICAL PERFORMANCE.
Heh heh heh ...
HE MUST HAVE SWORN THEM TO SECRECY SO HIS WIFE WOULDN'T FIND OUT, AND THE STORY HE TOLD WAS EMBELLISHED OVER THE YEARS.
NO, NO... THE DIARY AND POSTCARDS MUST BE THE CODE TO THE REAL MYSTERY!
FWP
WE HAD THEM ANALYZED BACKWARDS AND FORWARDS.
THEY'RE NOT.
THERE'S NO BOMBSHELL THAT'LL REIGNITE THE WAR.
LET'S JUST CALL THAT A VICTORY.

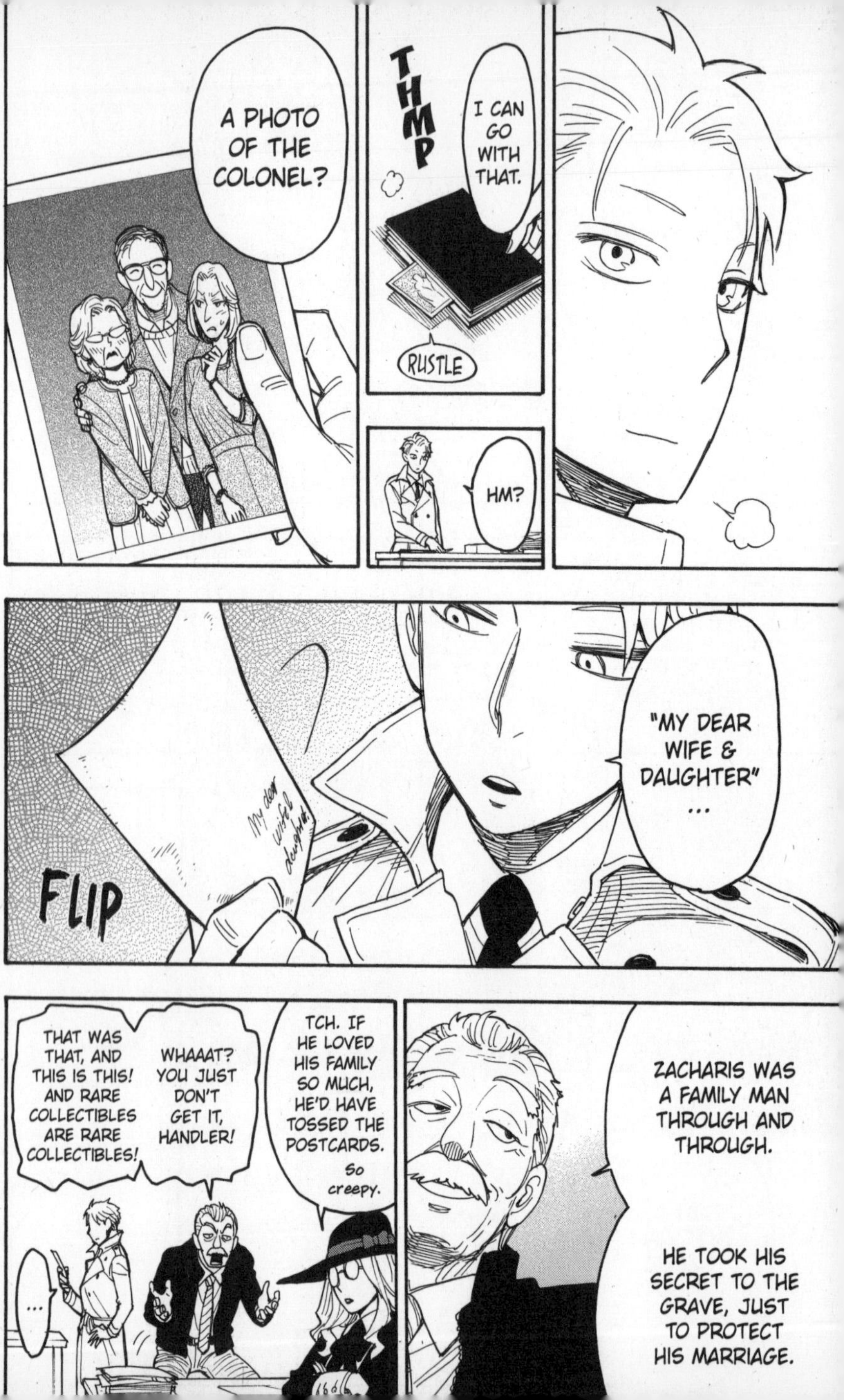

I CAN GO WITH THAT.
THMP
RUSTLE
HM?
A PHOTO OF THE COLONEL?
"MY DEAR WIFE & DAUGHTER" ...
My dear wife & daughter
FLIP
ZACHARIS WAS A FAMILY MAN THROUGH AND THROUGH.
HE TOOK HIS SECRET TO THE GRAVE, JUST TO PROTECT HIS MARRIAGE.
TCH. IF HE LOVED HIS FAMILY SO MUCH, HE'D HAVE TOSSED THE POSTCARDS.
So creepy.
WHAAAT? YOU JUST DON'T GET IT, HANDLER!
THAT WAS THAT, AND THIS IS THIS! AND RARE COLLECTIBLES ARE RARE COLLECTIBLES!
...

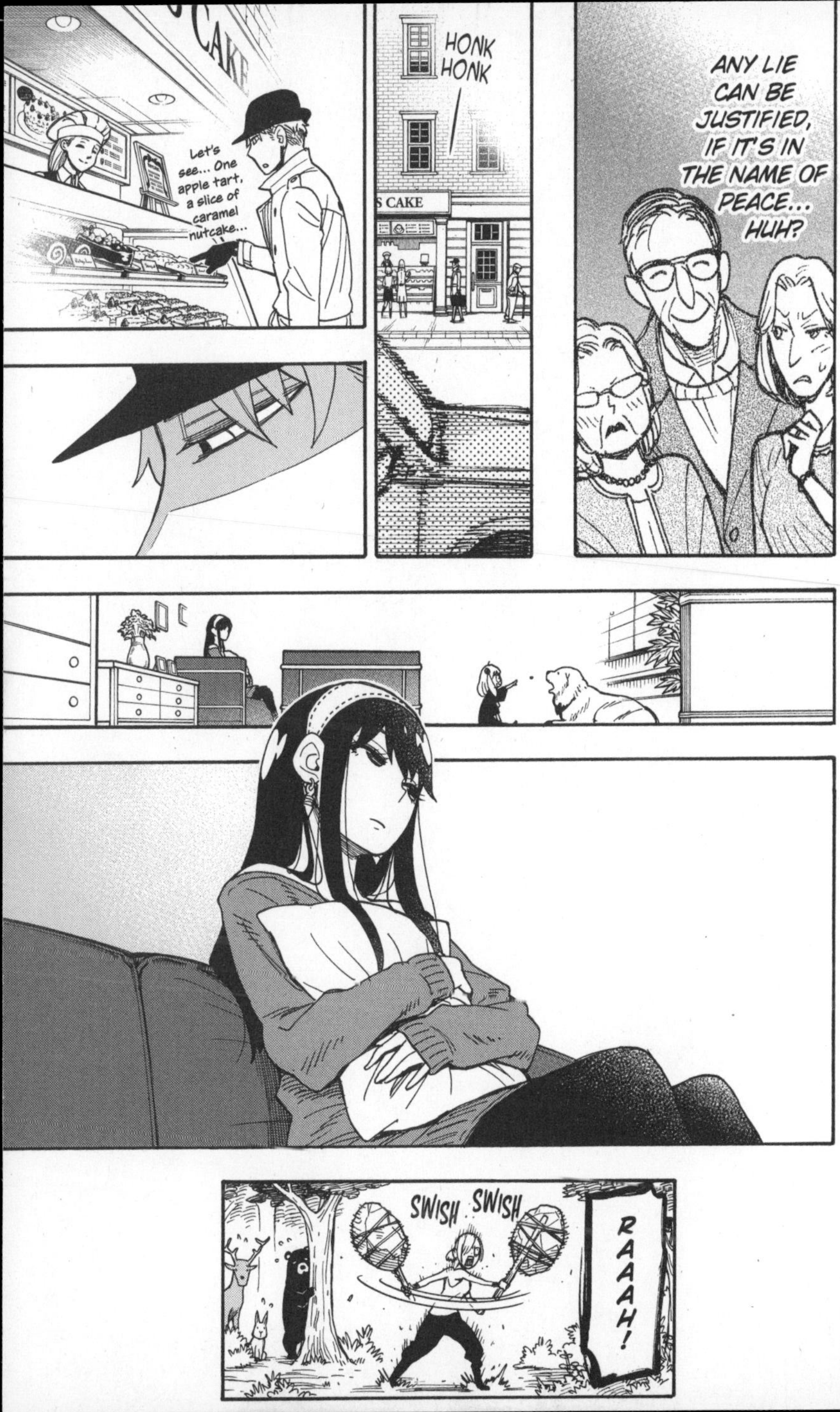
ANY LIE CAN BE JUSTIFIED, IF IT'S IN THE NAME OF PEACE... HUH?
HONK HONK
S CAKE
Let's see... One apple tart, a slice of caramel nutcake...
RAAAH!
SWISH SWISH

SPY×FAMILY

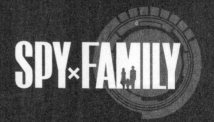

MISSION 35

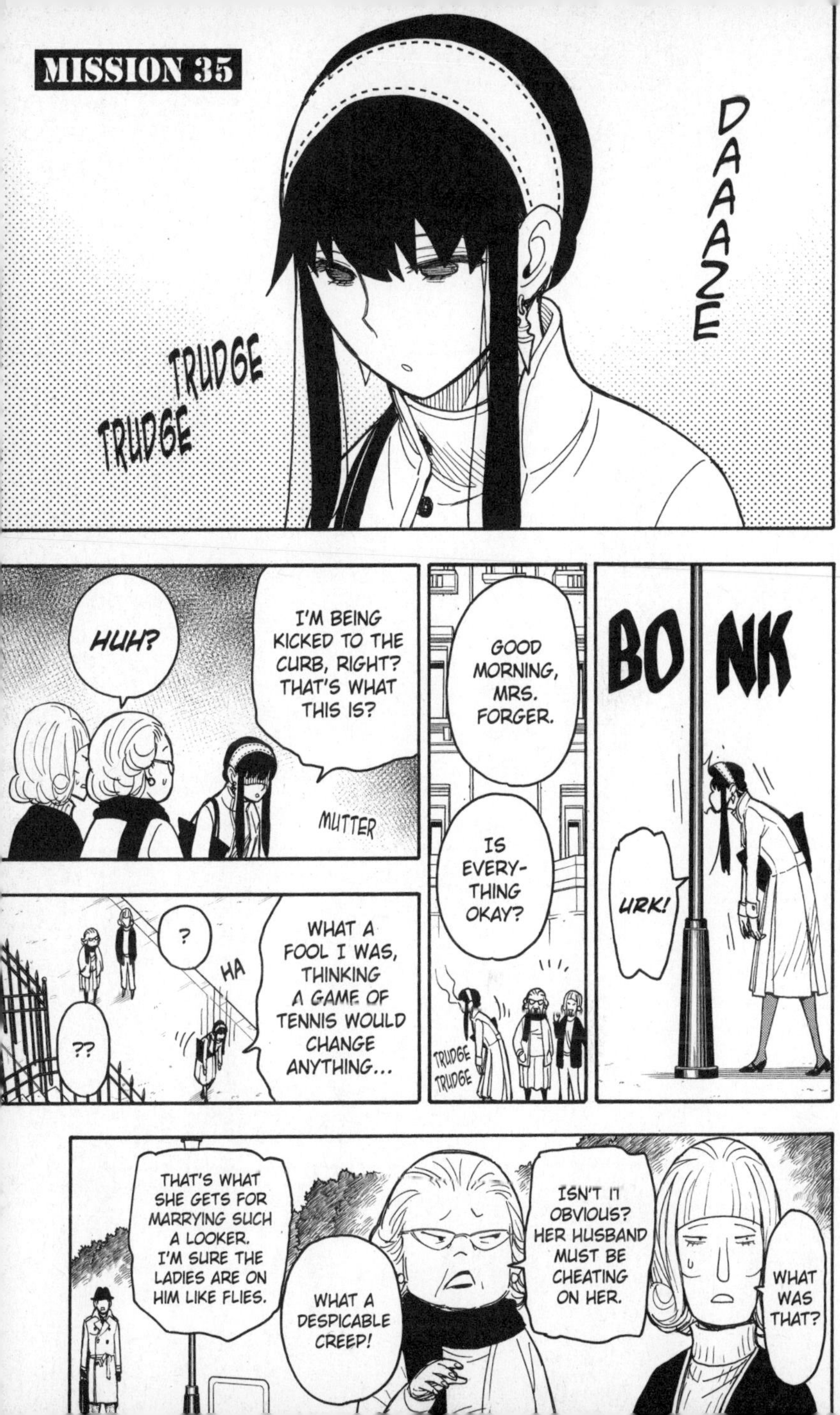
DAAAAZE
TRUDGE
TRUDGE
BONK
URK!
GOOD MORNING, MRS. FORGER.
IS EVERY-THING OKAY?
TRUDGE TRUDGE
I'M BEING KICKED TO THE CURB, RIGHT? THAT'S WHAT THIS IS?
MUTTER
HUH?
WHAT A FOOL I WAS, THINKING A GAME OF TENNIS WOULD CHANGE ANYTHING...
HA
?
??
WHAT WAS THAT?
ISN'T IT OBVIOUS? HER HUSBAND MUST BE CHEATING ON HER.
WHAT A DESPICABLE CREEP!
THAT'S WHAT SHE GETS FOR MARRYING SUCH A LOOKER. I'M SURE THE LADIES ARE ON HIM LIKE FLIES.

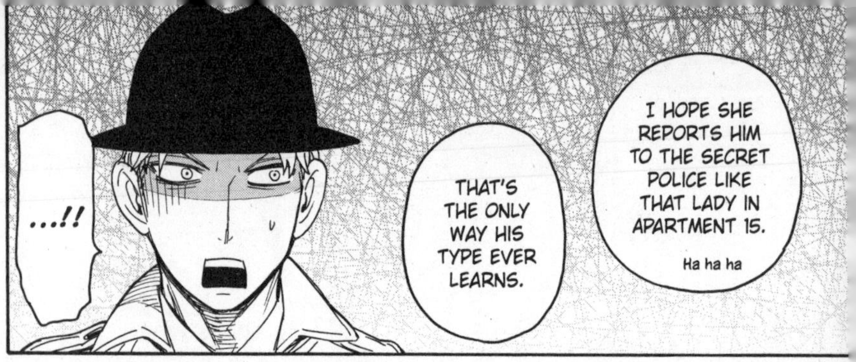
I HOPE SHE REPORTS HIM TO THE SECRET POLICE LIKE THAT LADY IN APARTMENT 15.
Ha ha ha
THAT'S THE ONLY WAY HIS TYPE EVER LEARNS.
...!!

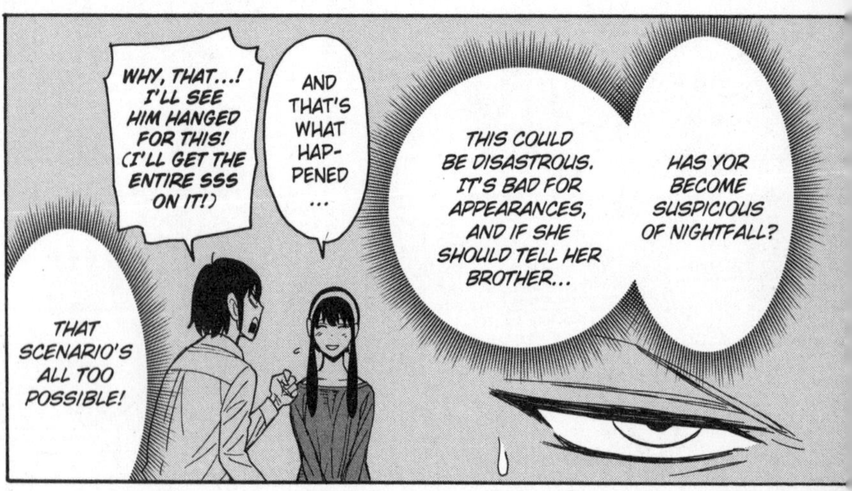
HAS YOR BECOME SUSPICIOUS OF NIGHTFALL?
THIS COULD BE DISASTROUS. IT'S BAD FOR APPEARANCES, AND IF SHE SHOULD TELL HER BROTHER...
AND THAT'S WHAT HAP-PENED...
WHY, THAT...! I'LL SEE HIM HANGED FOR THIS! (I'LL GET THE ENTIRE SSS ON IT!)
THAT SCENARIO'S ALL TOO POSSIBLE!

SPY×FAMILY

MISSION 35

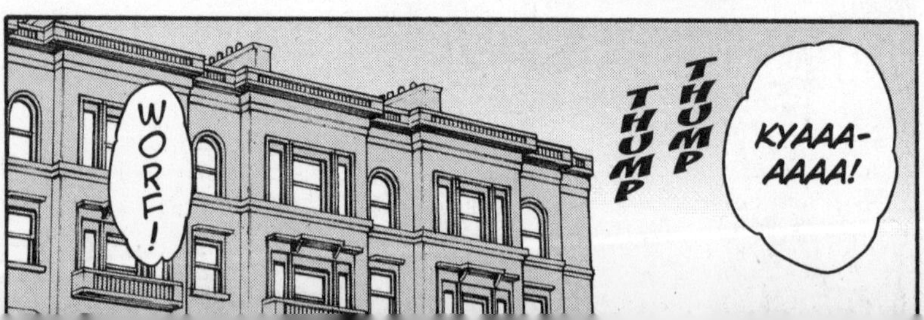
KYAAA-AAAA!
THUMP
THUMP
WORF!

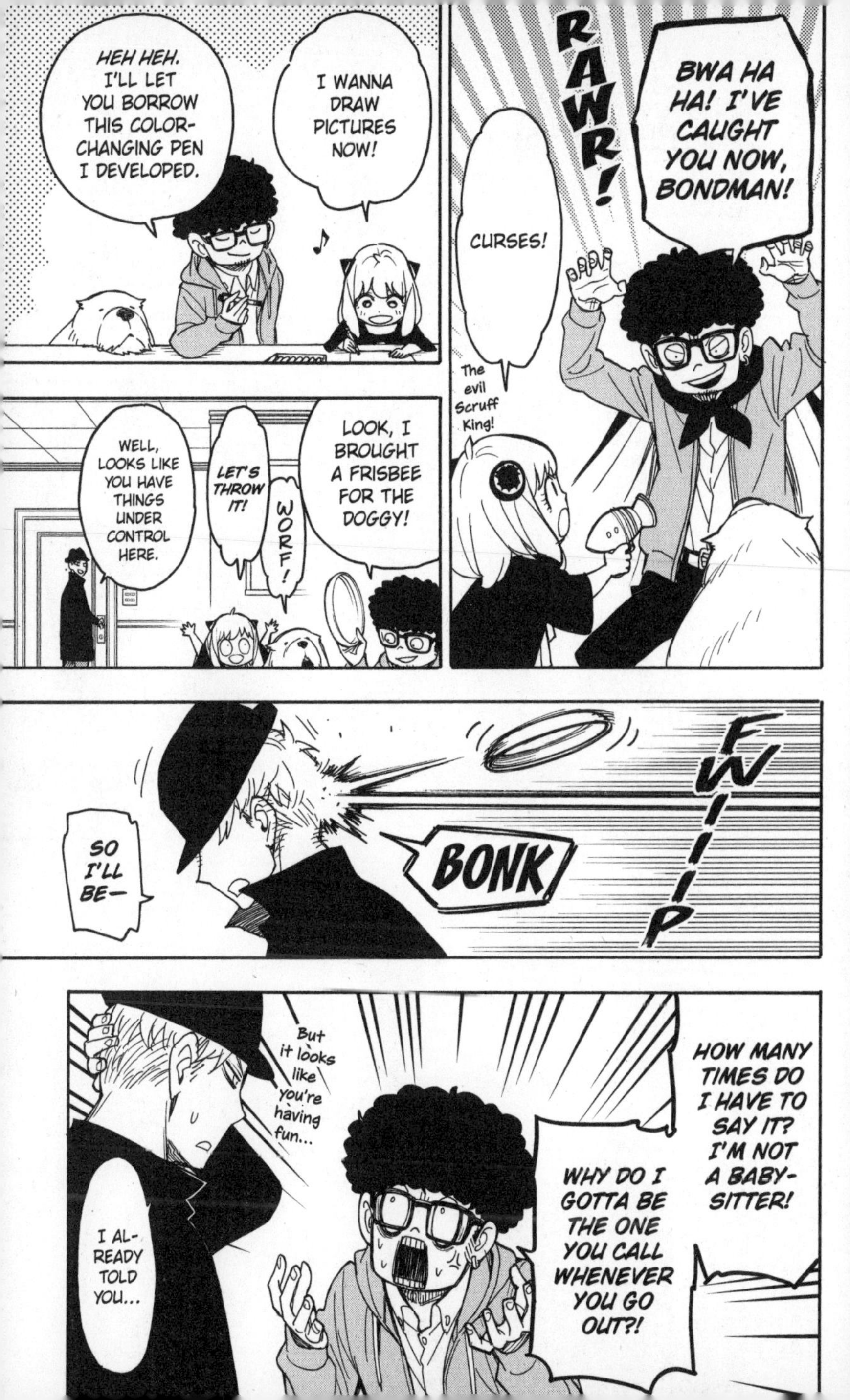
RAWR!
BWA HA HA! I'VE CAUGHT YOU NOW, BONDMAN!
CURSES!
The evil Scruff King!
I WANNA DRAW PICTURES NOW!
HEH HEH. I'LL LET YOU BORROW THIS COLOR-CHANGING PEN I DEVELOPED.
LOOK, I BROUGHT A FRISBEE FOR THE DOGGY!
WORF!
LET'S THROW IT!
WELL, LOOKS LIKE YOU HAVE THINGS UNDER CONTROL HERE.
FWIIIP
BONK
SO I'LL BE—
HOW MANY TIMES DO I HAVE TO SAY IT? I'M NOT A BABY-SITTER!
WHY DO I GOTTA BE THE ONE YOU CALL WHENEVER YOU GO OUT?!
But it looks like you're having fun...
I AL-READY TOLD YOU...

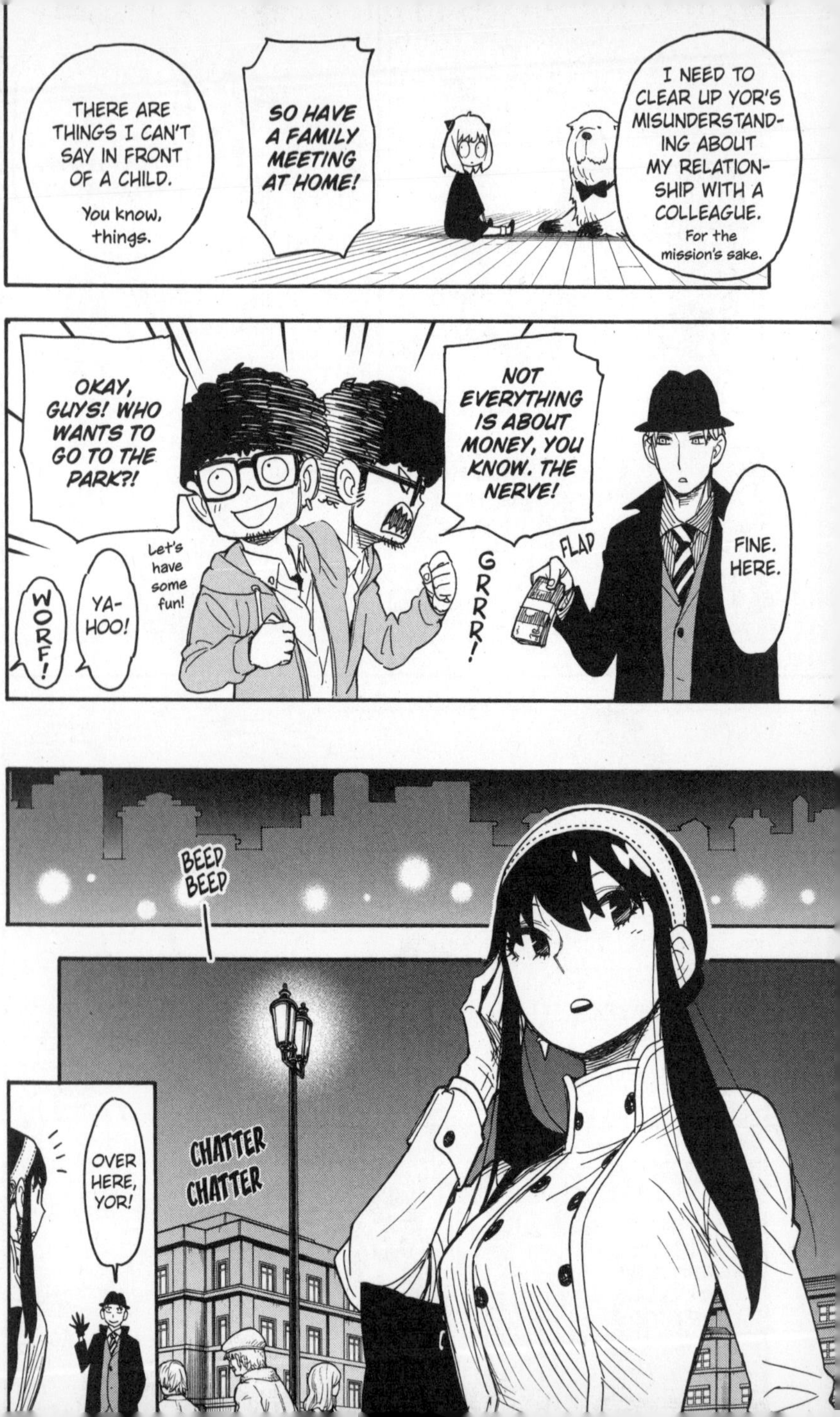
I NEED TO CLEAR UP YOR'S MISUNDERSTANDING ABOUT MY RELATIONSHIP WITH A COLLEAGUE.
For the mission's sake.
SO HAVE A FAMILY MEETING AT HOME!
THERE ARE THINGS I CAN'T SAY IN FRONT OF A CHILD.
You know, things.
FINE. HERE.
FLAP
GRRR!
NOT EVERYTHING IS ABOUT MONEY, YOU KNOW. THE NERVE!
OKAY, GUYS! WHO WANTS TO GO TO THE PARK?!
Let's have some fun!
YA-HOO!
WORF!
BEEP BEEP
CHATTER CHATTER
OVER HERE, YOR!

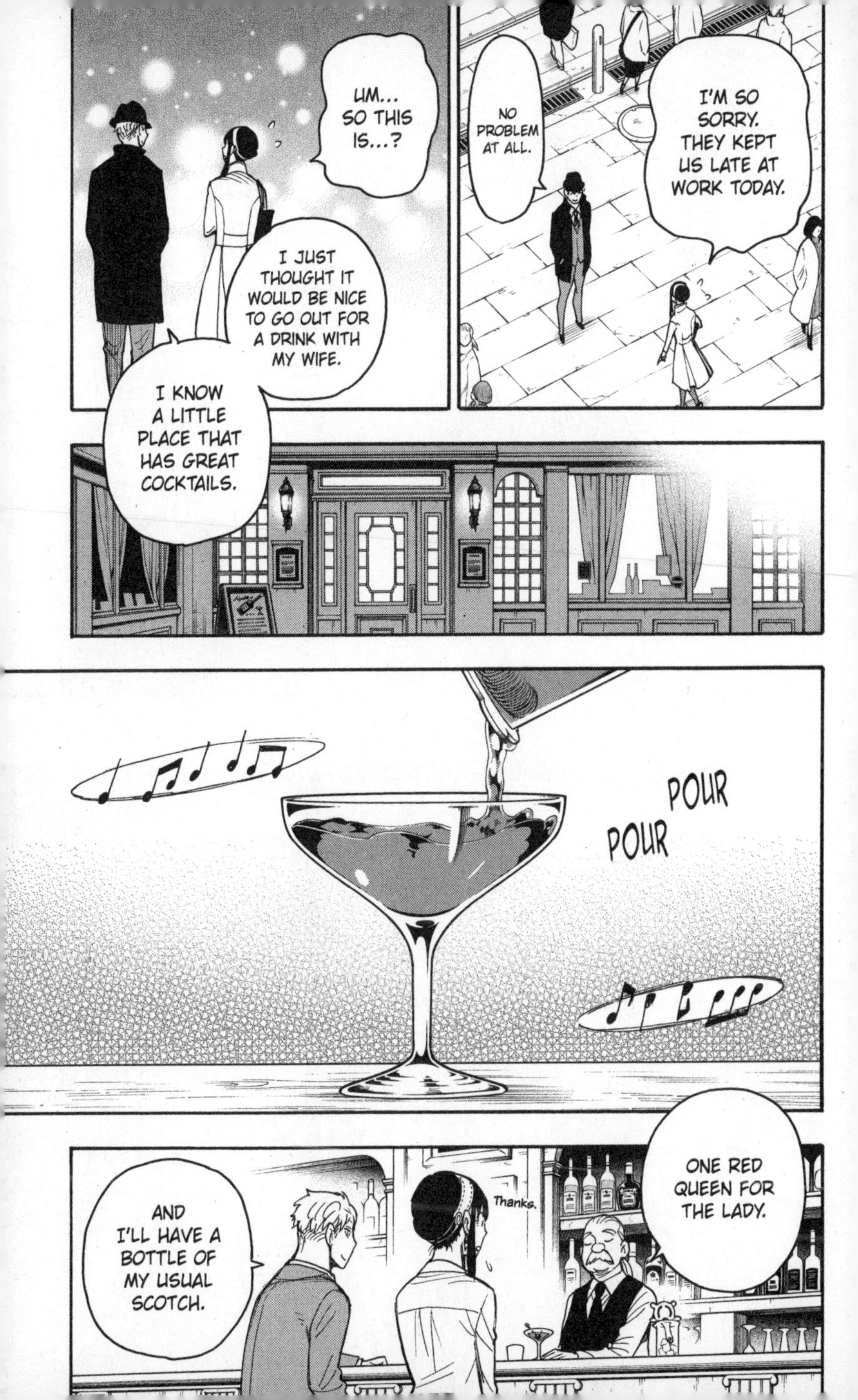
I'M SO SORRY. THEY KEPT US LATE AT WORK TODAY.
NO PROBLEM AT ALL.
UM... SO THIS IS...?
I JUST THOUGHT IT WOULD BE NICE TO GO OUT FOR A DRINK WITH MY WIFE.
I KNOW A LITTLE PLACE THAT HAS GREAT COCKTAILS.
POUR
POUR
ONE RED QUEEN FOR THE LADY.
Thanks.
AND I'LL HAVE A BOTTLE OF MY USUAL SCOTCH.

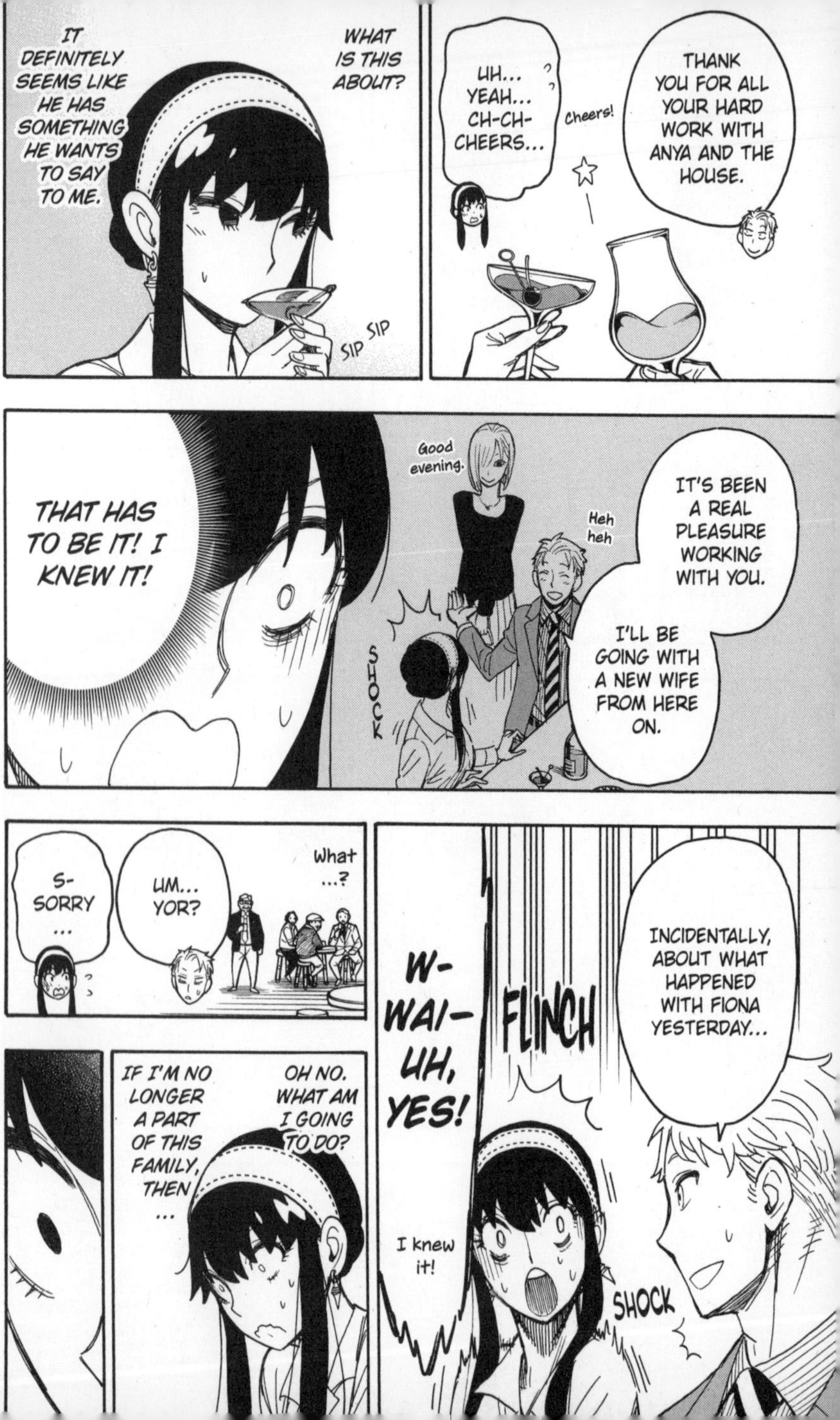
THANK YOU FOR ALL YOUR HARD WORK WITH ANYA AND THE HOUSE.
Cheers!
UH... YEAH... CH-CH-CHEERS...
WHAT IS THIS ABOUT?
IT DEFINITELY SEEMS LIKE HE HAS SOMETHING HE WANTS TO SAY TO ME.
SIP SIP
IT'S BEEN A REAL PLEASURE WORKING WITH YOU.
I'LL BE GOING WITH A NEW WIFE FROM HERE ON.
Heh heh
Good evening.
SHOCK
THAT HAS TO BE IT! I KNEW IT!
INCIDENTALLY, ABOUT WHAT HAPPENED WITH FIONA YESTERDAY...
FLINCH
W-WAI-UH, YES!
SHOCK
I knew it!
What ...?
UM... YOR?
S-SORRY ...
OH NO. WHAT AM I GOING TO DO?
IF I'M NO LONGER A PART OF THIS FAMILY, THEN ...

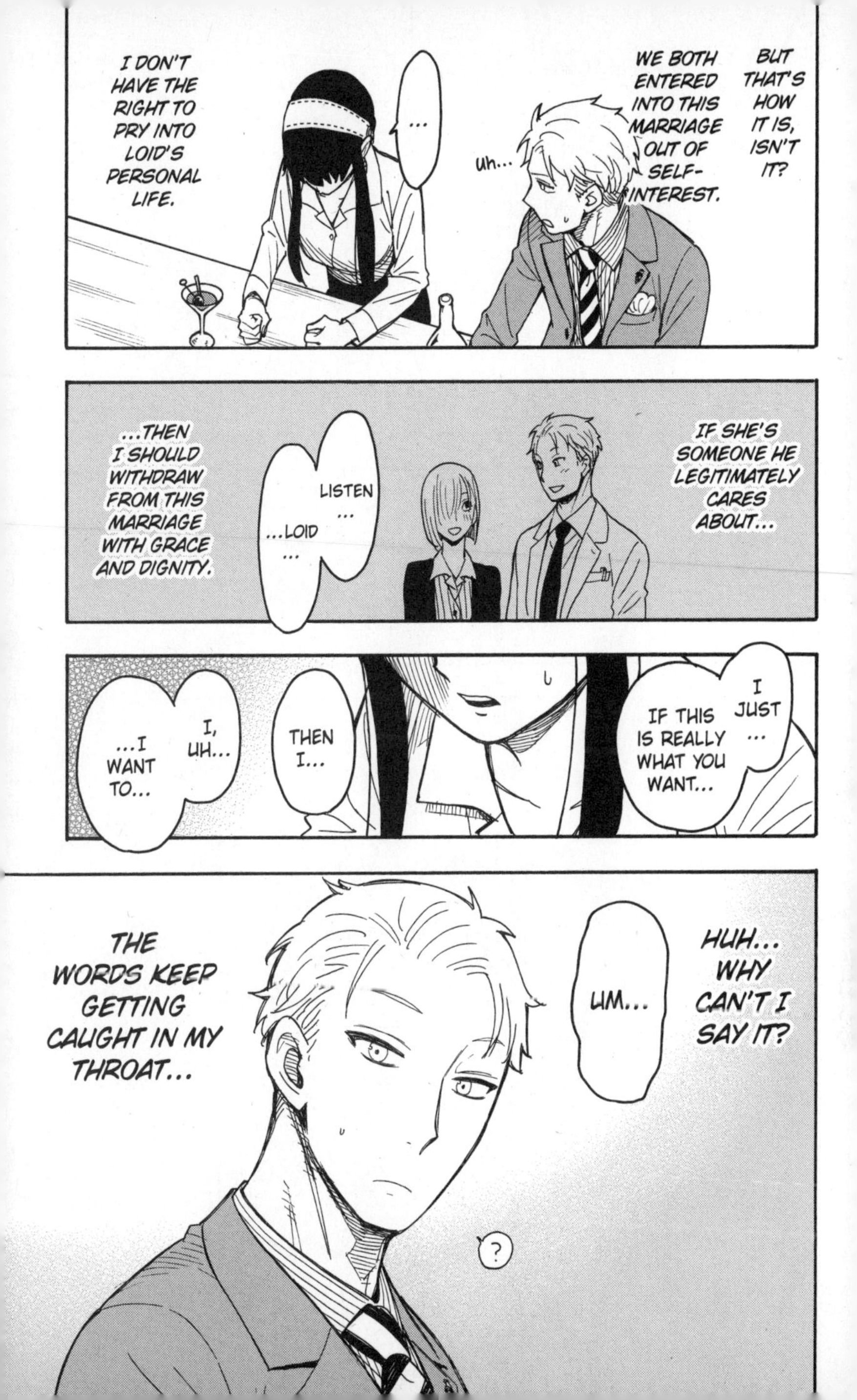

BUT THAT'S HOW IT IS, ISN'T IT?
WE BOTH ENTERED INTO THIS MARRIAGE OUT OF SELF-INTEREST.
uh...
...
I DON'T HAVE THE RIGHT TO PRY INTO LOID'S PERSONAL LIFE.
IF SHE'S SOMEONE HE LEGITIMATELY CARES ABOUT...
LISTEN ... ...LOID ...
...THEN I SHOULD WITHDRAW FROM THIS MARRIAGE WITH GRACE AND DIGNITY.
I JUST ...
IF THIS IS REALLY WHAT YOU WANT...
THEN I...
I, UH...
...I WANT TO...
HUH... WHY CAN'T I SAY IT?
UM...
THE WORDS KEEP GETTING CAUGHT IN MY THROAT...
?

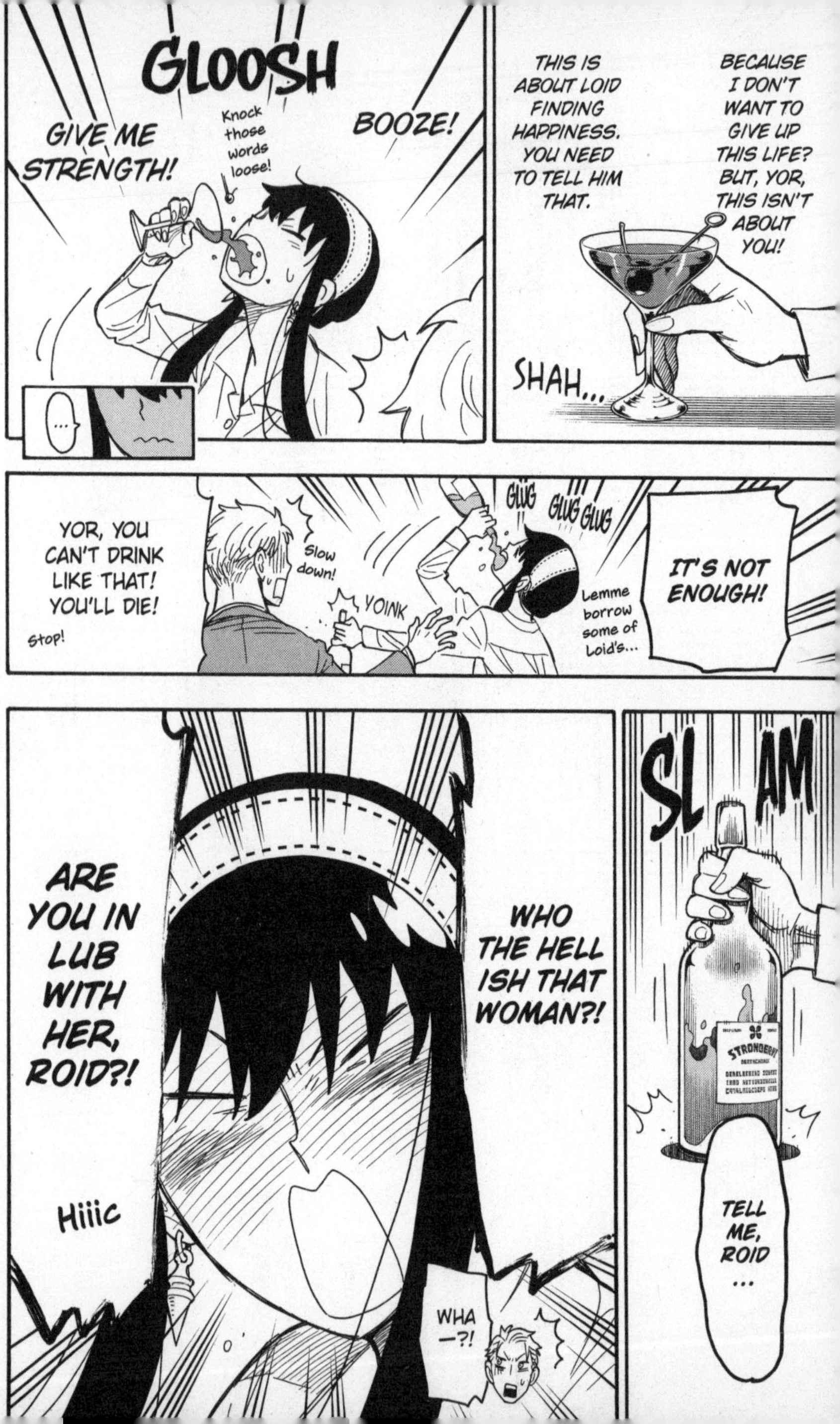
BECAUSE I DON'T WANT TO GIVE UP THIS LIFE? BUT, YOR, THIS ISN'T ABOUT YOU!
THIS IS ABOUT LOID FINDING HAPPINESS. YOU NEED TO TELL HIM THAT.
SHAH...
BOOZE!
GLOOSH
Knock those words loose!
GIVE ME STRENGTH!
...
IT'S NOT ENOUGH!
GLUG GLUG GLUG
Lemme borrow some of Loid's...
Slow down!
YOINK
YOR, YOU CAN'T DRINK LIKE THAT! YOU'LL DIE!
Stop!
SLAM
TELL ME, ROID...
WHO THE HELL ISH THAT WOMAN?!
ARE YOU IN LUB WITH HER, ROID?!
Hiiic
WHA—?!

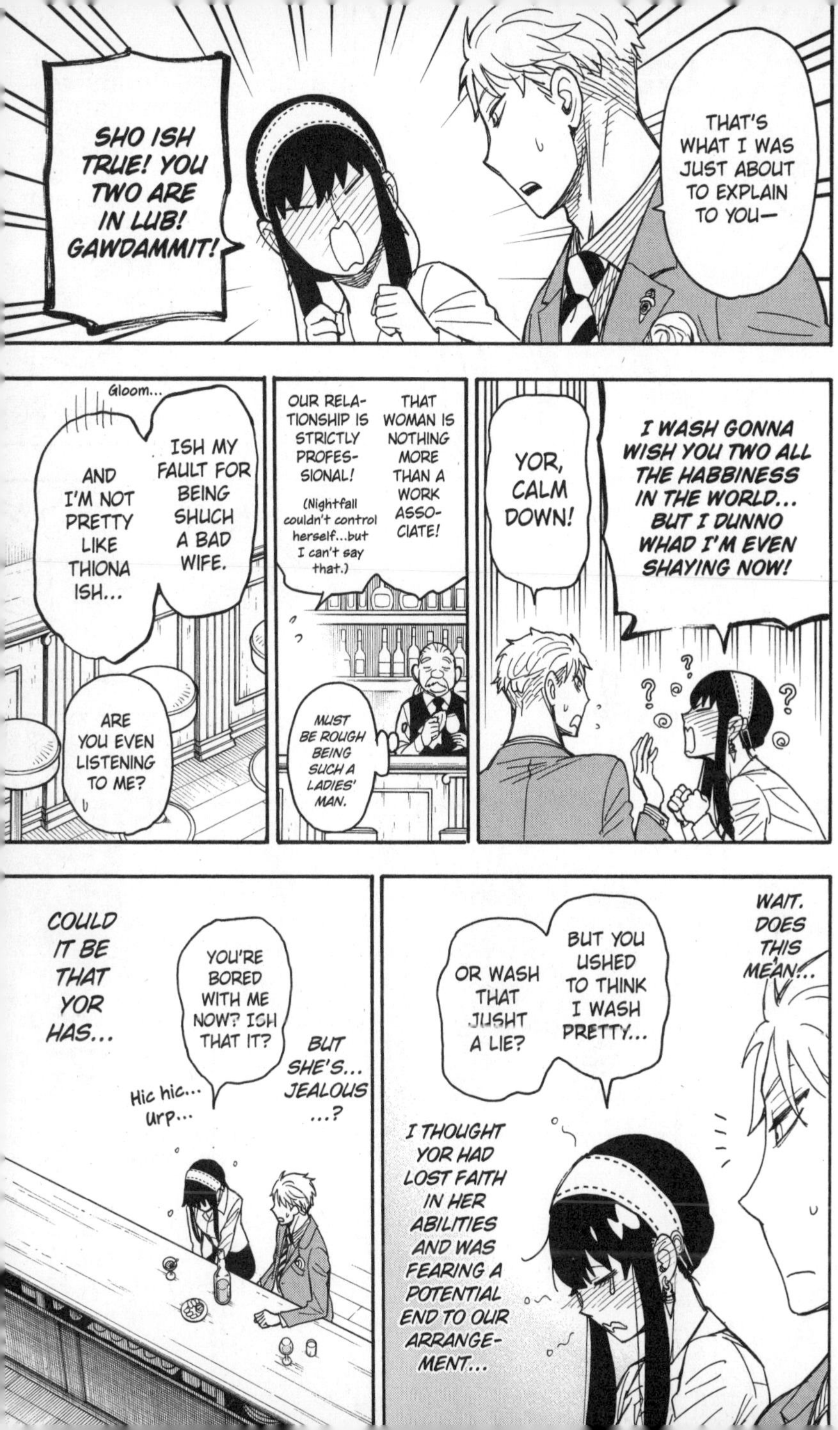
THAT'S WHAT I WAS JUST ABOUT TO EXPLAIN TO YOU—
SHO ISH TRUE! YOU TWO ARE IN LUB! GAWDAMMIT!
I WASH GONNA WISH YOU TWO ALL THE HABBINESS IN THE WORLD... BUT I DUNNO WHAD I'M EVEN SHAYING NOW!
YOR, CALM DOWN!
THAT WOMAN IS NOTHING MORE THAN A WORK ASSO-CIATE!
OUR RELA-TIONSHIP IS STRICTLY PROFES-SIONAL!
(Nightfall couldn't control herself...but I can't say that.)
MUST BE ROUGH BEING SUCH A LADIES' MAN.
Gloom...
ISH MY FAULT FOR BEING SHUCH A BAD WIFE.
AND I'M NOT PRETTY LIKE THIONA ISH...
ARE YOU EVEN LISTENING TO ME?
WAIT. DOES THIS MEAN...
BUT YOU USHED TO THINK I WASH PRETTY...
OR WASH THAT JUSHT A LIE?
I THOUGHT YOR HAD LOST FAITH IN HER ABILITIES AND WAS FEARING A POTENTIAL END TO OUR ARRANGE-MENT...
YOU'RE BORED WITH ME NOW? ISH THAT IT?
COULD IT BE THAT YOR HAS...
BUT SHE'S... JEALOUS ...?
Hic hic... Urp...

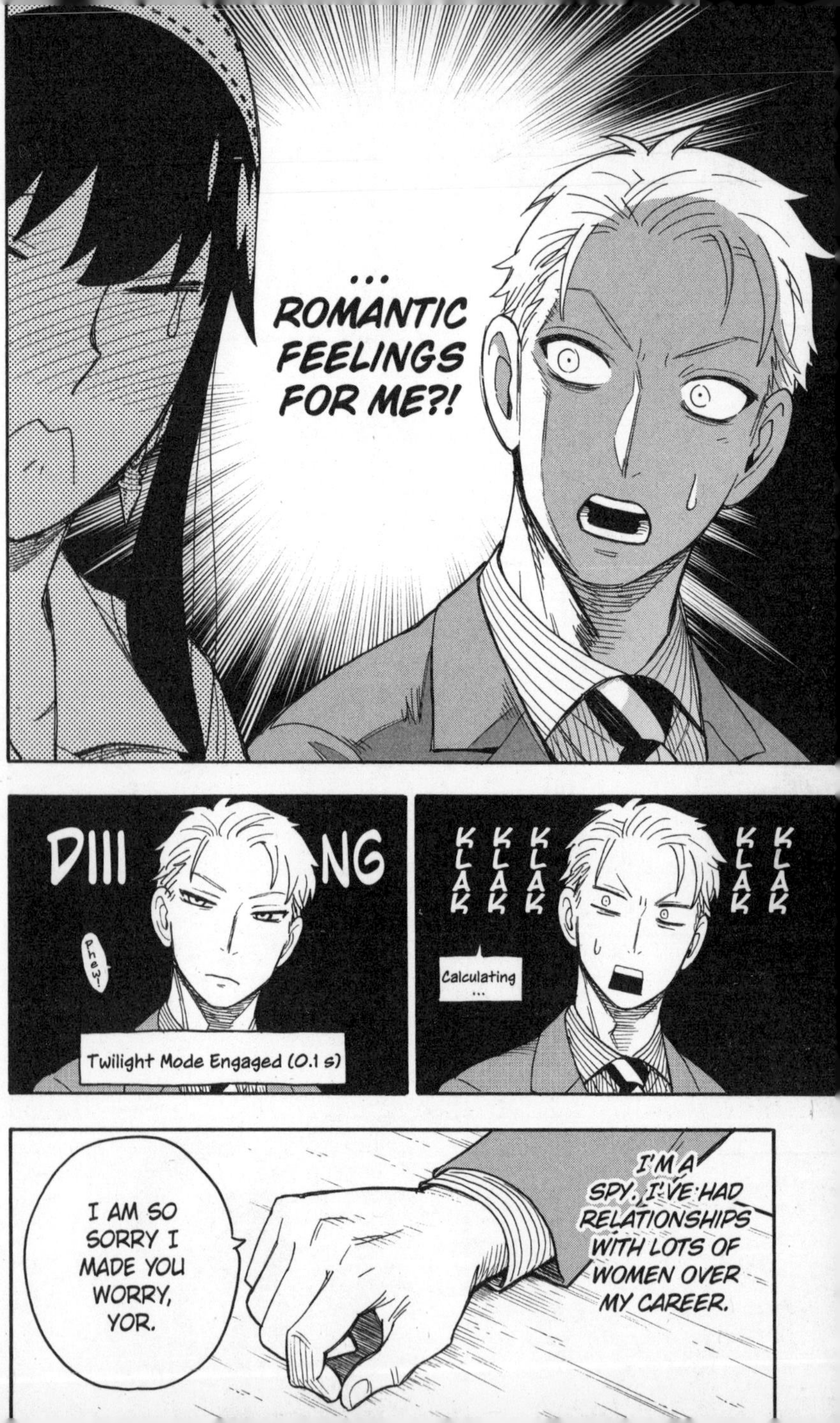
...ROMANTIC FEELINGS FOR ME?!
KLAK KLAK KLAK KLAK KLAK
Calculating...
DIIING
Phew!
Twilight Mode Engaged (0.1 s)
I'M A SPY. I'VE HAD RELATIONSHIPS WITH LOTS OF WOMEN OVER MY CAREER.
I AM SO SORRY I MADE YOU WORRY, YOR.

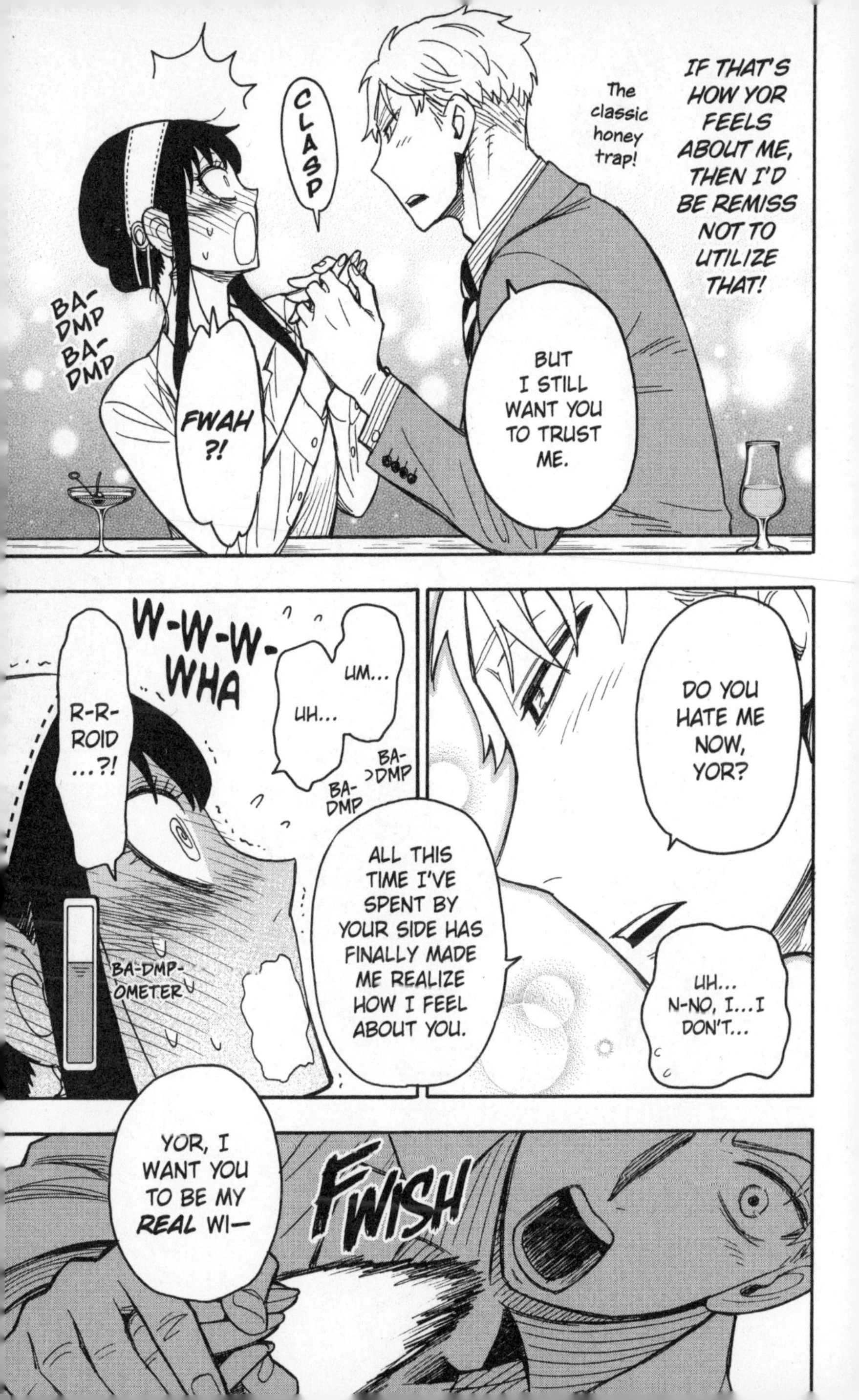
IF THAT'S HOW YOR FEELS ABOUT ME, THEN I'D BE REMISS NOT TO UTILIZE THAT!
The classic honey trap!
CLASP
BUT I STILL WANT YOU TO TRUST ME.
FWAH ?!
BA-DMP BA-DMP
DO YOU HATE ME NOW, YOR?
UH... N-NO, I...I DON'T...
ALL THIS TIME I'VE SPENT BY YOUR SIDE HAS FINALLY MADE ME REALIZE HOW I FEEL ABOUT YOU.
UM... UH...
BA-DMP
BA-DMP
W-W-W-WHA
R-R-ROID ...?!
BA-DMP-OMETER
YOR, I WANT YOU TO BE MY *REAL* WI—
FWISH

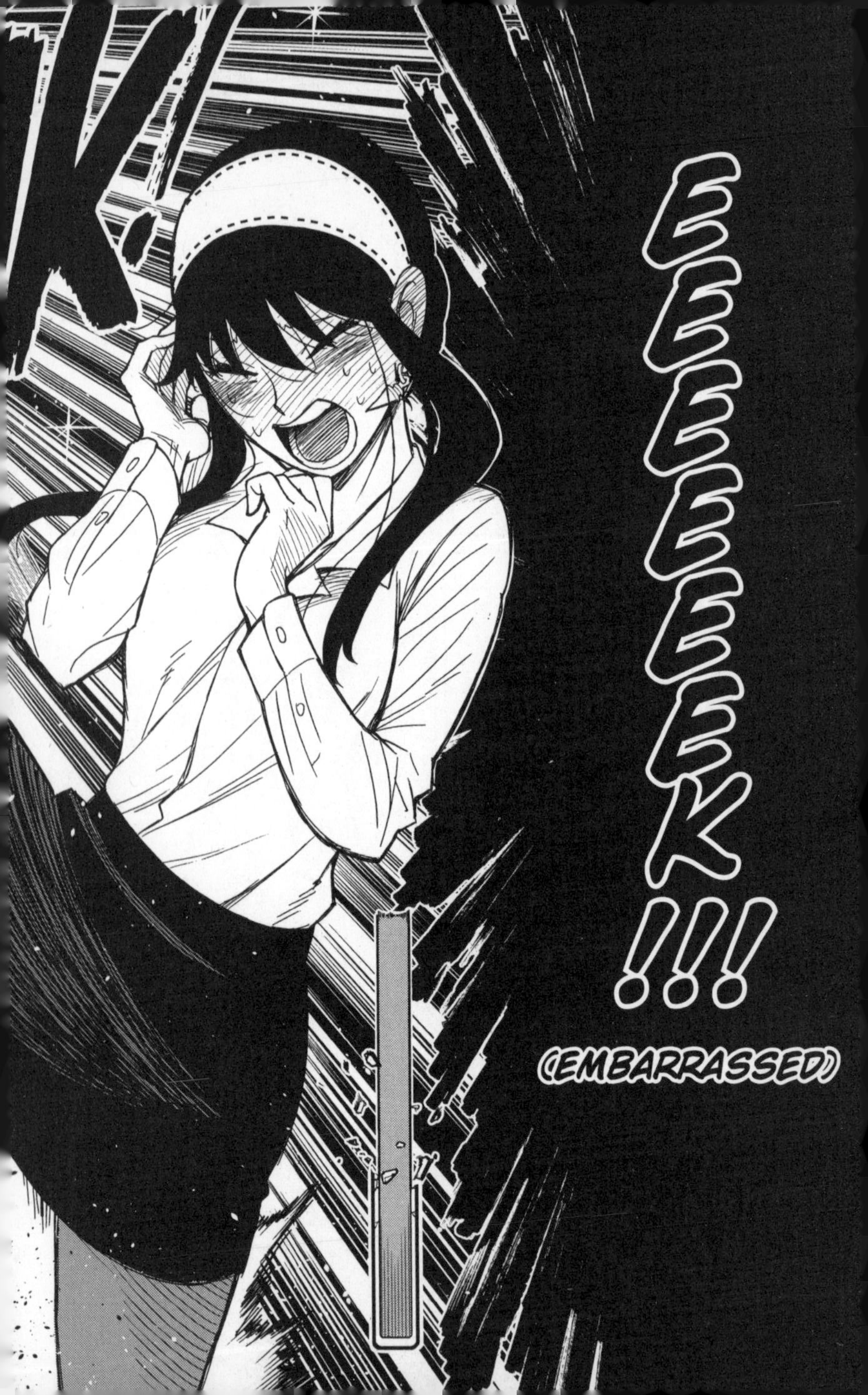
EEEEEEEK!!!
(EMBARRASSED)

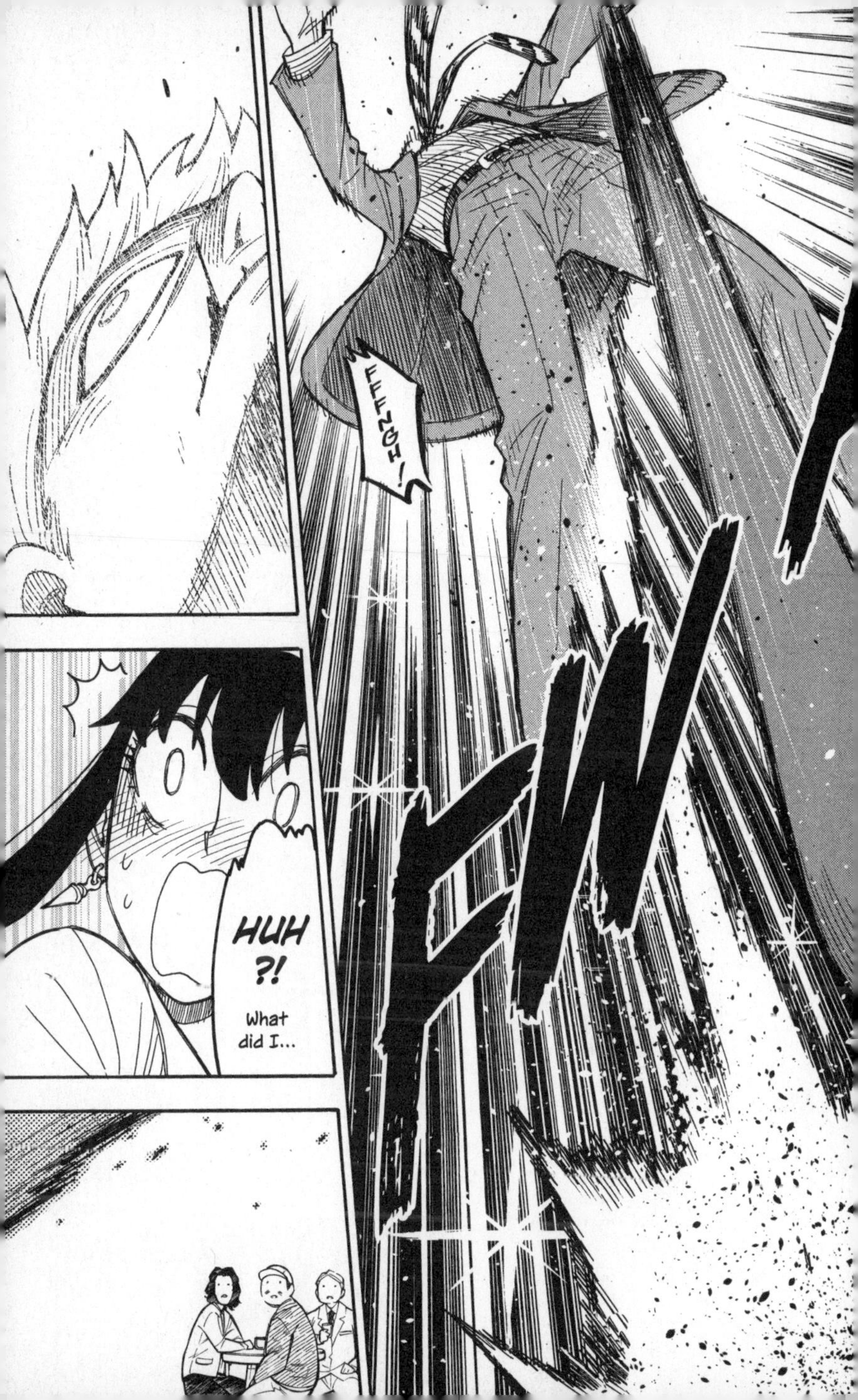
FFFNGH!
HUH ?!
What did I...

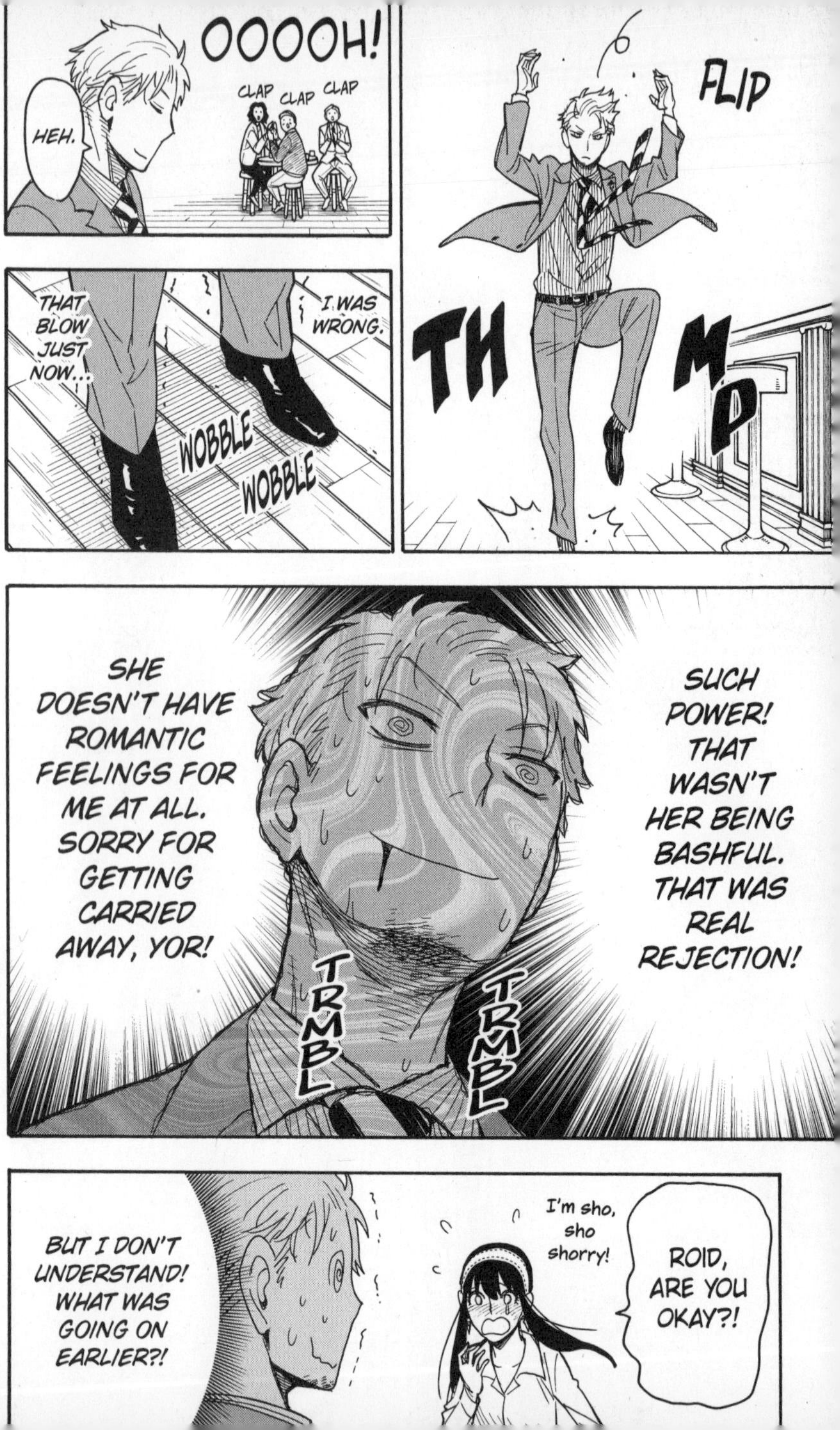
FLIP
OOOOH!
CLAP CLAP CLAP
HEH.
THMP
I WAS WRONG.
THAT BLOW JUST NOW...
WOBBLE WOBBLE
SUCH POWER! THAT WASN'T HER BEING BASHFUL. THAT WAS REAL REJECTION!
SHE DOESN'T HAVE ROMANTIC FEELINGS FOR ME AT ALL. SORRY FOR GETTING CARRIED AWAY, YOR!
TRMBL TRMBL
ROID, ARE YOU OKAY?!
I'm sho, sho shorry!
BUT I DON'T UNDERSTAND! WHAT WAS GOING ON EARLIER?!

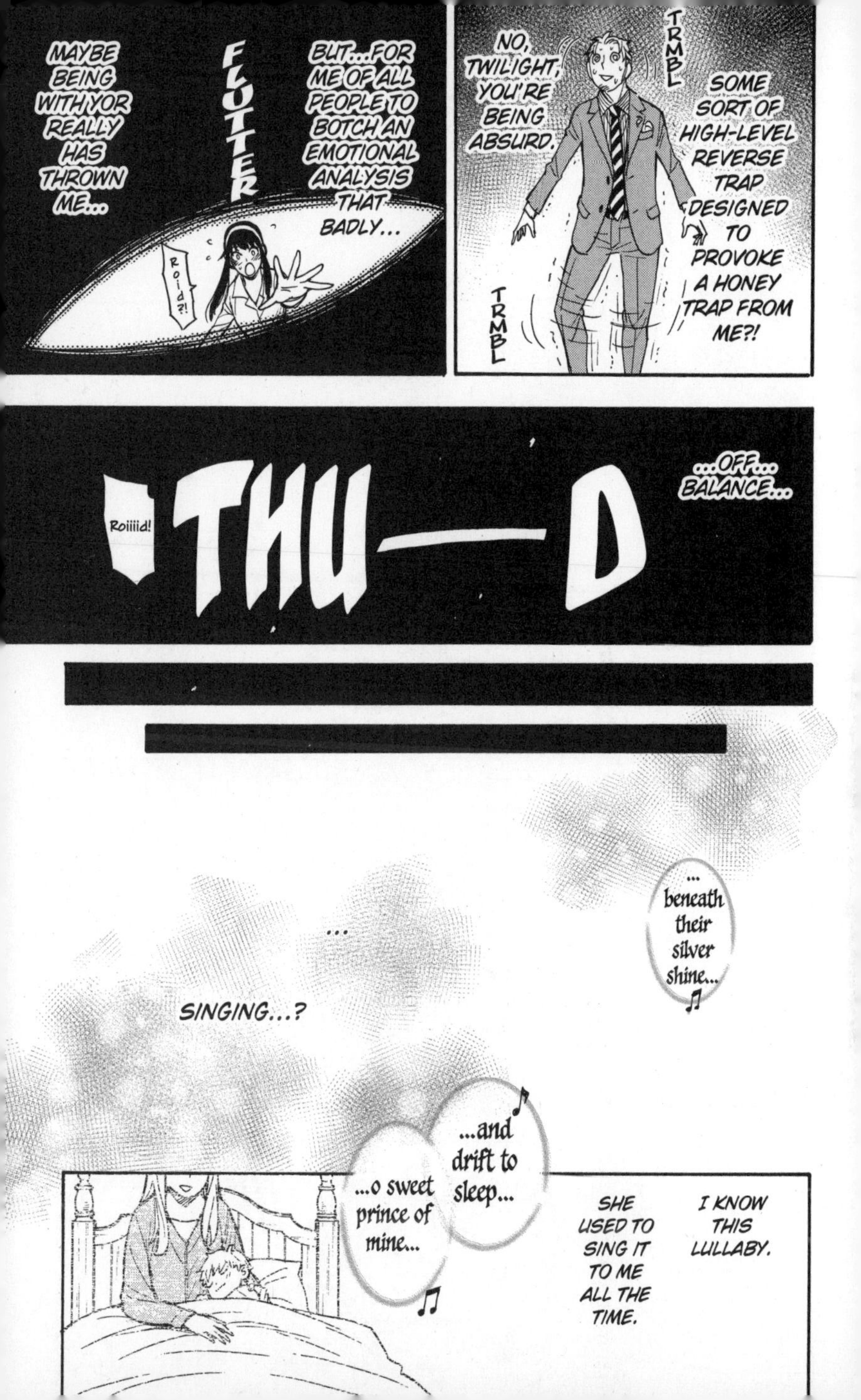
TRMBL
SOME SORT OF HIGH-LEVEL REVERSE TRAP DESIGNED TO PROVOKE A HONEY TRAP FROM ME?!
NO, TWILIGHT, YOU'RE BEING ABSURD.
TRMBL
BUT...FOR ME OF ALL PEOPLE TO BOTCH AN EMOTIONAL ANALYSIS THAT BADLY...
FLUTTER
MAYBE BEING WITH YOR REALLY HAS THROWN ME...
Roid?!
...OFF... BALANCE...
THU—D
Roiiiid!
...beneath their silver shine...♫
...
SINGING...?
I KNOW THIS LULLABY.
SHE USED TO SING IT TO ME ALL THE TIME.
...and drift to sleep...
...o sweet prince of mine...

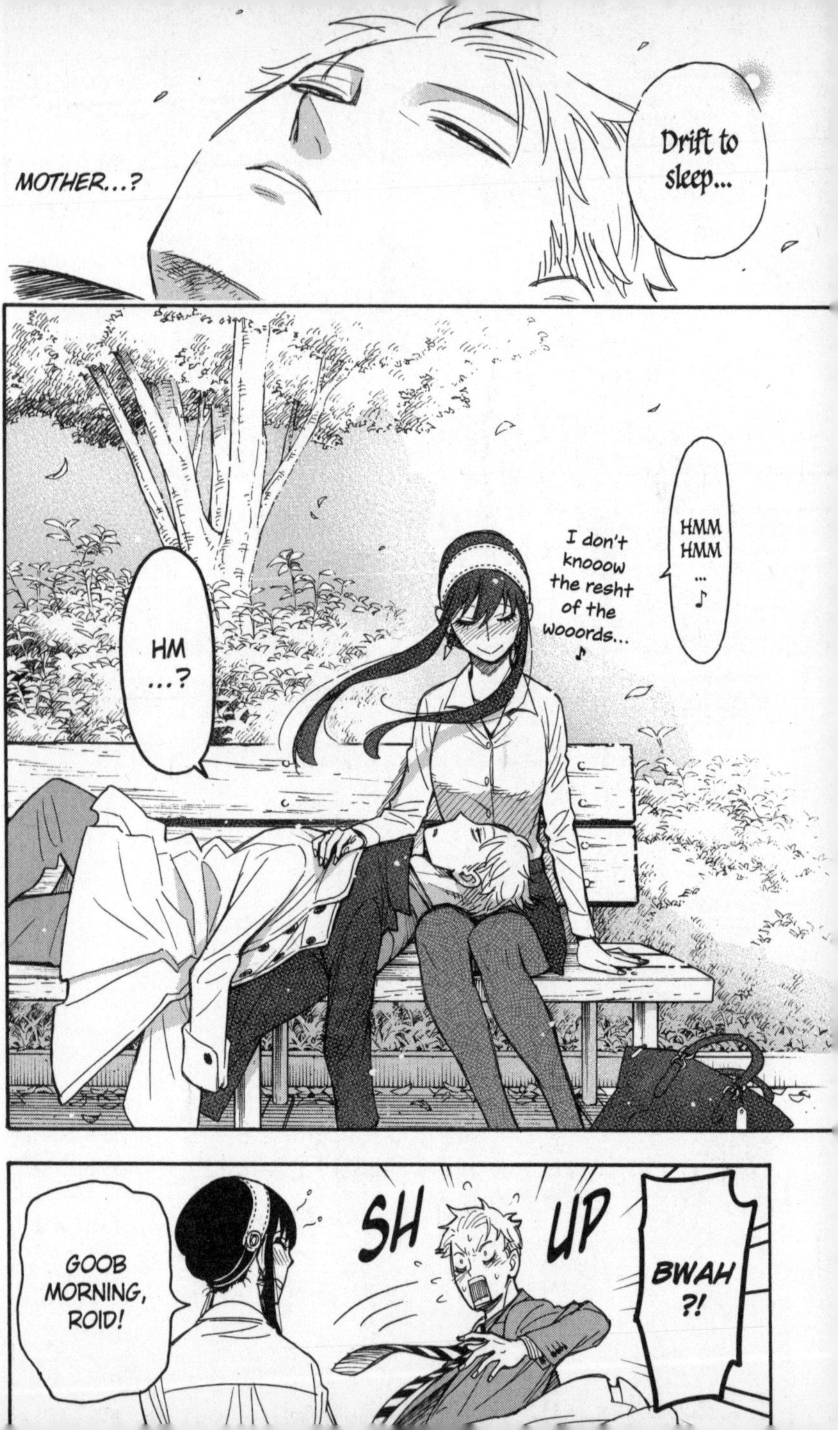
Drift to sleep...
MOTHER...?
HMM HMM ...♪
I don't knooow the resht of the wooords...♪
HM ...?
BWAH ?!
SH UP
GOOB MORNING, ROID!

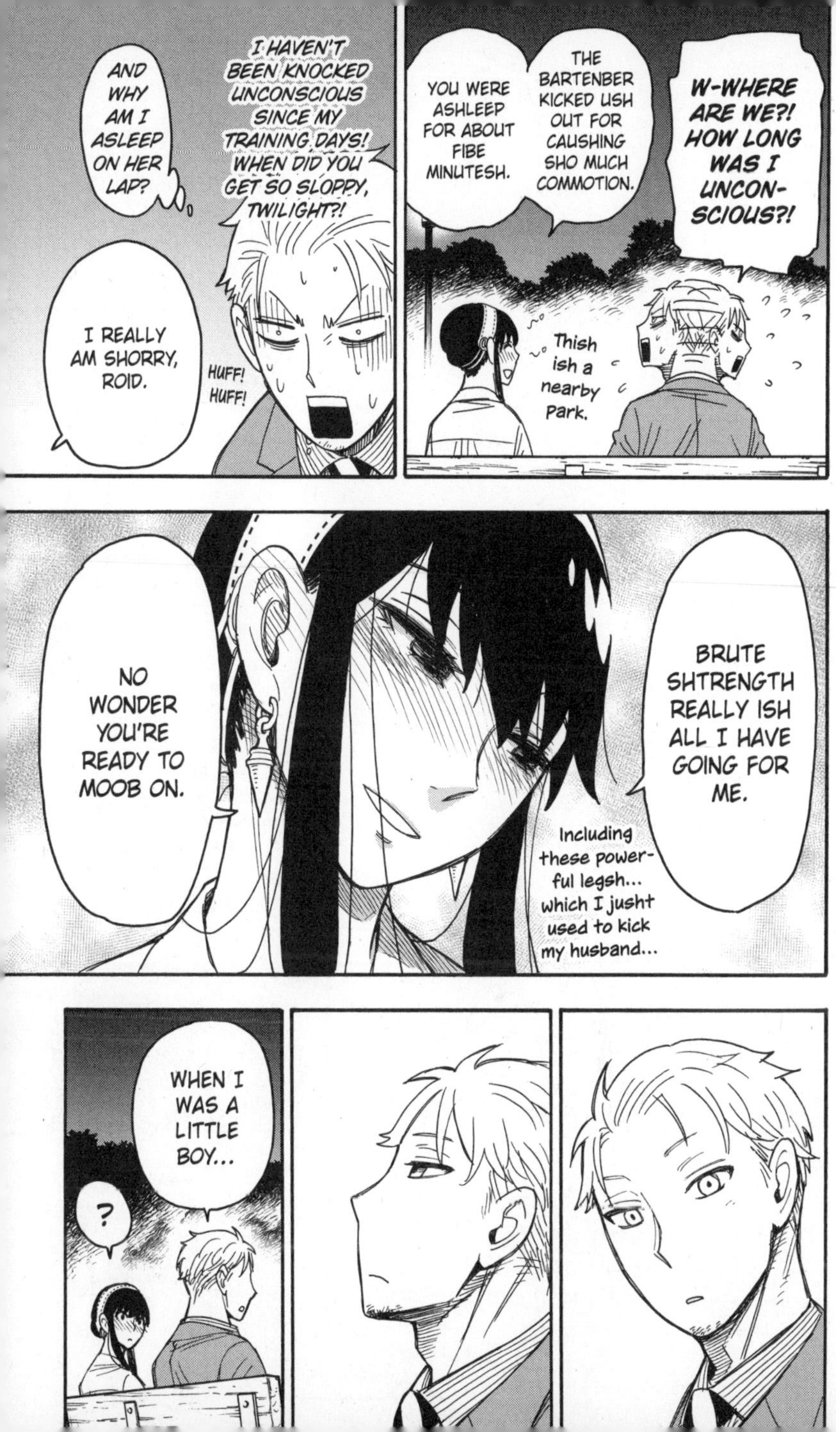
W-WHERE ARE WE?! HOW LONG WAS I UNCONSCIOUS?!
THE BARTENBER KICKED USH OUT FOR CAUSHING SHO MUCH COMMOTION.
YOU WERE ASHLEEP FOR ABOUT FIBE MINUTESH.
Thish ish a nearby Park.
I HAVEN'T BEEN KNOCKED UNCONSCIOUS SINCE MY TRAINING DAYS! WHEN DID YOU GET SO SLOPPY, TWILIGHT?!
AND WHY AM I ASLEEP ON HER LAP?
HUFF! HUFF!
I REALLY AM SHORRY, ROID.
BRUTE SHTRENGTH REALLY ISH ALL I HAVE GOING FOR ME.
Including these powerful legsh... which I jusht used to kick my husband...
NO WONDER YOU'RE READY TO MOOB ON.
WHEN I WAS A LITTLE BOY...
?

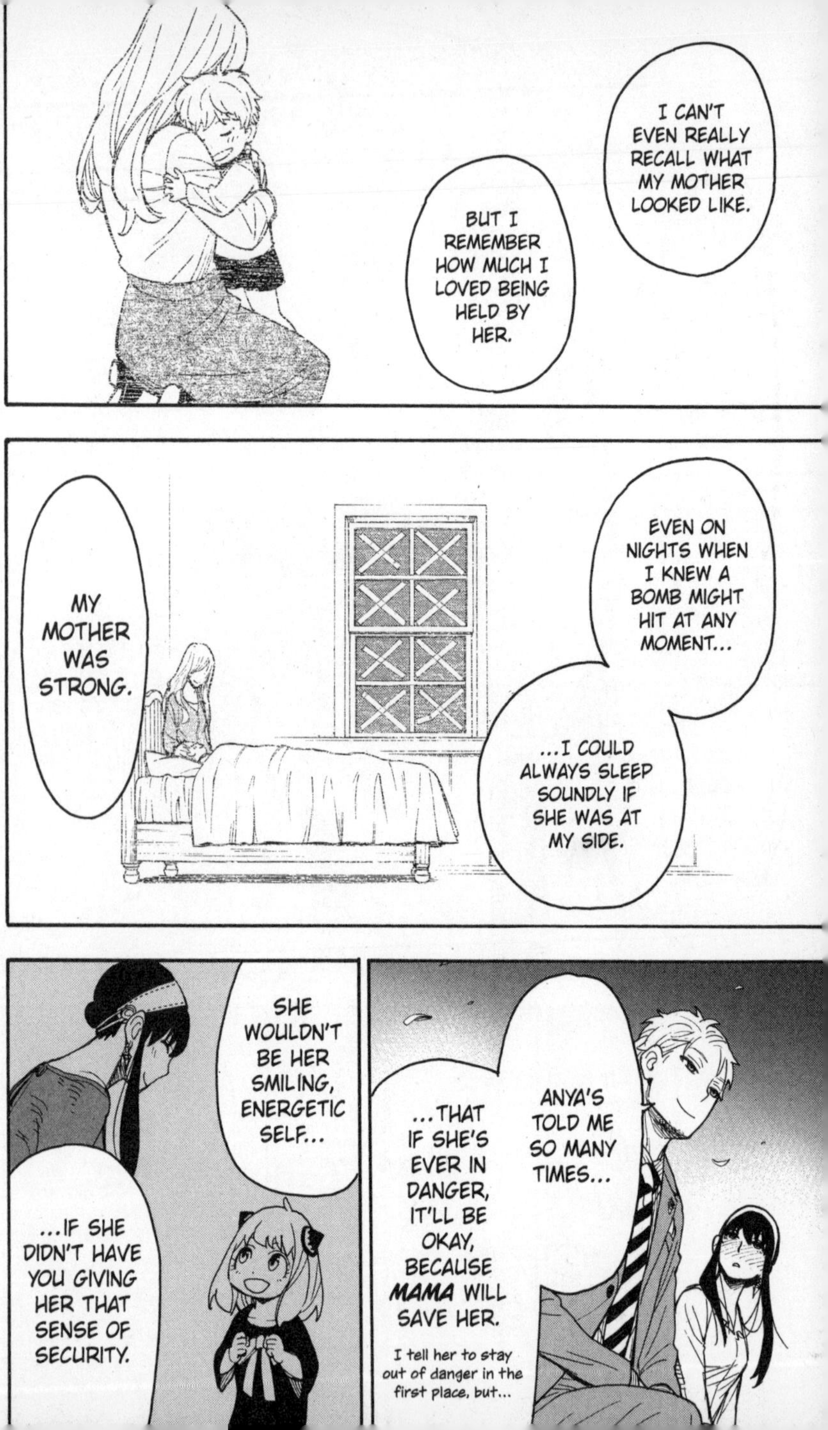
I CAN'T EVEN REALLY RECALL WHAT MY MOTHER LOOKED LIKE.
BUT I REMEMBER HOW MUCH I LOVED BEING HELD BY HER.
EVEN ON NIGHTS WHEN I KNEW A BOMB MIGHT HIT AT ANY MOMENT...
...I COULD ALWAYS SLEEP SOUNDLY IF SHE WAS AT MY SIDE.
MY MOTHER WAS STRONG.
ANYA'S TOLD ME SO MANY TIMES...
...THAT IF SHE'S EVER IN DANGER, IT'LL BE OKAY, BECAUSE *MAMA* WILL SAVE HER.
I tell her to stay out of danger in the first place, but...
SHE WOULDN'T BE HER SMILING, ENERGETIC SELF...
...IF SHE DIDN'T HAVE YOU GIVING HER THAT SENSE OF SECURITY.

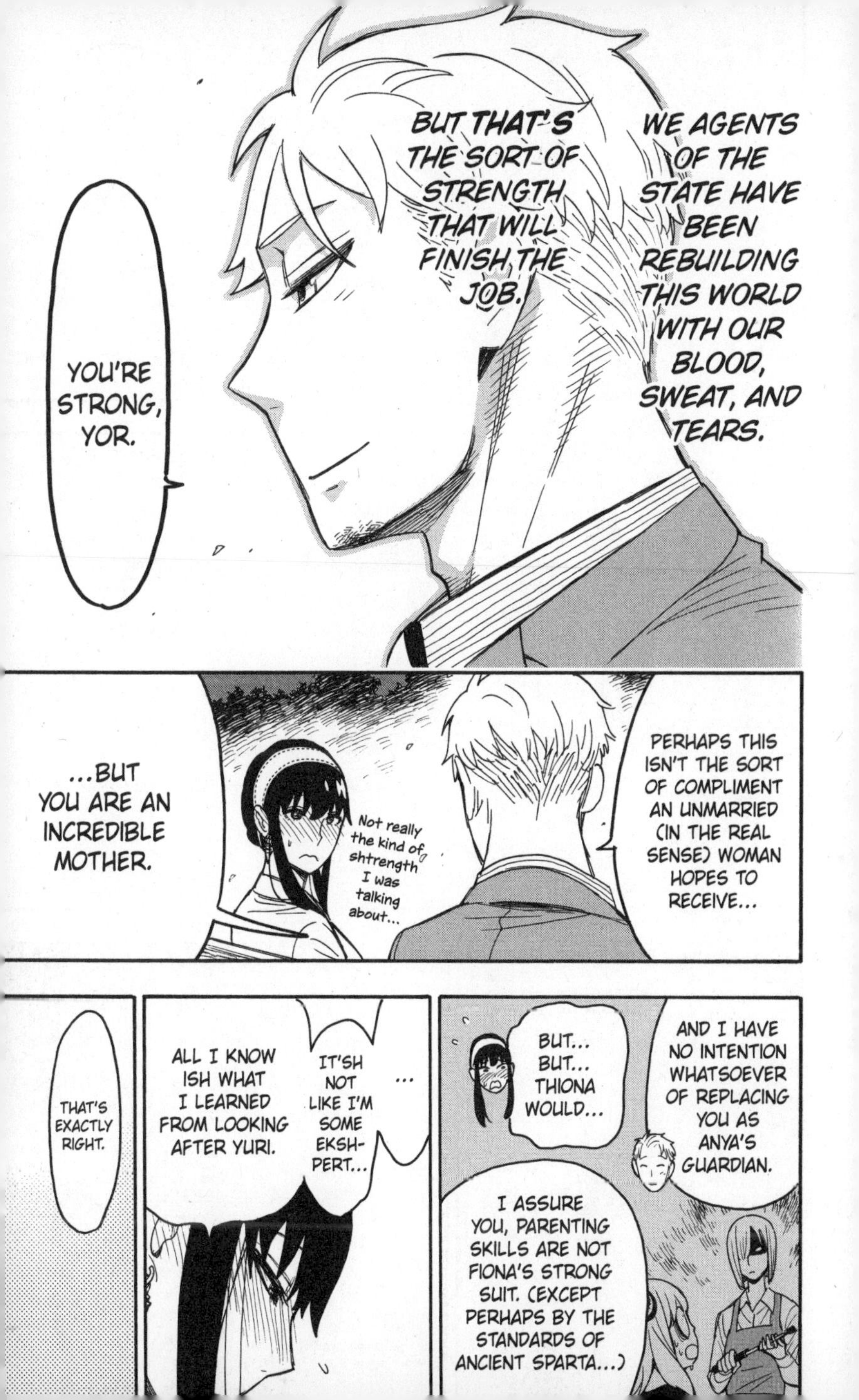
WE AGENTS OF THE STATE HAVE BEEN REBUILDING THIS WORLD WITH OUR BLOOD, SWEAT, AND TEARS.
BUT THAT'S THE SORT OF STRENGTH THAT WILL FINISH THE JOB.
YOU'RE STRONG, YOR.
PERHAPS THIS ISN'T THE SORT OF COMPLIMENT AN UNMARRIED (IN THE REAL SENSE) WOMAN HOPES TO RECEIVE...
Not really the kind of shtrength I was talking about...
...BUT YOU ARE AN INCREDIBLE MOTHER.
AND I HAVE NO INTENTION WHATSOEVER OF REPLACING YOU AS ANYA'S GUARDIAN.
BUT... BUT... THIONA WOULD...
I ASSURE YOU, PARENTING SKILLS ARE NOT FIONA'S STRONG SUIT. (EXCEPT PERHAPS BY THE STANDARDS OF ANCIENT SPARTA...)
...
IT'SH NOT LIKE I'M SOME EKSH-PERT...
ALL I KNOW ISH WHAT I LEARNED FROM LOOKING AFTER YURI.
THAT'S EXACTLY RIGHT.

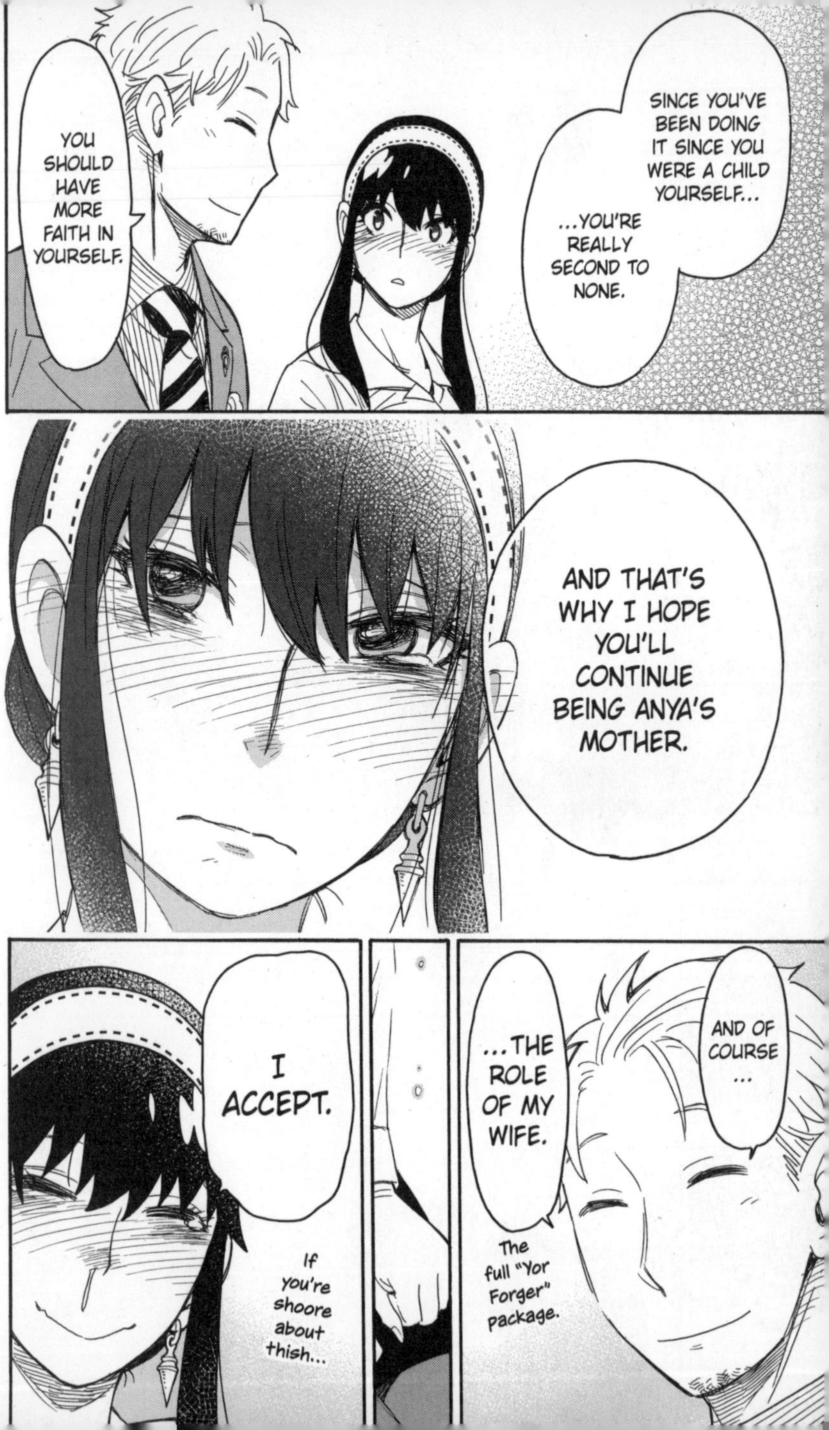
SINCE YOU'VE BEEN DOING IT SINCE YOU WERE A CHILD YOURSELF...
...YOU'RE REALLY SECOND TO NONE.
YOU SHOULD HAVE MORE FAITH IN YOURSELF.
AND THAT'S WHY I HOPE YOU'LL CONTINUE BEING ANYA'S MOTHER.
AND OF COURSE ...
...THE ROLE OF MY WIFE.
The full "Yor Forger" package.
I ACCEPT.
If you're shoore about thish...

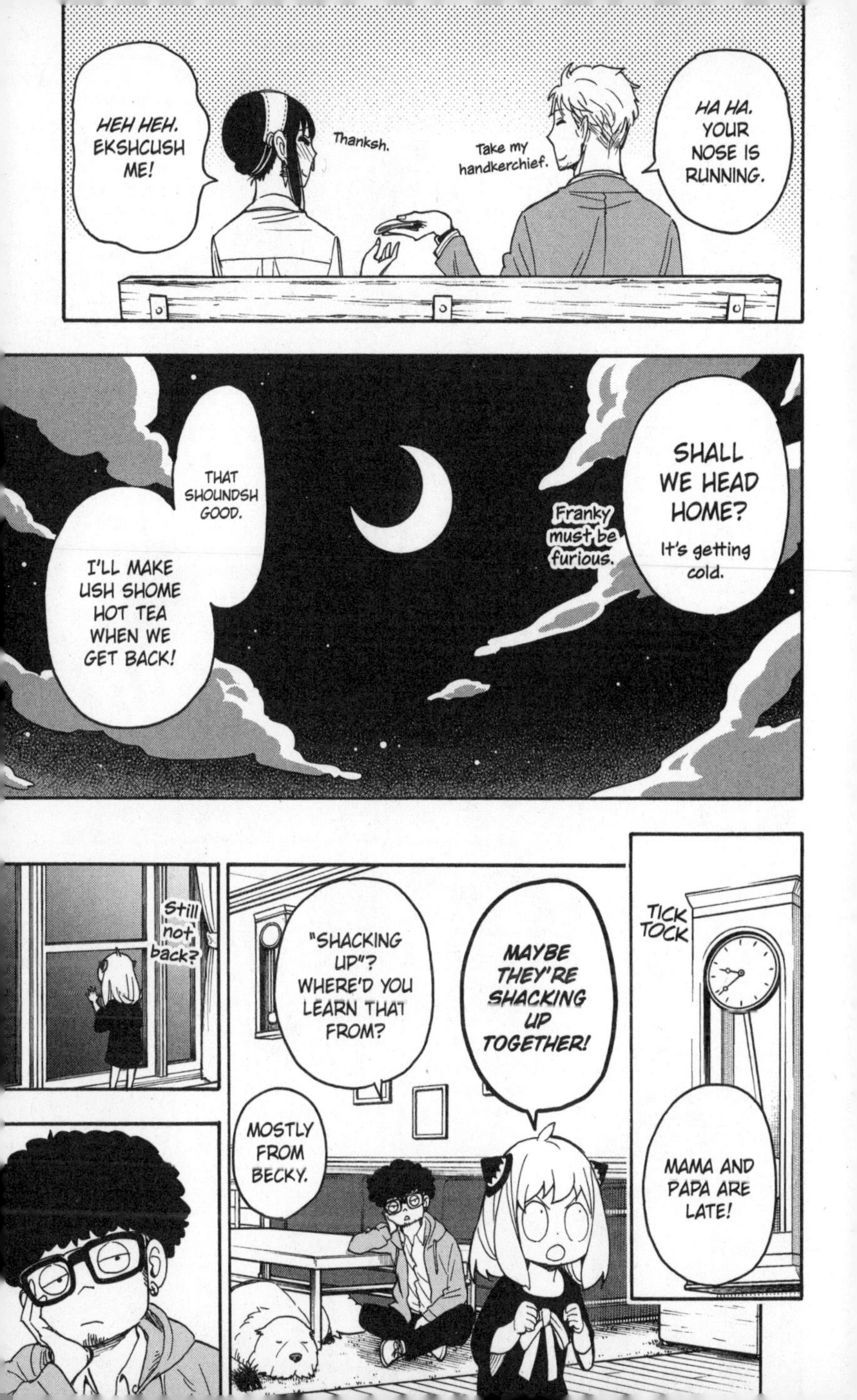
HA HA. YOUR NOSE IS RUNNING.
Take my handkerchief.
Thanksh.
HEH HEH. EKSHCUSH ME!
SHALL WE HEAD HOME?
It's getting cold.
Franky must be furious.
THAT SHOUNDSH GOOD.
I'LL MAKE USH SHOME HOT TEA WHEN WE GET BACK!
TICK TOCK
MAMA AND PAPA ARE LATE!
MAYBE THEY'RE SHACKING UP TOGETHER!
"SHACKING UP"? WHERE'D YOU LEARN THAT FROM?
MOSTLY FROM BECKY.
Still not back?

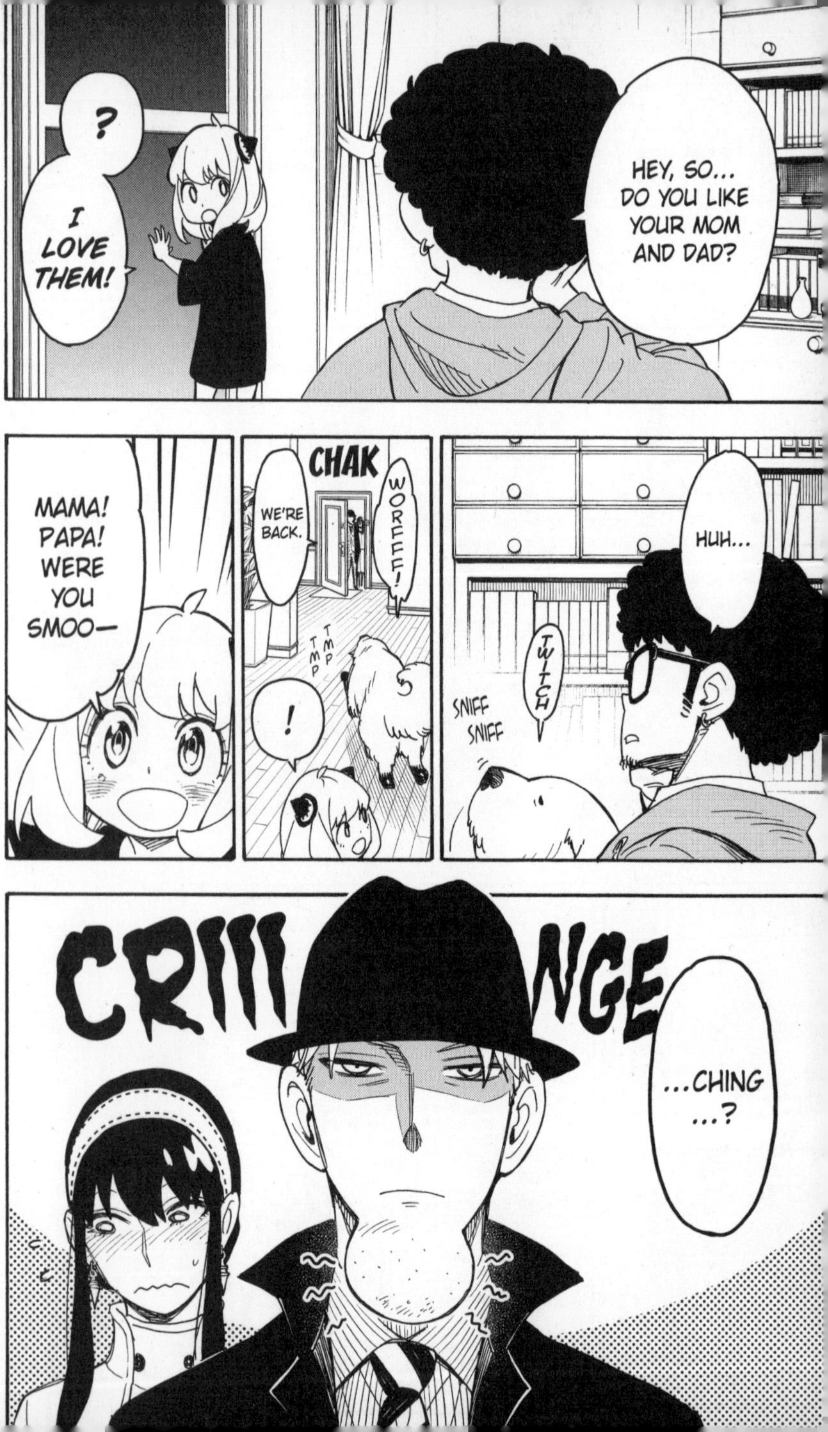
HEY, SO... DO YOU LIKE YOUR MOM AND DAD?
?
I LOVE THEM!
HUH...
TWITCH
SNIFF SNIFF
CHAK
WORFFF!
WE'RE BACK.
TMP TMP
!
MAMA! PAPA! WERE YOU SMOO—
CRIIINGE
...CHING ...?

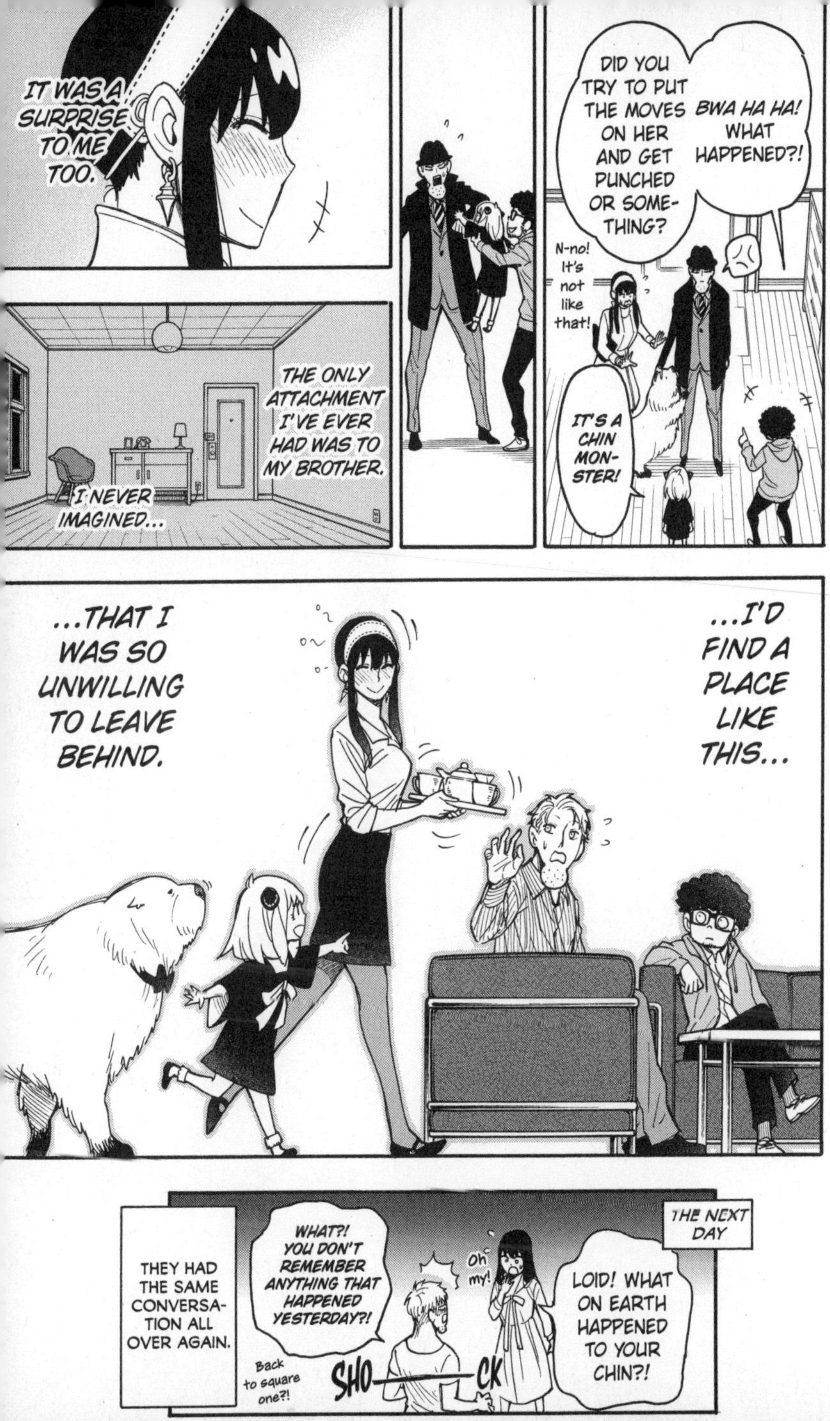
BWA HA HA! WHAT HAPPENED?!
DID YOU TRY TO PUT THE MOVES ON HER AND GET PUNCHED OR SOME-THING?
N-no! It's not like that!
IT'S A CHIN MON-STER!
IT WAS A SURPRISE TO ME TOO.
THE ONLY ATTACHMENT I'VE EVER HAD WAS TO MY BROTHER.
I NEVER IMAGINED...
...I'D FIND A PLACE LIKE THIS...
...THAT I WAS SO UNWILLING TO LEAVE BEHIND.
THE NEXT DAY
LOID! WHAT ON EARTH HAPPENED TO YOUR CHIN?!
Oh my!
WHAT?! YOU DON'T REMEMBER ANYTHING THAT HAPPENED YESTERDAY?!
SHO—CK
Back to square one?!
THEY HAD THE SAME CONVERSATION ALL OVER AGAIN.

SPY×FAMILY

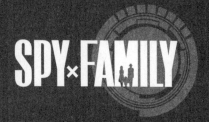

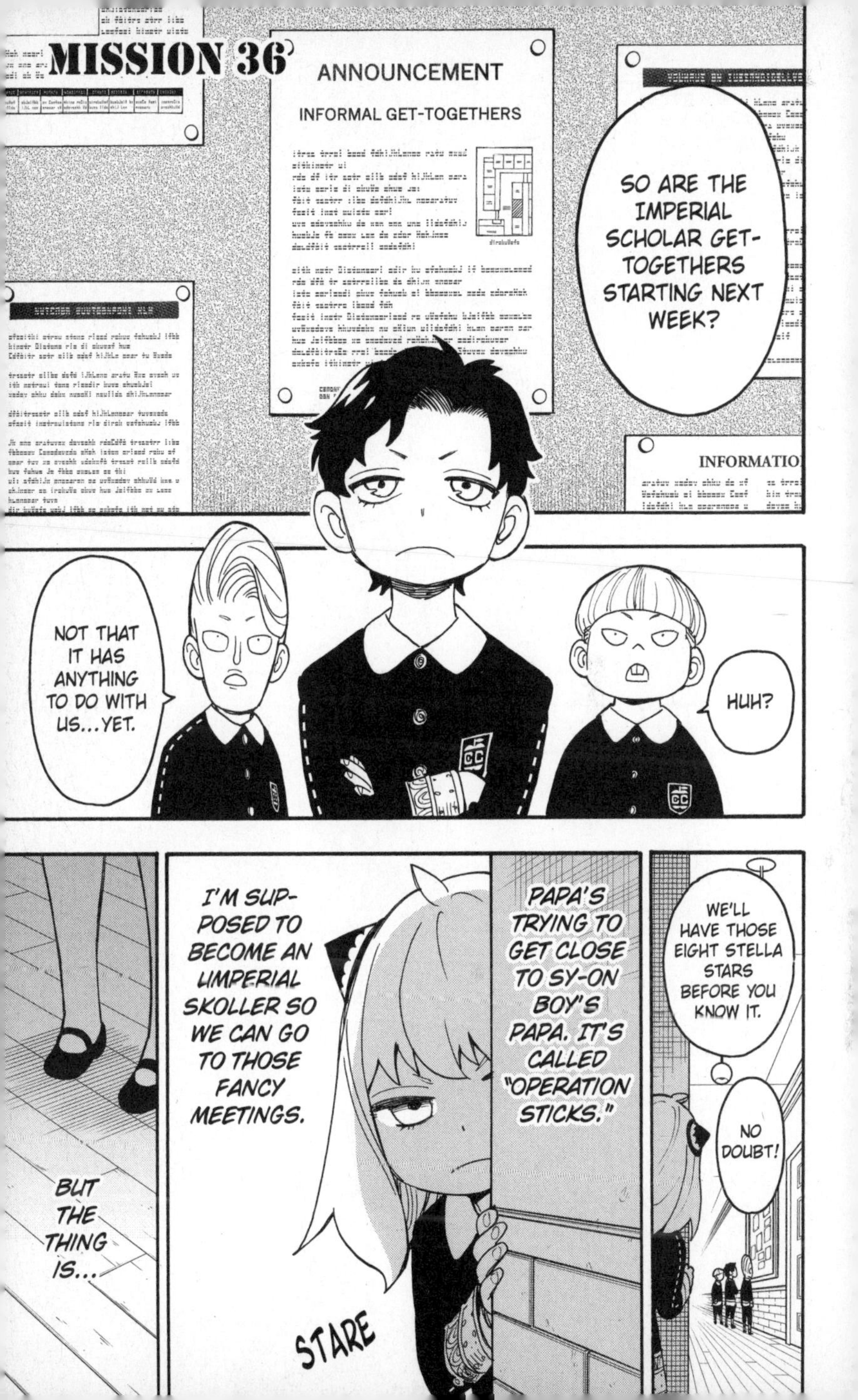
MISSION 36
ANNOUNCEMENT
INFORMAL GET-TOGETHERS
SO ARE THE IMPERIAL SCHOLAR GET-TOGETHERS STARTING NEXT WEEK?
INFORMATION
HUH?
NOT THAT IT HAS ANYTHING TO DO WITH US...YET.
WE'LL HAVE THOSE EIGHT STELLA STARS BEFORE YOU KNOW IT.
NO DOUBT!
PAPA'S TRYING TO GET CLOSE TO SY-ON BOY'S PAPA. IT'S CALLED "OPERATION STICKS."
I'M SUP-POSED TO BECOME AN UMPERIAL SKOLLER SO WE CAN GO TO THOSE FANCY MEETINGS.
STARE
BUT THE THING IS...

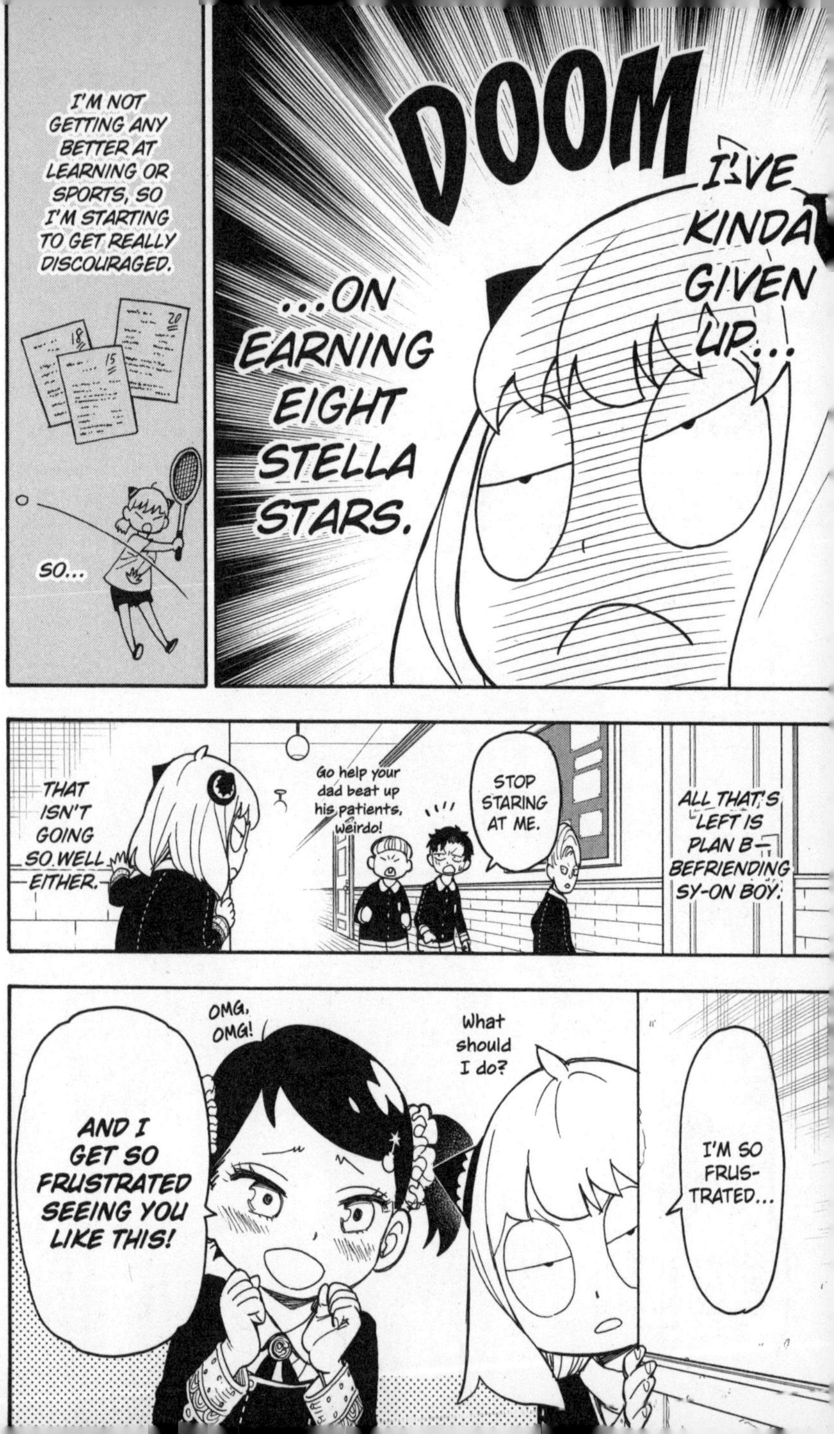
DOOM
I'VE KINDA GIVEN UP...
...ON EARNING EIGHT STELLA STARS.
I'M NOT GETTING ANY BETTER AT LEARNING OR SPORTS, SO I'M STARTING TO GET REALLY DISCOURAGED.
SO...
ALL THAT'S LEFT IS PLAN B—BEFRIENDING SY-ON BOY.
STOP STARING AT ME.
Go help your dad beat up his patients, weirdo!
THAT ISN'T GOING SO WELL EITHER.
I'M SO FRUS-TRATED...
What should I do?
OMG, OMG!
AND I GET SO FRUSTRATED SEEING YOU LIKE THIS!

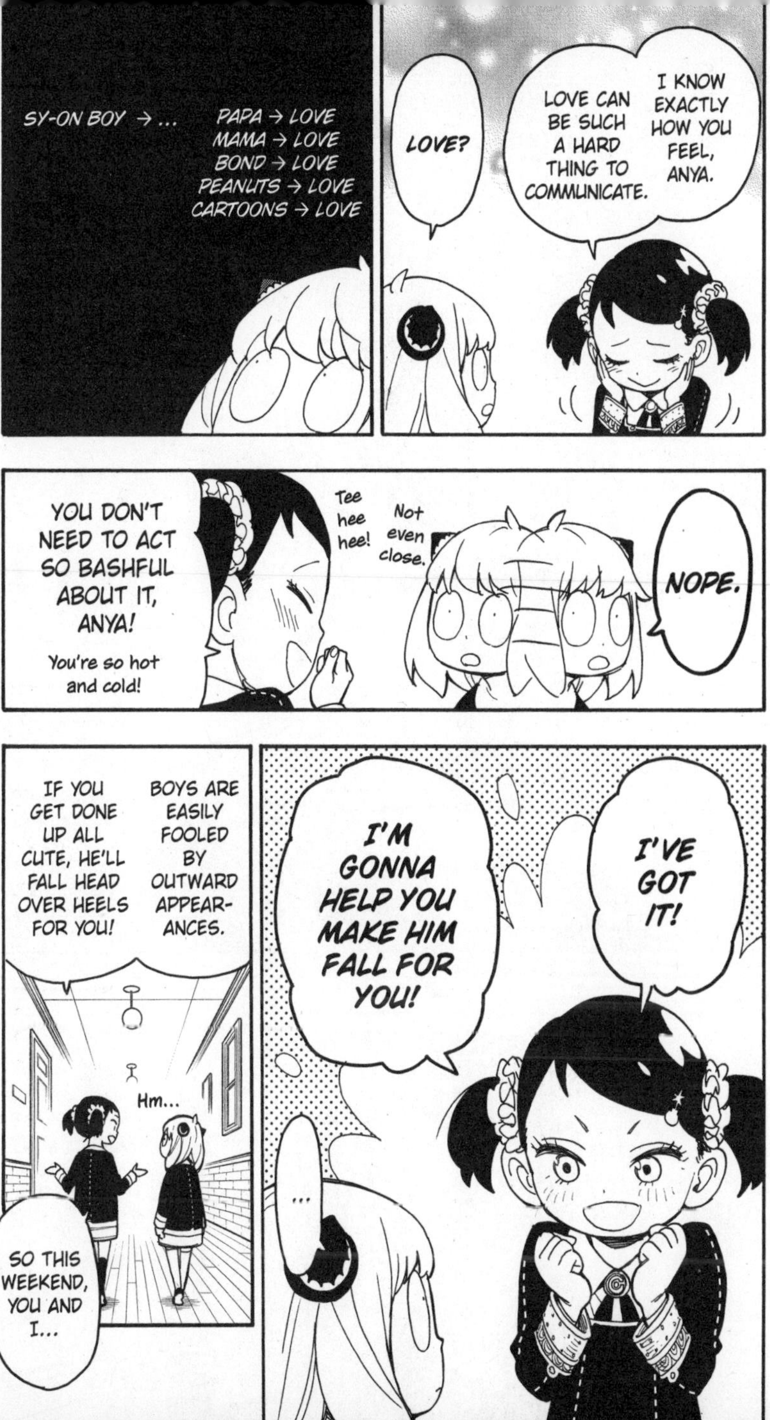
I KNOW EXACTLY HOW YOU FEEL, ANYA.
LOVE CAN BE SUCH A HARD THING TO COMMUNICATE.
LOVE?
PAPA → LOVE
MAMA → LOVE
BOND → LOVE
PEANUTS → LOVE
CARTOONS → LOVE
SY-ON BOY → ...
NOPE.
Not even close.
Tee hee hee!
YOU DON'T NEED TO ACT SO BASHFUL ABOUT IT, ANYA!
You're so hot and cold!
I'VE GOT IT!
I'M GONNA HELP YOU MAKE HIM FALL FOR YOU!
...
BOYS ARE EASILY FOOLED BY OUTWARD APPEAR-ANCES.
IF YOU GET DONE UP ALL CUTE, HE'LL FALL HEAD OVER HEELS FOR YOU!
Hm...
SO THIS WEEKEND, YOU AND I...

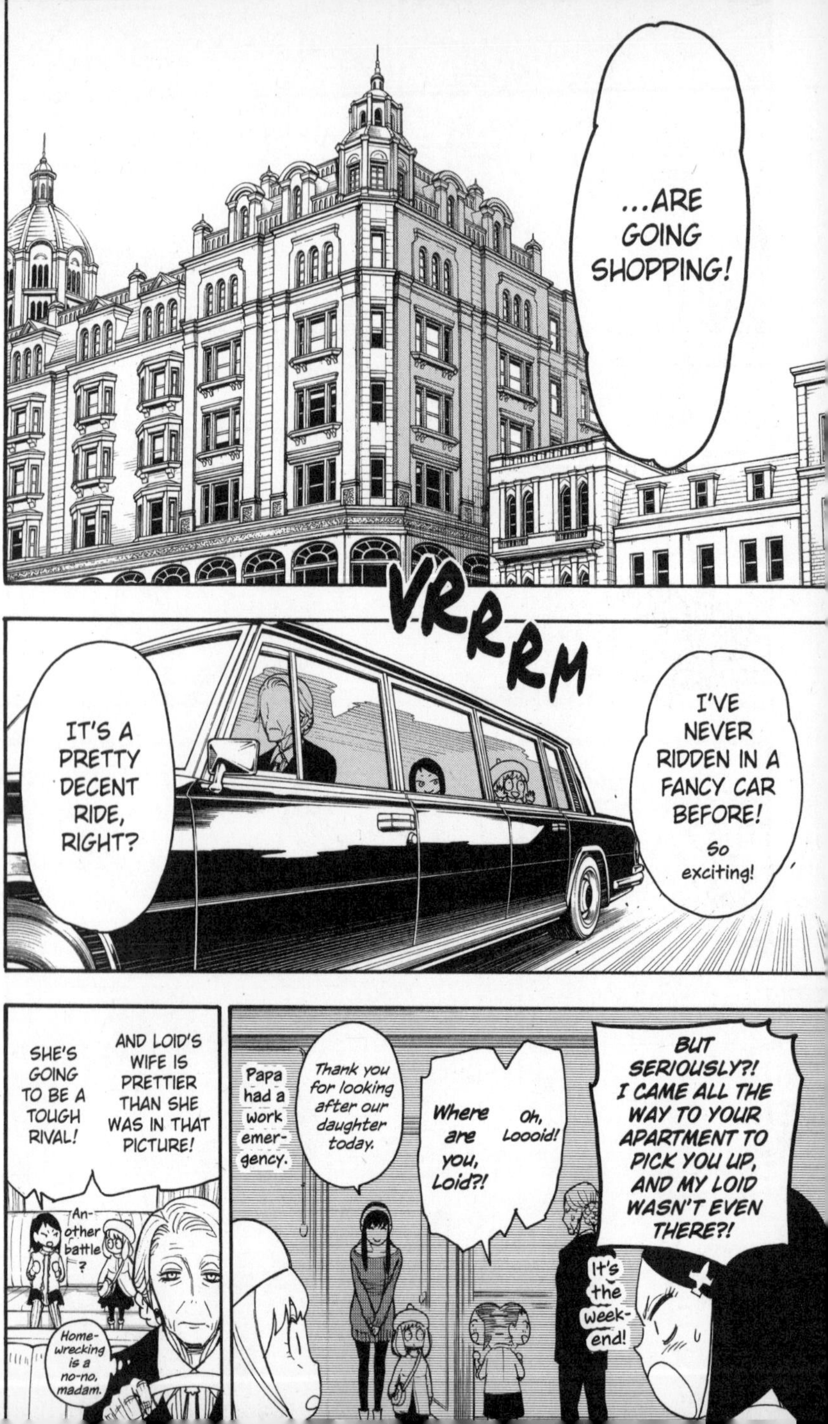
...ARE GOING SHOPPING!
I'VE NEVER RIDDEN IN A FANCY CAR BEFORE!
So exciting!
VRRRM
IT'S A PRETTY DECENT RIDE, RIGHT?
BUT SERIOUSLY?! I CAME ALL THE WAY TO YOUR APARTMENT TO PICK YOU UP, AND MY LOID WASN'T EVEN THERE?!
Oh, Loooid!
Where are you, Loid?!
Thank you for looking after our daughter today.
Papa had a work emer-gency.
It's the week-end!
AND LOID'S WIFE IS PRETTIER THAN SHE WAS IN THAT PICTURE!
SHE'S GOING TO BE A TOUGH RIVAL!
An-other battle?
Home-wrecking is a no-no, madam.

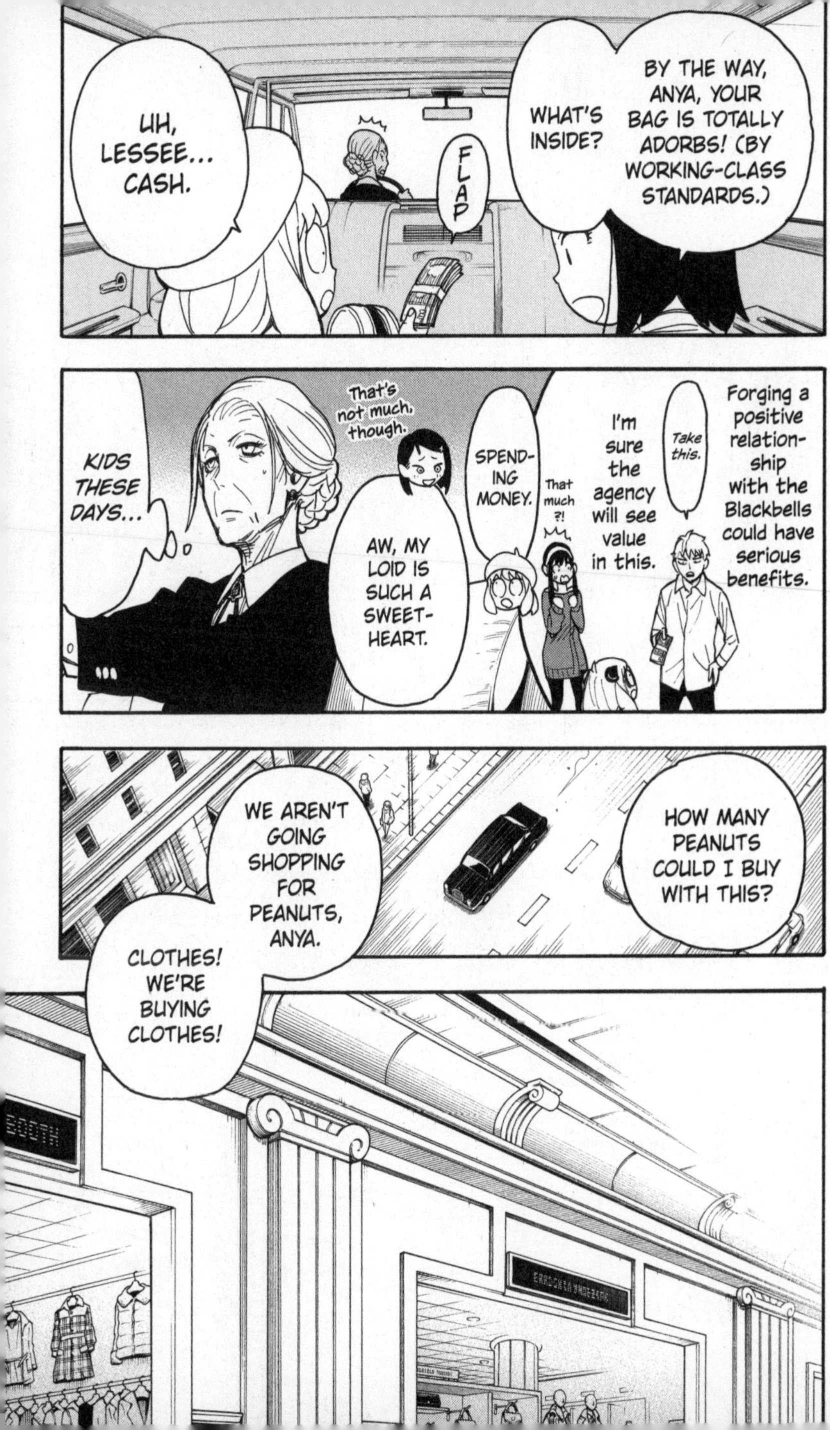
BY THE WAY, ANYA, YOUR BAG IS TOTALLY ADORBS! (BY WORKING-CLASS STANDARDS.)
WHAT'S INSIDE?
FLAP
UH, LESSEE... CASH.
Forging a positive relation-ship with the Blackbells could have serious benefits.
Take this.
I'm sure the agency will see value in this.
That much ?!
SPEND-ING MONEY.
That's not much, though.
AW, MY LOID IS SUCH A SWEET-HEART.
KIDS THESE DAYS...
HOW MANY PEANUTS COULD I BUY WITH THIS?
WE AREN'T GOING SHOPPING FOR PEANUTS, ANYA.
CLOTHES! WE'RE BUYING CLOTHES!

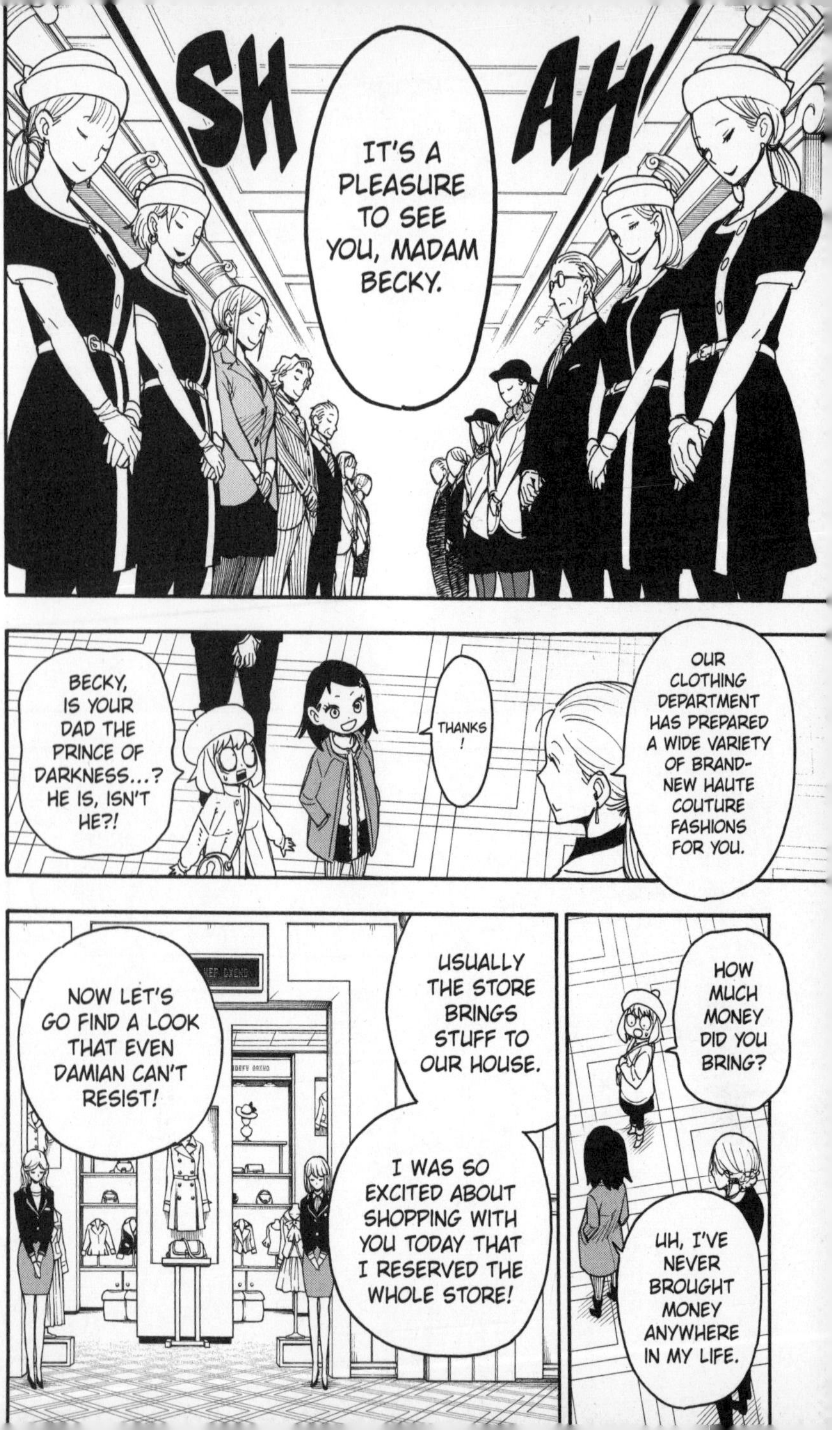
SH
AH
IT'S A PLEASURE TO SEE YOU, MADAM BECKY.
OUR CLOTHING DEPARTMENT HAS PREPARED A WIDE VARIETY OF BRAND-NEW HAUTE COUTURE FASHIONS FOR YOU.
THANKS!
BECKY, IS YOUR DAD THE PRINCE OF DARKNESS...? HE IS, ISN'T HE?!
HOW MUCH MONEY DID YOU BRING?
UH, I'VE NEVER BROUGHT MONEY ANYWHERE IN MY LIFE.
USUALLY THE STORE BRINGS STUFF TO OUR HOUSE.
I WAS SO EXCITED ABOUT SHOPPING WITH YOU TODAY THAT I RESERVED THE WHOLE STORE!
NOW LET'S GO FIND A LOOK THAT EVEN DAMIAN CAN'T RESIST!

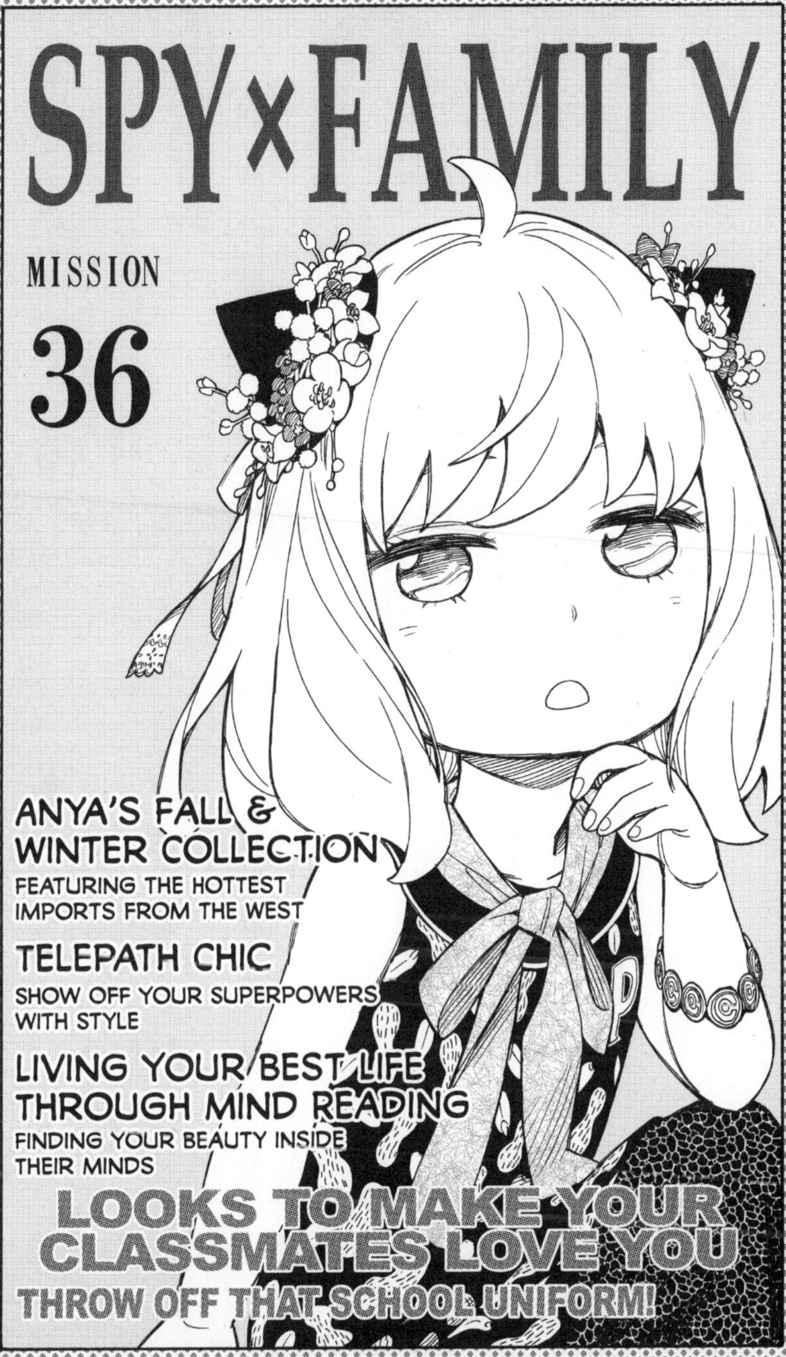
SPY×FAMILY
MISSION 36
ANYA'S FALL & WINTER COLLECTION
FEATURING THE HOTTEST IMPORTS FROM THE WEST
TELEPATH CHIC
SHOW OFF YOUR SUPERPOWERS WITH STYLE
LIVING YOUR BEST LIFE THROUGH MIND READING
FINDING YOUR BEAUTY INSIDE THEIR MINDS
LOOKS TO MAKE YOUR CLASSMATES LOVE YOU
THROW OFF THAT SCHOOL UNIFORM!

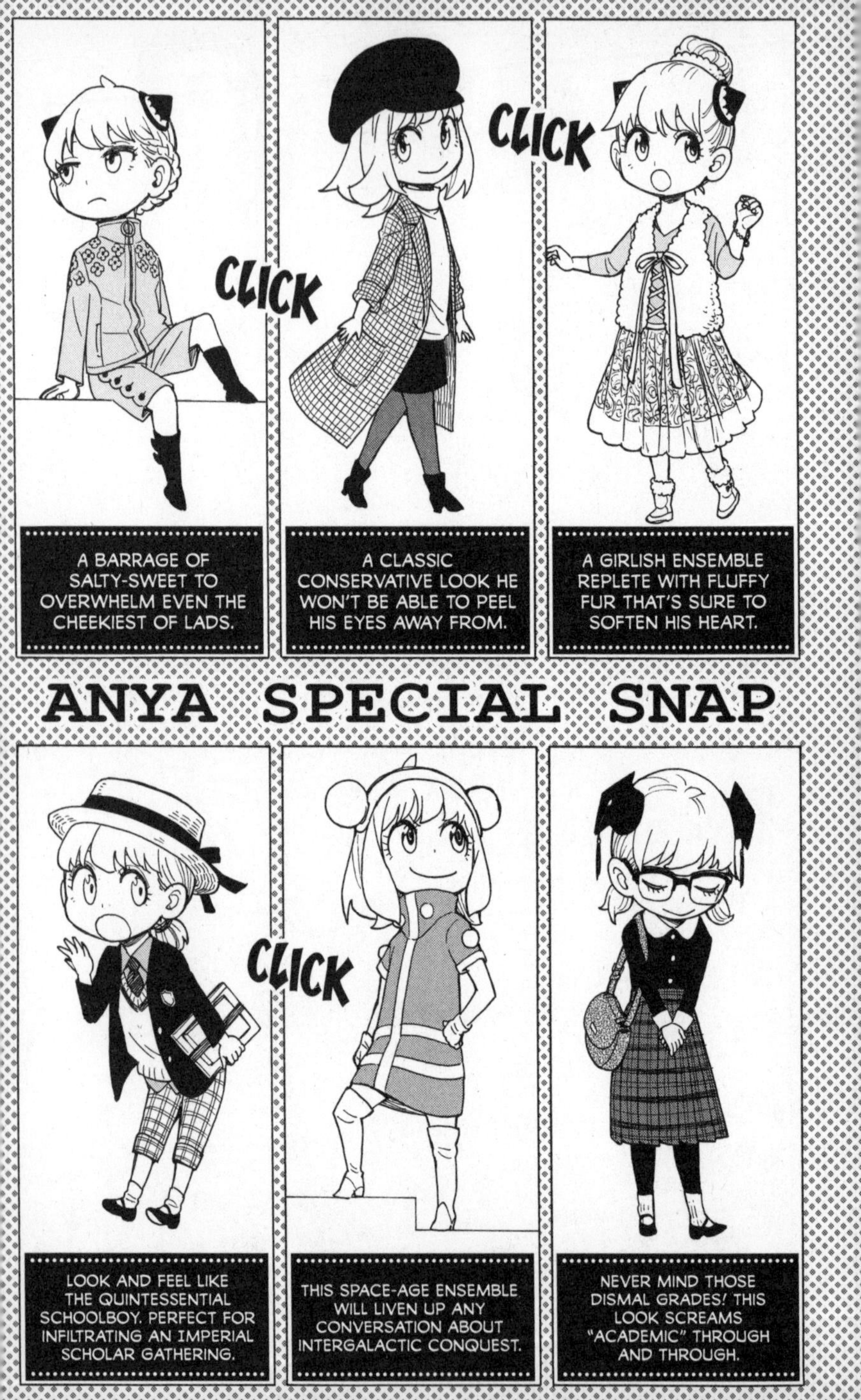
A GIRLISH ENSEMBLE REPLETE WITH FLUFFY FUR THAT'S SURE TO SOFTEN HIS HEART.
CLICK
A CLASSIC CONSERVATIVE LOOK HE WON'T BE ABLE TO PEEL HIS EYES AWAY FROM.
CLICK
A BARRAGE OF SALTY-SWEET TO OVERWHELM EVEN THE CHEEKIEST OF LADS.
ANYA SPECIAL SNAP
NEVER MIND THOSE DISMAL GRADES! THIS LOOK SCREAMS "ACADEMIC" THROUGH AND THROUGH.
THIS SPACE-AGE ENSEMBLE WILL LIVEN UP ANY CONVERSATION ABOUT INTERGALACTIC CONQUEST.
CLICK
LOOK AND FEEL LIKE THE QUINTESSENTIAL SCHOOLBOY. PERFECT FOR INFILTRATING AN IMPERIAL SCHOLAR GATHERING.

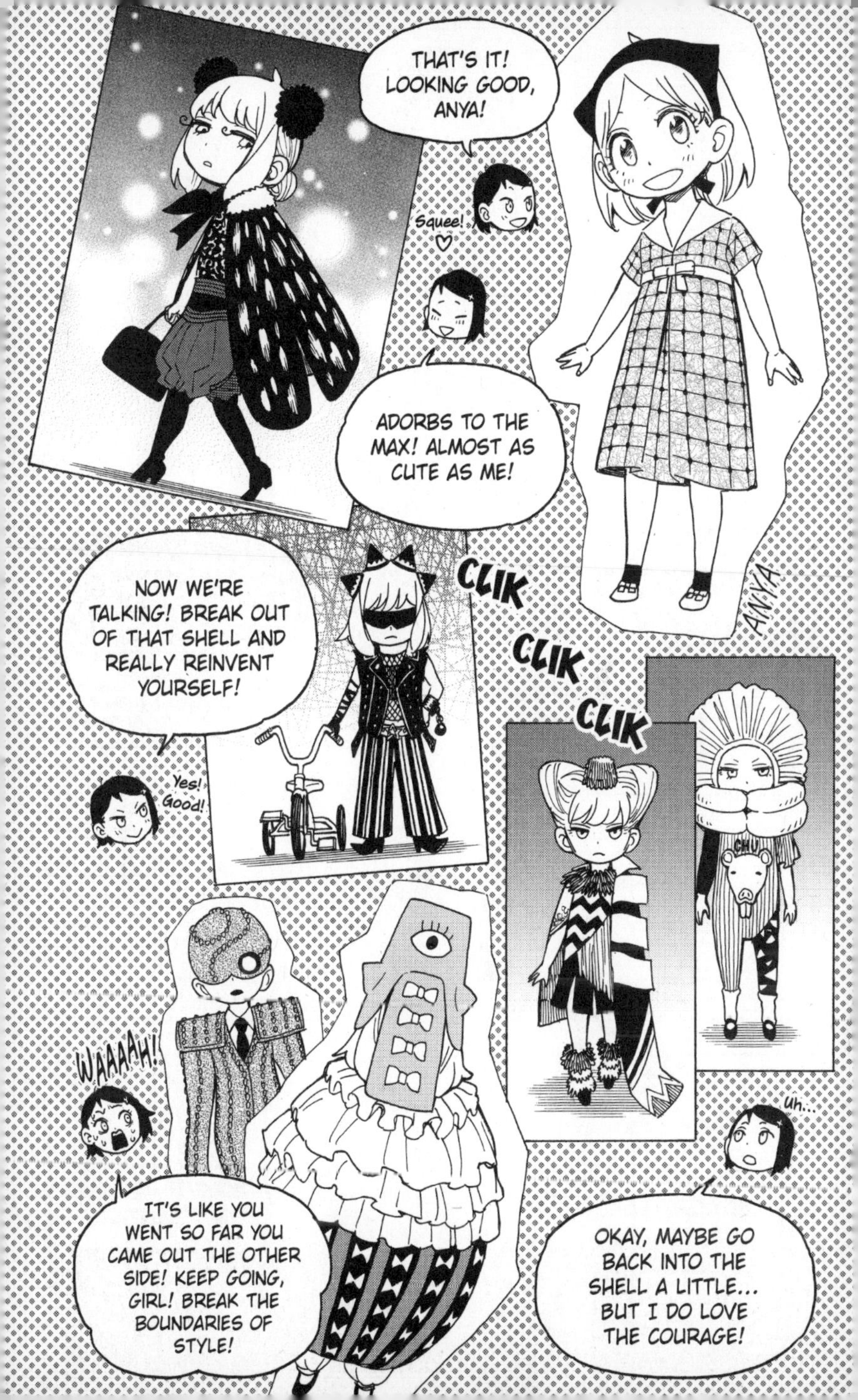
THAT'S IT! LOOKING GOOD, ANYA!
Squee! ♡
ADORBS TO THE MAX! ALMOST AS CUTE AS ME!
ANYA
CLIK
CLIK
CLIK
NOW WE'RE TALKING! BREAK OUT OF THAT SHELL AND REALLY REINVENT YOURSELF!
Yes! Good!
CHU
uh...
OKAY, MAYBE GO BACK INTO THE SHELL A LITTLE... BUT I DO LOVE THE COURAGE!
WAAAAH!
IT'S LIKE YOU WENT SO FAR YOU CAME OUT THE OTHER SIDE! KEEP GOING, GIRL! BREAK THE BOUNDARIES OF STYLE!

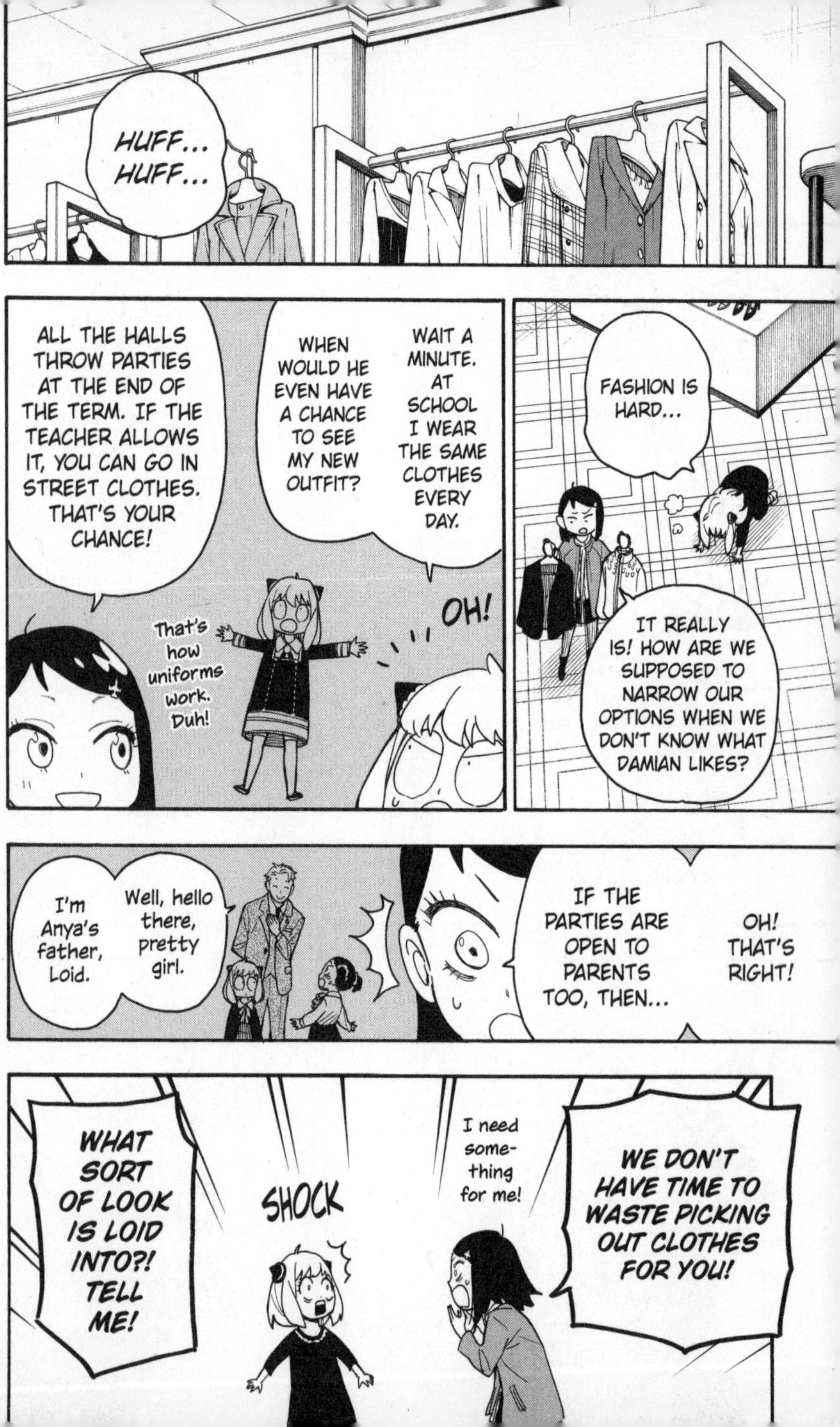
HUFF... HUFF...
FASHION IS HARD...
IT REALLY IS! HOW ARE WE SUPPOSED TO NARROW OUR OPTIONS WHEN WE DON'T KNOW WHAT DAMIAN LIKES?
WAIT A MINUTE. AT SCHOOL I WEAR THE SAME CLOTHES EVERY DAY.
WHEN WOULD HE EVEN HAVE A CHANCE TO SEE MY NEW OUTFIT?
OH!
That's how uniforms work. Duh!
ALL THE HALLS THROW PARTIES AT THE END OF THE TERM. IF THE TEACHER ALLOWS IT, YOU CAN GO IN STREET CLOTHES. THAT'S YOUR CHANCE!
OH! THAT'S RIGHT!
IF THE PARTIES ARE OPEN TO PARENTS TOO, THEN...
Well, hello there, pretty girl.
I'm Anya's father, Loid.
WE DON'T HAVE TIME TO WASTE PICKING OUT CLOTHES FOR YOU!
I need something for me!
SHOCK
WHAT SORT OF LOOK IS LOID INTO?! TELL ME!

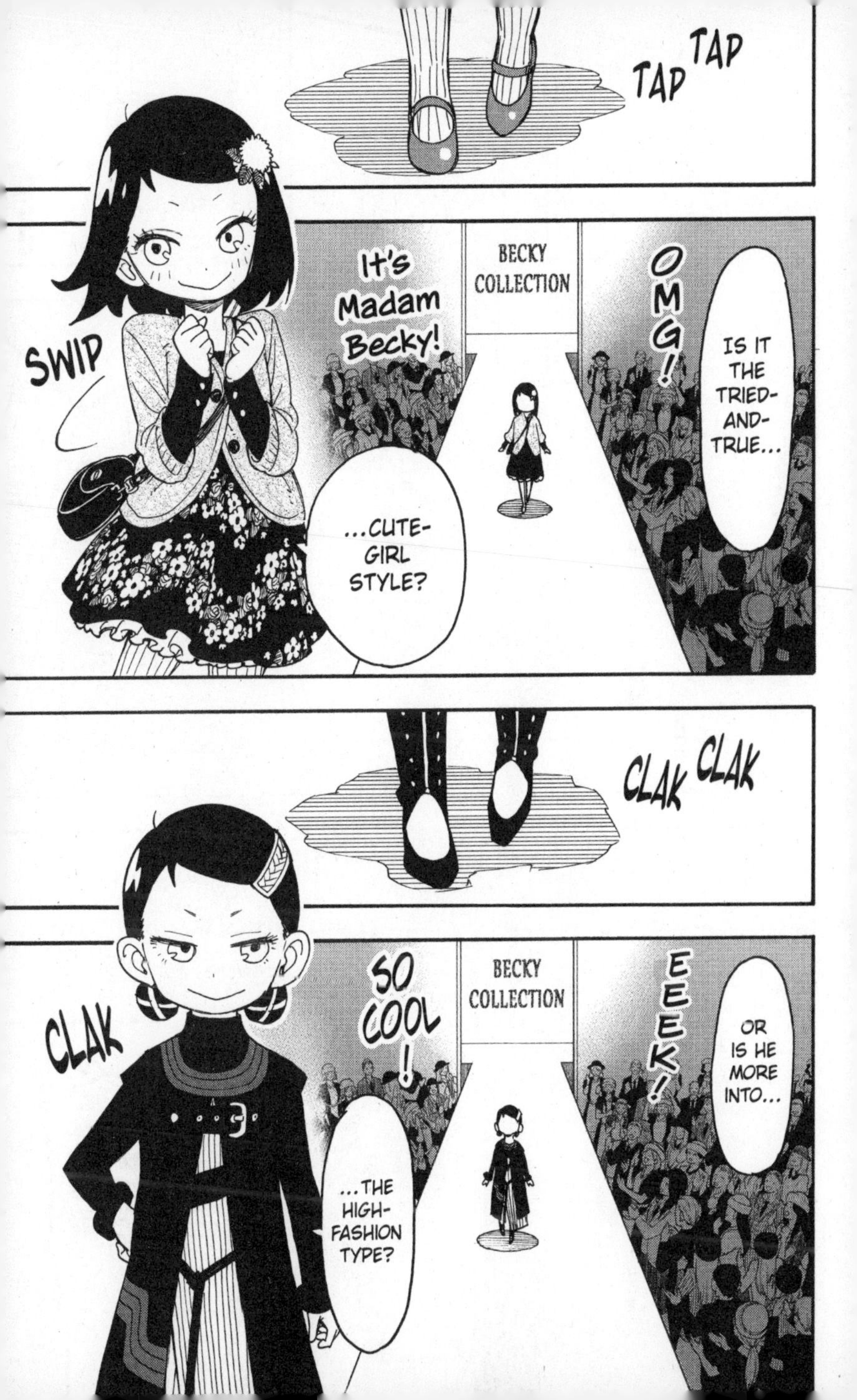
TAP TAP
OMG!
IS IT THE TRIED-AND-TRUE...
BECKY COLLECTION
It's Madam Becky!
...CUTE-GIRL STYLE?
SWIP
CLAK CLAK
EEEK!
OR IS HE MORE INTO...
BECKY COLLECTION
SO COOL!
...THE HIGH-FASHION TYPE?
CLAK

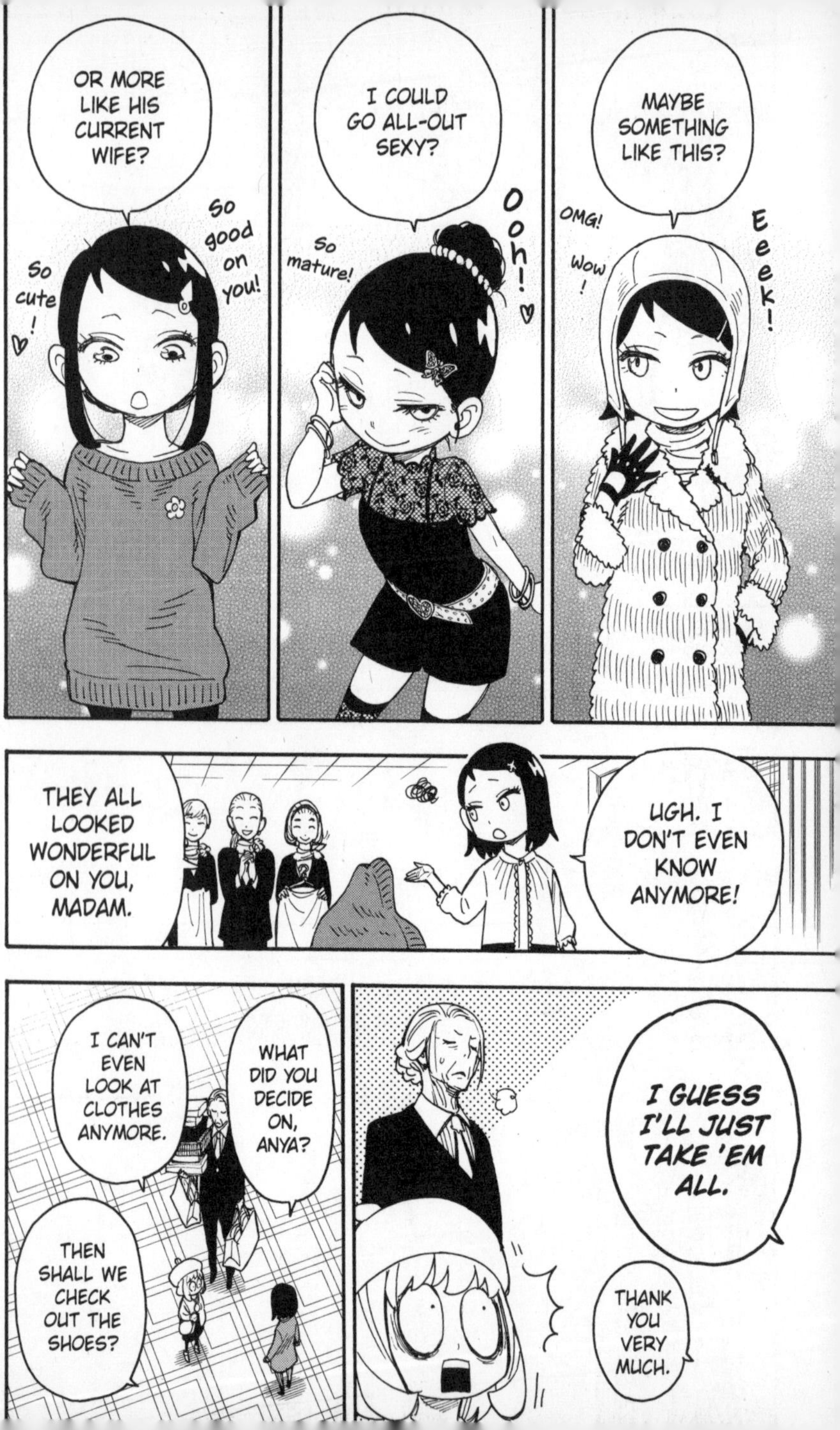
MAYBE SOMETHING LIKE THIS?
Eeek!
OMG!
Wow!
I COULD GO ALL-OUT SEXY?
Oooh!
So mature!
OR MORE LIKE HIS CURRENT WIFE?
So good on you!
So cute!
UGH. I DON'T EVEN KNOW ANYMORE!
THEY ALL LOOKED WONDERFUL ON YOU, MADAM.
I GUESS I'LL JUST TAKE 'EM ALL.
THANK YOU VERY MUCH.
WHAT DID YOU DECIDE ON, ANYA?
I CAN'T EVEN LOOK AT CLOTHES ANYMORE.
THEN SHALL WE CHECK OUT THE SHOES?

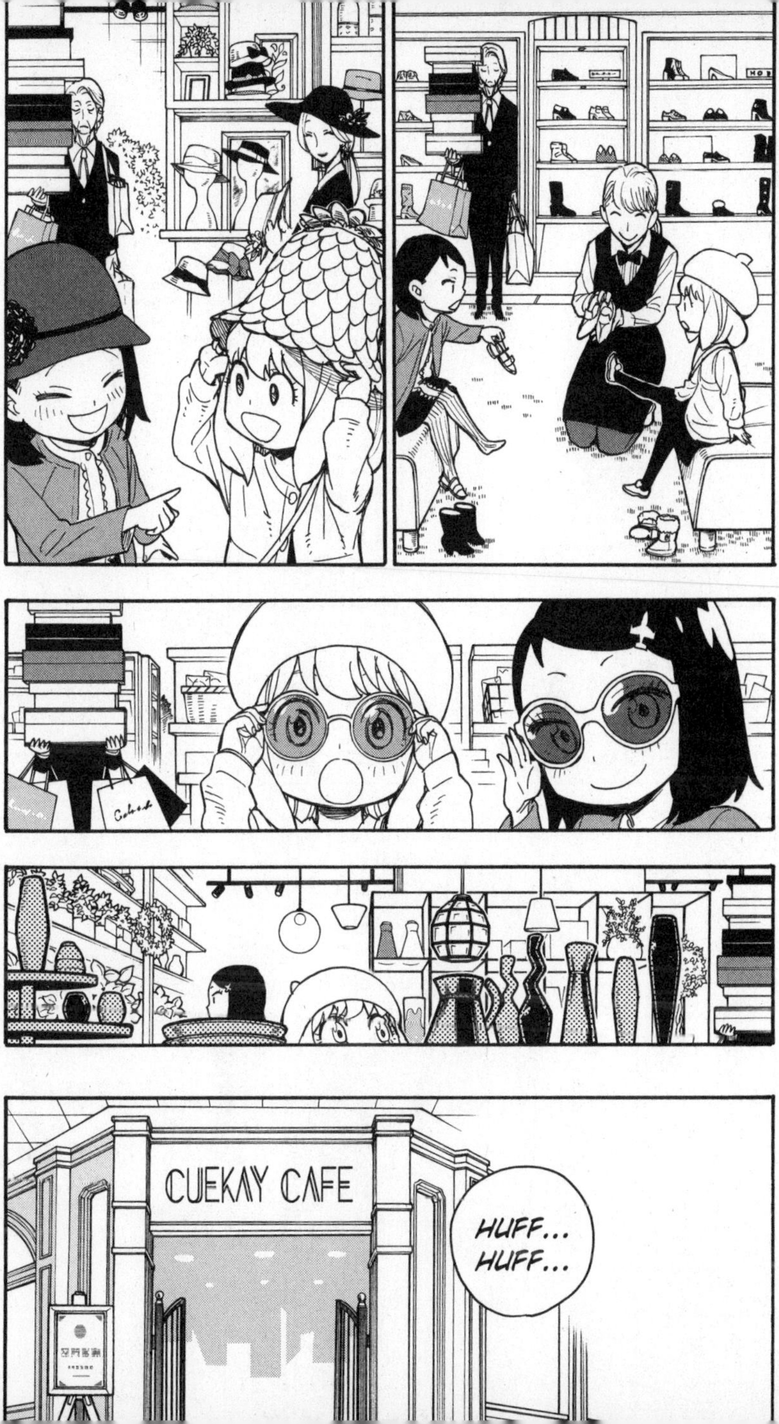
CUEKAY CAFE
HUFF... HUFF...

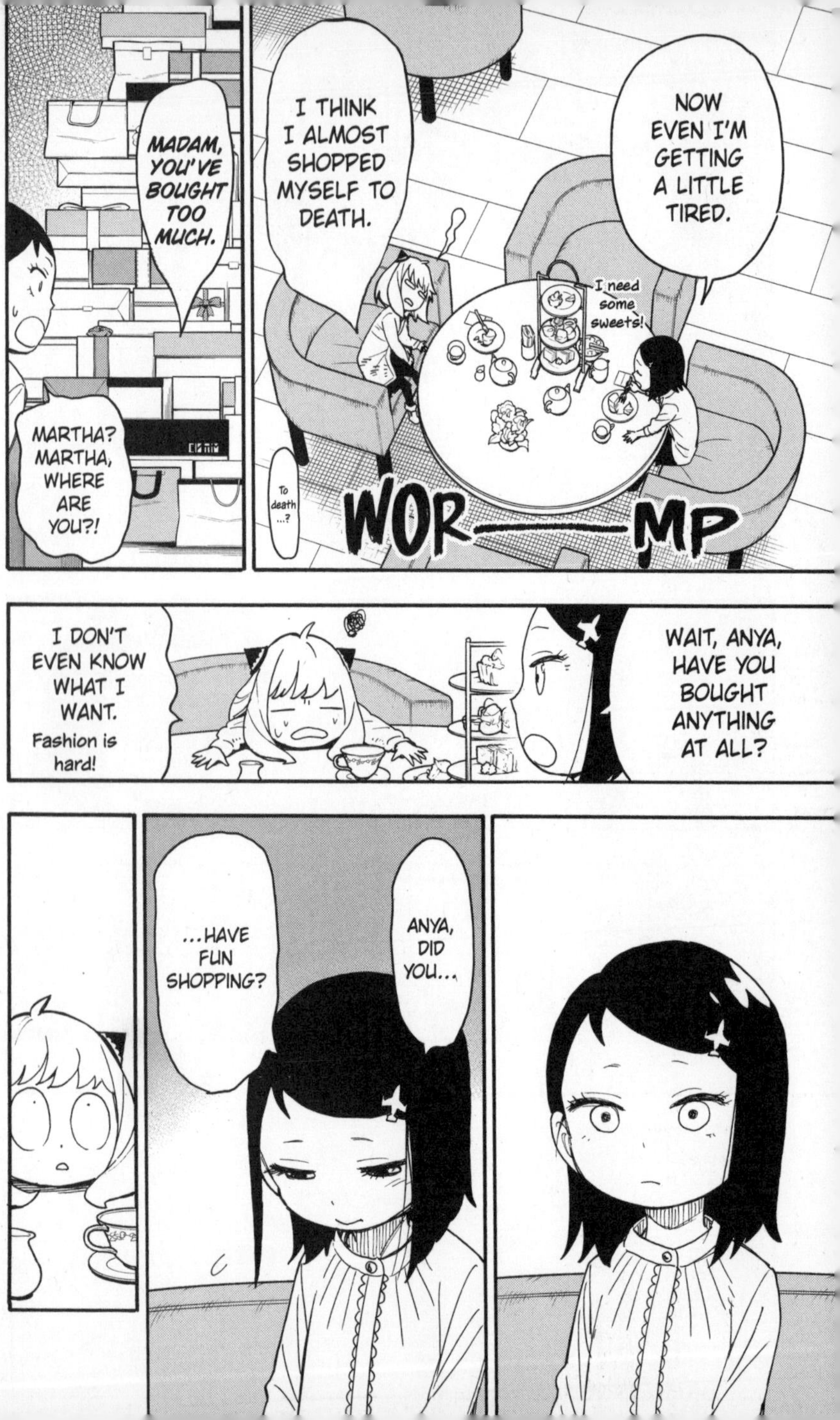
NOW EVEN I'M GETTING A LITTLE TIRED.
I need some sweets!
I THINK I ALMOST SHOPPED MYSELF TO DEATH.
WOR——MP
To death ...?
MADAM, YOU'VE BOUGHT TOO MUCH.
MARTHA? MARTHA, WHERE ARE YOU?!
WAIT, ANYA, HAVE YOU BOUGHT ANYTHING AT ALL?
I DON'T EVEN KNOW WHAT I WANT.
Fashion is hard!
ANYA, DID YOU...
...HAVE FUN SHOPPING?

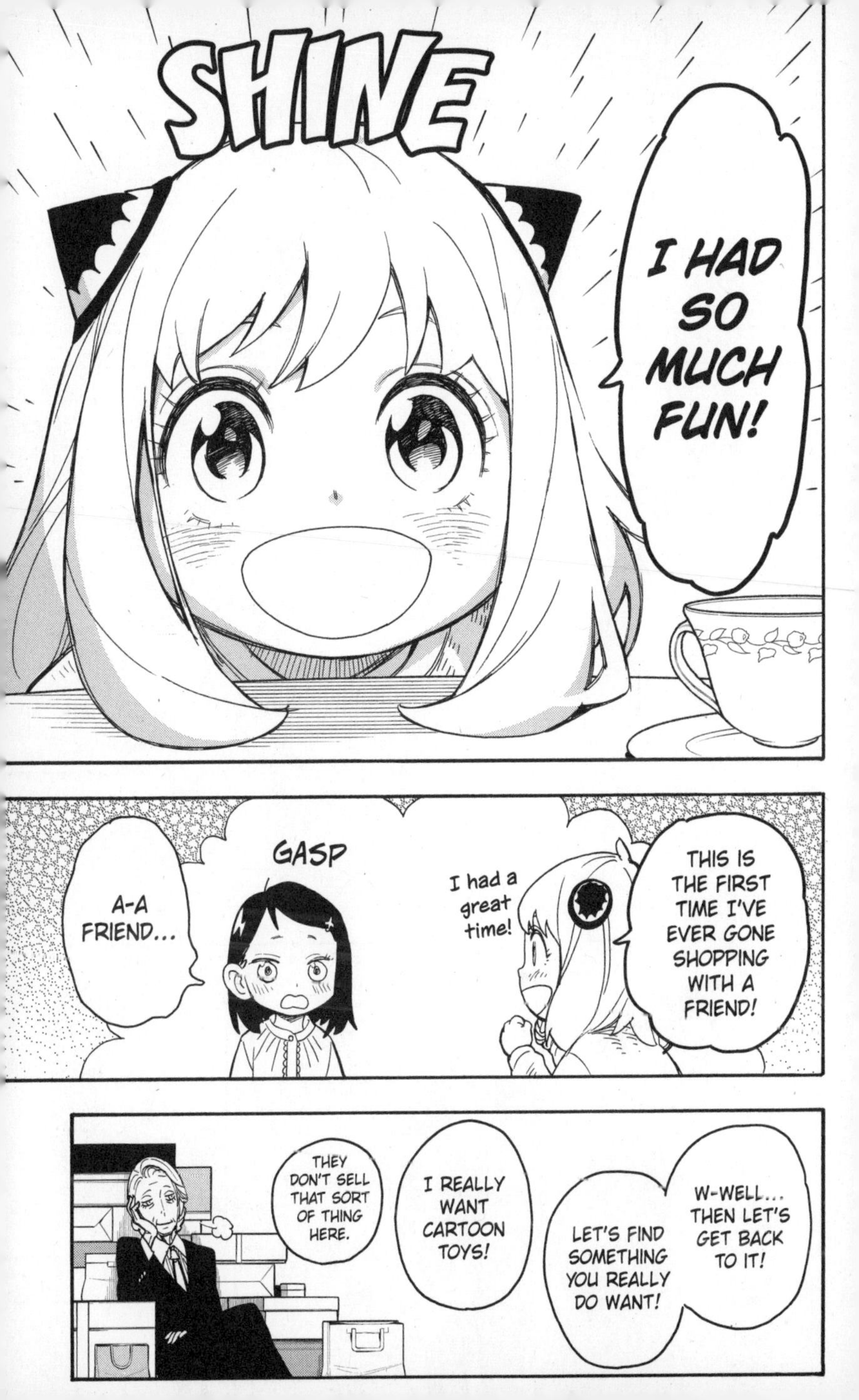
SHINE
I HAD SO MUCH FUN!
THIS IS THE FIRST TIME I'VE EVER GONE SHOPPING WITH A FRIEND!
I had a great time!
GASP
A-A FRIEND...
W-WELL... THEN LET'S GET BACK TO IT!
LET'S FIND SOMETHING YOU REALLY DO WANT!
I REALLY WANT CARTOON TOYS!
THEY DON'T SELL THAT SORT OF THING HERE.

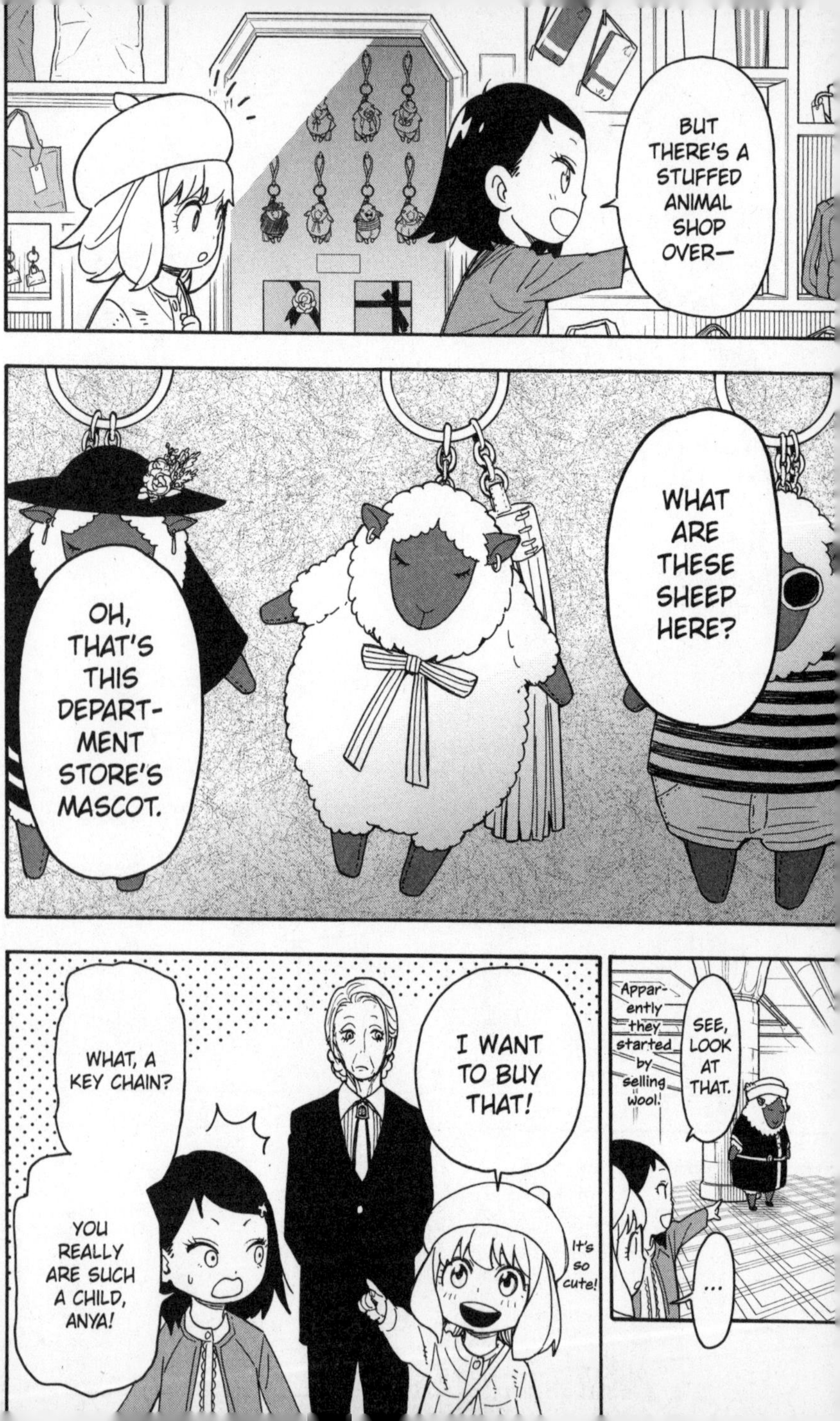
BUT THERE'S A STUFFED ANIMAL SHOP OVER—
WHAT ARE THESE SHEEP HERE?
OH, THAT'S THIS DEPART-MENT STORE'S MASCOT.
SEE, LOOK AT THAT.
Appar-ently they started by selling wool!
...
I WANT TO BUY THAT!
It's so cute!
WHAT, A KEY CHAIN?
YOU REALLY ARE SUCH A CHILD, ANYA!

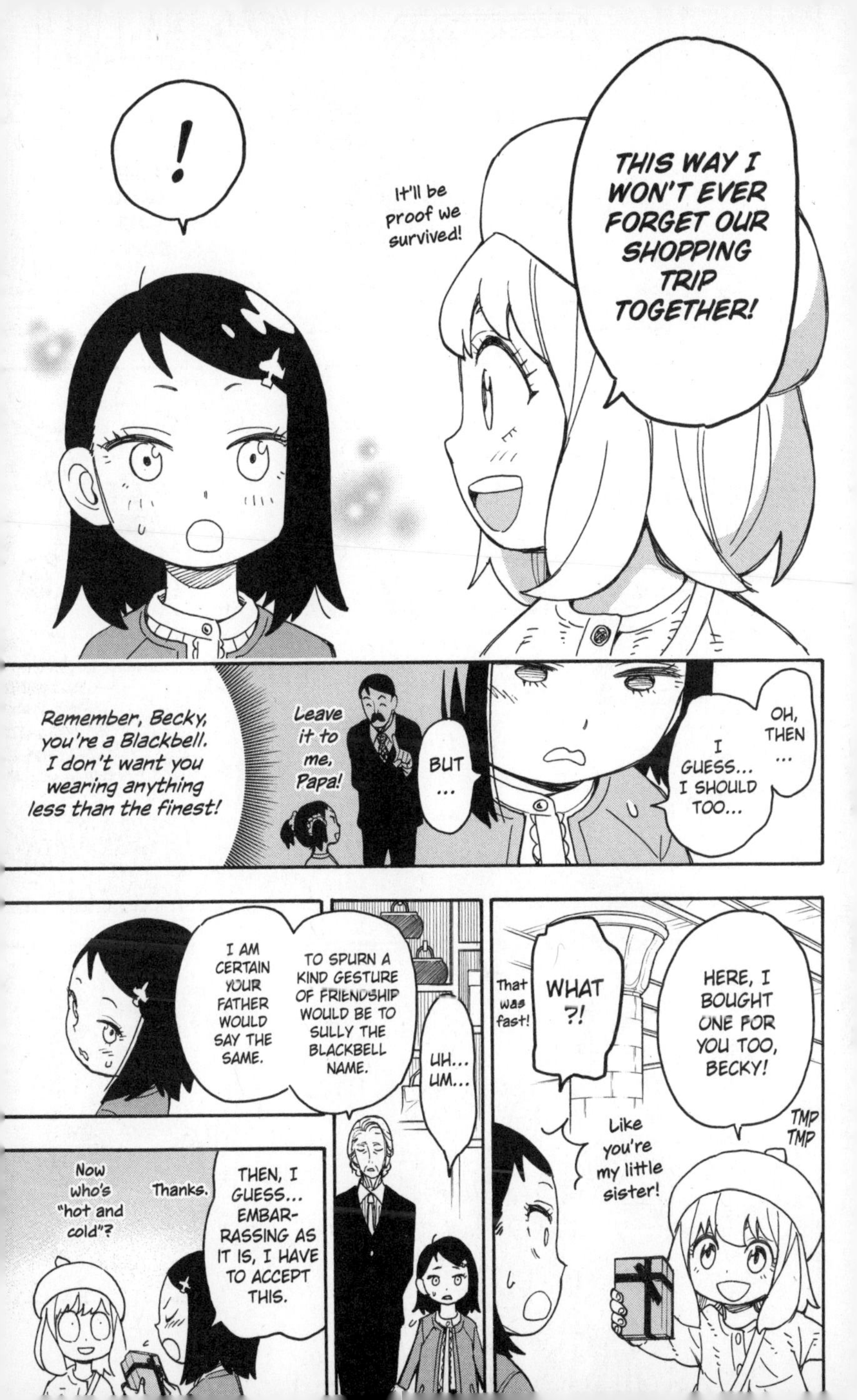
THIS WAY I WON'T EVER FORGET OUR SHOPPING TRIP TOGETHER!
It'll be proof we survived!
!
OH, THEN ...
I GUESS... I SHOULD TOO...
BUT ...
Leave it to me, Papa!
Remember, Becky, you're a Blackbell. I don't want you wearing anything less than the finest!
HERE, I BOUGHT ONE FOR YOU TOO, BECKY!
TMP TMP
Like you're my little sister!
WHAT ?!
That was fast!
UH... UM...
TO SPURN A KIND GESTURE OF FRIENDSHIP WOULD BE TO SULLY THE BLACKBELL NAME.
I AM CERTAIN YOUR FATHER WOULD SAY THE SAME.
THEN, I GUESS... EMBAR-RASSING AS IT IS, I HAVE TO ACCEPT THIS.
Thanks.
Now who's "hot and cold"?

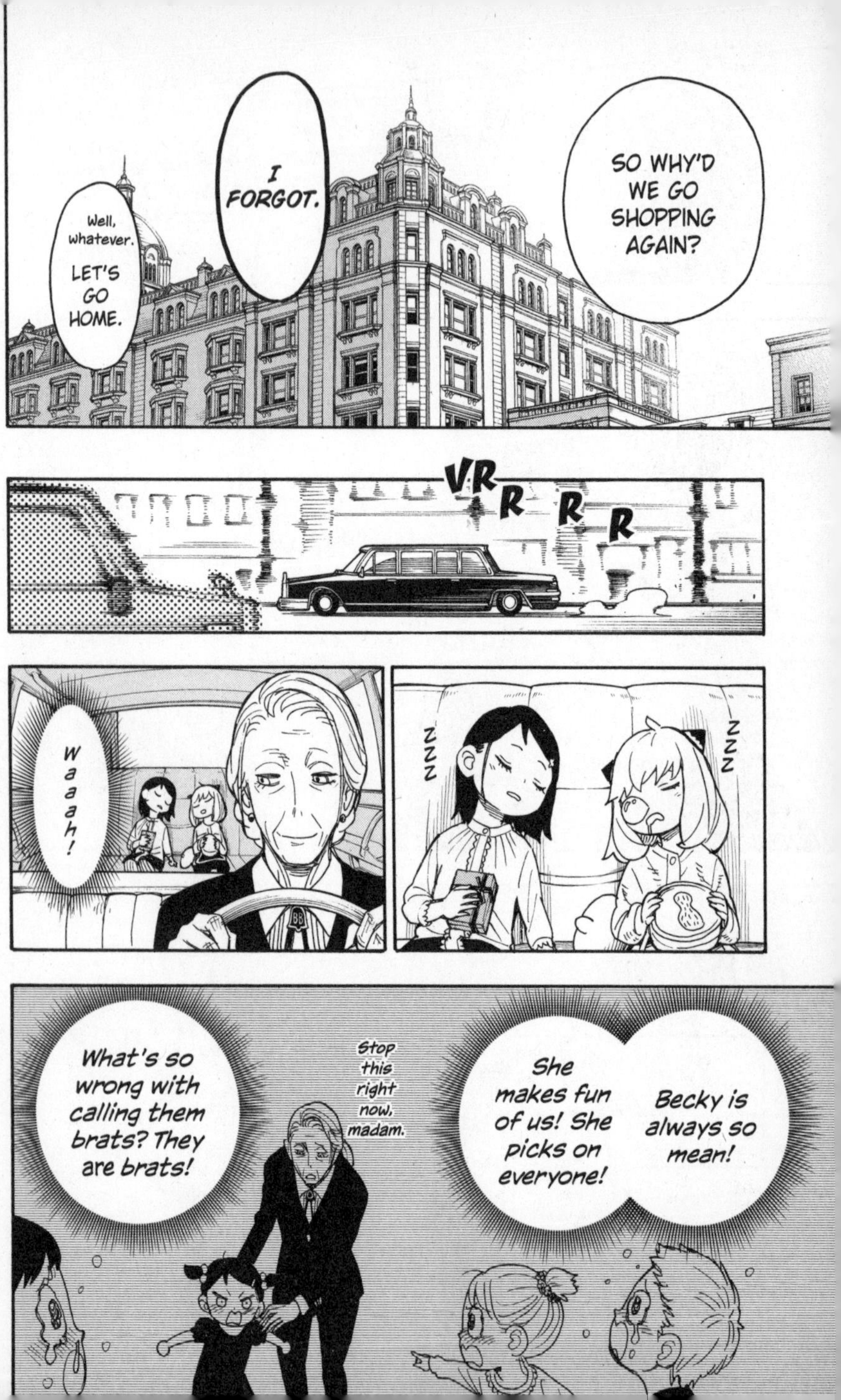
SO WHY'D WE GO SHOPPING AGAIN?
I FORGOT.
Well, whatever. LET'S GO HOME.
VRRRRR
ZZZ
ZZZ
Waaaah!
Becky is always so mean!
She makes fun of us! She picks on everyone!
Stop this right now, madam.
What's so wrong with calling them brats? They are brats!

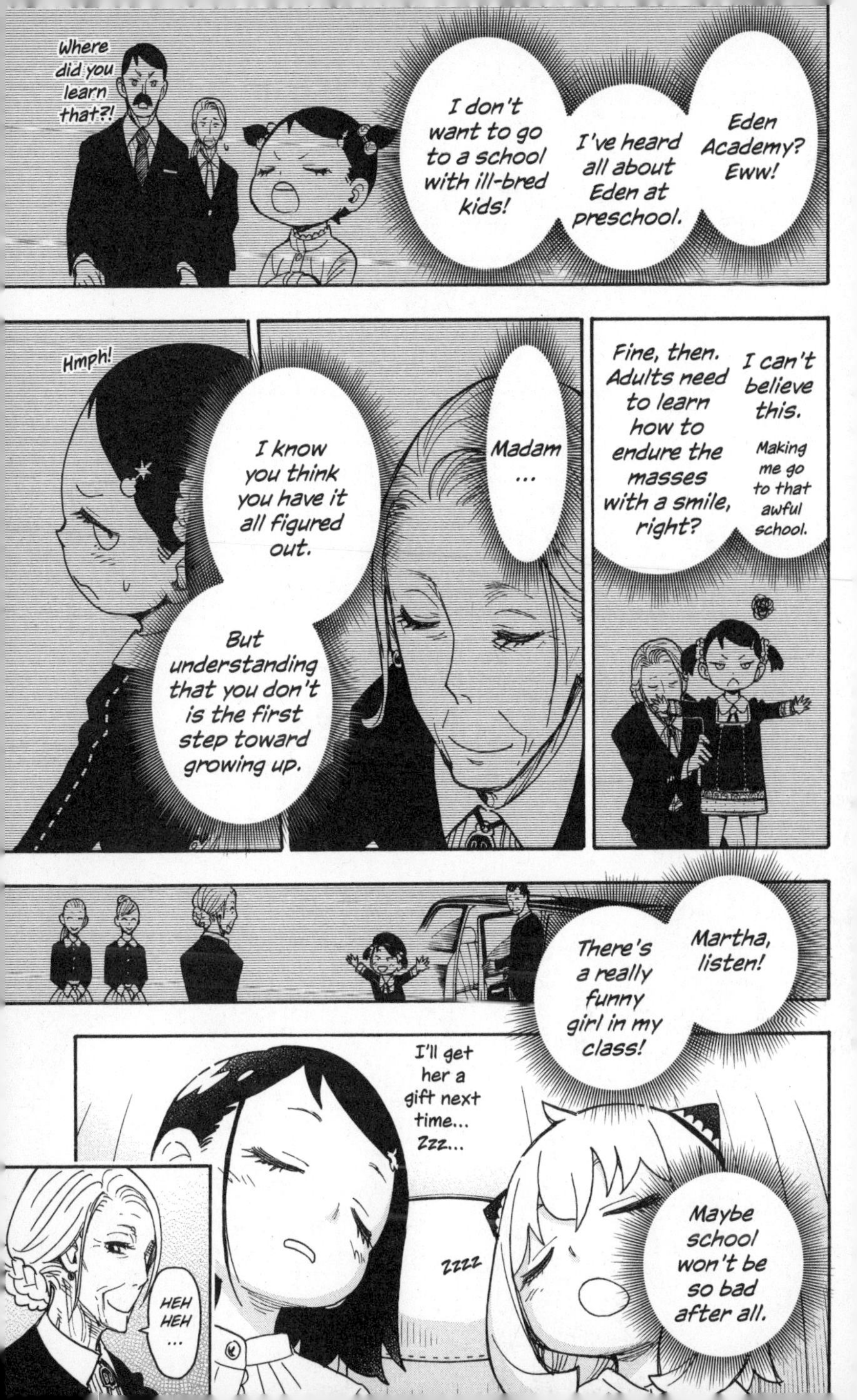

Eden Academy? Eww!
I've heard all about Eden at preschool.
I don't want to go to a school with ill-bred kids!
Where did you learn that?!
I can't believe this.
Making me go to that awful school.
Fine, then. Adults need to learn how to endure the masses with a smile, right?
Madam...
I know you think you have it all figured out.
But understanding that you don't is the first step toward growing up.
Hmph!
Martha, listen!
There's a really funny girl in my class!
Maybe school won't be so bad after all.
I'll get her a gift next time... Zzz...
zzzz
HEH HEH...

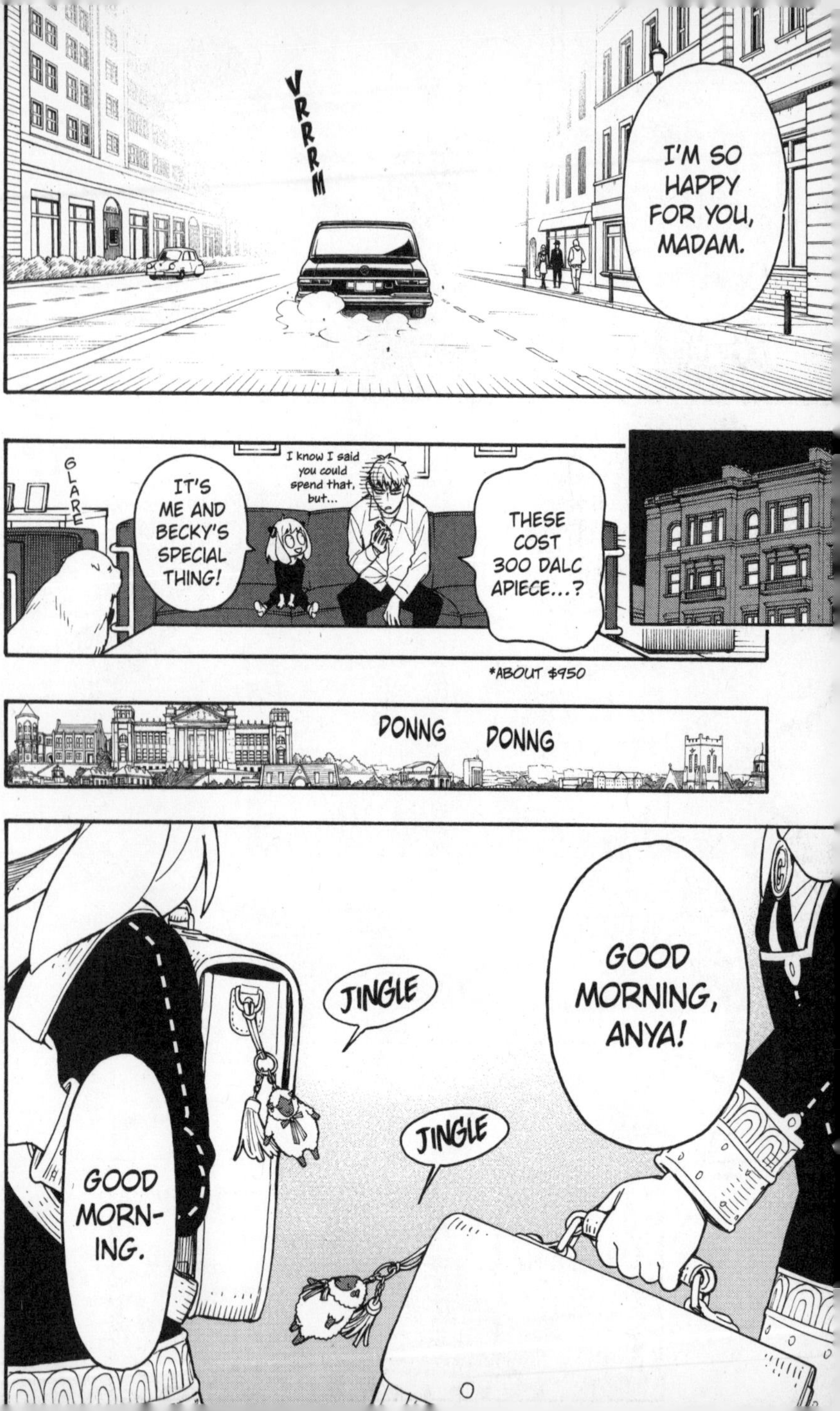
VRRRM
I'M SO HAPPY FOR YOU, MADAM.
THESE COST 300 DALC APIECE...?
I know I said you could spend that, but...
IT'S ME AND BECKY'S SPECIAL THING!
GLARE
*ABOUT $950
DONNG DONNG
GOOD MORNING, ANYA!
JINGLE
JINGLE
GOOD MORN-ING.

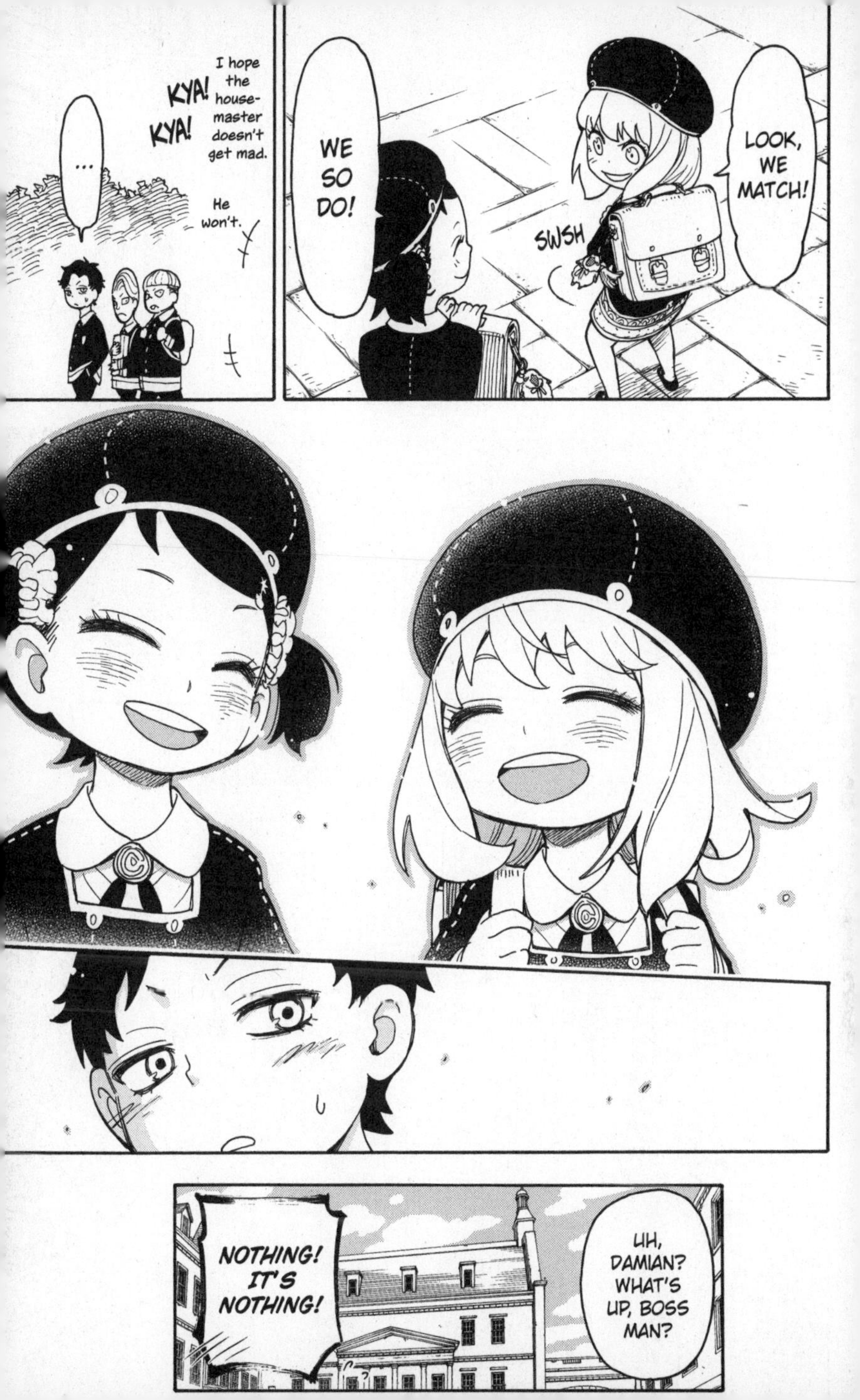
LOOK, WE MATCH!
SWSH
WE SO DO!
I hope the house-master doesn't get mad.
KYA! KYA!
He won't.
...
UH, DAMIAN? WHAT'S UP, BOSS MAN?
NOTHING! IT'S NOTHING!

SPY×FAMILY

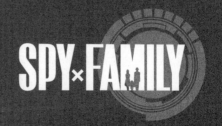

MISSION 37

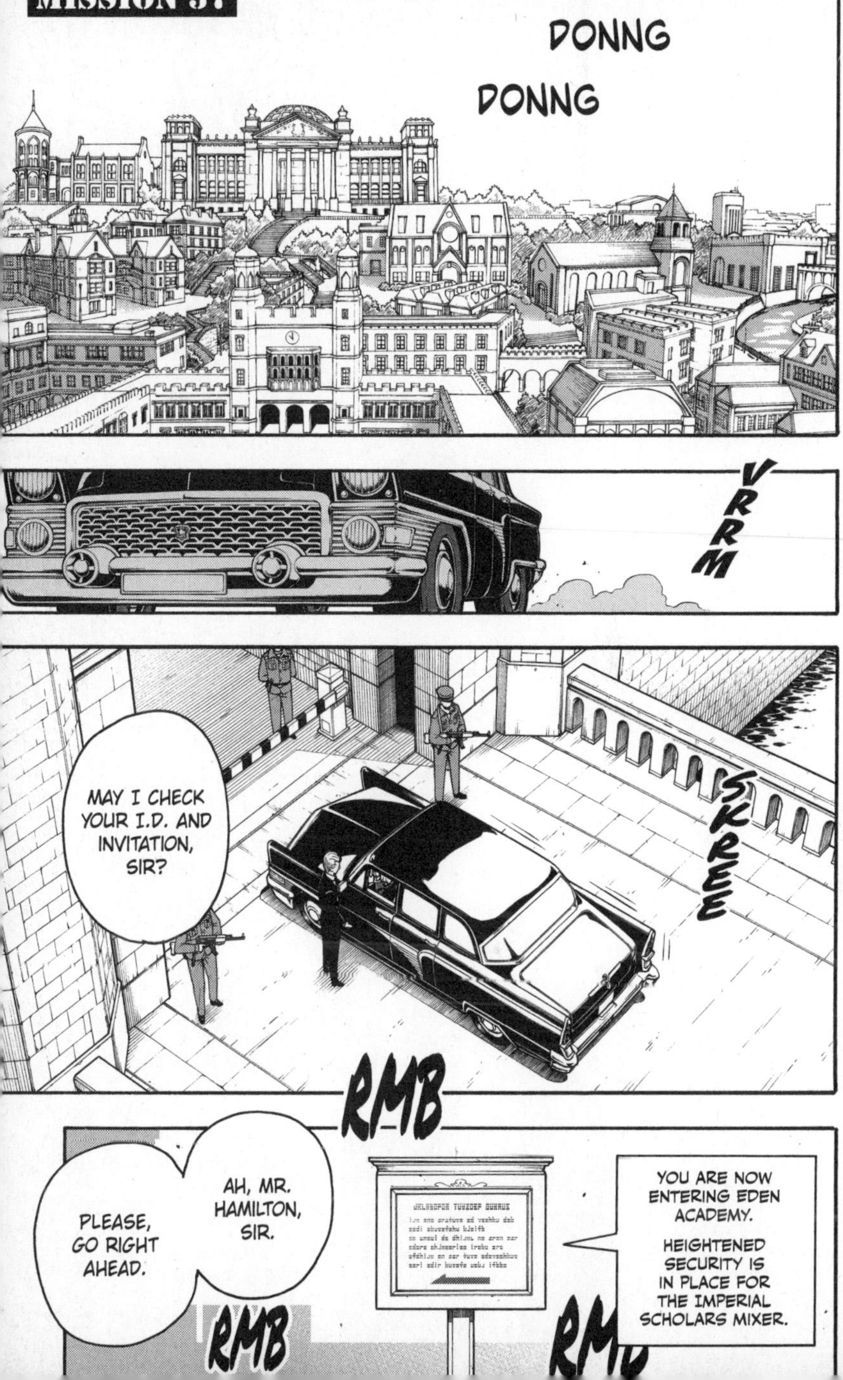
DONNG
DONNG
VRRM
SKREE
MAY I CHECK YOUR I.D. AND INVITATION, SIR?
RMB
YOU ARE NOW ENTERING EDEN ACADEMY.
HEIGHTENED SECURITY IS IN PLACE FOR THE IMPERIAL SCHOLARS MIXER.
RMB
AH, MR. HAMILTON, SIR.
PLEASE, GO RIGHT AHEAD.
RMB

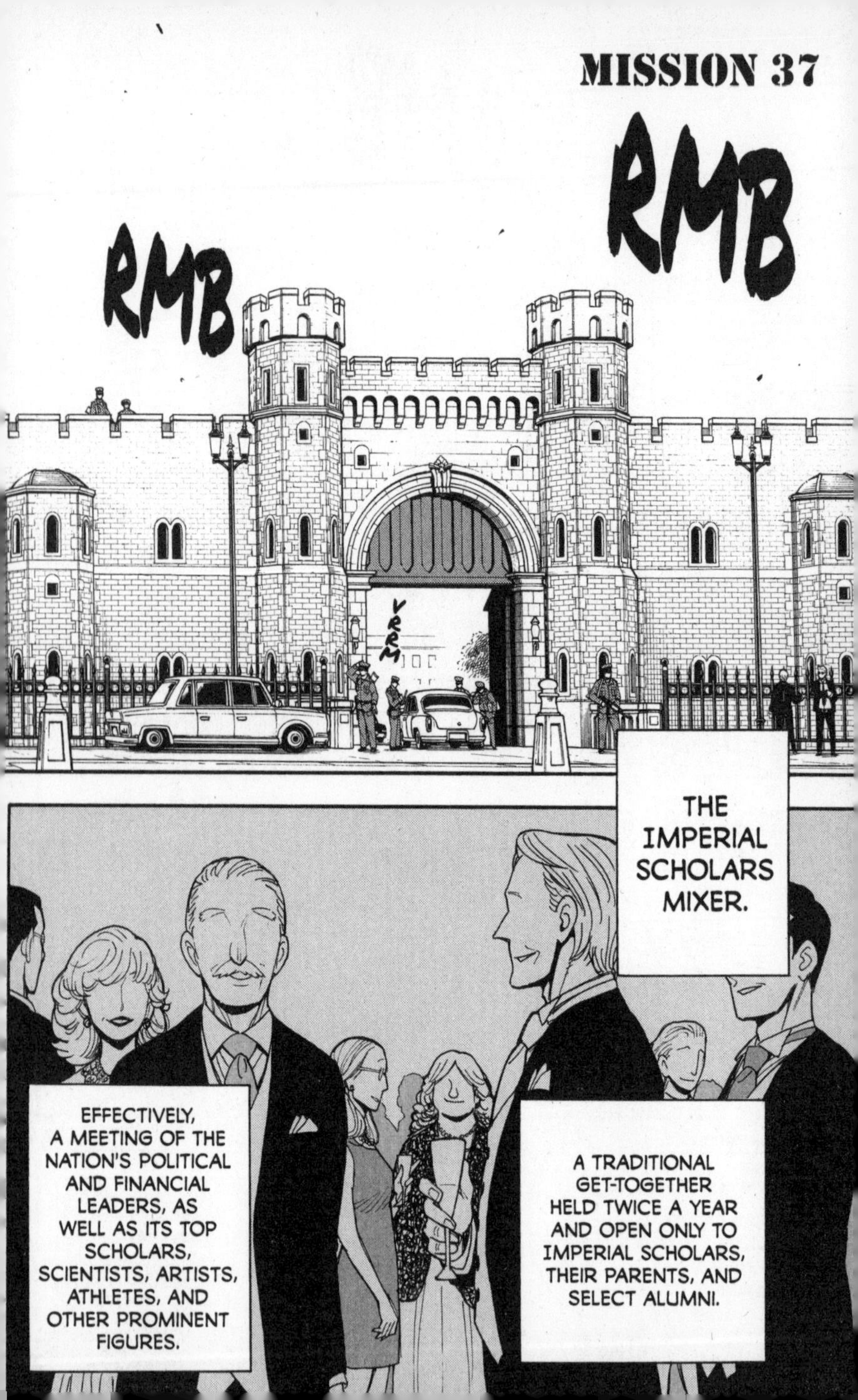
MISSION 37
RMB
RMB
VRRM
THE IMPERIAL SCHOLARS MIXER.
A TRADITIONAL GET-TOGETHER HELD TWICE A YEAR AND OPEN ONLY TO IMPERIAL SCHOLARS, THEIR PARENTS, AND SELECT ALUMNI.
EFFECTIVELY, A MEETING OF THE NATION'S POLITICAL AND FINANCIAL LEADERS, AS WELL AS ITS TOP SCHOLARS, SCIENTISTS, ARTISTS, ATHLETES, AND OTHER PROMINENT FIGURES.

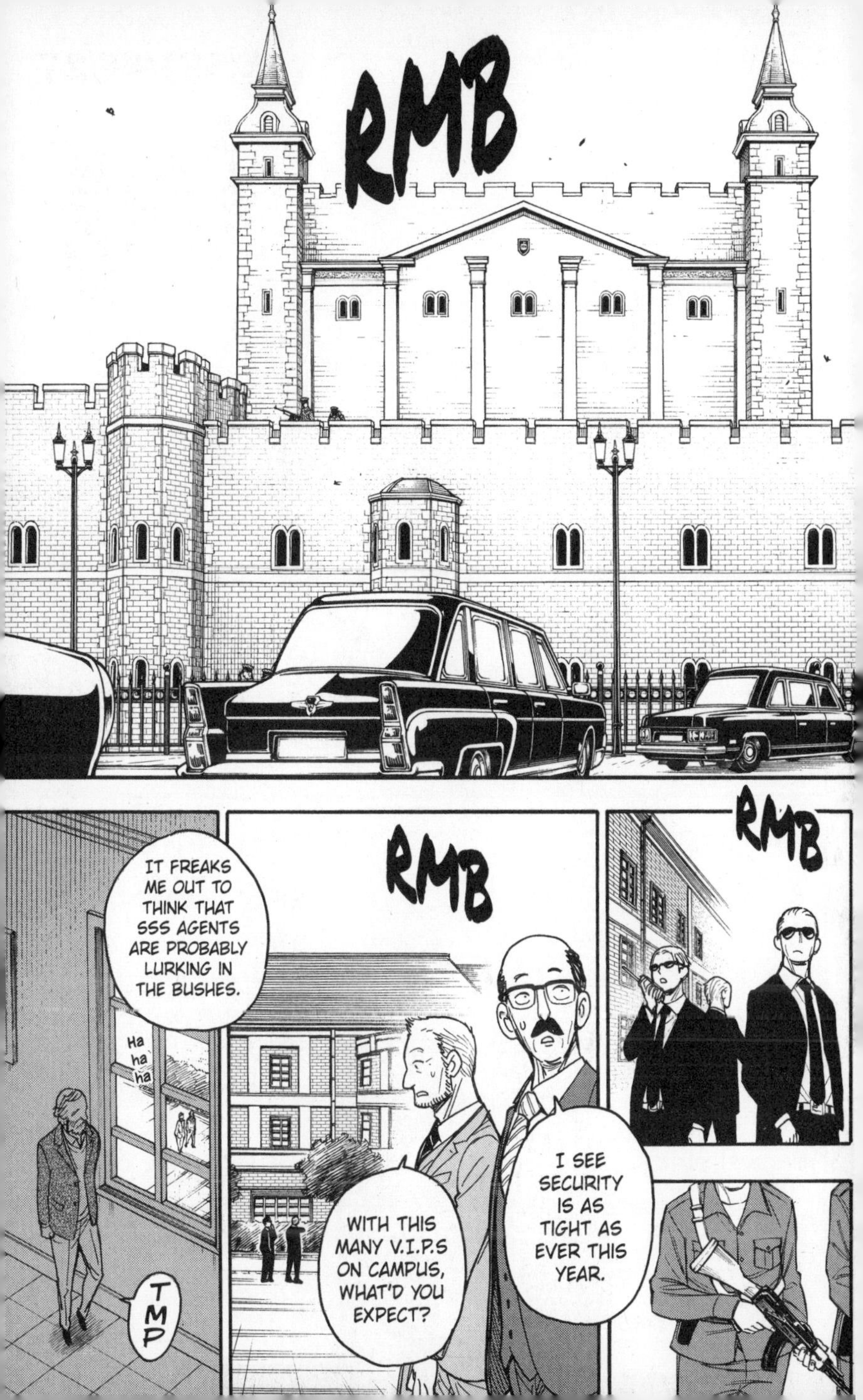
RMB
RMB
RMB
I SEE SECURITY IS AS TIGHT AS EVER THIS YEAR.
WITH THIS MANY V.I.P.S ON CAMPUS, WHAT'D YOU EXPECT?
IT FREAKS ME OUT TO THINK THAT SSS AGENTS ARE PROBABLY LURKING IN THE BUSHES.
Ha ha ha
TMP

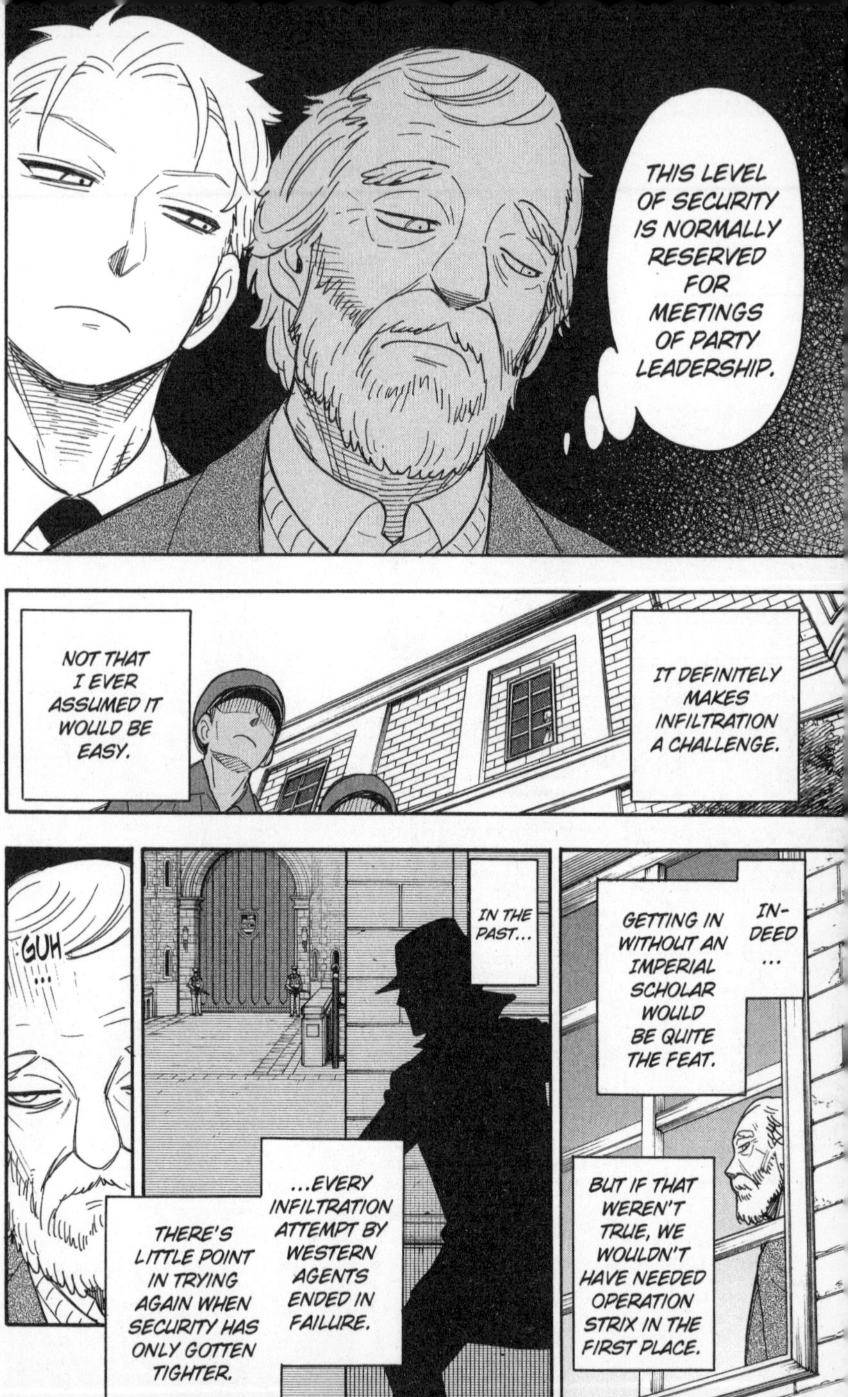
THIS LEVEL OF SECURITY IS NORMALLY RESERVED FOR MEETINGS OF PARTY LEADERSHIP.
IT DEFINITELY MAKES INFILTRATION A CHALLENGE.
NOT THAT I EVER ASSUMED IT WOULD BE EASY.
IN-DEED...
GETTING IN WITHOUT AN IMPERIAL SCHOLAR WOULD BE QUITE THE FEAT.
BUT IF THAT WEREN'T TRUE, WE WOULDN'T HAVE NEEDED OPERATION STRIX IN THE FIRST PLACE.
IN THE PAST...
...EVERY INFILTRATION ATTEMPT BY WESTERN AGENTS ENDED IN FAILURE.
GUH...
THERE'S LITTLE POINT IN TRYING AGAIN WHEN SECURITY HAS ONLY GOTTEN TIGHTER.

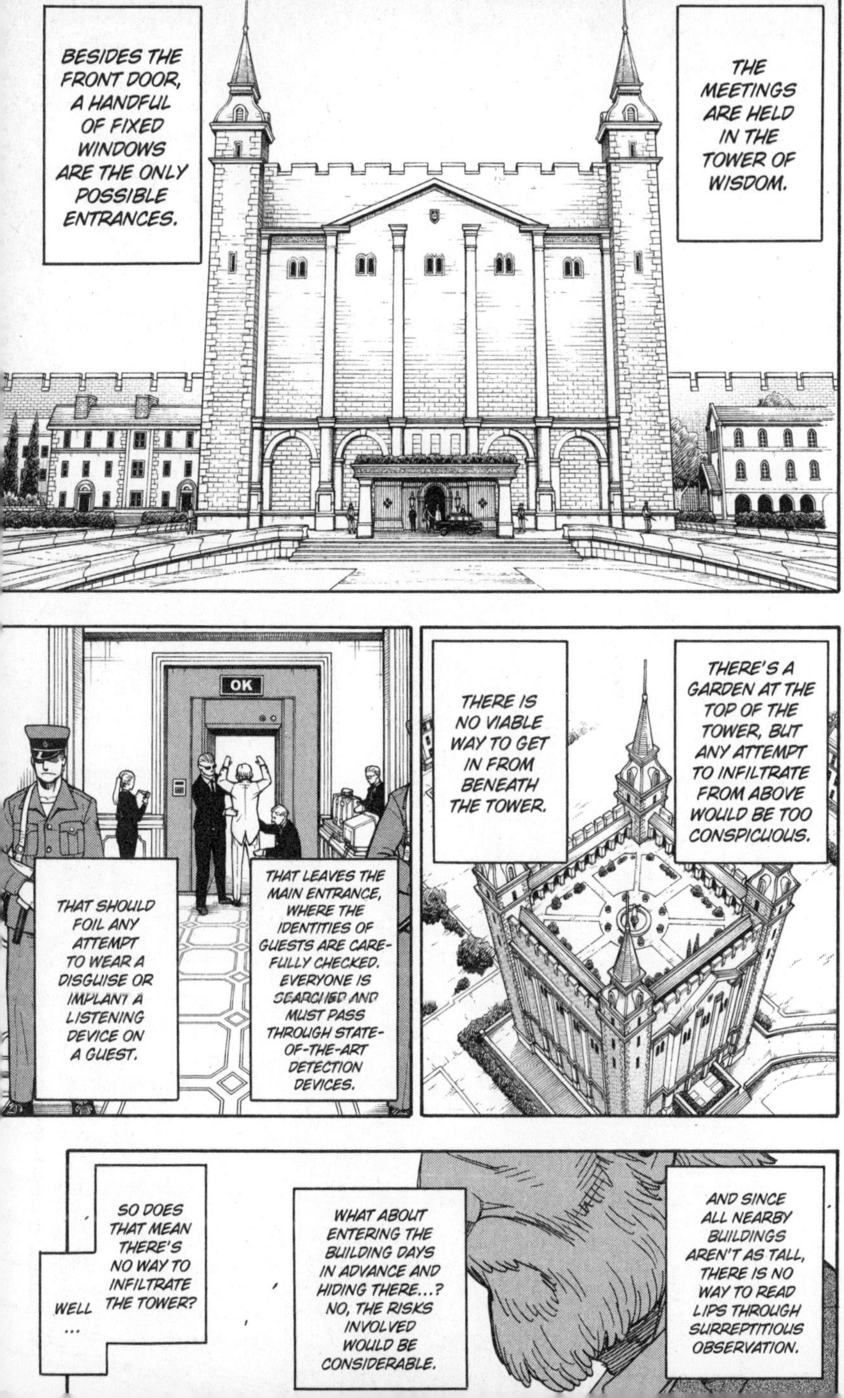
THE MEETINGS ARE HELD IN THE TOWER OF WISDOM.
BESIDES THE FRONT DOOR, A HANDFUL OF FIXED WINDOWS ARE THE ONLY POSSIBLE ENTRANCES.
THERE'S A GARDEN AT THE TOP OF THE TOWER, BUT ANY ATTEMPT TO INFILTRATE FROM ABOVE WOULD BE TOO CONSPICUOUS.
THERE IS NO VIABLE WAY TO GET IN FROM BENEATH THE TOWER.
OK
THAT LEAVES THE MAIN ENTRANCE, WHERE THE IDENTITIES OF GUESTS ARE CAREFULLY CHECKED. EVERYONE IS SEARCHED AND MUST PASS THROUGH STATE-OF-THE-ART DETECTION DEVICES.
THAT SHOULD FOIL ANY ATTEMPT TO WEAR A DISGUISE OR IMPLANT A LISTENING DEVICE ON A GUEST.
AND SINCE ALL NEARBY BUILDINGS AREN'T AS TALL, THERE IS NO WAY TO READ LIPS THROUGH SURREPTITIOUS OBSERVATION.
WHAT ABOUT ENTERING THE BUILDING DAYS IN ADVANCE AND HIDING THERE...? NO, THE RISKS INVOLVED WOULD BE CONSIDERABLE.
SO DOES THAT MEAN THERE'S NO WAY TO INFILTRATE THE TOWER?
WELL ...

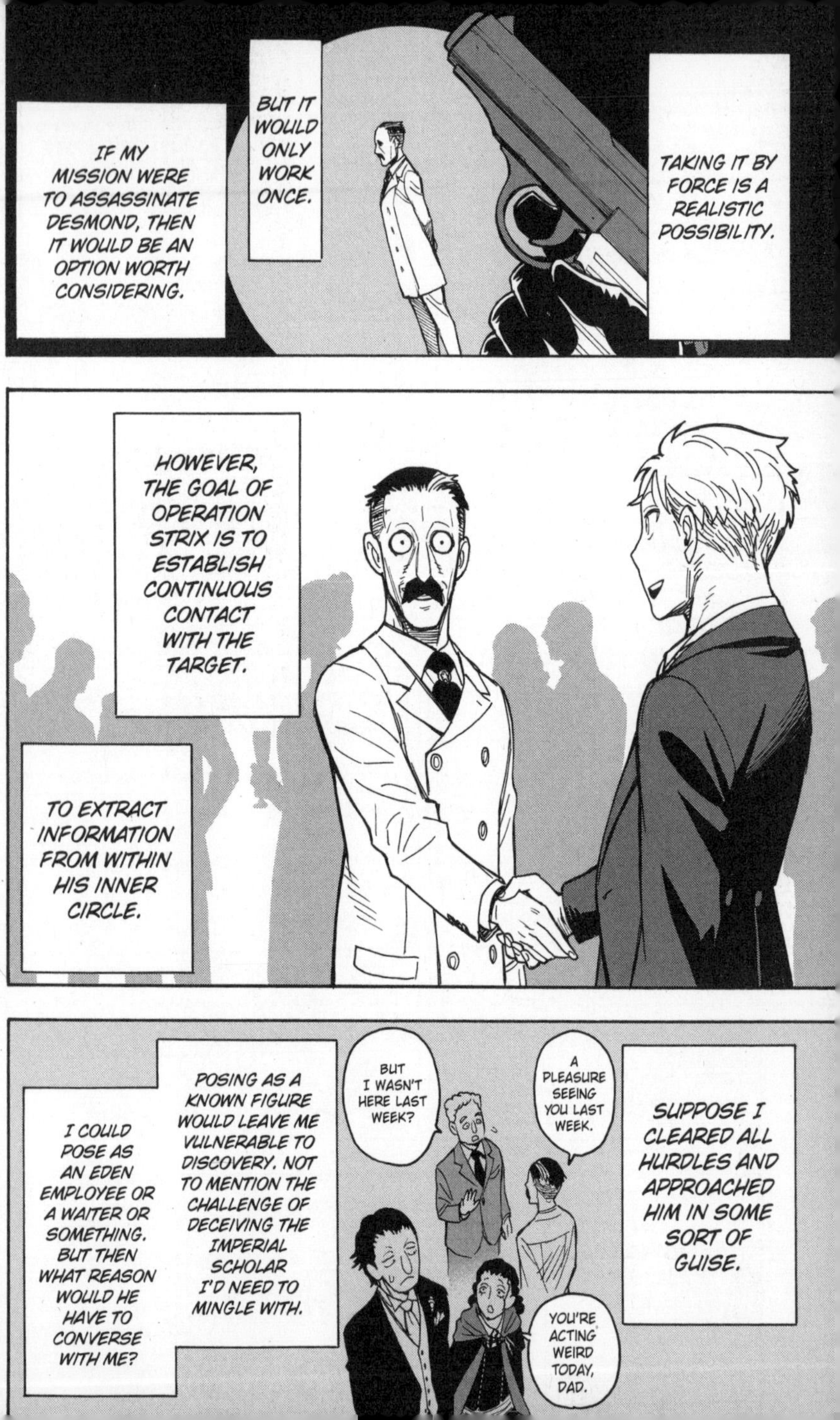
TAKING IT BY FORCE IS A REALISTIC POSSIBILITY.
BUT IT WOULD ONLY WORK ONCE.
IF MY MISSION WERE TO ASSASSINATE DESMOND, THEN IT WOULD BE AN OPTION WORTH CONSIDERING.
HOWEVER, THE GOAL OF OPERATION STRIX IS TO ESTABLISH CONTINUOUS CONTACT WITH THE TARGET.
TO EXTRACT INFORMATION FROM WITHIN HIS INNER CIRCLE.
SUPPOSE I CLEARED ALL HURDLES AND APPROACHED HIM IN SOME SORT OF GUISE.
A PLEASURE SEEING YOU LAST WEEK.
BUT I WASN'T HERE LAST WEEK?
YOU'RE ACTING WEIRD TODAY, DAD.
POSING AS A KNOWN FIGURE WOULD LEAVE ME VULNERABLE TO DISCOVERY. NOT TO MENTION THE CHALLENGE OF DECEIVING THE IMPERIAL SCHOLAR I'D NEED TO MINGLE WITH.
I COULD POSE AS AN EDEN EMPLOYEE OR A WAITER OR SOMETHING. BUT THEN WHAT REASON WOULD HE HAVE TO CONVERSE WITH ME?

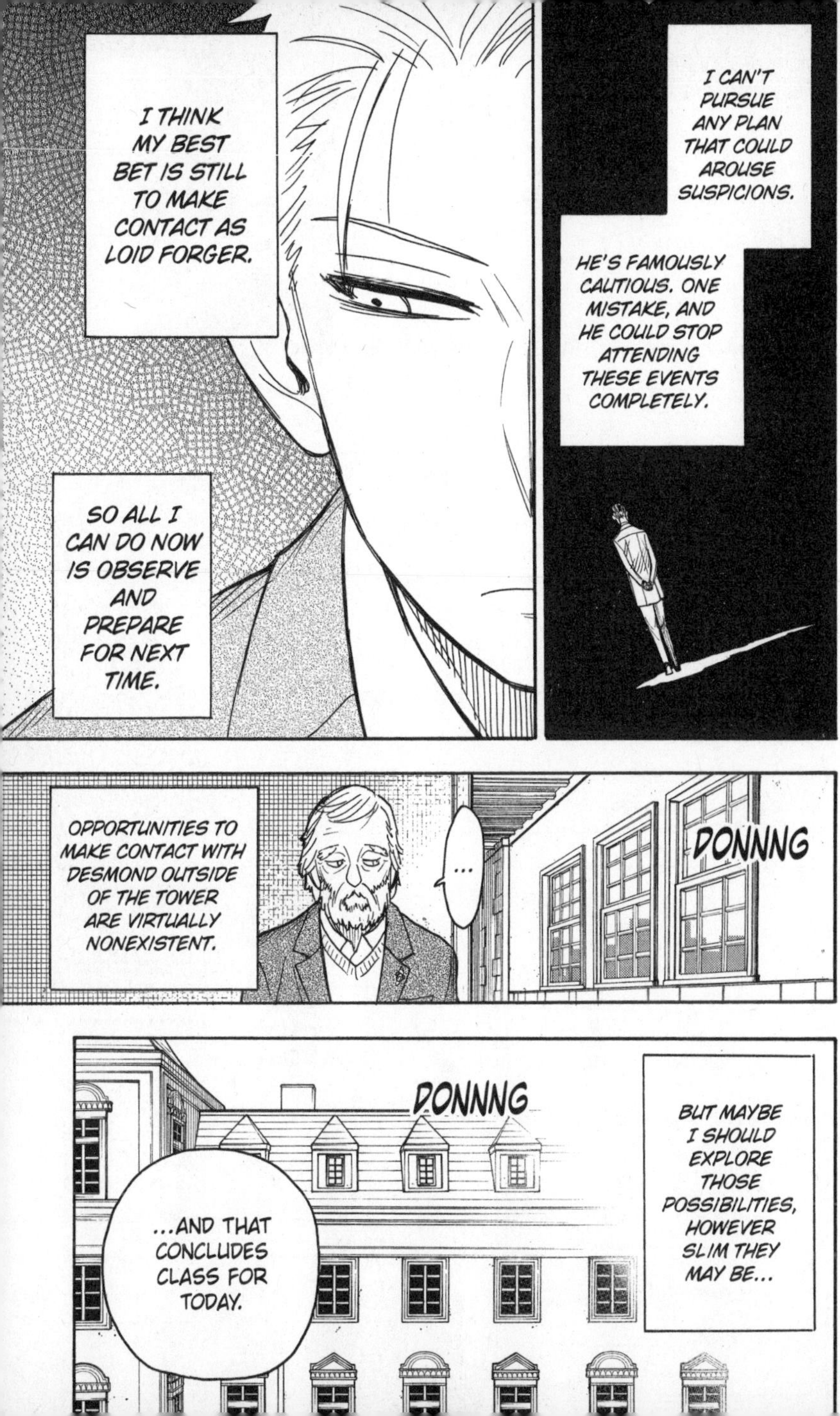
I CAN'T PURSUE ANY PLAN THAT COULD AROUSE SUSPICIONS.
HE'S FAMOUSLY CAUTIOUS. ONE MISTAKE, AND HE COULD STOP ATTENDING THESE EVENTS COMPLETELY.
I THINK MY BEST BET IS STILL TO MAKE CONTACT AS LOID FORGER.
SO ALL I CAN DO NOW IS OBSERVE AND PREPARE FOR NEXT TIME.
DONNNG
...
OPPORTUNITIES TO MAKE CONTACT WITH DESMOND OUTSIDE OF THE TOWER ARE VIRTUALLY NONEXISTENT.
BUT MAYBE I SHOULD EXPLORE THOSE POSSIBILITIES, HOWEVER SLIM THEY MAY BE...
DONNNG
...AND THAT CONCLUDES CLASS FOR TODAY.

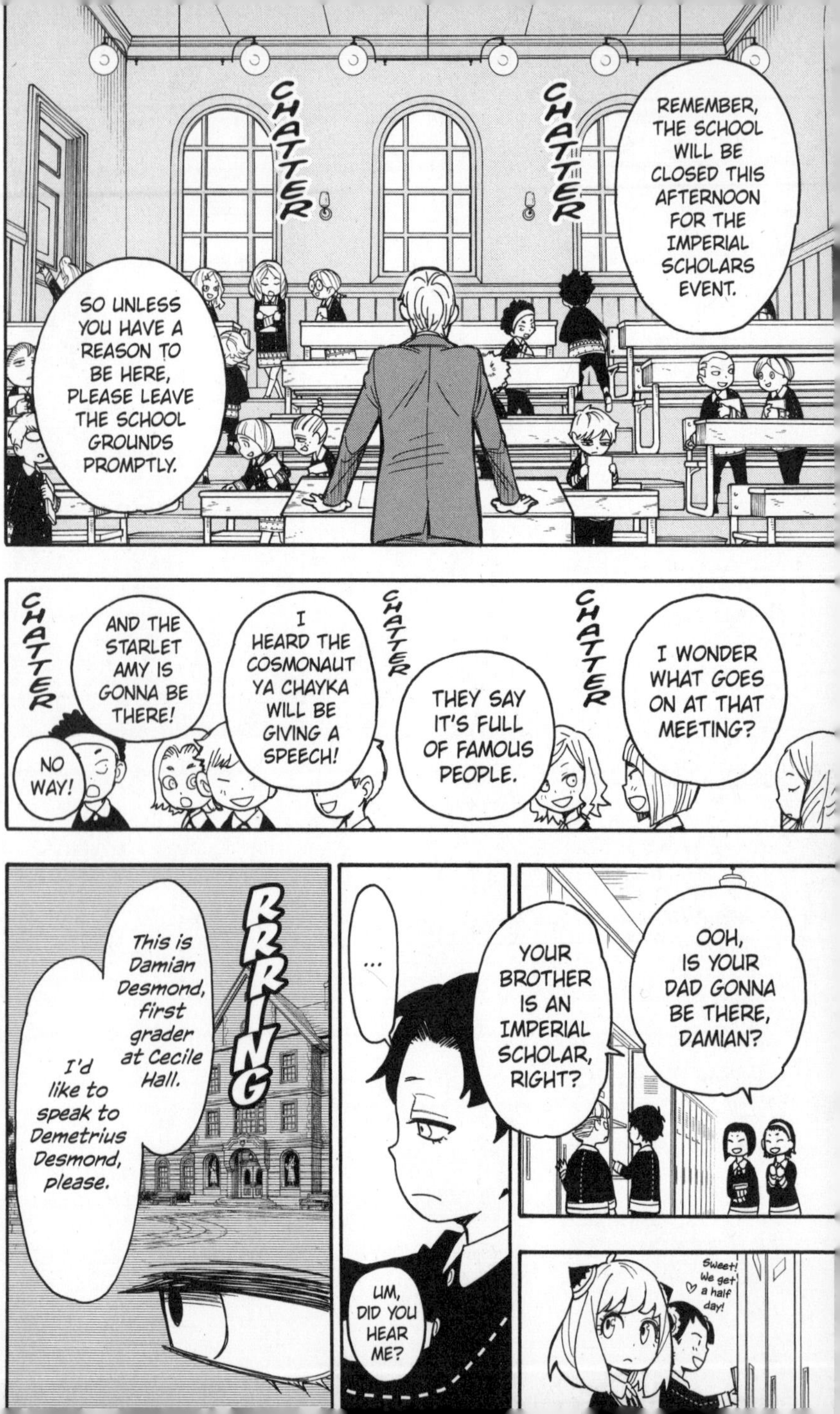
CHATTER
CHATTER
REMEMBER, THE SCHOOL WILL BE CLOSED THIS AFTERNOON FOR THE IMPERIAL SCHOLARS EVENT.
SO UNLESS YOU HAVE A REASON TO BE HERE, PLEASE LEAVE THE SCHOOL GROUNDS PROMPTLY.
CHATTER
I WONDER WHAT GOES ON AT THAT MEETING?
THEY SAY IT'S FULL OF FAMOUS PEOPLE.
CHATTER
I HEARD THE COSMONAUT YA CHAYKA WILL BE GIVING A SPEECH!
AND THE STARLET AMY IS GONNA BE THERE!
CHATTER
NO WAY!
OOH, IS YOUR DAD GONNA BE THERE, DAMIAN?
YOUR BROTHER IS AN IMPERIAL SCHOLAR, RIGHT?
Sweet! We get a half day!
...
UM, DID YOU HEAR ME?
RRRING
This is Damian Desmond, first grader at Cecile Hall.
I'd like to speak to Demetrius Desmond, please.

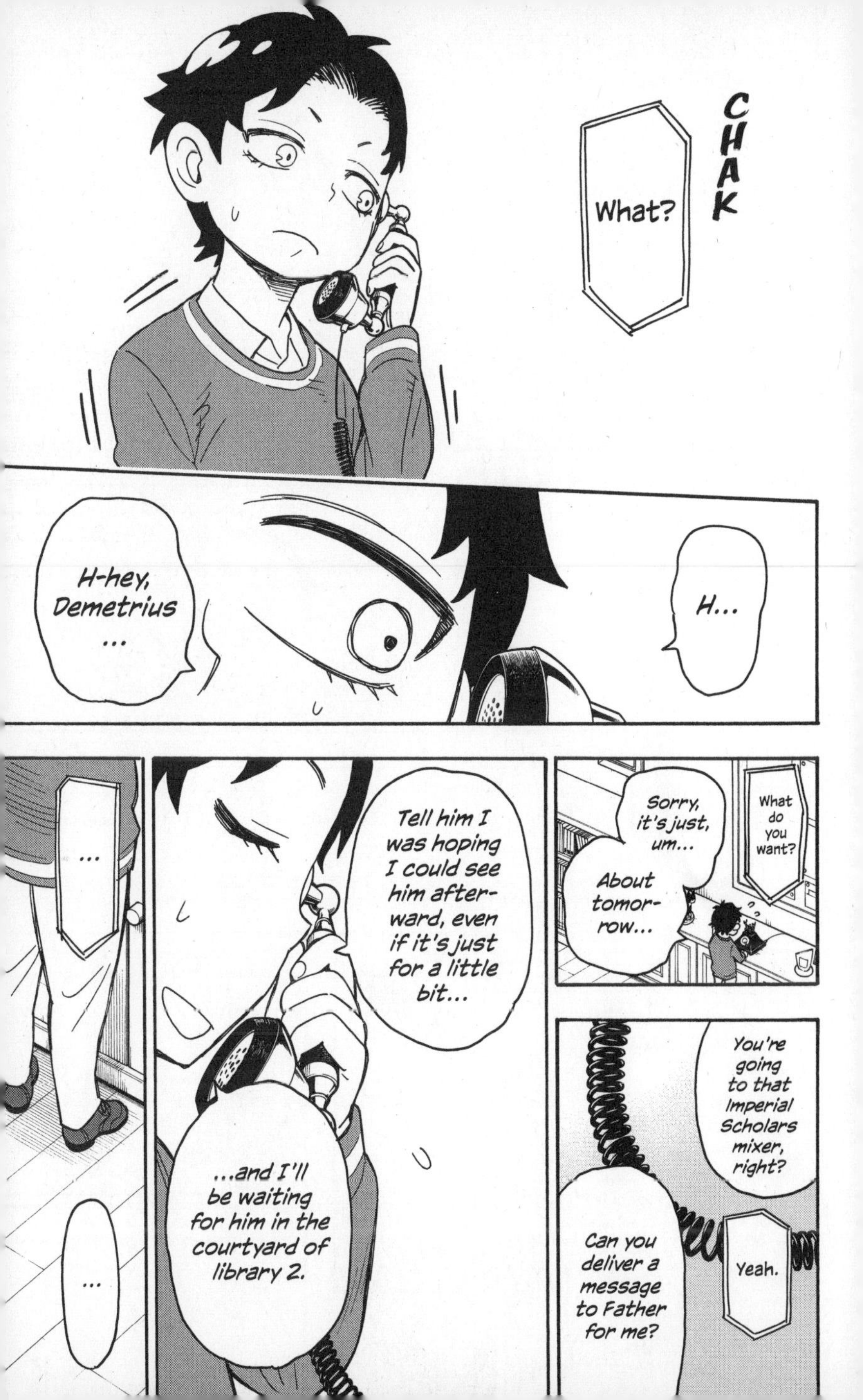
CHAK
What?
H...
H-hey, Demetrius ...
What do you want?
Sorry, it's just, um...
About tomorrow...
You're going to that Imperial Scholars mixer, right?
Yeah.
Can you deliver a message to Father for me?
Tell him I was hoping I could see him afterward, even if it's just for a little bit...
...and I'll be waiting for him in the courtyard of library 2.
...
...

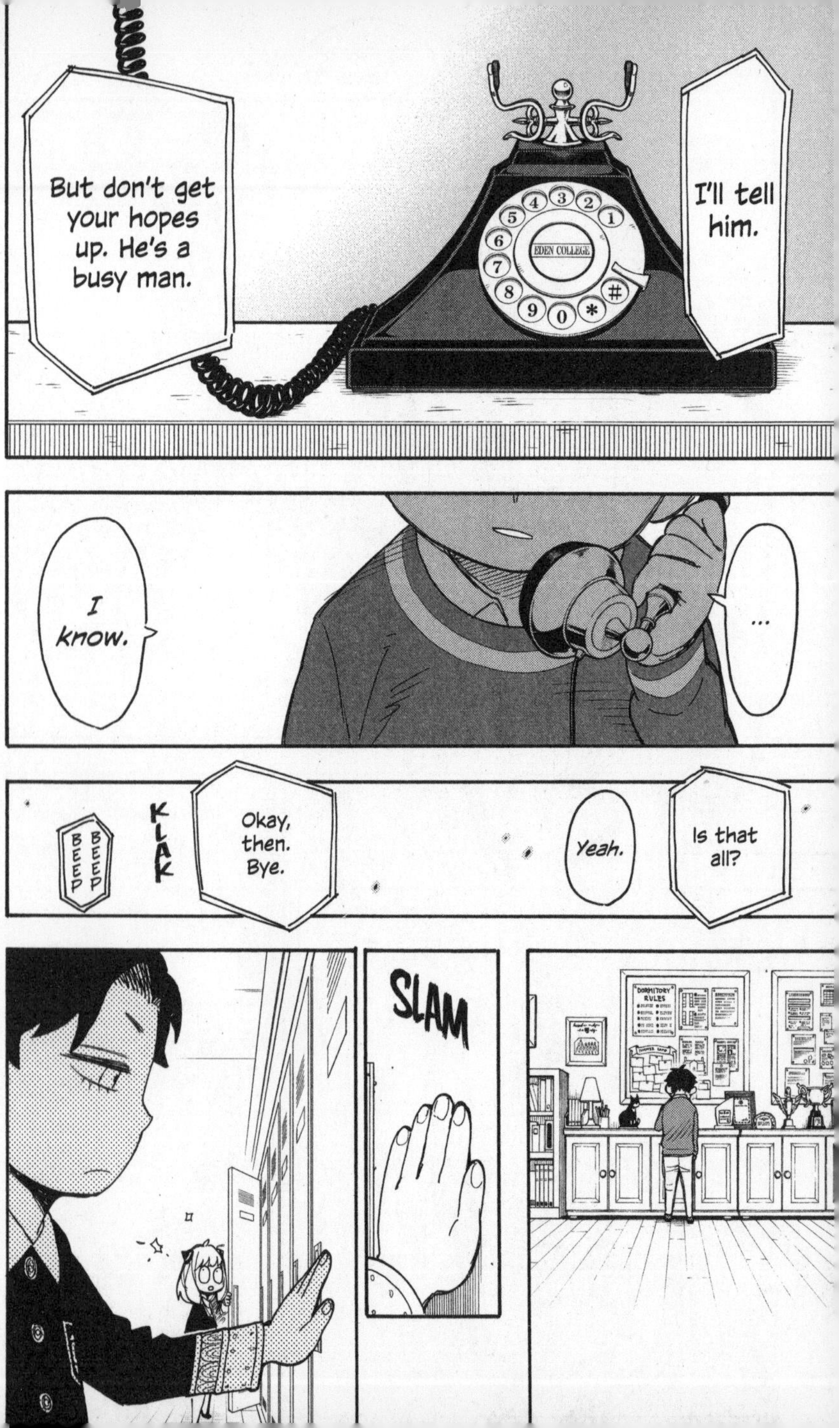
I'll tell him.
EDEN COLLEGE
But don't get your hopes up. He's a busy man.
...
I know.
Is that all?
Yeah.
Okay, then. Bye.
KLAK
BEEP BEEP
DORMITORY RULES
SLAM

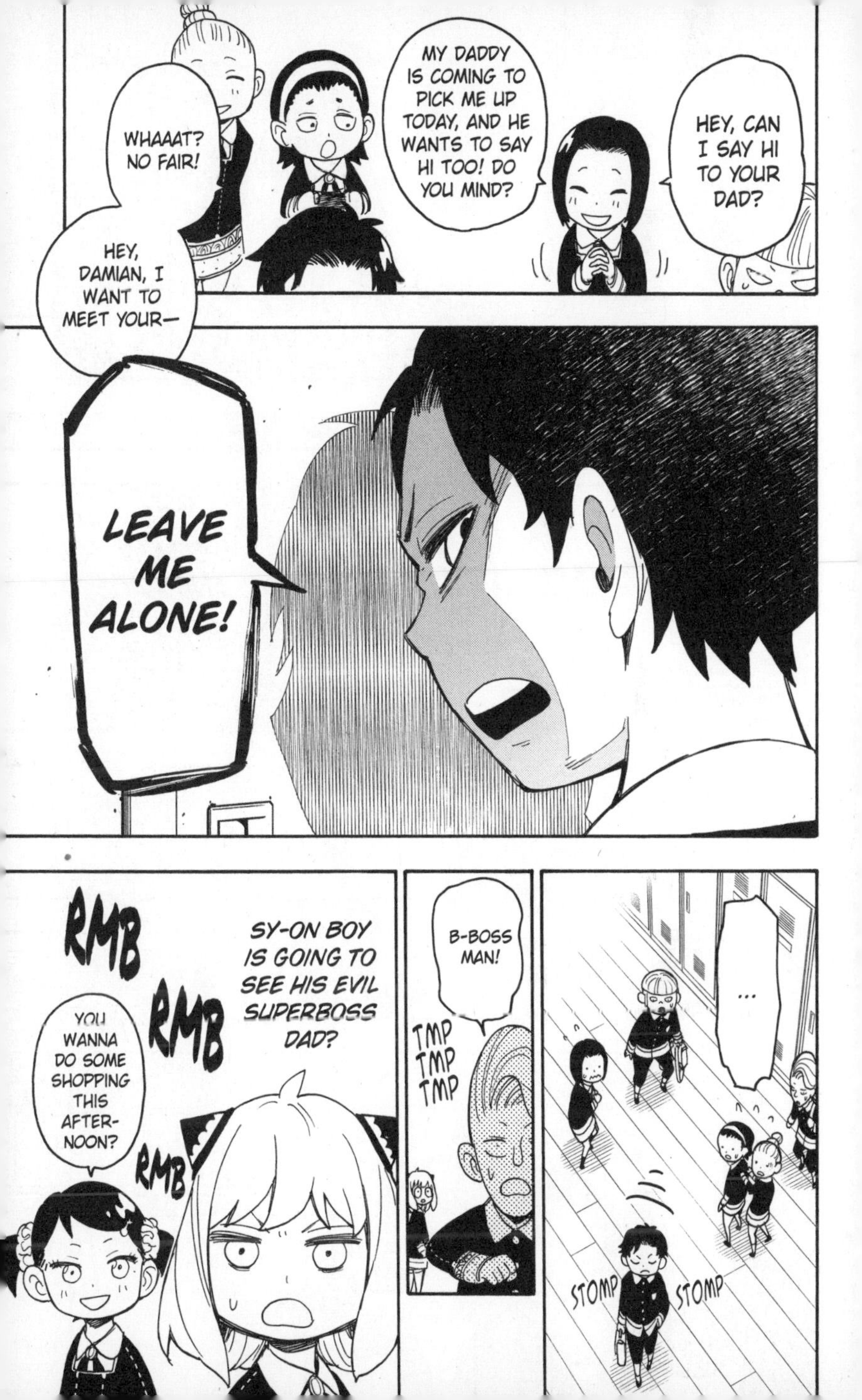
HEY, CAN I SAY HI TO YOUR DAD?
MY DADDY IS COMING TO PICK ME UP TODAY, AND HE WANTS TO SAY HI TOO! DO YOU MIND?
WHAAAT? NO FAIR!
HEY, DAMIAN, I WANT TO MEET YOUR—
LEAVE ME ALONE!
...
STOMP
STOMP
B-BOSS MAN!
TMP TMP TMP
SY-ON BOY IS GOING TO SEE HIS EVIL SUPERBOSS DAD?
RMB
RMB
YOU WANNA DO SOME SHOPPING THIS AFTER-NOON?
RMB

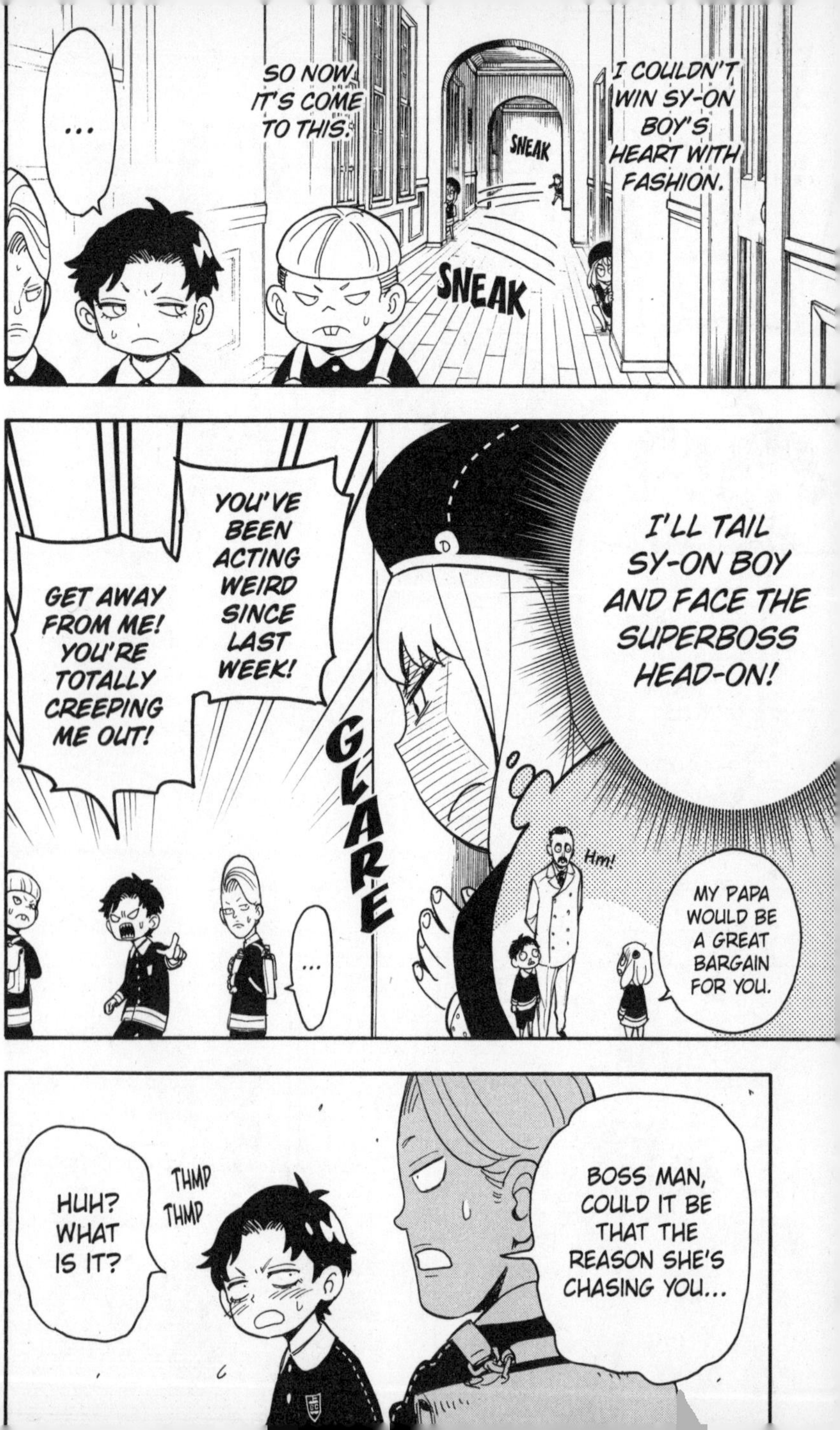
I COULDN'T WIN SY-ON BOY'S HEART WITH FASHION.
SNEAK
SNEAK
SO NOW IT'S COME TO THIS.
...
I'LL TAIL SY-ON BOY AND FACE THE SUPERBOSS HEAD-ON!
Hm!
MY PAPA WOULD BE A GREAT BARGAIN FOR YOU.
GLARE
YOU'VE BEEN ACTING WEIRD SINCE LAST WEEK!
GET AWAY FROM ME! YOU'RE TOTALLY CREEPING ME OUT!
...
BOSS MAN, COULD IT BE THAT THE REASON SHE'S CHASING YOU...
THMP THMP
HUH? WHAT IS IT?

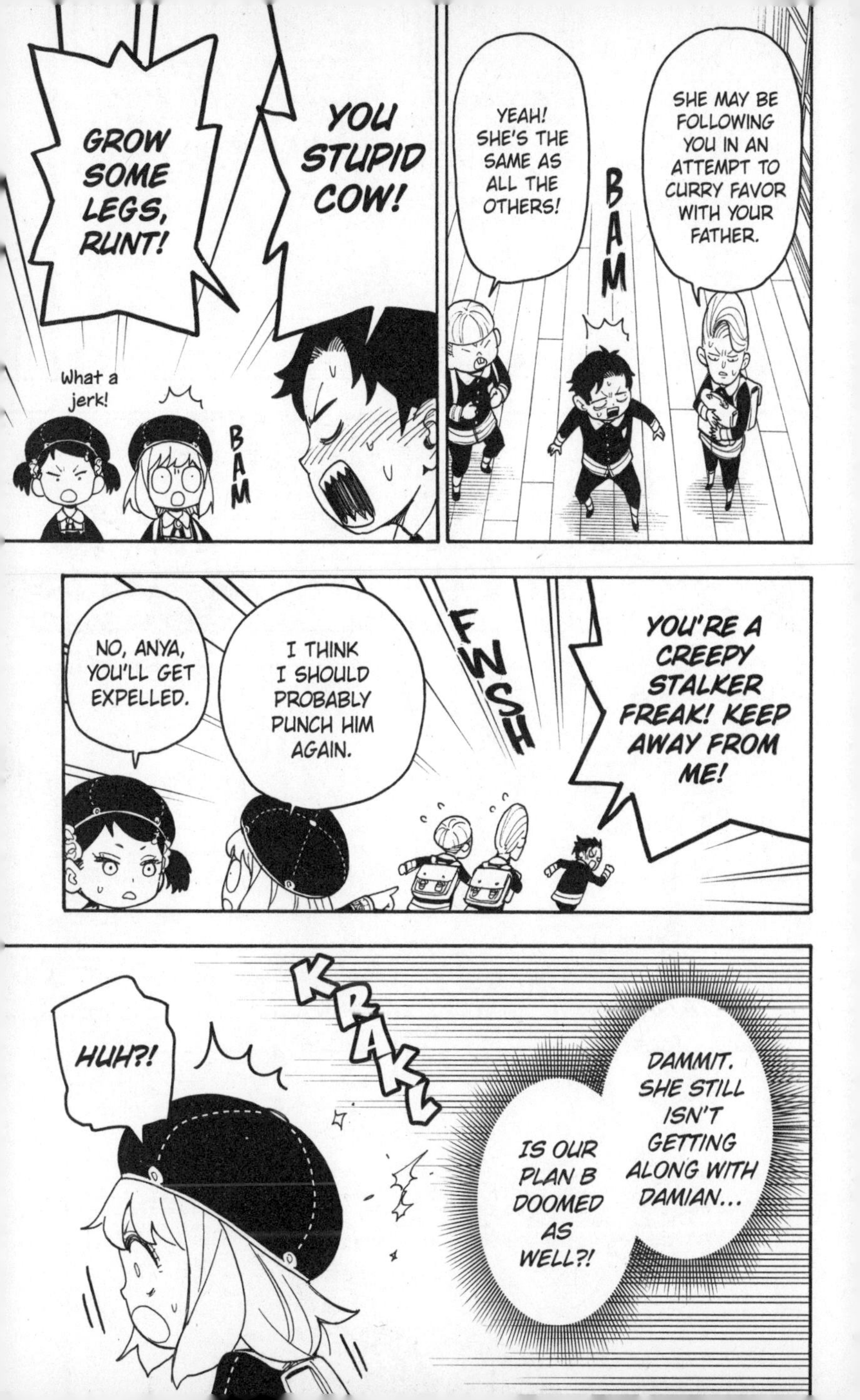
SHE MAY BE FOLLOWING YOU IN AN ATTEMPT TO CURRY FAVOR WITH YOUR FATHER.
BAM
YEAH! SHE'S THE SAME AS ALL THE OTHERS!
YOU STUPID COW!
GROW SOME LEGS, RUNT!
BAM
What a jerk!
YOU'RE A CREEPY STALKER FREAK! KEEP AWAY FROM ME!
FWSH
I THINK I SHOULD PROBABLY PUNCH HIM AGAIN.
NO, ANYA, YOU'LL GET EXPELLED.
DAMMIT. SHE STILL ISN'T GETTING ALONG WITH DAMIAN...
IS OUR PLAN B DOOMED AS WELL?!
KRAKL
HUH?!

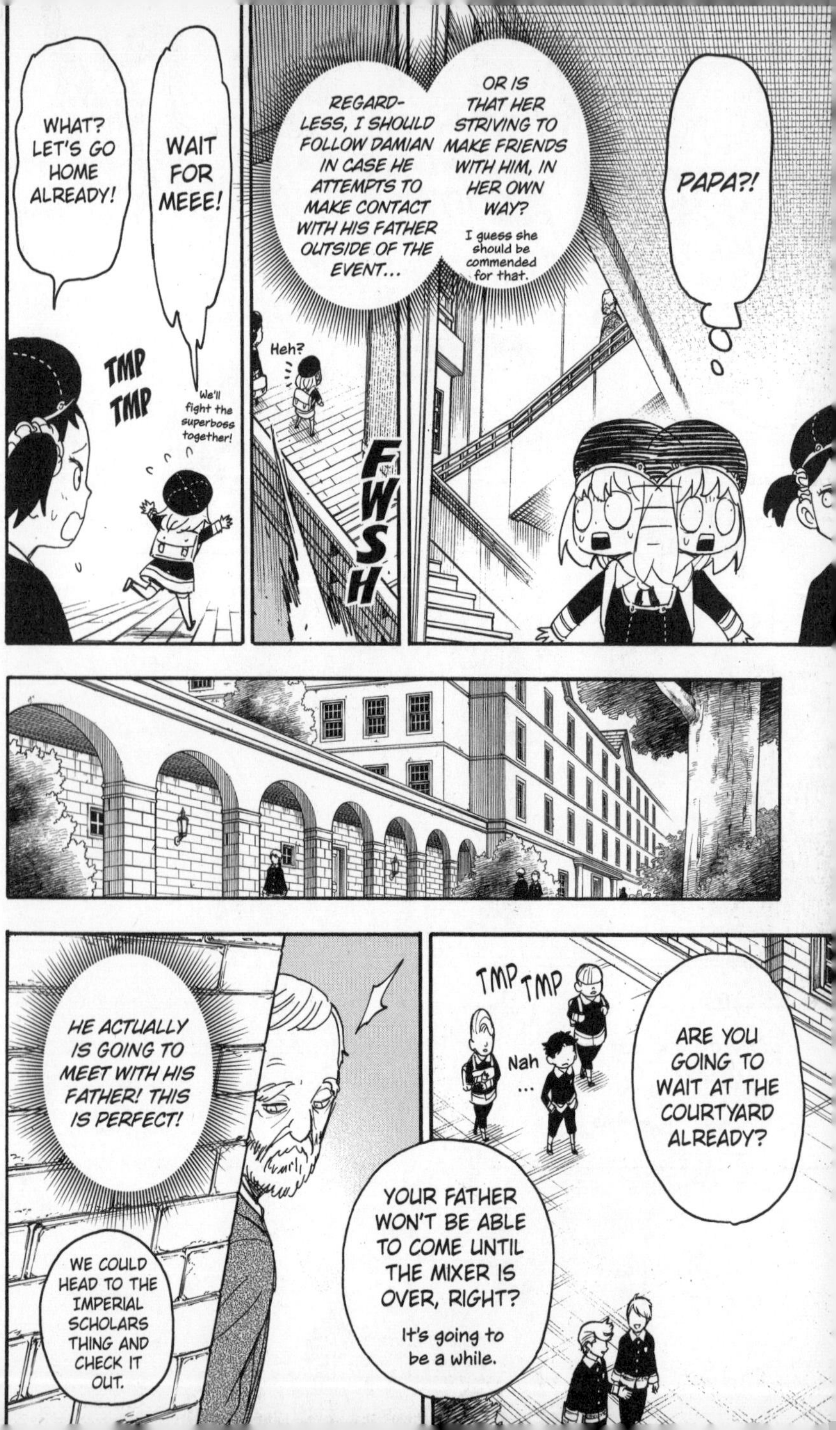
PAPA?!
OR IS THAT HER STRIVING TO MAKE FRIENDS WITH HIM, IN HER OWN WAY?
I guess she should be commended for that.
REGARDLESS, I SHOULD FOLLOW DAMIAN IN CASE HE ATTEMPTS TO MAKE CONTACT WITH HIS FATHER OUTSIDE OF THE EVENT...
Heh?
FWSH
WAIT FOR MEEE!
We'll fight the superboss together!
TMP TMP
WHAT? LET'S GO HOME ALREADY!
ARE YOU GOING TO WAIT AT THE COURTYARD ALREADY?
TMP TMP
Nah ...
YOUR FATHER WON'T BE ABLE TO COME UNTIL THE MIXER IS OVER, RIGHT?
It's going to be a while.
WE COULD HEAD TO THE IMPERIAL SCHOLARS THING AND CHECK IT OUT.
HE ACTUALLY IS GOING TO MEET WITH HIS FATHER! THIS IS PERFECT!

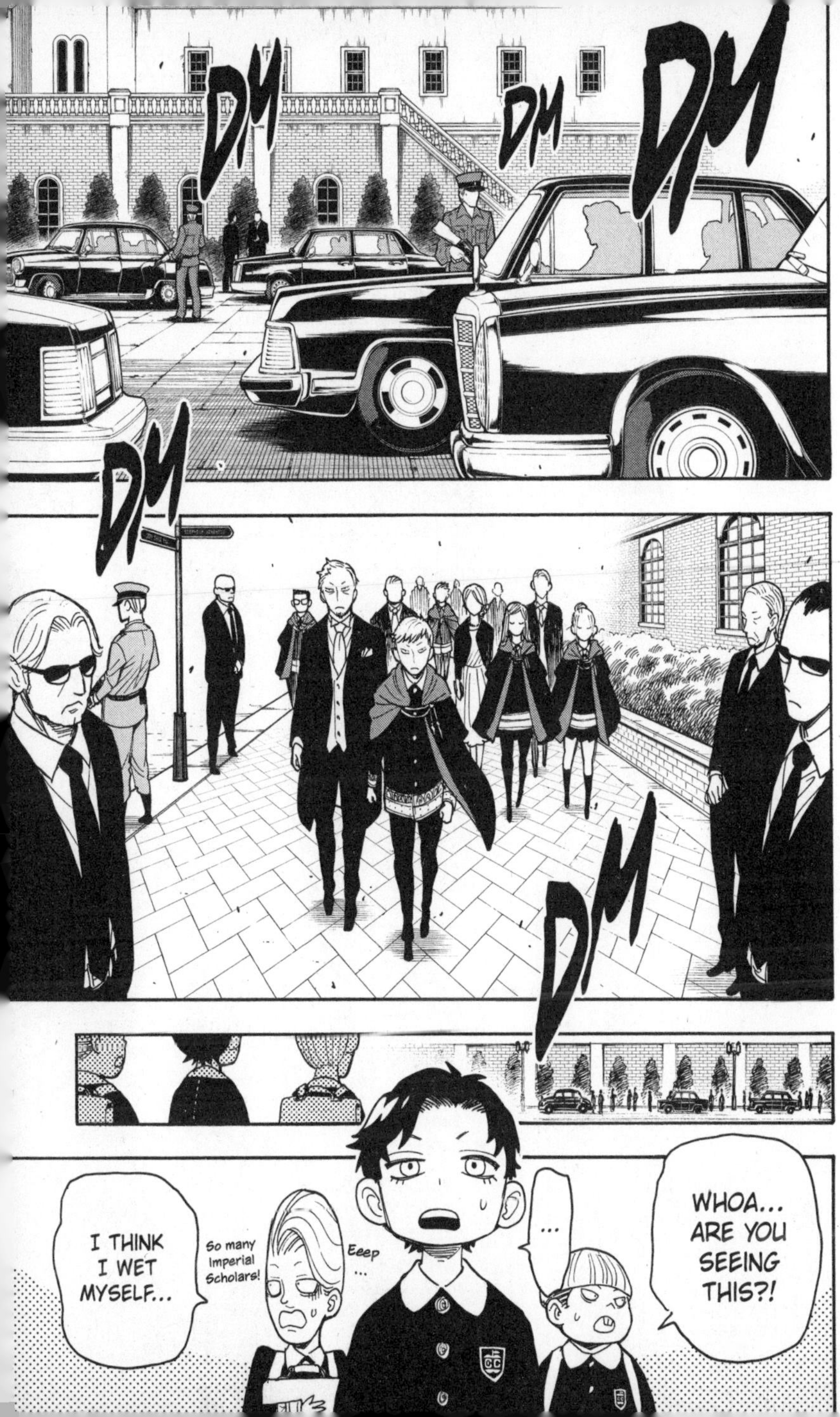
DM
DM
DM
DM
DM
WHOA... ARE YOU SEEING THIS?!
...
Eeep ...
So many Imperial Scholars!
I THINK I WET MYSELF...

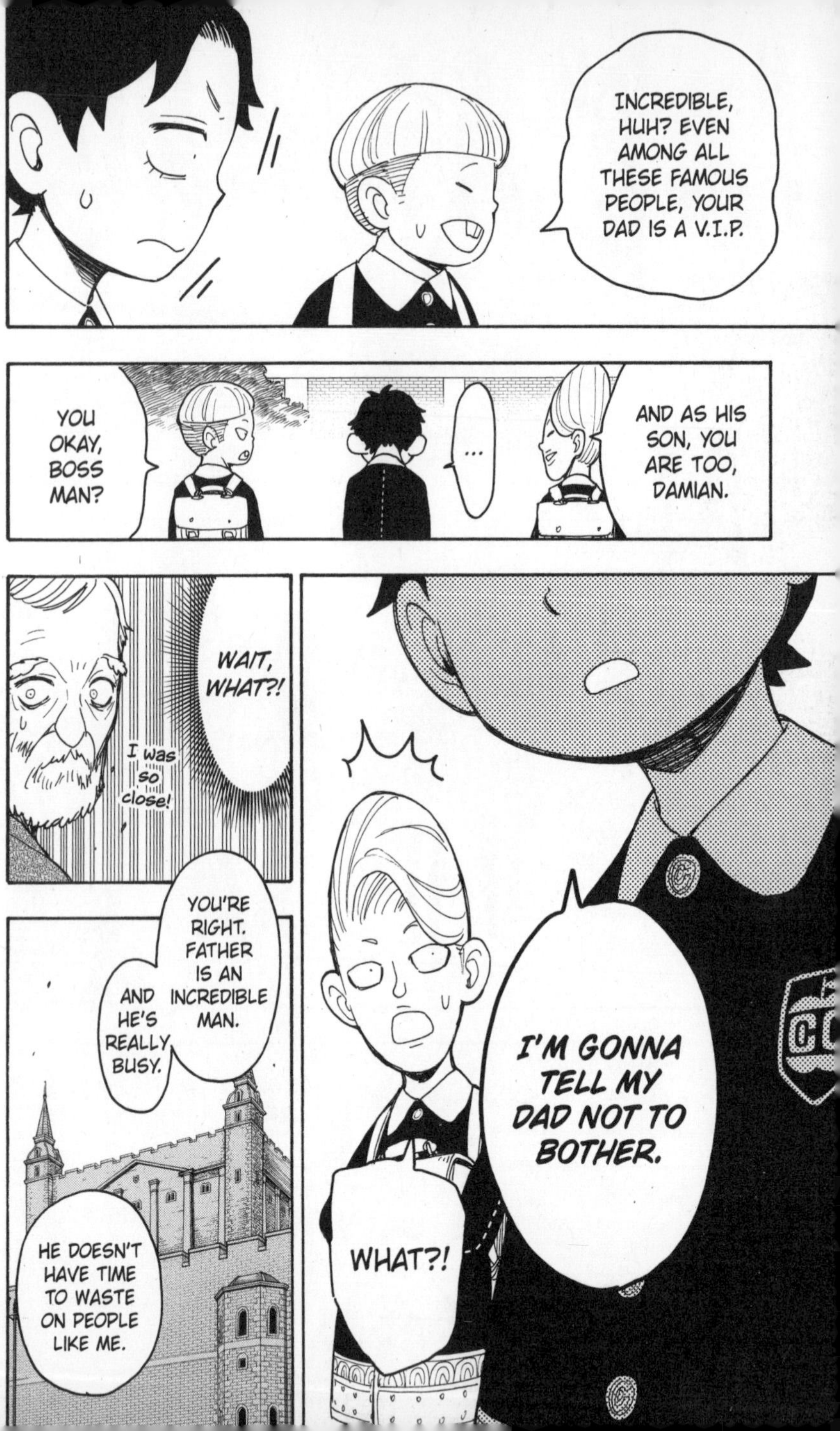
INCREDIBLE, HUH? EVEN AMONG ALL THESE FAMOUS PEOPLE, YOUR DAD IS A V.I.P.
AND AS HIS SON, YOU ARE TOO, DAMIAN.
...
YOU OKAY, BOSS MAN?
I'M GONNA TELL MY DAD NOT TO BOTHER.
WHAT?!
WAIT, WHAT?!
I was so close!
YOU'RE RIGHT. FATHER IS AN INCREDIBLE MAN.
AND HE'S REALLY BUSY.
HE DOESN'T HAVE TIME TO WASTE ON PEOPLE LIKE ME.

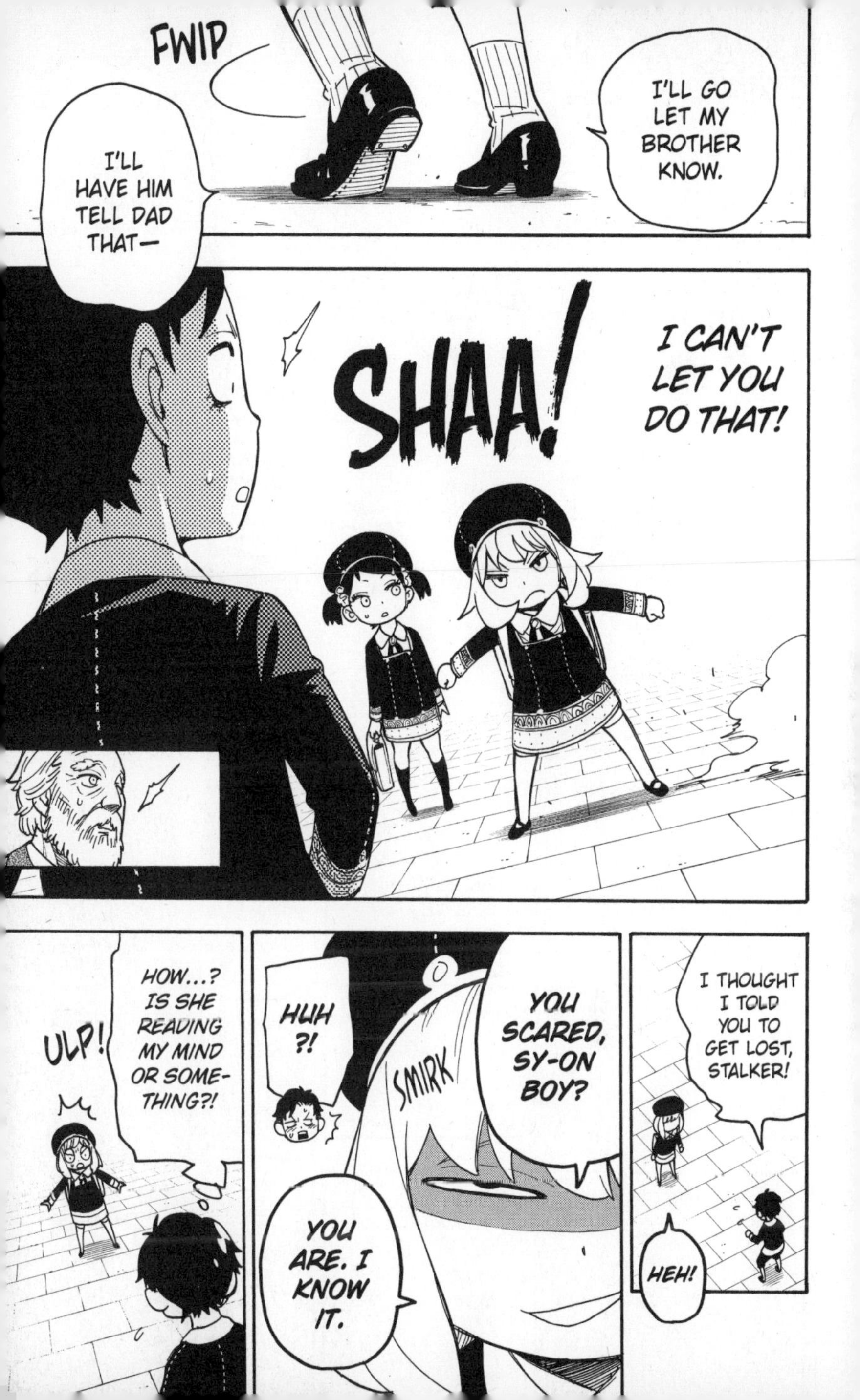
I'LL GO LET MY BROTHER KNOW.
FWIP
I'LL HAVE HIM TELL DAD THAT—
I CAN'T LET YOU DO THAT!
SHAA!
I THOUGHT I TOLD YOU TO GET LOST, STALKER!
HEH!
YOU SCARED, SY-ON BOY?
SMIRK
HUH ?!
YOU ARE. I KNOW IT.
HOW...? IS SHE READING MY MIND OR SOME-THING?!
ULP!

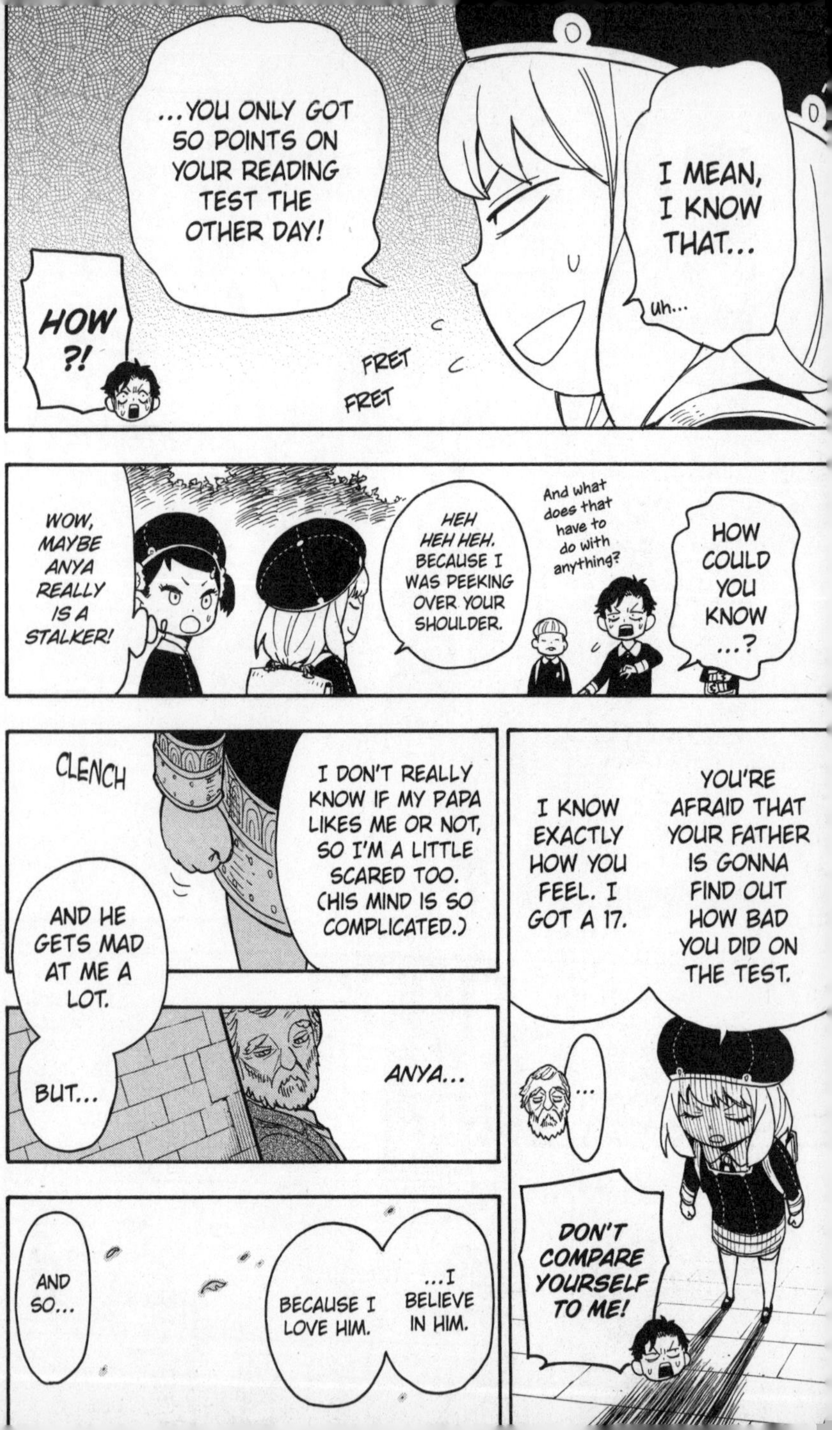
I MEAN, I KNOW THAT...
...YOU ONLY GOT 50 POINTS ON YOUR READING TEST THE OTHER DAY!
uh...
FRET
FRET
HOW?!
HOW COULD YOU KNOW ...?
And what does that have to do with anything?
HEH HEH HEH. BECAUSE I WAS PEEKING OVER YOUR SHOULDER.
WOW, MAYBE ANYA REALLY IS A STALKER!
YOU'RE AFRAID THAT YOUR FATHER IS GONNA FIND OUT HOW BAD YOU DID ON THE TEST.
I KNOW EXACTLY HOW YOU FEEL. I GOT A 17.
...
DON'T COMPARE YOURSELF TO ME!
I DON'T REALLY KNOW IF MY PAPA LIKES ME OR NOT, SO I'M A LITTLE SCARED TOO. (HIS MIND IS SO COMPLICATED.)
CLENCH
AND HE GETS MAD AT ME A LOT.
ANYA...
BUT...
...I BELIEVE IN HIM.
BECAUSE I LOVE HIM.
AND SO...

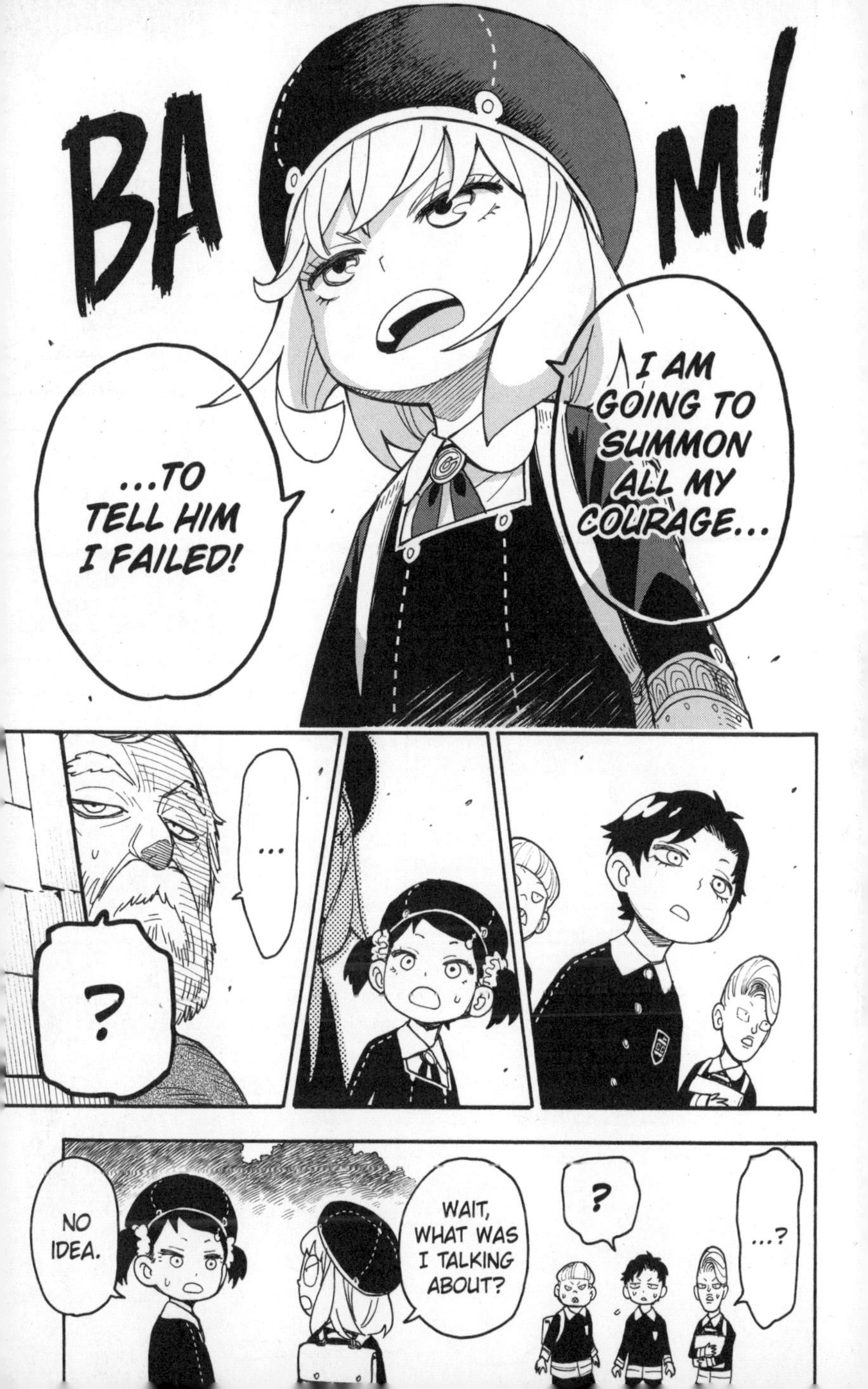
BAM!
I AM GOING TO SUMMON ALL MY COURAGE...
...TO TELL HIM I FAILED!
...
?
...?
?
WAIT, WHAT WAS I TALKING ABOUT?
NO IDEA.

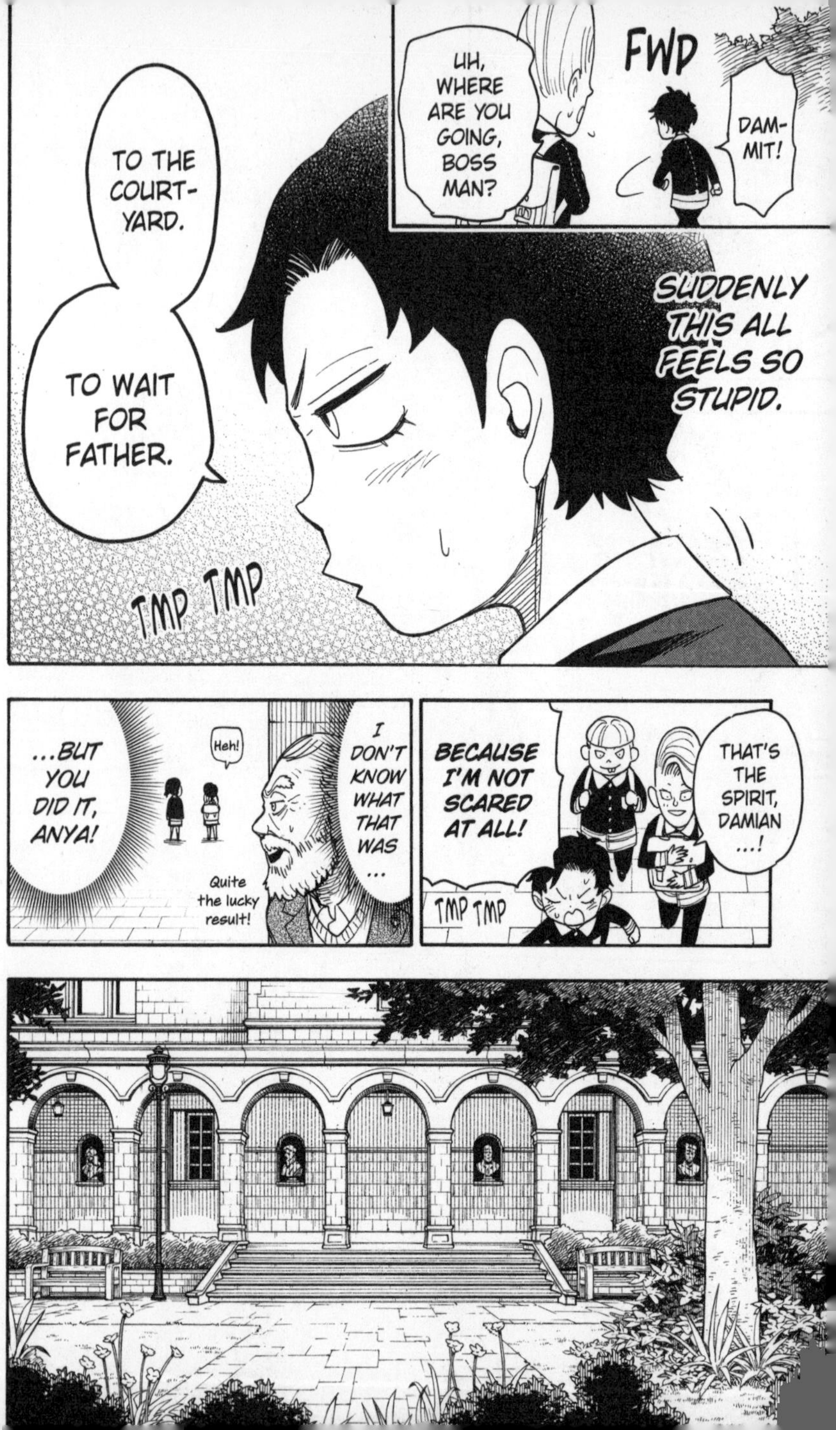
DAM-MIT!
FWD
UH, WHERE ARE YOU GOING, BOSS MAN?
SUDDENLY THIS ALL FEELS SO STUPID.
TO THE COURT-YARD.
TO WAIT FOR FATHER.
TMP TMP
THAT'S THE SPIRIT, DAMIAN...!
BECAUSE I'M NOT SCARED AT ALL!
TMP TMP
I DON'T KNOW WHAT THAT WAS...
Heh!
Quite the lucky result!
...BUT YOU DID IT, ANYA!

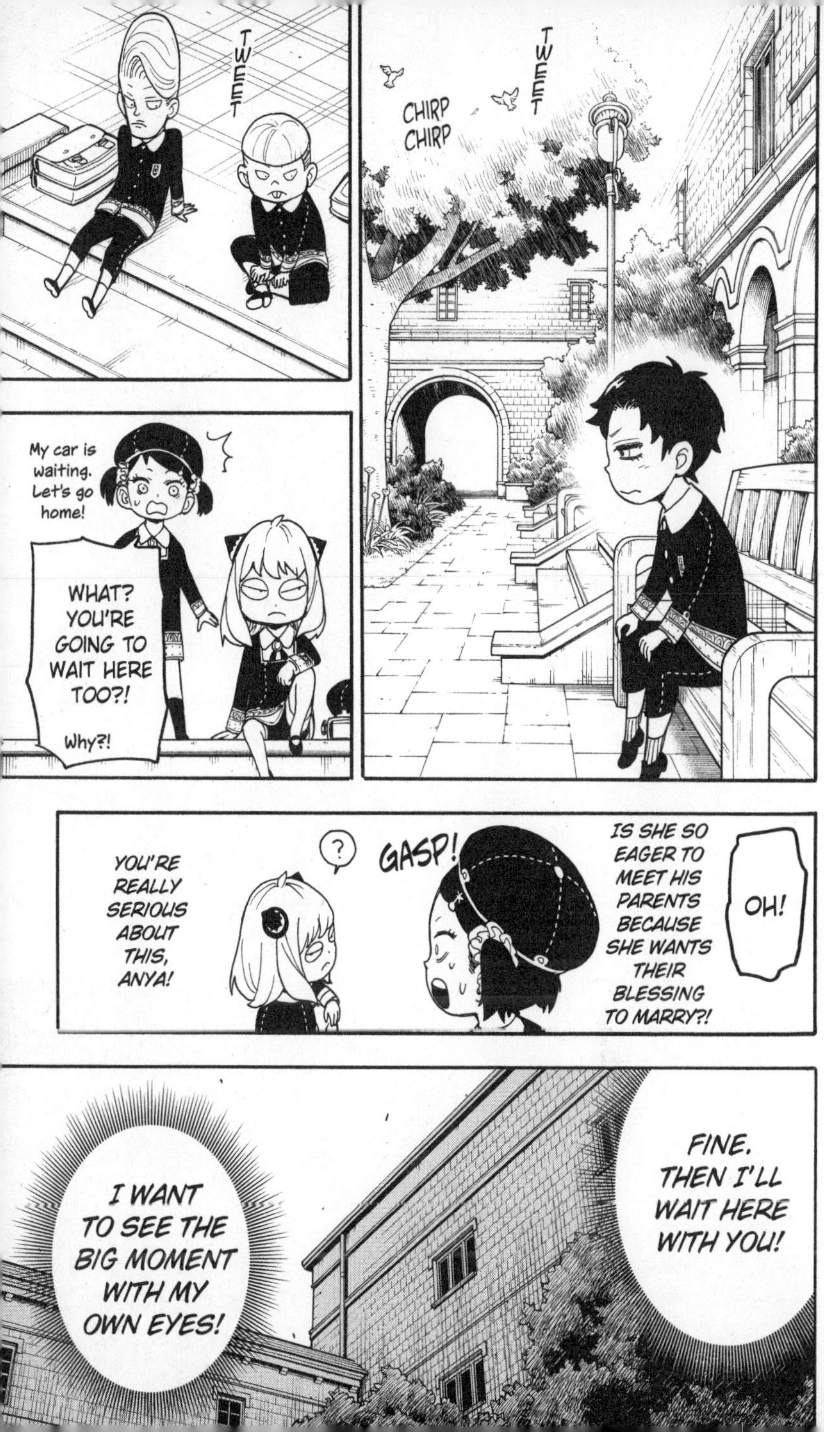
TWEET
CHIRP CHIRP
TWEET
My car is waiting. Let's go home!
WHAT? YOU'RE GOING TO WAIT HERE TOO?!
Why?!
OH!
IS SHE SO EAGER TO MEET HIS PARENTS BECAUSE SHE WANTS THEIR BLESSING TO MARRY?!
GASP!
?
YOU'RE REALLY SERIOUS ABOUT THIS, ANYA!
FINE. THEN I'LL WAIT HERE WITH YOU!
I WANT TO SEE THE BIG MOMENT WITH MY OWN EYES!

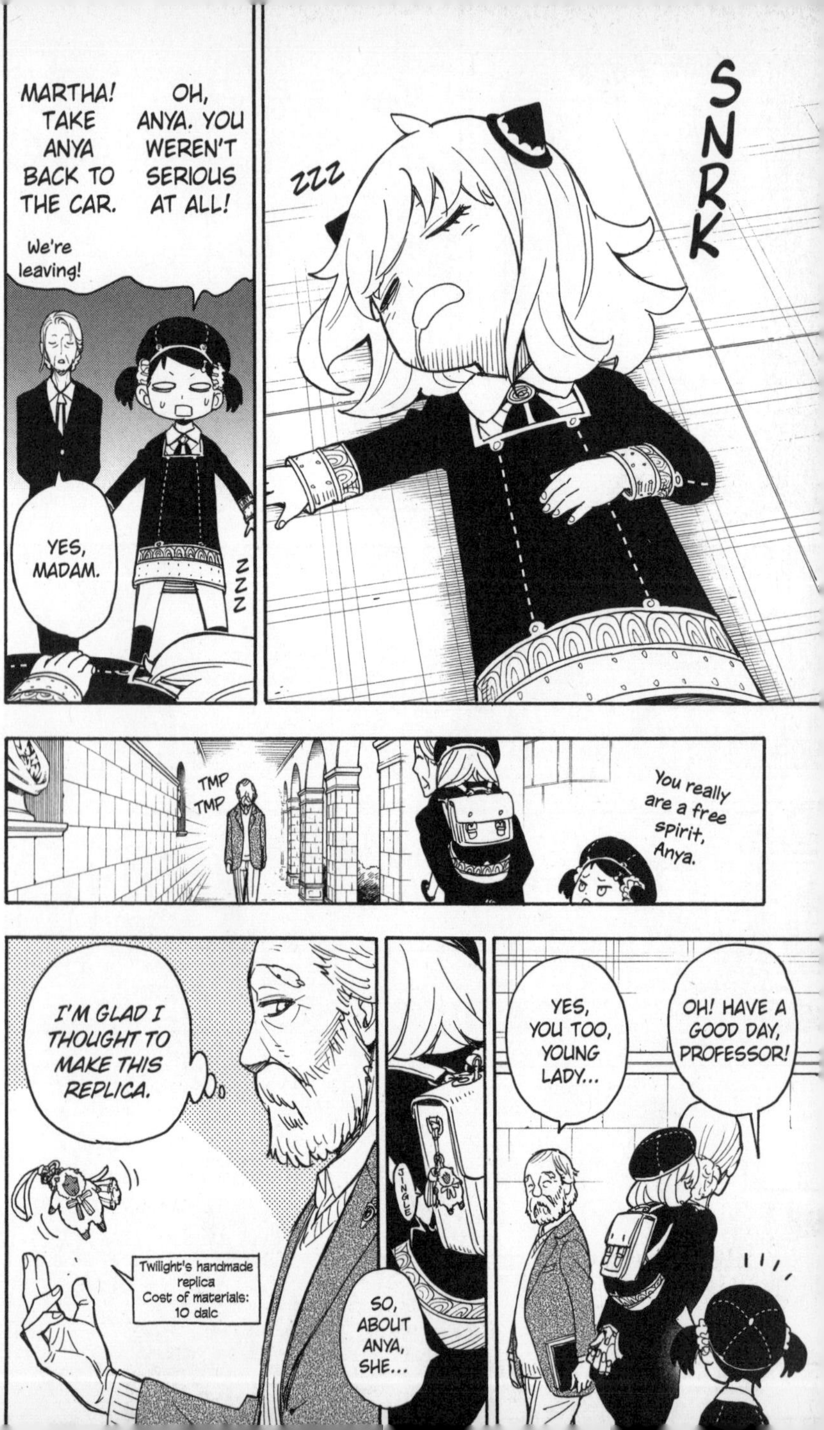
SNRK
ZZZ
OH, ANYA. YOU WEREN'T SERIOUS AT ALL!
MARTHA! TAKE ANYA BACK TO THE CAR.
We're leaving!
YES, MADAM.
ZZZ
You really are a free spirit, Anya.
TMP TMP
OH! HAVE A GOOD DAY, PROFESSOR!
YES, YOU TOO, YOUNG LADY...
JINGLE
SO, ABOUT ANYA, SHE...
I'M GLAD I THOUGHT TO MAKE THIS REPLICA.
Twilight's handmade replica
Cost of materials: 10 dalc

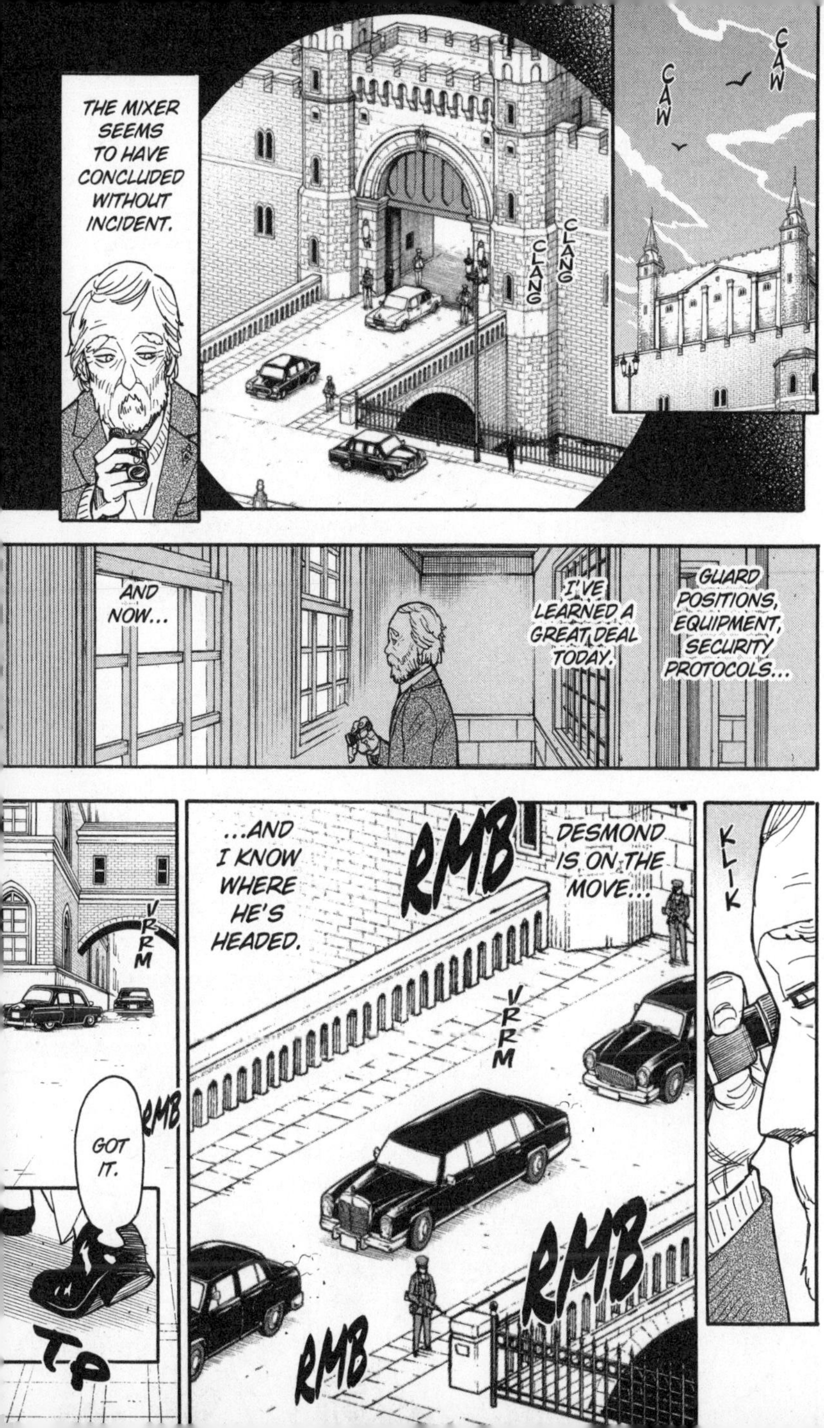
CAW
CAW
CLANG
CLANG
THE MIXER SEEMS TO HAVE CONCLUDED WITHOUT INCIDENT.
GUARD POSITIONS, EQUIPMENT, SECURITY PROTOCOLS...
I'VE LEARNED A GREAT DEAL TODAY.
AND NOW...
KLIK
DESMOND IS ON THE MOVE...
RMB
...AND I KNOW WHERE HE'S HEADED.
VRRM
RMB
RMB
VRRM
RMB
GOT IT.
TP

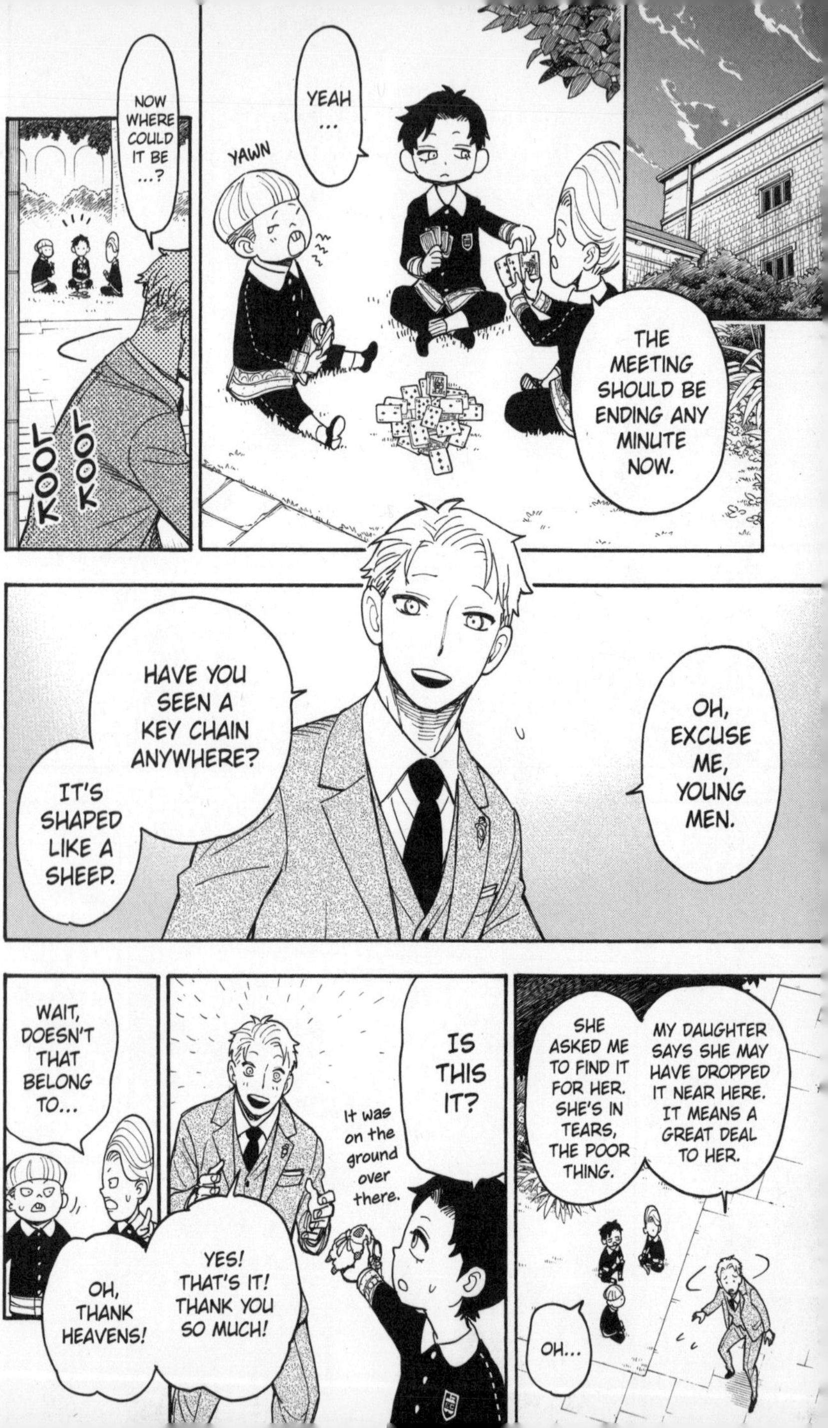
THE MEETING SHOULD BE ENDING ANY MINUTE NOW.
YEAH ...
YAWN
NOW WHERE COULD IT BE ...?
LOOK LOOK
OH, EXCUSE ME, YOUNG MEN.
HAVE YOU SEEN A KEY CHAIN ANYWHERE?
IT'S SHAPED LIKE A SHEEP.
MY DAUGHTER SAYS SHE MAY HAVE DROPPED IT NEAR HERE. IT MEANS A GREAT DEAL TO HER.
SHE ASKED ME TO FIND IT FOR HER. SHE'S IN TEARS, THE POOR THING.
OH...
IS THIS IT?
It was on the ground over there.
YES! THAT'S IT! THANK YOU SO MUCH!
OH, THANK HEAVENS!
WAIT, DOESN'T THAT BELONG TO...

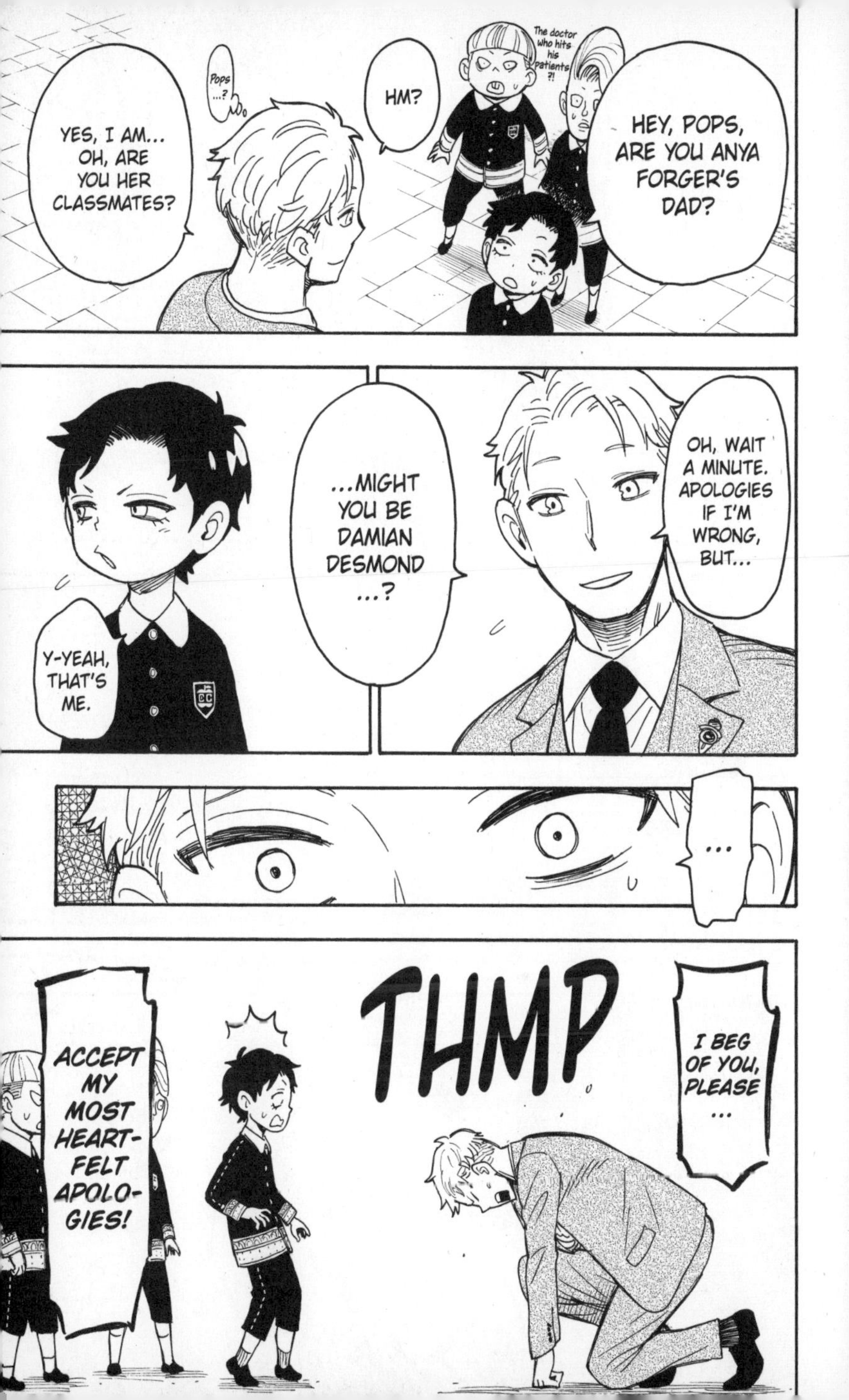
HEY, POPS, ARE YOU ANYA FORGER'S DAD?
The doctor who hits his patients?!
HM?
Pops...?
YES, I AM... OH, ARE YOU HER CLASSMATES?
OH, WAIT A MINUTE. APOLOGIES IF I'M WRONG, BUT...
...MIGHT YOU BE DAMIAN DESMOND...?
Y-YEAH, THAT'S ME.
...
I BEG OF YOU, PLEASE...
THMP
ACCEPT MY MOST HEART-FELT APOLOGIES!

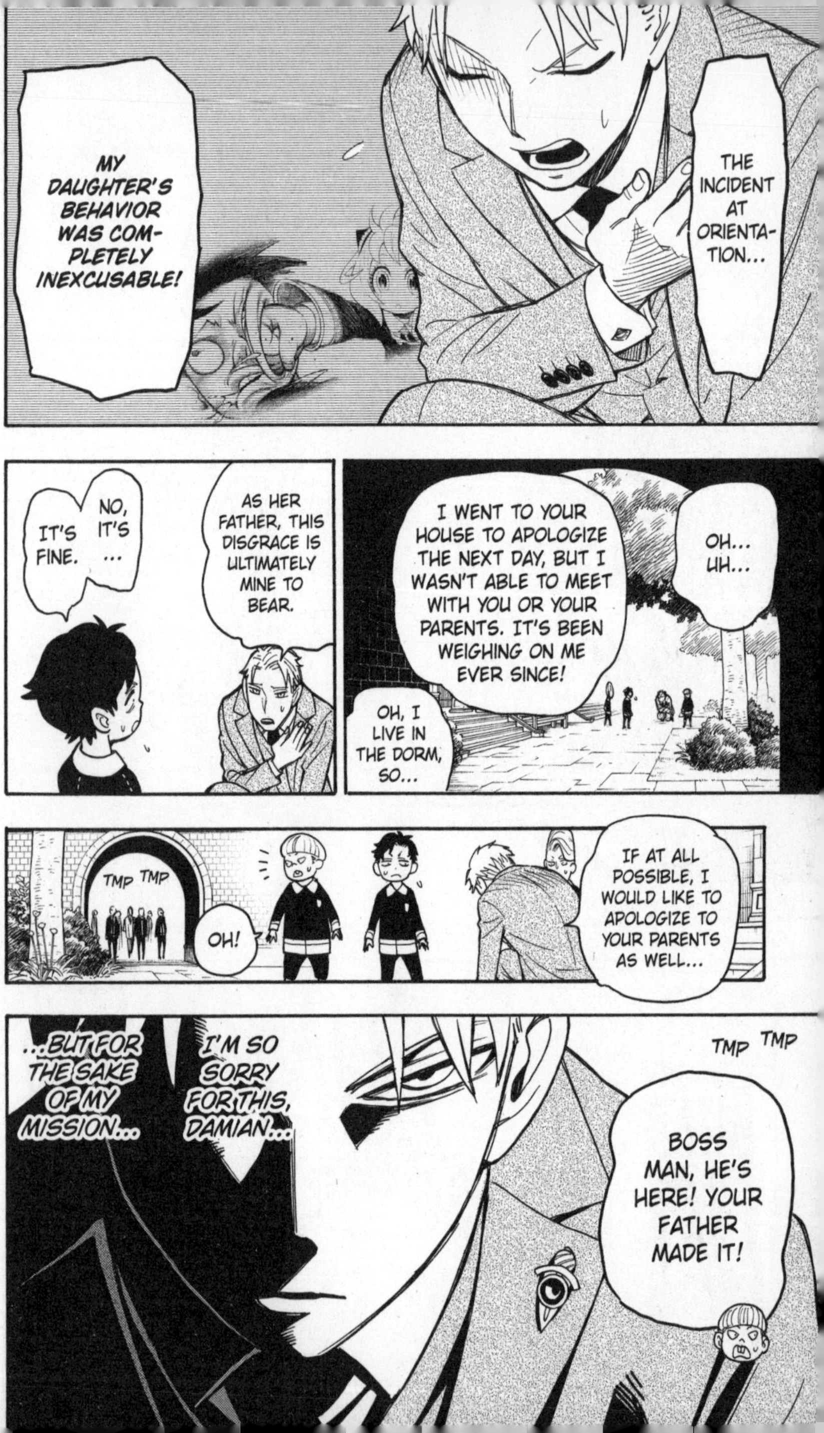
THE INCIDENT AT ORIENTATION...
MY DAUGHTER'S BEHAVIOR WAS COMPLETELY INEXCUSABLE!
I WENT TO YOUR HOUSE TO APOLOGIZE THE NEXT DAY, BUT I WASN'T ABLE TO MEET WITH YOU OR YOUR PARENTS. IT'S BEEN WEIGHING ON ME EVER SINCE!
OH... UH...
OH, I LIVE IN THE DORM, SO...
AS HER FATHER, THIS DISGRACE IS ULTIMATELY MINE TO BEAR.
NO, IT'S ...
IT'S FINE.
IF AT ALL POSSIBLE, I WOULD LIKE TO APOLOGIZE TO YOUR PARENTS AS WELL...
OH!
TMP TMP
TMP TMP
BOSS MAN, HE'S HERE! YOUR FATHER MADE IT!
I'M SO SORRY FOR THIS, DAMIAN...
...BUT FOR THE SAKE OF MY MISSION...

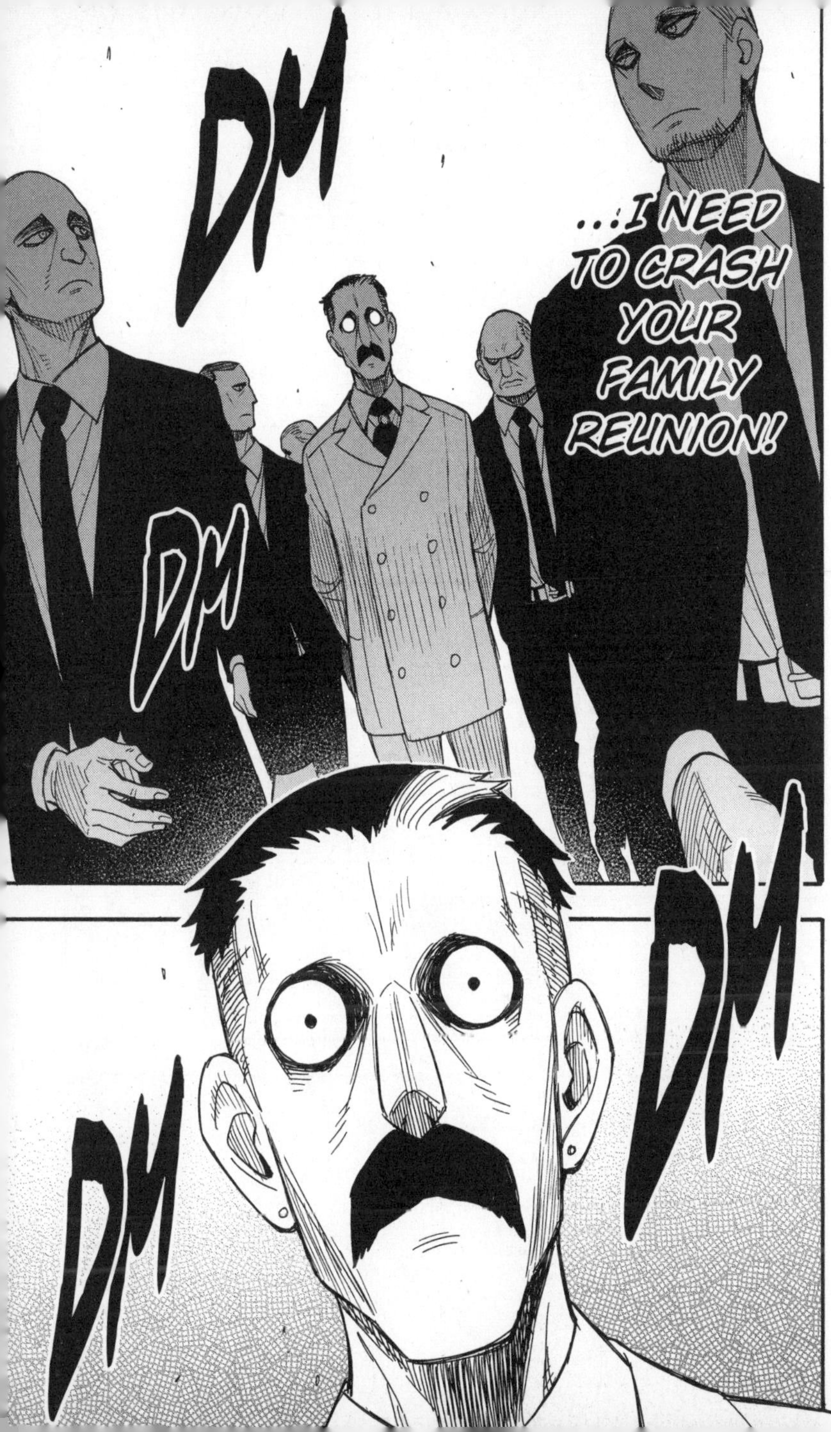
...I NEED TO CRASH YOUR FAMILY REUNION!
DM
DM
DM
DM

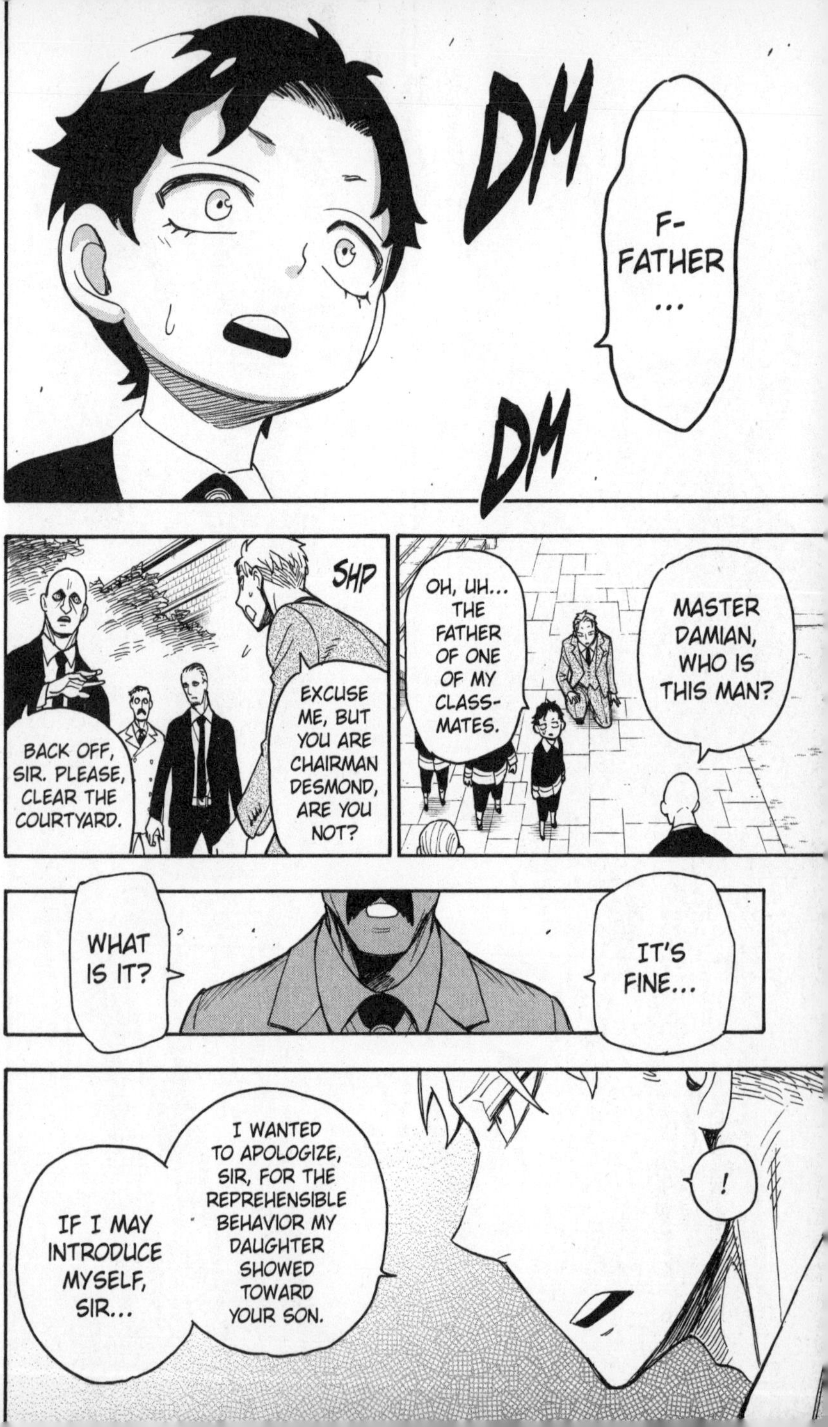
F-FATHER...
DM
DM
MASTER DAMIAN, WHO IS THIS MAN?
OH, UH... THE FATHER OF ONE OF MY CLASSMATES.
SHP
EXCUSE ME, BUT YOU ARE CHAIRMAN DESMOND, ARE YOU NOT?
BACK OFF, SIR. PLEASE, CLEAR THE COURTYARD.
IT'S FINE...
WHAT IS IT?
!
I WANTED TO APOLOGIZE, SIR, FOR THE REPREHENSIBLE BEHAVIOR MY DAUGHTER SHOWED TOWARD YOUR SON.
IF I MAY INTRODUCE MYSELF, SIR...

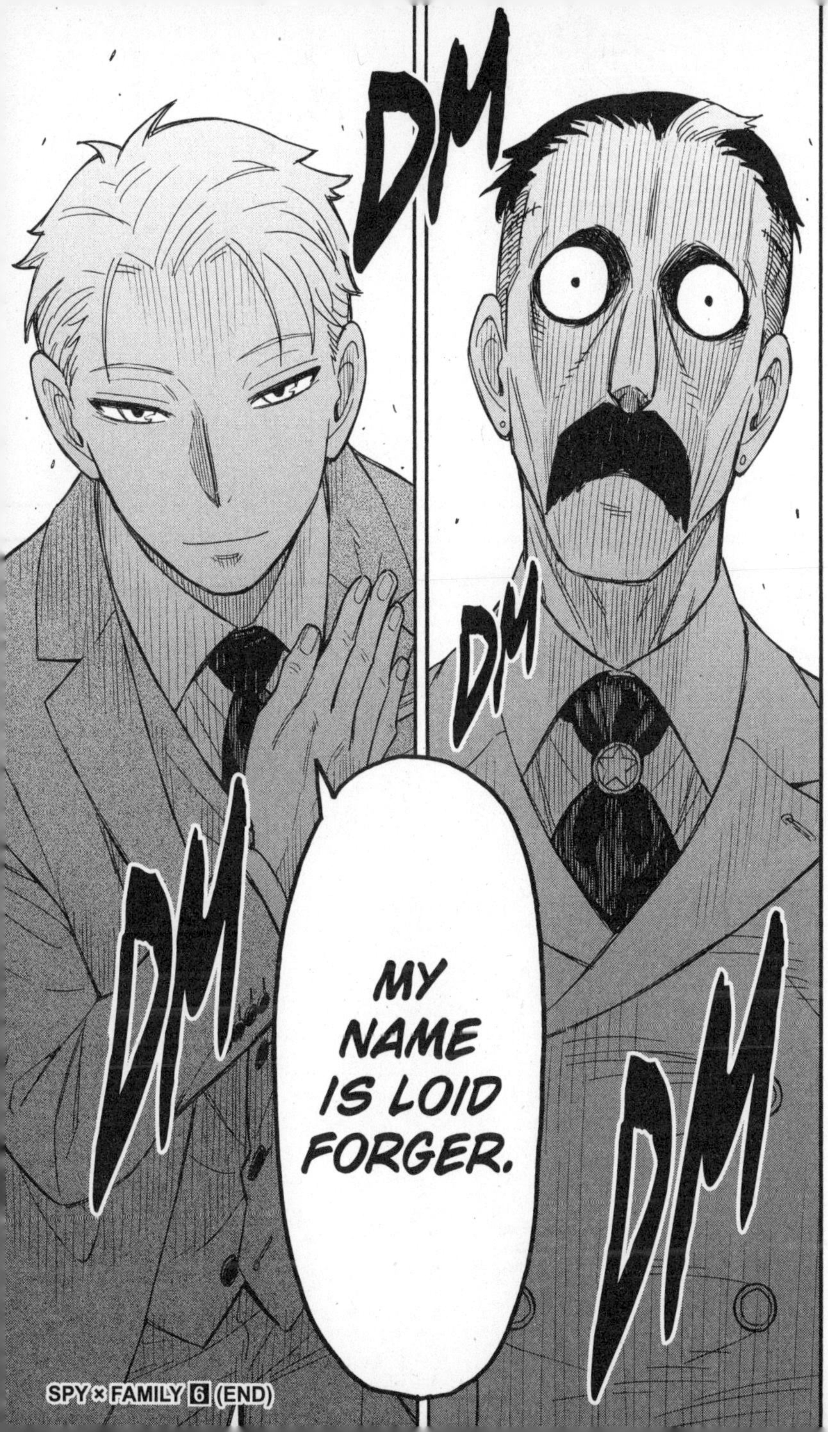
DM
DM
DM
MY NAME IS LOID FORGER.
DM

SPY×FAMILY

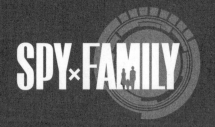

SHORT MISSION 4

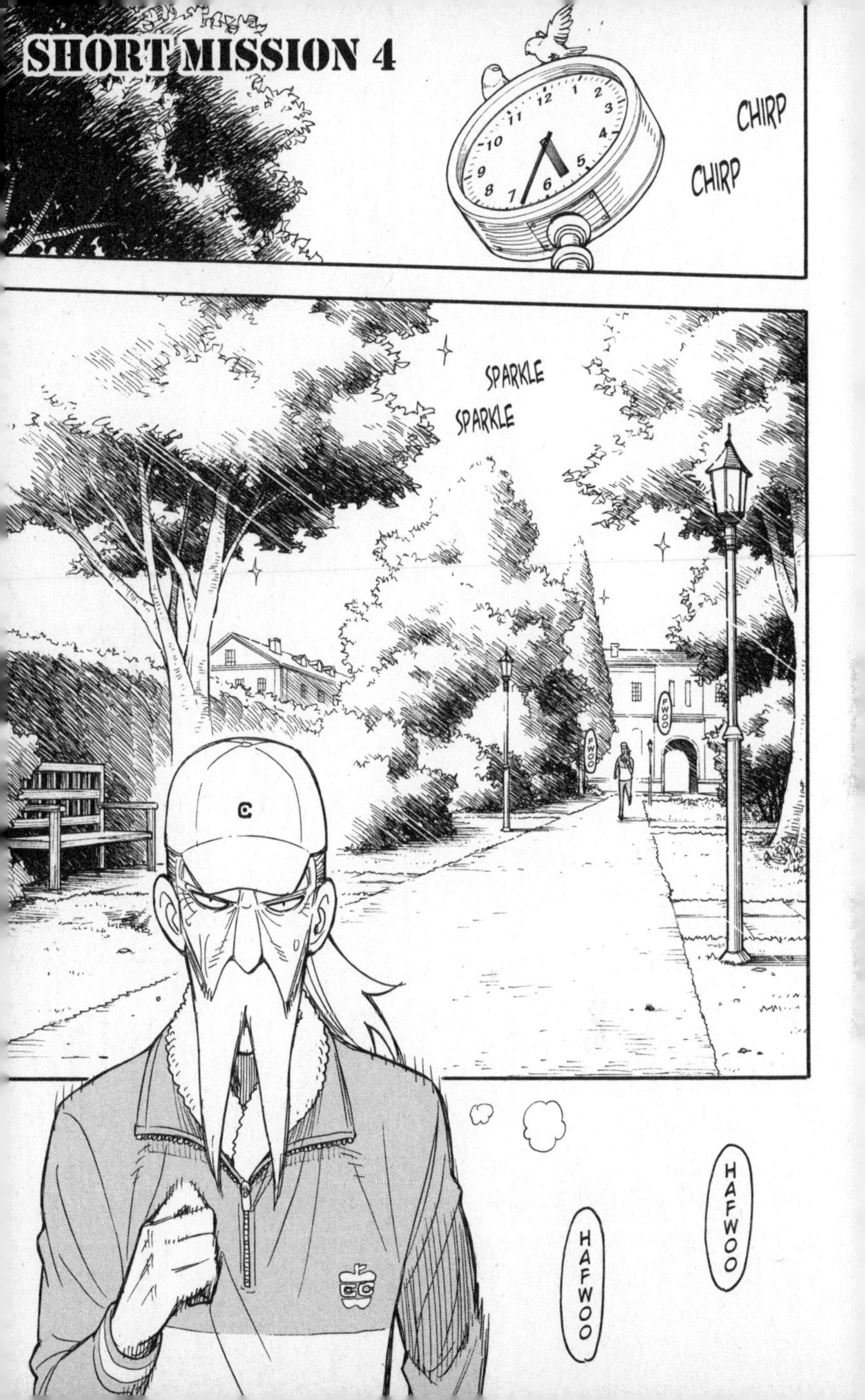
CHIRP
CHIRP
SPARKLE
SPARKLE
FWOO
FWOO
HAFWOO
HAFWOO

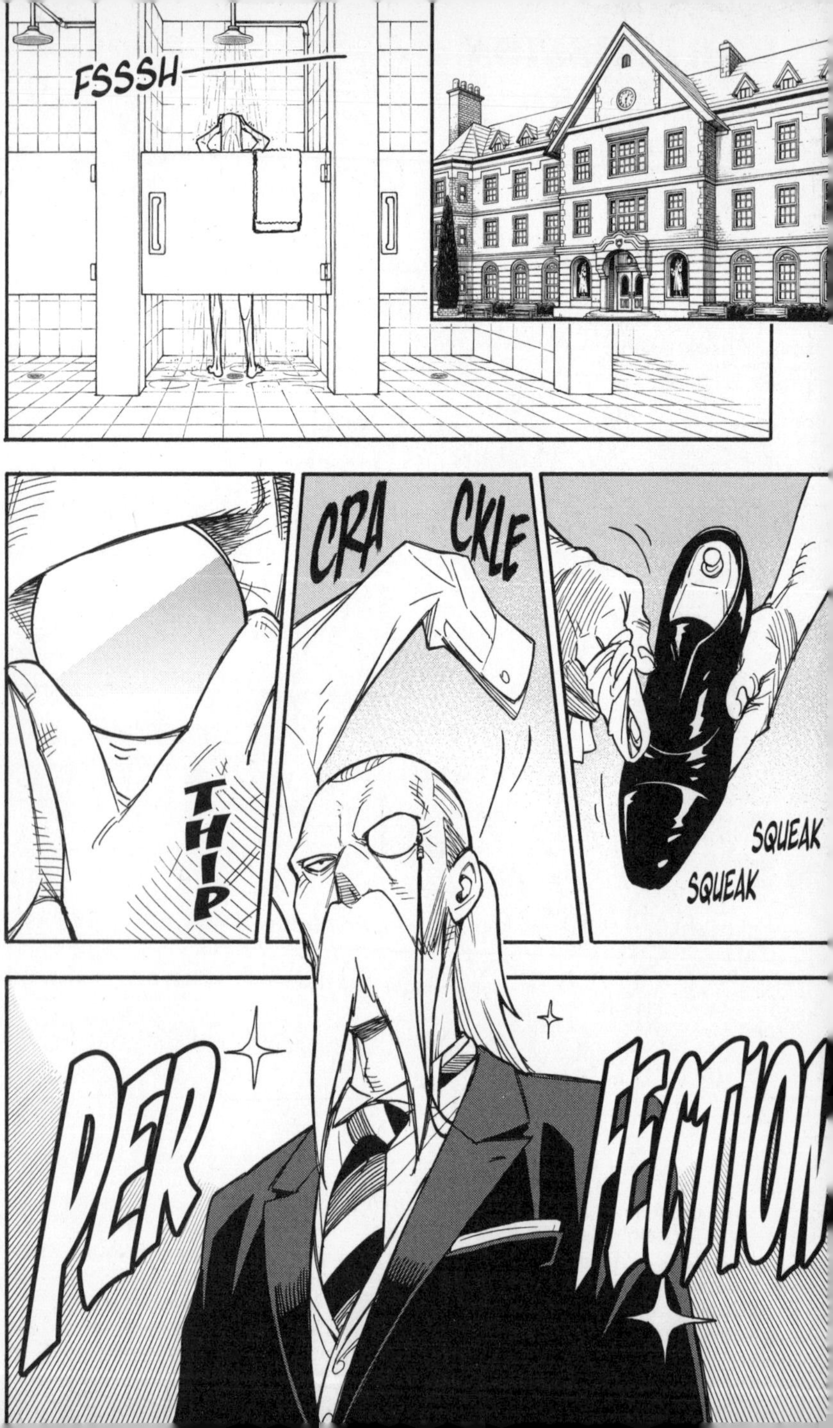
FSSSH
SQUEAK
SQUEAK
CRACKLE
THIP
PERFECTION

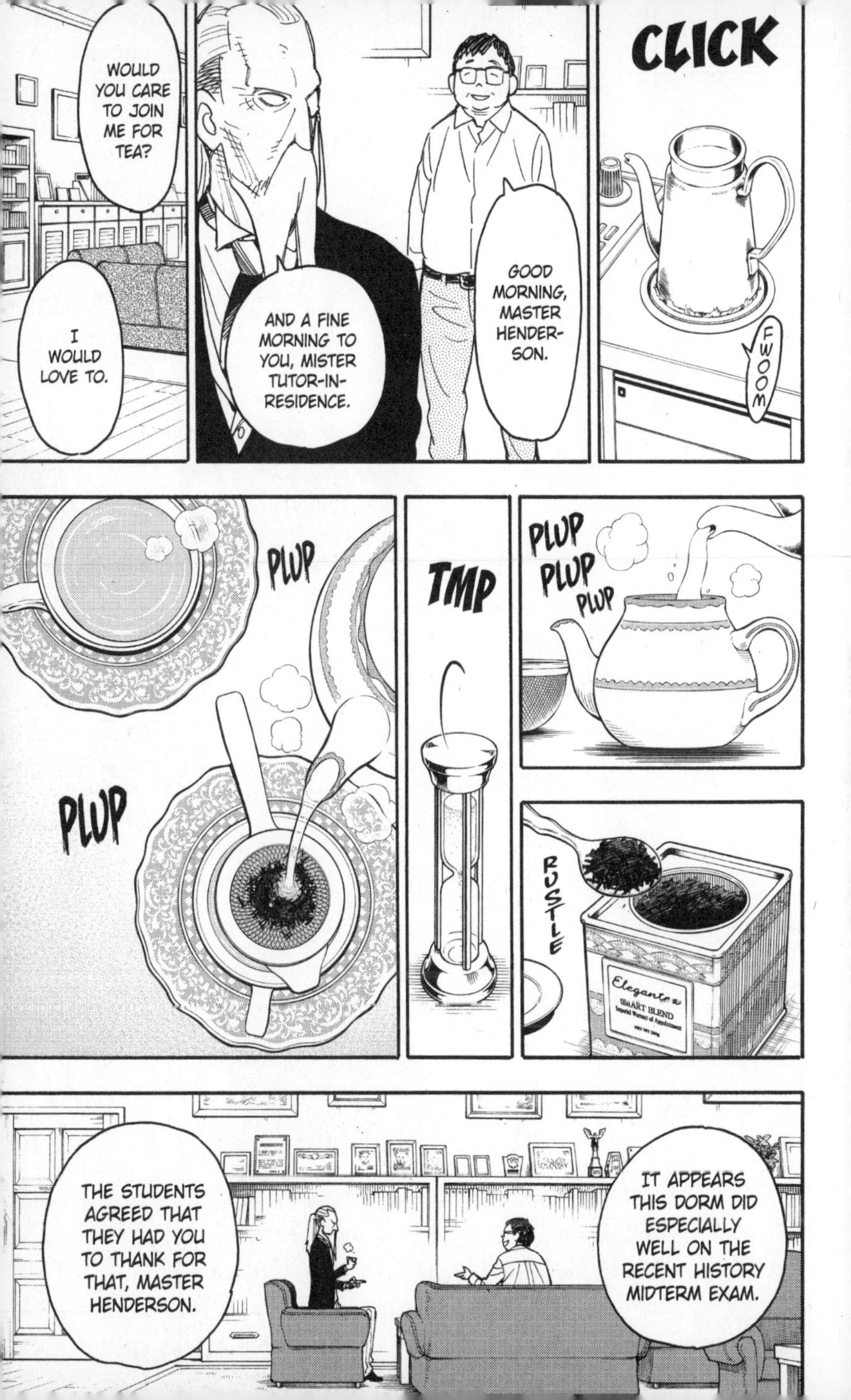
CLICK
FWOOM
GOOD MORNING, MASTER HENDER-SON.
AND A FINE MORNING TO YOU, MISTER TUTOR-IN-RESIDENCE.
WOULD YOU CARE TO JOIN ME FOR TEA?
I WOULD LOVE TO.
PLUP PLUP PLUP
RUSTLE
TMP
PLUP
PLUP
IT APPEARS THIS DORM DID ESPECIALLY WELL ON THE RECENT HISTORY MIDTERM EXAM.
THE STUDENTS AGREED THAT THEY HAD YOU TO THANK FOR THAT, MASTER HENDERSON.

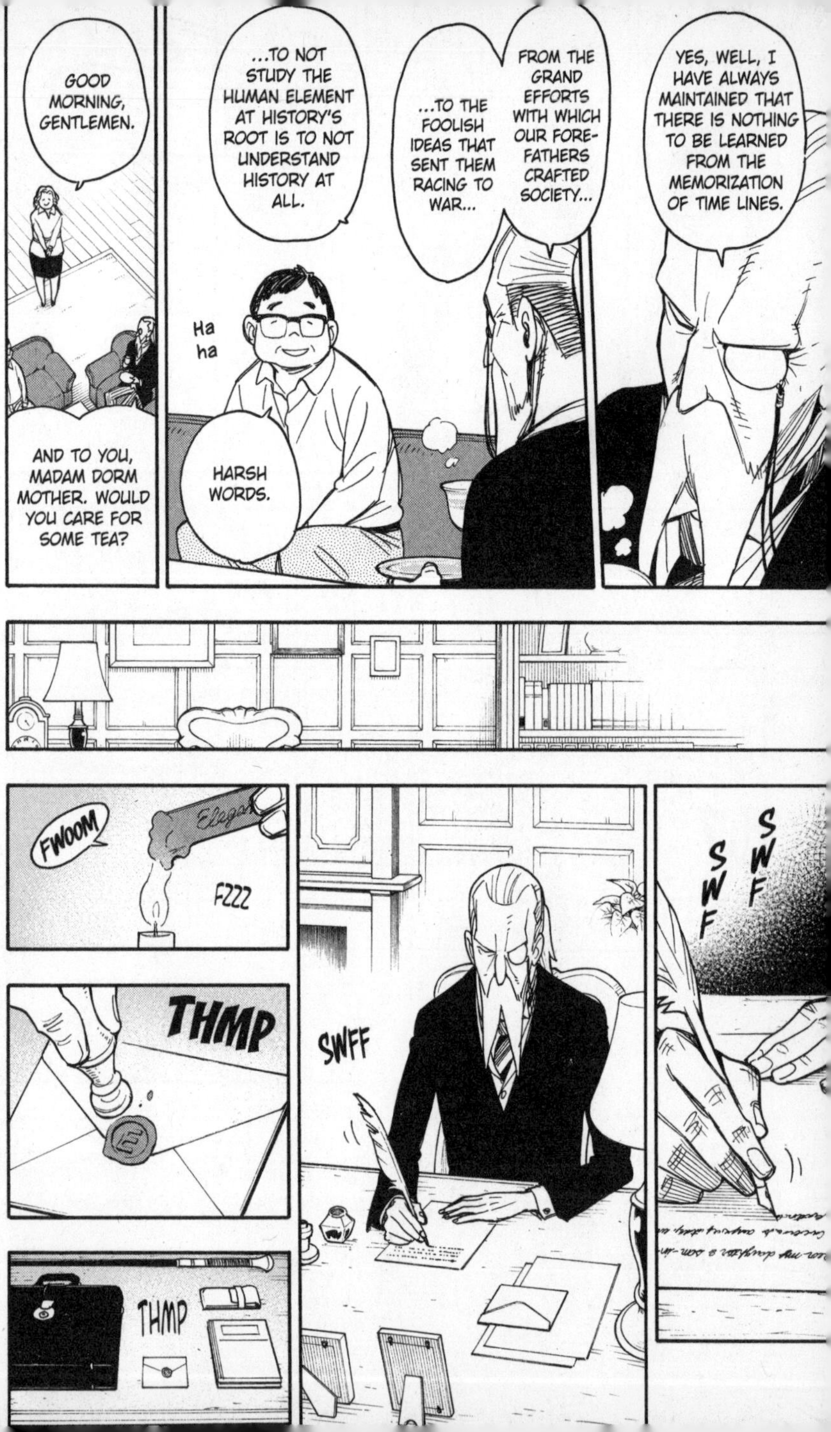
YES, WELL, I HAVE ALWAYS MAINTAINED THAT THERE IS NOTHING TO BE LEARNED FROM THE MEMORIZATION OF TIME LINES.
FROM THE GRAND EFFORTS WITH WHICH OUR FORE-FATHERS CRAFTED SOCIETY...
...TO THE FOOLISH IDEAS THAT SENT THEM RACING TO WAR...
...TO NOT STUDY THE HUMAN ELEMENT AT HISTORY'S ROOT IS TO NOT UNDERSTAND HISTORY AT ALL.
Ha ha
HARSH WORDS.
GOOD MORNING, GENTLEMEN.
AND TO YOU, MADAM DORM MOTHER. WOULD YOU CARE FOR SOME TEA?
SWF
SWF
SWFF
FWOOM
FZZZ
THMP
THMP

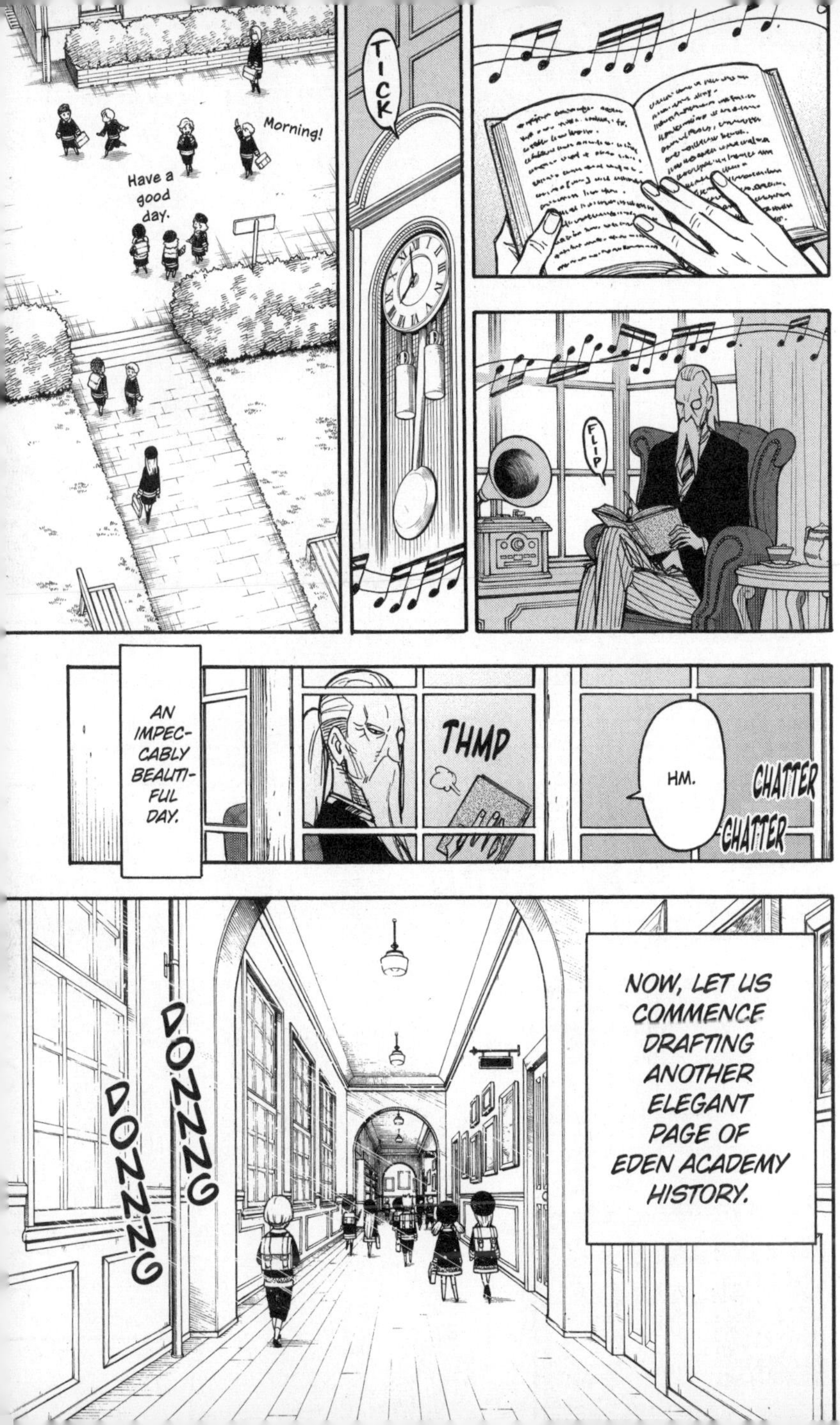
FLIP
TICK
Morning!
Have a good day.
CHATTER
CHATTER
HM.
THMP
AN IMPEC-CABLY BEAUTI-FUL DAY.
NOW, LET US COMMENCE DRAFTING ANOTHER ELEGANT PAGE OF EDEN ACADEMY HISTORY.
DONNG
DONNG

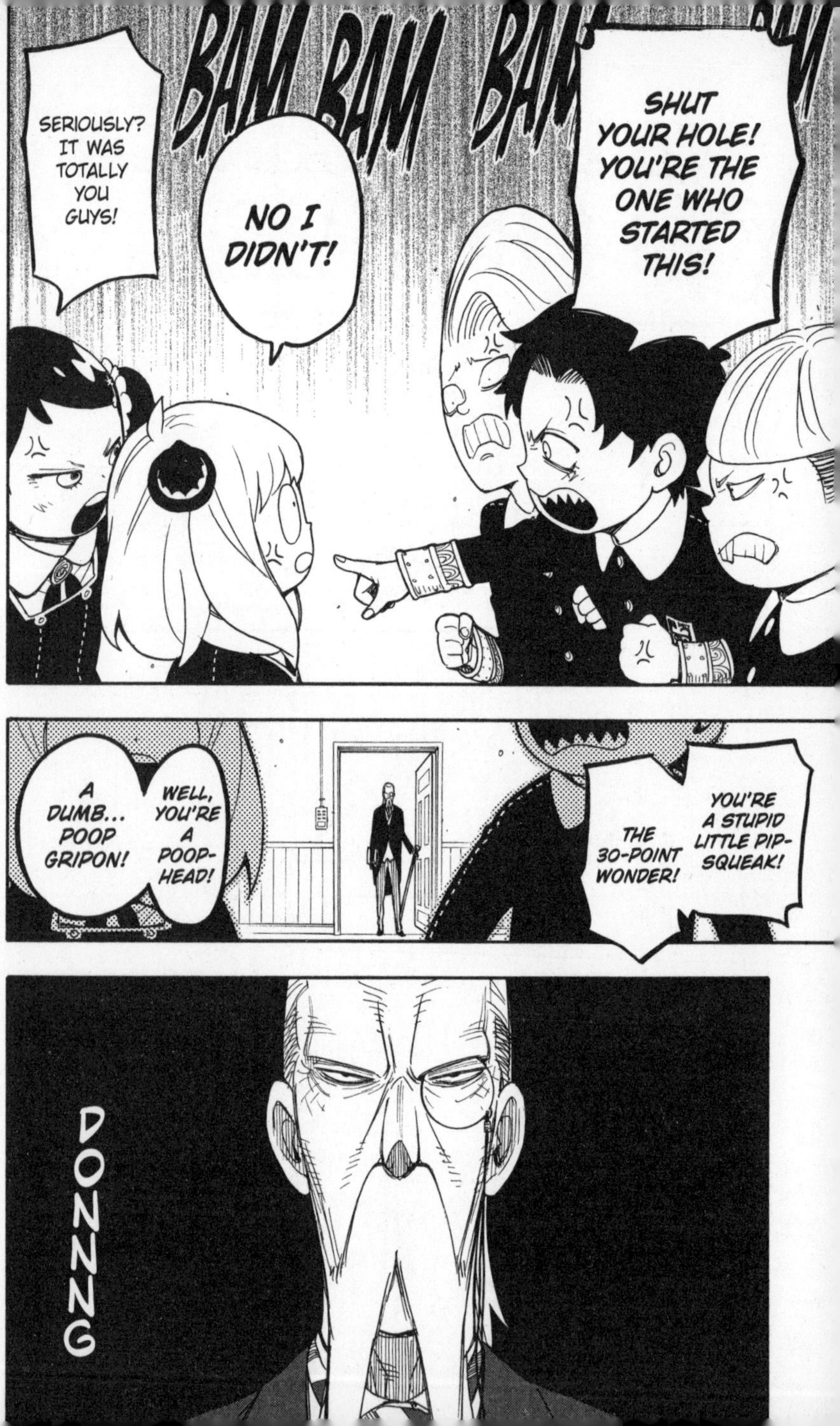

BAM BAM BAM
SHUT YOUR HOLE! YOU'RE THE ONE WHO STARTED THIS!
NO I DIDN'T!
SERIOUSLY? IT WAS TOTALLY YOU GUYS!
YOU'RE A STUPID LITTLE PIP-SQUEAK!
THE 30-POINT WONDER!
WELL, YOU'RE A POOP-HEAD!
A DUMB... POOP GRIPON!
DONNNG

SPYxFAMILY CONFIDENTIAL FILES (BONUS)

TOP SECRET
EYES ONLY

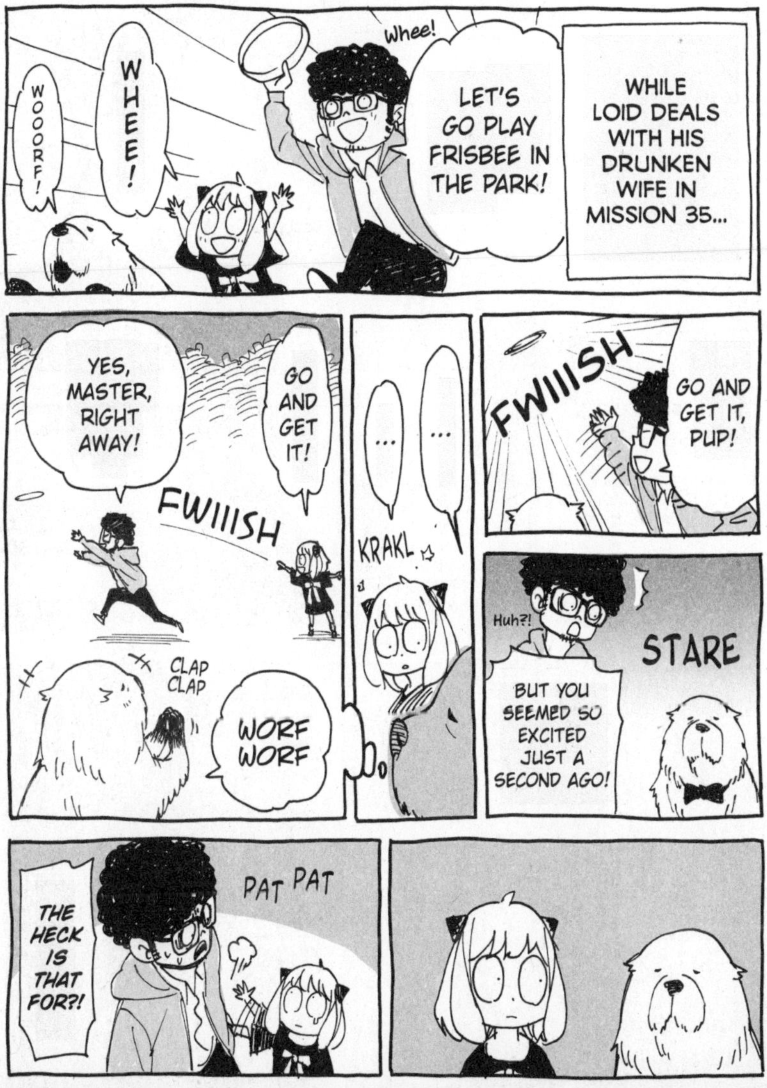
WHILE LOID DEALS WITH HIS DRUNKEN WIFE IN MISSION 35...
Whee!
LET'S GO PLAY FRISBEE IN THE PARK!
WHEE!
WOOORF!
FWIIISH
GO AND GET IT, PUP!
Huh?!
STARE
BUT YOU SEEMED SO EXCITED JUST A SECOND AGO!
...
...
KRAKL
GO AND GET IT!
YES, MASTER, RIGHT AWAY!
FWIIISH
CLAP CLAP
WORF WORF
PAT PAT
THE HECK IS THAT FOR?!

FRANKY'S SECRET FILES

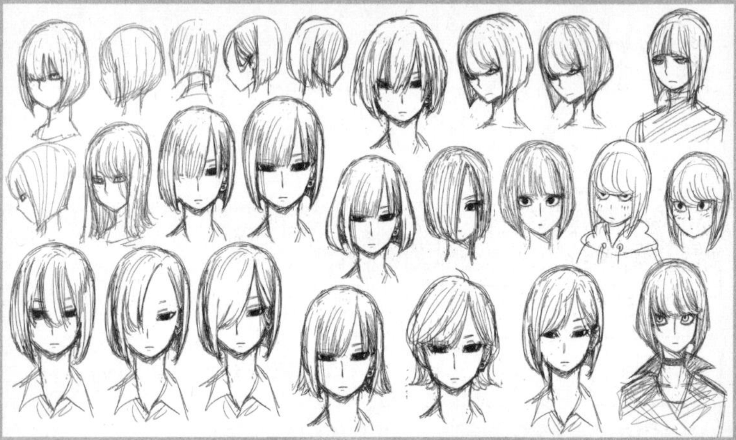

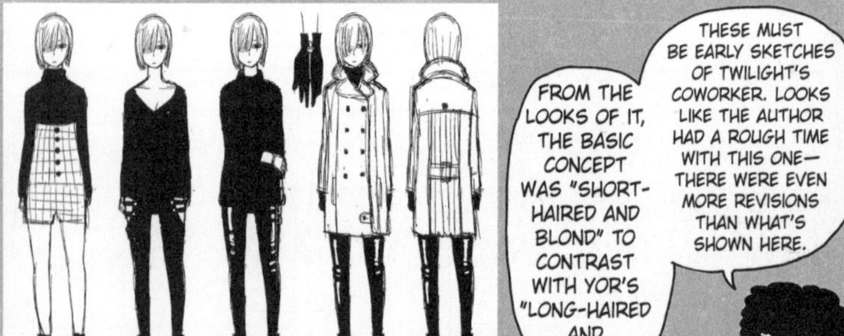
THESE MUST BE EARLY SKETCHES OF TWILIGHT'S COWORKER. LOOKS LIKE THE AUTHOR HAD A ROUGH TIME WITH THIS ONE—THERE WERE EVEN MORE REVISIONS THAN WHAT'S SHOWN HERE.
FROM THE LOOKS OF IT, THE BASIC CONCEPT WAS "SHORT-HAIRED AND BLOND" TO CONTRAST WITH YOR'S "LONG-HAIRED AND BLACK."

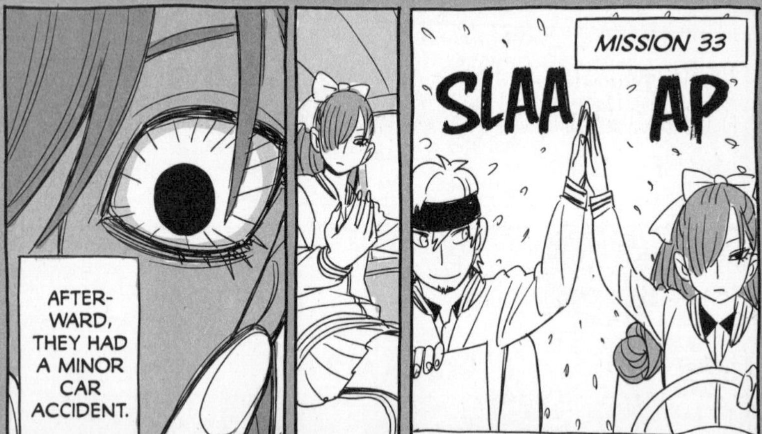
MISSION 33
SLAA AP
AFTER-WARD, THEY HAD A MINOR CAR ACCIDENT.

SPY×FAMILY VOL. 6
SPECIAL THANKS LIST

·CLASSIFIED·

ART ASSISTANCE	
SATOSHI KIMURA	KAZUKI NONAKA
AMASHIMA	MAFUYU KONISHI
YUICHI OZAKI	MAEHATA
HIKARI SUEHIRO	MIO AYATSUKA
MASAHITO SASAKI	
GRAPHIC NOVEL DESIGN	
HIDEAKI SHIMADA	ERI ARAKAWA
GRAPHIC NOVEL EDITOR	
KANAKO YANAGIDA	
MANAGING EDITOR	
SHIHEI LIN	

MY FIRST-EVER VOLUME 6! I AM SO GRATEFUL!
THE YEAR 2020 WAS FULL OF VARIOUS CHALLENGES. I HOPE 2021 WILL
SHINE BRIGHTER THAN LAST YEAR AND THAT MY HUMBLE EFFORTS WILL
BRING EVERYONE A LITTLE JOY.

—TATSUYA ENDO

EYES ONLY   READ & ~~DESTROY~~   EYES ONLY

SPY×FAMILY

6

STORY AND ART BY
TATSUYA ENDO

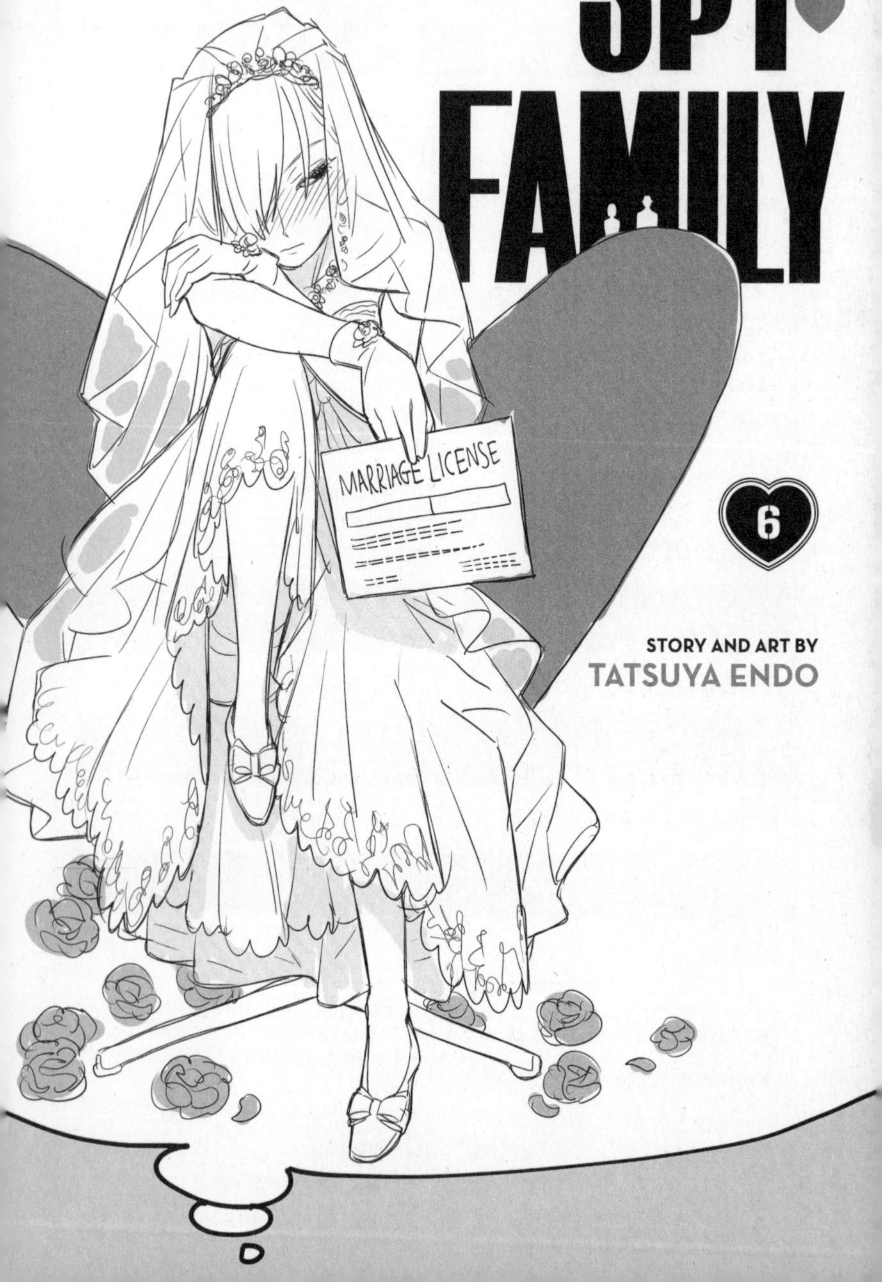
MARRIAGE LICENSE

I draw this manga with the idea that it's set in the sixties or seventies, but it ends up as a mishmash of the present and past. This happens because I frequently have to ask myself if something existed during that time period, and if I can't find the answer, I just shrug it off and think, "Well, this *is* a fictional country..."

—TATSUYA ENDO

Tatsuya Endo was born in Ibaraki Prefecture, Japan, on July 23, 1980. He debuted as a manga artist with the one-shot "Soibu Yugi" (Western Game), which ran in the Spring 2000 issue of *Akamaru Jump*. He is the author of *TISTA* and *Gekka Bijin* (Moon Flower Beauty). *Spy x Family* is his first work published in English.

SPY×FAMILY ⑥

SHONEN JUMP Edition

STORY AND ART BY **TATSUYA ENDO**

Translation **CASEY LOE**

Touch-Up Art & Lettering **RINA MAPA**

Design **JIMMY PRESLER**

Editor **JOHN BAE**

SPY x FAMILY © 2019 by Tatsuya Endo
All rights reserved.
First published in Japan in 2019 by SHUEISHA Inc., Tokyo.
English translation rights arranged by SHUEISHA Inc.

The stories, characters and incidents mentioned in this publication are entirely fictional.

Printed in Italy

Published by VIZ Media, LLC
P.O. Box 77010
San Francisco, CA 94107

10 9 8
First printing, October 2021
Eighth printing, October 2022

PARENTAL ADVISORY
SPY x FAMILY is rated T+ for Older Teen and is recommended for ages 16 and up. This volume contains realistic violence.

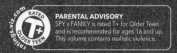

viz.com

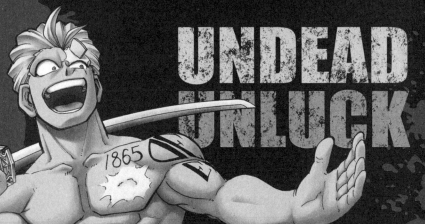

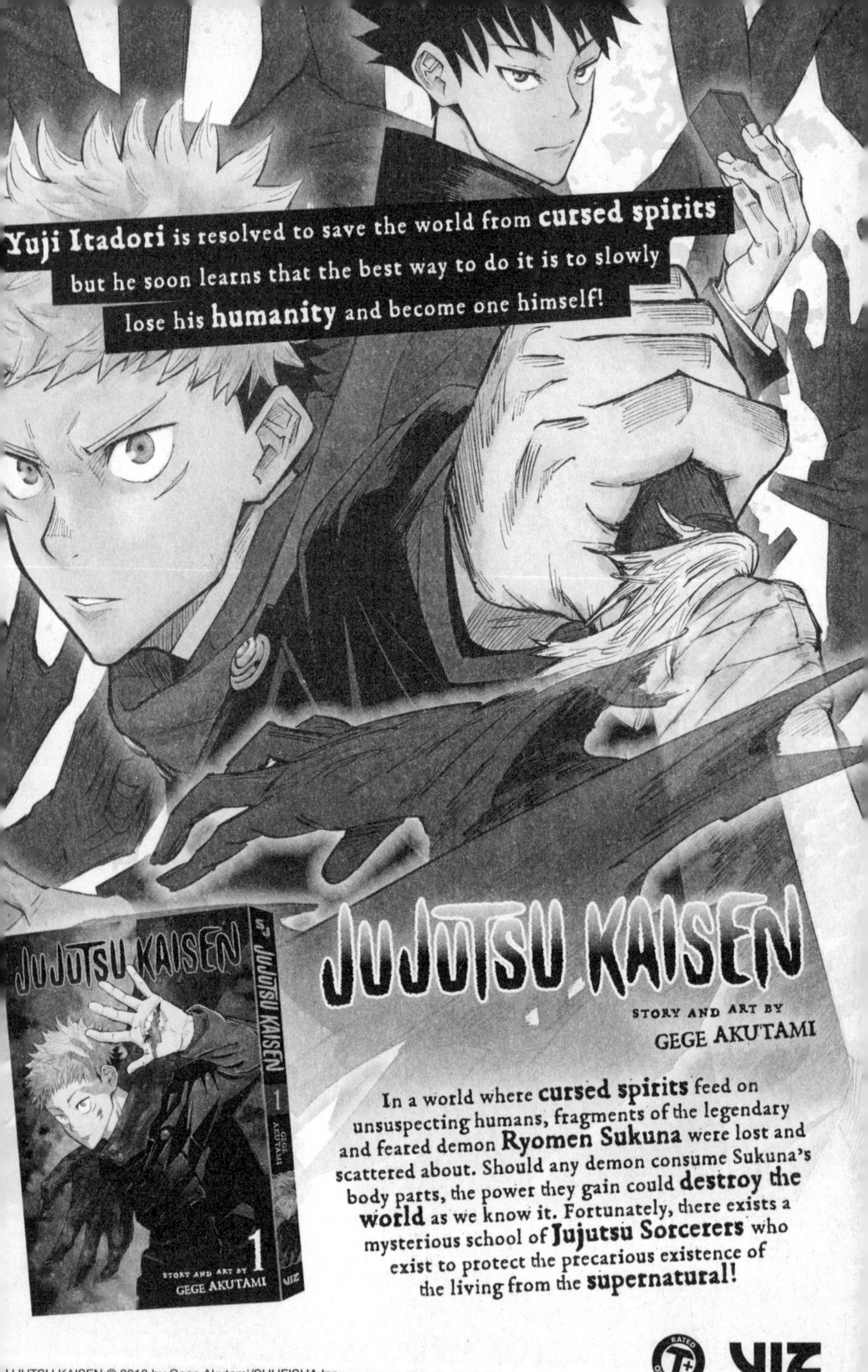
Yuji Itadori is resolved to save the world from cursed spirits
but he soon learns that the best way to do it is to slowly
lose his humanity and become one himself!
JUJUTSU KAISEN
1
STORY AND ART BY
GEGE AKUTAMI
VIZ
JUJUTSU KAISEN
STORY AND ART BY
GEGE AKUTAMI
In a world where cursed spirits feed on unsuspecting humans, fragments of the legendary and feared demon Ryomen Sukuna were lost and scattered about. Should any demon consume Sukuna's body parts, the power they gain could destroy the world as we know it. Fortunately, there exists a mysterious school of Jujutsu Sorcerers who exist to protect the precarious existence of the living from the supernatural!
RATED T+ OLDER TEEN
VIZ

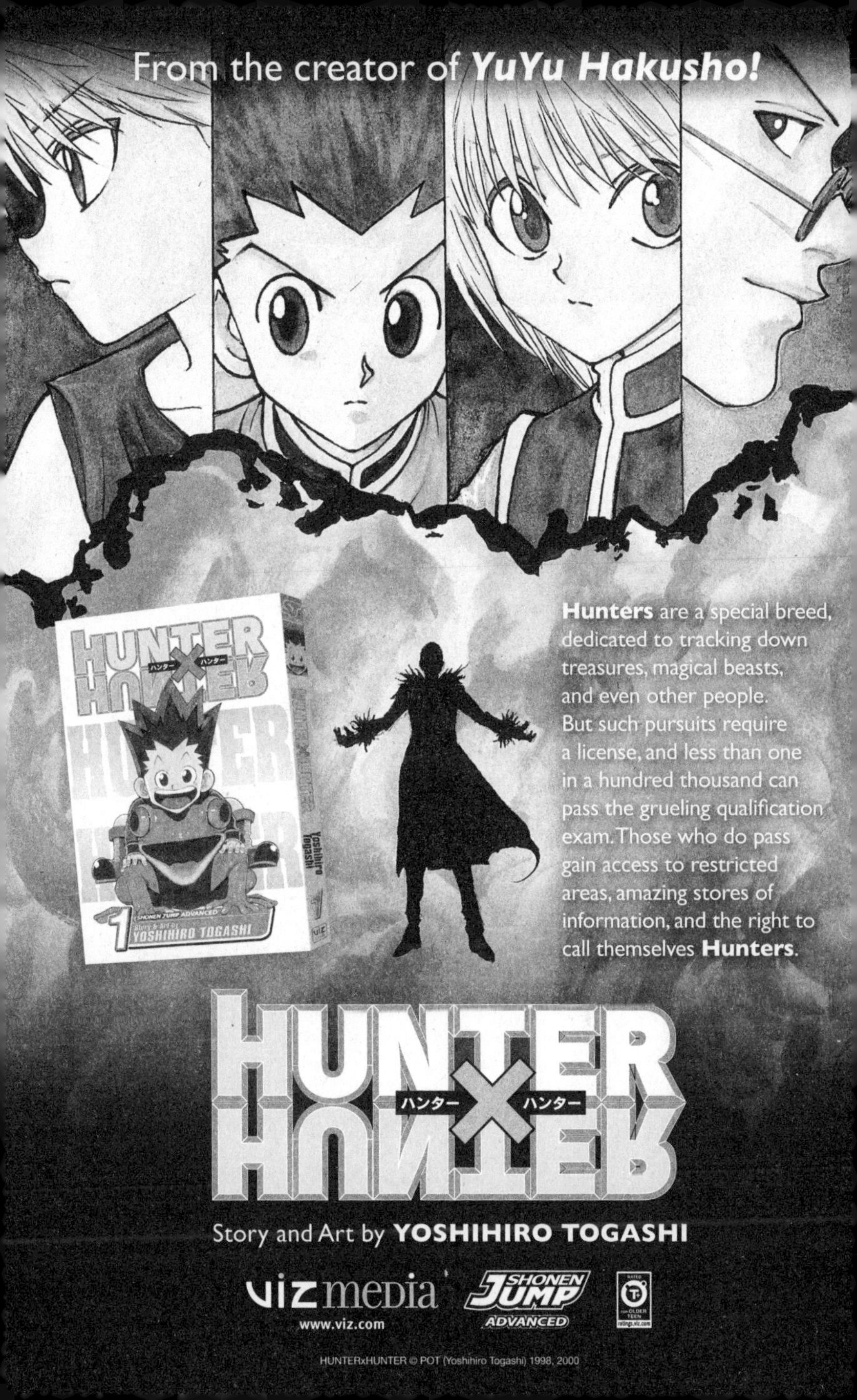
From the creator of YuYu Hakusho!
Hunters are a special breed, dedicated to tracking down treasures, magical beasts, and even other people. But such pursuits require a license, and less than one in a hundred thousand can pass the grueling qualification exam. Those who do pass gain access to restricted areas, amazing stores of information, and the right to call themselves Hunters.
HUNTER × HUNTER
ハンター ハンター
Story and Art by YOSHIHIRO TOGASHI
viz media
www.viz.com
SHONEN JUMP ADVANCED
HUNTERxHUNTER © POT (Yoshihiro Togashi) 1998, 2000

ASSASSINATION
CLASSROOM

COMPLETE BOX SET

STORY AND ART BY YUSEI MATSUI

The complete bestselling *Assassination Classroom* series is now available in a boldly designed, value-priced box set!

· Includes all 21 volumes of this unique tale of a mysterious, smiley-faced, tentacled, superpowered teacher who guides a group of misfit students to find themselves—while doing their best to assassinate him.

· Also includes an exclusive, full-color, mini "yearbook" filled with images of favorite characters in different art styles and contexts (previously unreleased in the English editions).

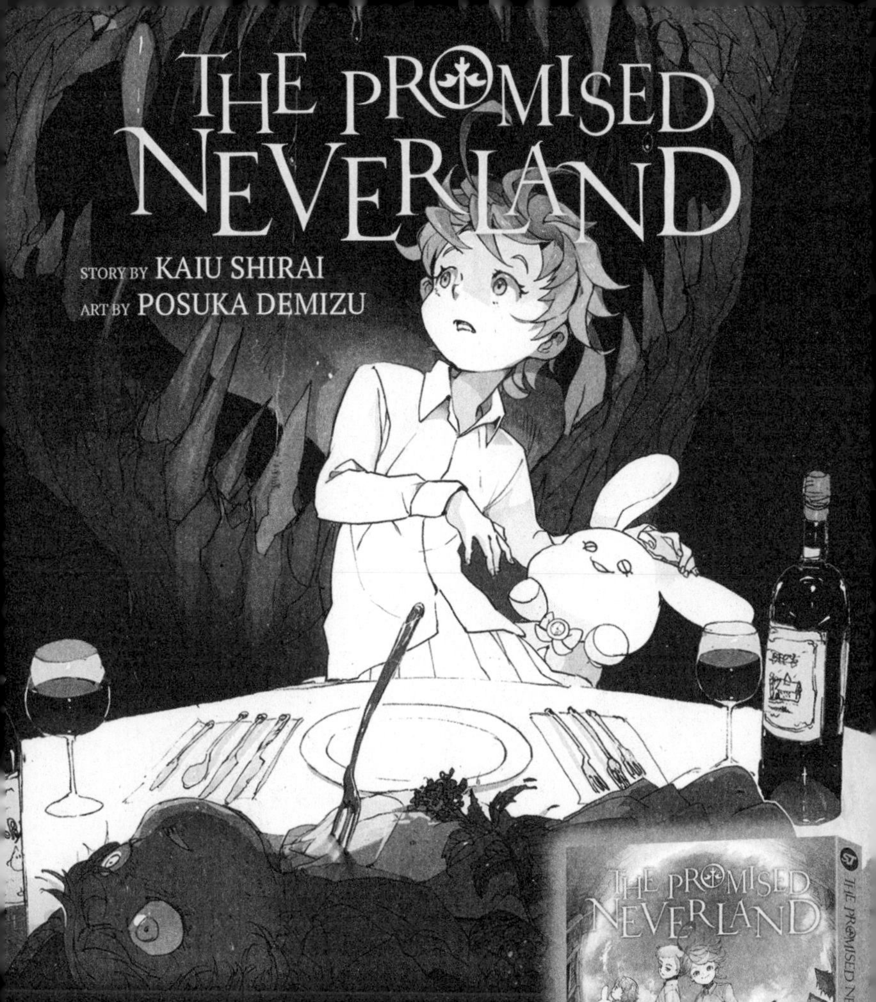

THE PROMISED NEVERLAND
STORY BY KAIU SHIRAI
ART BY POSUKA DEMIZU

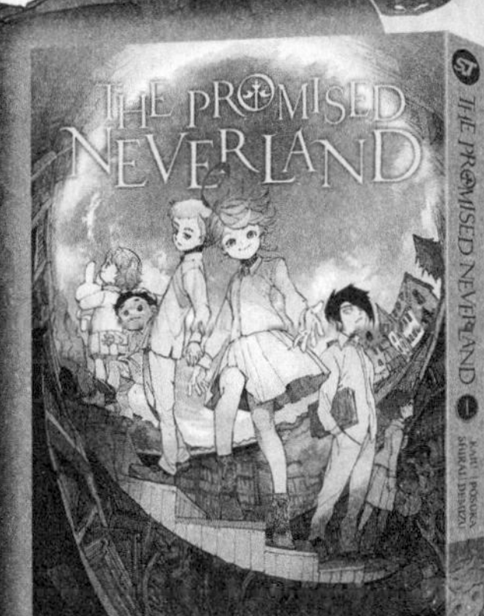

THE PROMISED NEVERLAND
STORY BY KAIU SHIRAI
ART BY POSUKA DEMIZU
1

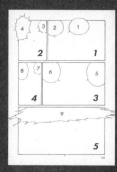

YOU'RE READING THE WRONG WAY!

SPY x FAMILY reads from right to left, starting in the upper-right corner. Japanese is read from right to left, meaning that action, sound effects and word-balloon order are completely reversed from English order.